THE PENGUIN CLASSICS

FOUNDER EDITOR (1944–64): E. V. RIEU

Editor: Betty Radice

PLUTARCH was one of the last of the classical Greek historians. He was born in about A.D. 46 at Chaeronea in Boeotia, where he later had a school, and in middle age he took up a priesthood at near-by Delphi.

When Nero visited Greece in A.D. 66, Plutarch was a student at Athens. He became a philosopher, a man capable of lecturing and discussing on many learned topics, and wrote a large number of essays and dialogues on philosophical, scientific and literary subjects (the *Moralia*). He adopted the philosophical standpoint of a Platonist, and frequently attacked both Stoics and Epicureans. He wrote his historical works somewhat late in life, and his *Parallel Lives* of eminent Greeks and Romans is probably his best-known and most influential work. (North's translation was used by Shakespeare as a source for his Roman plays).

Plutarch travelled in Egypt and also went to Rome, where he had many distinguished friends. The Emperor Hadrian honoured him with a government appointment in Greece, yet he always remained strongly attached to his native Chaeronea. His death probably occurred some years after A.D. 120.

IAN SCOTT-KILVERT is Director of the Literature Department of the British Council. He has translated, for the Penguin Classics, Plutarch's *The Rise and Fall of Athens* and *Makers of Rome: Nine Lives*.

THE AGE OF
ALEXANDER

NINE GREEK LIVES BY
PLUTARCH

AGESILAUS · PELOPIDAS

DION · TIMOLEON

DEMOSTHENES

PHOCION · ALEXANDER

DEMETRIUS · PYRRHUS

TRANSLATED AND ANNOTATED BY
Ian Scott-Kilvert

INTRODUCTION BY
G. T. Griffith

PENGUIN BOOKS

Penguin Books Ltd, Harmondsworth, Middlesex, England
Penguin Books, 40 West 23rd Street, New York, New York 10010, U.S.A.
Penguin Books Australia Ltd, Ringwood, Victoria, Australia
Penguin Books Canada Ltd, 2801 John Street, Markham, Ontario, Canada L3R 1B4
Penguin Books (N.Z.) Ltd, 182–190 Wairau Road, Auckland 10, New Zealand

—

This translation first published 1973
Reprinted 1977, 1979, 1980, 1982, 1983

—

Translation and notes copyright © Ian Scott-Kilvert, 1973
Introduction copyright © G. T. Griffith, 1973
All rights reserved

—

Made and printed in Great Britain
by Hazell Watson & Viney Ltd,
Aylesbury, Bucks
Set in Monotype Bembo

CONTENTS

* *
*

Introduction		7
Translator's Foreword		12
Chronological Table		18
1.	AGESILAUS	25
2.	PELOPIDAS	69
3.	DION	104
4.	TIMOLEON	151
5.	DEMOSTHENES	188
6.	PHOCION	218
7.	ALEXANDER	252
8.	DEMETRIUS	335
9.	PYRRHUS	384
	Appendix	426
	Maps	433
	Biographical Notes	438

INTRODUCTION

* *
*

IN the fifth century B.C. the Greek world, organized in its multi-
plicity of self-governing city-states, had produced already many of
its best things, in literature, in the arts and in politics. The Greeks
having repelled attacks from great foreign powers (Persia and Carthage), were able to continue their experiments in the arts of self-
government into the new medium of democracy. Here Athens, the
great leader, might even have united Greece politically had her
leadership been acceptable to most of the rest. The successful reaction
against Athenian imperialism did not end democracy, but it deferred
indefinitely any unification of Greece by a dominant leadership of
any one of the cities themselves. After 400 B.C. the attempts to
dominate, first by Sparta, presently by Thebes, were brief because
they were beyond their powers. From about 460 onwards a century
of wars had sown, in sum, enmities nearly irreconcilable, which
together with a class war latent inside the cities themselves, were
reducing the Greek political genius to something which in practical
terms looked like a wasting asset, as the contemporary Isocrates saw
and said. One of the symptoms of this malady was the growth of a
class of mercenary soldiers, men either unemployed or preferring war
to work, who can be seen taking a part, occasionally a spectacular
one, in nearly all the wars of this time. Persia naturally became a
leading employer, and the overthrow of Persia by Alexander opened
up new worlds for mercenaries, especially when his own death
presented his empire as a prize to be fought over and divided. Thousands of Greeks who went abroad as soldiers stayed as settlers.

To Greek political thinkers Sparta became something like what the
modern Ideas Man is to his boss; a thesaurus of things admirable,
formidable, lunatic, superhuman, all (at Sparta) the work of one
divinely-inspired lawgiver; but of things, above all, which were
thought to have started well for the Spartans and then to have gone

sour on them. In this rich setting of the Spartan background the two great men of this time stand out worthily: the magnificent Lysander (whose *Life* closes *The Rise and Fall of Athens*): the supremely able and active Agesilaus,[1] lucky ever to become king, but deserving his luck because no king at Sparta ever knew so well what a king could do there, if he went about it in the right way. Between them they steered Sparta into and through victory, empire and disaster in the space of one human generation. They had nearly everything except what Thucydides called *gnomē*, that order of political intelligence which included among other things (and perhaps above all things) *le tact des choses possibles*. Thebes and Boeotia, the overthrower of Spartan domination, offered nothing comparable to Lycurgus and *le mirage Spartiate* for the intellectuals to analyse or romanticize, though to us moderns their federal institutions are interesting enough. But for Plutarch (a Boeotian himself) it is the brief military glory of the Thebans that seems the thing that he most would have us remember. Pelopidas[2] is an outstanding soldier even in Plutarch's galaxy of military stars, and as winning a personality as any in the series. His premature death in action was a blow both to Thebes and to Greece, both of whom badly lacked a great soldier in the following years which saw the rise of Macedonia.

The maladies and defects in the Greek scene of the fourth century were not hard to find. But its great and overriding merit is summed up in the word 'freedom'. With allowance made for the infinite variety promoted by so many independent governments, Greece was still broadly speaking a free country. This freedom was threatened and in the end extinguished by the coming of the great Macedonians. Macedonia (and to a lesser degree Epirus, the kingdom of Pyrrhus later) can be called 'backward' in the sense that the peoples there were still organized in tribes ruled by kings in the archaic fashion of the Greeks some centuries before. In Macedonia the luxury of self-government in city-states had never developed, probably because the relative security of the Greek peninsula was missing. Here was a harder, tougher world in which the neighbouring peoples were big and strong and near, and the Macedonians needed the strong rule of kings in order to survive. In order to prosper they needed the rule of a king who could control the smaller princes and unite the regional tribes to form one Macedonian people. It was this that Philip the father of

1. Translated in this volume pp. 25ff.   2. pp. 69ff.

Alexander finally achieved, and the resultant surge of power in the north flooded down over Greece and out into Asia to the Indus. This was the political lifetime of Demosthenes[1] and Phocion[2] at Athens, the one abominating and resisting the expansion of the 'barbarians' as damaging to Athenian interests abroad and in the end to Greek freedom itself, the other recognizing that the 'barbarian' king and his nobles had very much in common with Greek aristocrats, and that this new power was something that Athens and Greece must learn to live with, if only because there was really no choice. In political realism the Athenian who was elected to the office of general far more often than any other (including those great ones Pericles and Cimon) surpassed the professional politician who became the greatest of Greek orators, and who stirs us paradoxically by his ability to persuade the Athenians to fight for their freedom, when we can see that they lacked now the power and the will to fight and win.

The great Macedonians themselves (and for most purposes Pyrrhus can be counted as one of them) pose no such problems, for even Alexander was above everything the soldier and great commander; Demetrius 'the Besieger' and Pyrrhus were nothing else. One of the achievements of Alexander's conquests in Asia was to make the world safe for great Macedonians, so long as they did not exterminate each other. They did their very best to do just this, and none more whole-heartedly than Demetrius[3] and Pyrrhus,[4] each with great military talents which in this new world clearly entitled him (he judged) to be a king on as grand a scale as he could achieve. Pyrrhus' challenge to Rome was a piece of professionalism like something in the career of the modern tycoon who flits from one megalith to the next in the world of the great companies and the boards of nationalized industries. To us it can seem a little crazy. But not so to the Greeks, whose history as an effective people flashed by with the thrill of war, for worse or better, seldom far away, and for whose historiography war kept for centuries all the fascination which 'the economy' now holds for some few of us. Demetrius the Besieger earned his place in Plutarch's gallery, even though for Plutarch's ethical purposes he had to serve as a bad example instead of a good one.

Alexander's was perhaps the *Heldenleben* in a closer sense than is obvious immediately. Though it was recorded by contemporaries and eye witnesses, it does not yield up his personality easily; sympathies

1. pp. 188ff.   2. pp. 218ff.   3. pp. 335ff.   4. pp. 384ff.

and antipathies were too intimately involved in the record from the start. In action his success and its results were almost fabulous, yet punctuated now by acts of great generosity or of policy that look enlightened, now by the most atrocious crimes. Nor is it easy to detect a master-planner here; rather the man of action gifted with a fine sense of priorities. If, as is said, he saw himself in the early days as Achilles, there seems in truth much of the Homeric hero in his unsparing pursuit of reputation, and his unforgiving malice towards those, even friends, who opposed or endangered his purposes. That his character and temper grew worse as his power grew greater seems to us clear, and Plutarch does not deny it, but in general he is kinder to the hero than most modern interpreters, and interested though he was in what we would call his psychology, he does not treat it with the subtlety and the sense of balance that are needed to capture it in full. Judged by his achievements, by their effects and influence, and by his personal character, Alexander was truly awe-inspiring: this at least Plutarch saw and communicated in the *Life*[1] – one of his fullest and best.

Finally the Greeks in Sicily had their troubles, too, and in the fourth century they were not small ones. Dion[2] and Timoleon,[3] whose *Lives* by Plutarch are such welcome additions to our scanty sources of information on the Greeks of the West, belonged clearly to a period in which a sense of disintegration comes through even more strongly than for Greece itself. In Sicily the Greeks shared the island with a strong power, Carthage. Wars with Carthage combined with intercity wars and with a keen class warfare inside the cities to make these Greeks peculiarly susceptible to the form of monarchy which they called tyranny and which we call dictatorship. Dion and Timoleon were heroes because they were 'liberators'. Dion was also the friend of Plato, Timoleon was also the spectacular vanquisher of the Carthaginians. The ingredients are here, plainly, for a tradition uncritically favourable to this pair, and something of this unquestionably survives in the two *Lives* of Plutarch. Nevertheless, there is no doubt that the Greek decline in Sicily was arrested, and even reversed. The evidence of archaeology points to a notable revival in prosperity in the last quarter of the fourth century, and for this the basis can have been laid only by Timoleon's restoration of peace and stable government and his programme of repopulation at Syracuse and elsewhere.

1. pp. 252ff.   2. pp. 104ff.   3. pp. 151ff.

Probably it was most of all Timoleon's indifference to personal aggrandizement that made him most revered; a Solon-like figure who more even than Solon deserved his reputation for effectiveness at least. This is the stuff that sages are made of. Incidentally, of the nine lives in this volume, only Timoleon's ended peacefully at home and in bed.

G. T. GRIFFITH

TRANSLATOR'S FOREWORD

* *
*

SIR THOMAS NORTH entitled his great translation of Plutarch *The Lives of The Noble Grecians and Romans. Noble* was his own importation, but it was a well-chosen epithet, for it serves to emphasize the qualities which distinguish Plutarch from the Greek historians of the golden age. It reminds us of the distance which separates him from his subjects and of the heroic aura which had grown up around them in the meanwhile. Plutarch is, as it were, a backward-looking writer standing on the last range which divided the pagan civilization from the Christian. He lacks the startlingly original and impersonal quality of Periclean literature, just as that literature lacks his intimacy on the one hand and the breadth of his tolerance and philanthropy on the other. He was no Thucydides, applying a ruthlessly objective analysis to uncover the historical process. He was a lover of tradition, and his prime object was at once to cherish and understand the greatness of the past and to re-assert it as a living ideal.

Plutarch's life-time of some seventy-five years stretches from the middle forties A.D. to the beginning of Hadrian's reign. It is the period at which the blend of Greek and Roman culture reached its highest point of development; almost all the major writers had done their work and Plutarch's writings are in many ways a summing up of that culture. He came of an ancient Theban family and he never strayed for long from his home-town of Chaeronea, a small city lying in the midst of the great Boeotian plain, which the Greeks called 'the dancing-floor of Ares' and which had witnessed the decisive battles of Haliartus, Leuctra, Chaeronea itself, and many more. Not that his own outlook was provincial in any narrowing sense. He studied philosophy in Athens as a young man, travelled in Greece and Egypt, earned a high reputation both as a scholar and a diplomat in Rome, making many influential friends in the process, and may even have been granted honorary consular rank.

Plutarch himself assiduously practised the ideal of the city-state, that the educated man should play his part in public life; and he held a succession of magistracies at Chaeronea and a priesthood at Delphi. In any political sense, of course, Greece had lost the last vestiges of her independence at the sack of Corinth two centuries before. Meanwhile not only had her population shrunk, but the riches and other material rewards of Italy and Asia had attracted many of her ablest soldiers, administrators, and scholars to emigrate, so that in his own time, according to Plutarch's estimate, Greece could scarcely have put three thousand armed men into the field. In the directly practical sphere no Greek could do anything to alter these realities, and yet it was no mere antiquarian sentiment which influenced Plutarch to keep his Hellenism as intact as possible rather than embark, say, on the career of an imperial civil servant. For the governing class of his day Roman and Greek education had become inseparably intermingled, and in the Roman Empire, which was now beginning to enjoy the benefits of stable government and yet possessed neither a moral nor an intellectual centre, a teacher of Plutarch's stature could still hope to benefit his fellow-men by inspiration and example.

The form of Plutarch's writings suggests that his gifts were for the essay rather than the full-length history. Apart from the *Lives* his other major work, the *Moralia*, is a collection of comparatively short treatises and dialogues which cover an immense range of subjects, literary, ethical, political, and scientific.[1] Plutarch never attempted any single work on a large scale and his themes are not developed organically, but rather as a series of factual statements followed by comments. Both in the *Moralia* and the *Lives* his main object is didactic. When he turned to history, he set out not only to convince the Greeks that the annals of Rome deserved their attention, but also to remind the Romans that Greece had possessed soldiers and statesmen who could challenge comparison with their own. He wrote only of men of action and he explains at the beginning of the *Life of Pericles* why he chose these rather than artists or philosophers. It was perhaps because of his firm belief that the two races should draw mutual profit from their traditions that he named the series *Parallel Lives* and grouped his Greeks and Romans in pairs. He liked to regard Greek and Roman history as complementary in a sense, and this arrangement of his material allowed him to sum up his heroes' moral qualities and

1. See Plutarch, *Moral Essays*, Penguin Books, 1971.

measure their achievements in the formal essay of comparison with which he concludes most of the pairs of *Lives*. But these resemblances were often more coincidental than real, and Plutarch does not in fact pursue them very far; indeed he could not have done so without seriously distorting his material.

The order of composition of the *Lives* is still much disputed, but there are signs that they were written in four distinct groups. One series contained the lives of Sertorius and Eumenes, Cimon and Lucullus, Lysander and Sulla, Demosthenes and Cicero, Agis and Cleomenes and Tiberius and Caius Gracchus, Pelopidas and Marcellus, Phocion and Cato the Younger, and Aristides and Cato the Elder. This series Plutarch undertook, he tells us, at the request of his friends, and it may also have included the lost Epaminondas, Plutarch's favourite hero, paired here with Scipio Africanus. A second group was composed for his own satisfaction, and it consists of great men chosen as object-lessons in a particular virtue: Pericles and Fabius Maximus, Nicias and Crassus, Dion and Brutus, Timoleon and Aemilius Paulus, Philopoemen and Titus Flamininus, Themistocles and Camillus, Alexander and Julius Caesar, Agis and Pompey, Pyrrhus and Marius and Solon and Publicola. A third group was chosen to comprise those whose career may serve as a warning. It contains Demetrius and Mark Antony and Alcibiades and Coriolanus, and here, paradoxically, Plutarch achieved from the literary point of view three of his most brilliant portraits. Lastly he turned to the semi-mythical and wrote of the founding fathers and legislators of Greece and Rome, Theseus and Romulus, and Lycurgus and Numa.

The present selection has been made on the same principle as that adopted for the other volumes of the *Lives* in the Penguin Classics. Instead of reproducing Plutarch's arrangement of Greeks and Romans in pairs, I have grouped nine of the *Lives* in chronological order so as to trace a crucial phase of ancient history, in this case the period which extends from the collapse of Athenian supremacy at the end of the Peloponnesian War to the transformation of mainland Greece and the Eastern Mediterranean by the rise of Macedonia: the selection ends with the death of one of the last of the successors of Alexander, Pyrrhus of Epirus.

By Plutarch's time a conventional form of biography already existed. It began with an account of the subject's birth, family, and education, went on to delineate his character and recount the most important and typical events of his career, and concluded with an account of his posterity and influence. Plutarch followed this organization of his material fairly closely, but he employed it with far greater skill and variety than his predecessors. He freed his *Lives* from the rhetorical and argumentative nature of Greek biography and from the ponderous eulogy of the Roman *laudatio*; above all he impressed on them the charm of his personality and the depth of his insight into human nature. He was a conscientious collector of material, and he draws upon a very wide range of authorities, although these are of distinctly unequal value, for he was better at amassing evidence than at sifting it. The task as he saw it, working over material which was already familiar in outline to his readers, was not so much to evaluate facts as to create an inspiring portrait. Moreover, as he reminds us at the beginning of his *Life of Alexander*, he is writing biography, not history. The record he provides of the major battles and campaigns is thus sketchy by comparison with Arrian's *History*. The *Life* consists in fact of a highly selective sequence of episodes and personal anecdotes culled from significant phases of Alexander's career. The intention is plainly to emphasize Alexander's moderation and self-control and to counter-balance other interpretations of his life-story as that of a man corrupted by the unimaginably swift growth of his fortunes and power. It is, of course, noteworthy that he pairs Alexander with Julius Caesar, whose career likewise rendered him vulnerable to the temptations that beset the holders of supreme power. But whether Plutarch saw a parallel in this respect we cannot know, since we do not have the customary essay of comparison summing up the actions and qualities of the two men.

With the exception of Alexander and Demosthenes, the subjects of this group of *Lives* are much less familiar to the general reader than those which comprise *The Rise and Fall of Athens:* on the other hand the present selection contains many of Plutarch's finest descriptions of war, revolution and scenes of action. There is Agesilaus' undaunted defence of Lacedaemon when his home-land is attacked – the first time in six hundred years that an invader had set his foot on Spartan soil; there is the deliverance of Thebes by the young Pelopidas and his fellow-conspirators disguised as girls; Dion's race against time to rescue a burning Syracuse from the mercenaries of the tyrant Dionysius II; Timoleon's great victory over the Carthaginians won amid mist and thunderstorm; Pyrrhus' annihilating battles with the Romans, the first clash between Greek and Roman arms.

This period also witnesses the decline of the city-state, the final failure of the Greek communities to combine effectively enough to preserve their cherished independence against the larger power-units, first of Persia and Carthage, then of Macedon, ultimately of Rome. Plutarch passes judgement on these events and the subsequent collapse of Greek liberties in a memorable passage from another biography, his *Life of Flamininus*.

For if we except the victory at Marathon, the sea-fight at Salamis, the battles of Plataea and Thermopylae and Cimon's exploits at Eurymedon ... Greece fought all her battles against and to enslave herself. Every one of her trophies stands as a memorial to her own shame and misfortune, and she owed her ruin above all to the misdeeds and the rivalries of her leaders.

Still it is not the cycle of history which really engages Plutarch's attention, and his habit of seeing all events in personal terms is at once his weakness and his strength. He brought to history a Platonist's conviction that knowledge is virtue and that cause and effect are really only operative in the sphere of Ideas: hence he tends to describe his statesmen's policies simply in terms of their personalities and to judge public conduct by the ethical standards of private life. He forgets that a statesman is far more often faced with a conflict of opposing interests than with a straight choice between right and wrong, and he seems to regard the past as a completely separate world, rather than as a continuum, which merges imperceptibly into present and future.

On the other hand it is just this boundless interest in the individual character which has given the *Lives* their enduring popularity from age to age. Plutarch has an unerring sense of the drama of men in great situations. His eye ranges over a wider field of human action than any of the classical historians. He surveys men's conduct in war, in council, in love, in the use of money – always a vital test in Greek eyes of a man's capacities – in religion, in the family, and he judges as a man of wide tolerance and ripe experience. Believing implicitly in the stature of his heroes, he has a genius for making greatness stand out in small actions. We think of Alexander handing to his physician the paper denouncing him as an assassin and in the same gesture drinking off the physic the man had prepared him; or of Demosthenes finding in the hour of his death the courage which had deserted him on the battlefield: these and countless other scenes Plutarch has engraved on the memory of posterity for all time. It was surely this power of his to epitomize the moral grandeur of the ancient world which appealed most strongly to Shakespeare and Montaigne and inspired the gigantic outlines of such typically Renaissance heroes as Coriolanus and Mark Antony, and which later prompted Mme Roland's remark that the *Lives* are the pasturage of great souls.

*

Among classical authors Plutarch does not rank high as a stylist. He can tell a story or dramatize a scene to great effect – witness his account of the Theban *coup d'état*, or the comedy of the dialogue between Pyrrhus and his diplomatic and philosophical adviser Cineas. He is at his most original, both in thought and vocabulary, when he sets out to analyse characters, motives, or states of mind. But often the structure of his sentences is too loose and unwieldy to allow of a close rendering into English, and the translator is constantly obliged to shorten or re-shape them if the narrative is to flow freely or smoothly. A new translation was certainly overdue, and my main concern here has been to bring the resources of the modern idiom to express Plutarch's thought as faithfully as possible. There is on the other hand a deliberate sententiousness about his choice of words which restrains the translator from an excess of informality. Where a phrase has seemed to me exactly right, I have not hesitated to borrow from Langhorne, Clough or other translators.

In conclusion I should like to express my very warm thanks to Mr G. T. Griffith of Gonville and Caius College, Cambridge, who has provided innumerable helpful criticisms of the translation and notes and made valuable constructive suggestions.

I.S.-K.

CHRONOLOGICAL TABLE

* *
*

405 Athenian fleet defeated at Aegospotami.
Dionysius I seizes power in Syracuse.

404 Surrender of Athens. The Long Walls demolished. Rule of the Thirty.

403 Spartan garrison in Athens. Revolt of Thrasybulus.
Fall of the Thirty.

402 Birth of Phocion.

401 Rebellion of Cyrus in Persia. March of the Ten Thousand.

398 Accession of Agesilaus as King of Sparta.

396 Agesilaus assembles expedition to invade Persia.

395 Agesilaus invades Lydia. Death of Tissaphernes.
Agesilaus invades Phrygia and makes terms with Pharnabazus.
Battle of Haliartus (near Thebes). Death of Lysander.
Coalition of Athens, Corinth, and Thebes against Sparta.

394 Athens begins to rebuild Long Walls. Agesilaus recalled.
(July) Sparta defeats the opposing alliance at battles of Corinth and Coronea. (August) Athenian and Persian fleets defeat Spartans at Cnidus.

393 Completion of the Long Walls.

392 Sparta at war with Corinth and Argos. Iphicrates, Athenian
391 general, trains a light infantry corps for the allies against Sparta. Sparta captures Lechaeum, the Corinthian port. First diplomatic mission to Persia of the Spartan Antalcidas.

390 Agesilaus defeats Corinthians and Argives, celebrates Isthmian Games. Iphicrates defeats Spartans at Lechaeum.

389 Thrasybulus sails to Hellespont and wins over Thasos, Samothrace, Byzantium and Chalcedon to alliance with Athens.

388 Second diplomatic mission of Antalcidas to Persia.

387 'The King's Peace': a settlement negotiated mainly between Sparta and Persia and imposed by Sparta on the other Greek states.

385 First visit of Plato to Dionysius I of Syracuse.

384 Birth of Demosthenes.

382 The Cadmeia, citadel of Thebes, seized with Spartan connivance.

380 Accession of King Cleombrotus at Sparta.

379 Liberation of Thebes by Pelopidas and others.

378 Failure of Sphodrias' raid on Piraeus.
Alliance between Athens and Thebes. Agesilaus invades Boeotia.

377 Second invasion of Thebes by Agesilaus.

376 Athenian fleet under Chabrias defeats Spartans off Naxos.

375 Spartan force defeated by Thebans at Tegyra.

372 Alliance between Thebes and Jason of Pherae (Thessaly).

371 Peace of Callias signed by Sparta, Athens and other Greek states. Sparta challenges Thebes' hegemony over other Boeotian cities and declares war. (August) Spartans defeated at Leuctra by Epaminondas and Pelopidas. King Cleombrotus killed.

370 Arcadia, Mantinea, Tegea, states hitherto dominated by Sparta, re-shape their constitutions. Death of Jason of Pherae.
Allied army under Epaminondas invades Sparta.

369 Resettlement of Messenia despite Spartan opposition.
Second allied invasion of Sparta. Pelopidas' first expedition to Thessaly. The young Philip of Macedon in Thebes as hostage.

368 Pelopidas' second expedition to Thessaly: he is imprisoned by Alexander of Pherae.

367 Epaminondas sent to Thessaly: secures release of Pelopidas. Death of Dionysius I at Syracuse. Plato's second visit. Return of Philistus to Syracuse. Pelopidas returns to Thebes and is sent on a diplomatic mission to Persia; he achieves success.

366 Dion exiled from Syracuse by Dionysius II.

364 Pelopidas' third expedition to Thessaly: he is killed at battle of Cynoscephalae.

362 Epaminondas killed at battle of Mantinea.

361 Plato's final visit to Syracuse and return. Agesilaus in Egypt.

360 Death of Agesilaus in Egypt.

357 Dion's expedition assembled at Zacynthus. (August) Dion lands in Sicily: enters Syracuse: Dionysius II besieged on Ortygia: Heraclides arrives with his squadron: Syracusans build a fleet.

356 The new Syracusan fleet defeats Dionysius' ships. Philistus killed. Birth of Alexander the Great.

355 Dionysius II escapes from Syracuse. His son Apollocrates surrenders.

354 Murder of Dion.

348 Phocion's campaign in Euboea against the Macedonians.

347 Dionysius II regains power in Syracuse.

345 Syracusans appeal for help to Corinth. Timoleon chosen to lead a small expedition.

344 Timoleon sails from Leucas: evades Carthaginians at Rhegium; lands at Tauromenium: defeats Hicetas at Adranum: enters Syracuse: receives surrender of Dionysius II.

343 Reinforcements sent to Timoleon. Dionysius settles in Corinth. Repopulation of Syracuse begins.
Aristotle becomes Alexander's tutor.

342 Timoleon expels Leptines from Apollonia.

341 Carthaginian expedition arrives at Lilybaeum. (June) Timoleon defeats Carthaginians at battle of Crimisus.

340 Athenian expedition to assist Byzantium against Philip of Macedon.

339 Timoleon makes peace with Carthage. Hicetas and Mamercus captured and executed. Liberation of Sicily completed.

338 General coalition of Greek states goes to war with Philip of Macedon and is decisively defeated by Philip and Alexander at Chaeronea.

337 Death of Timoleon. Hellenic League convened at Corinth supports Philip's plans for invasion of Persia.

336 Accession of Darius in Persia. Assassination of Philip.
Alexander establishes control of Macedonia.

335 Thebes revolts against Alexander and is destroyed.

334 (Spring) Alexander invades Asia Minor: (May) wins battle of the Granicus: receives surrender of Sardis: encourages demo-cratic regimes among Greek cities of Asia Minor: captures Miletus: (autumn) captures Halicarnassus: (winter) advances through Lydia and Pamphylia.

333 Alexander marches on Celaenae: cuts the knot at Gordium: death of Memnon, the Persians' most able Greek commander. Persians mobilize another army at Babylon: (Summer) Alexander advances to the Cilician Gates: (Sept.) victory over Darius at Issus. Alexander advances through Phoenicia. First peace offer by Darius.

332 (Jan.–Feb.) Surrender of Byblos and Sidon: (March) siege of
     Tyre begun: second peace offer from Darius: (July) fall of
     Tyre: (Sept.) Gaza captured: (Nov.) Alexander crowned as
     Pharaoh at Memphis.

331 (March) Alexander visits oracle of Zeus Ammon at Siwa:
     (April) founds Alexandria: marches north through Syria:
     (Sept.) defeats Darius at Gaugamela: (December) enters Susa.

330 (January) Alexander enters and sacks Persepolis: (June) sets out
     for Ecbatana and renews pursuit of Darius: (July) Darius found
     murdered at Hecatompylos: (August) Alexander advances to
     Drangiana: (autumn) conspiracy of Philotas discovered:
     execution of Philotas and Parmenio: (winter) advances through
     Arachosia.

329 (March) Alexander turns north and crosses Hindu Khush by
     Khawak Pass: (May) advances north into Bactria in pursuit
     of Bessus: Macedonian veterans and Thessalian volunteers
     posted home: (June) Bessus captured: advances to Samarkand.
     Local revolt of Spitamenes in Sogdiana: Alexander takes up
     winter quarters in Bactria.

328 Execution of Bessus: campaign against Spitamenes: (summer)
     killing of Cleitus at Samarkand.

327 Alexander married to Roxane. Recruitment of 30,000 young
     Persians: conspiracy of the pages: execution of Callisthenes:
     (early summer) Alexander launches invasion of India; wel-
     comed by envoys from Taxila: divides his force with Perdiccas
     and spends the rest of the year in reconnaissance campaigns.

326 (March) Alexander regroups in Taxila and whole army advances
     against Porus: (July) defeats Porus at the Hydaspes river, but
     with heavy losses: death of Bucephalus: army mutinies at the
     Beas river and refuses to go further east: (Nov.) fleet and army
     sail down the Indus.

325 Alexander campaigns against the Brahman cities: Alexander
     severely wounded by the Mallians: (August) reaches the mouth
     of the Indus: army marches through the Gedrosian desert:
     (winter) is rejoined by Nearchus with the fleet.

324 Alexander returns to Susa: restoration of order and reorganiza-
     tion of army and administration: arrival of the 30,000 young
     Persian recruits, 'the Successors': mass marriages of Greeks
     and Persians in Susa.

Amnesty declared for all exiles from Greek cities, including mainland Greece: mainland Greeks required to recognize Alexander as a god.

(Summer) Army rebels against scheme for partial demobilization. Craterus appointed regent in Greece to replace Antipater, and entrusted with leading Macedonian veterans home.

(Autumn) Death of Hephaestion.

323 (Spring) campaign against the Cossaeans: plans for circumnavigation of Africa and Arabia: Alexander returns to Babylon: (May) contracts fever: (June) dies in Babylon.

Philip Arrhidaeus and Alexander's infant son by Roxane proclaimed kings: Craterus guardian of Philip: Antipater regent in Greece. Coalition of Greek states formed against Macedon. Antipater besieged in Lamia.

322 Leonnatus reaches Antipater with reinforcements but is killed: (Aug.) Battle of Crannon: Greek coalition collapses: surrender of Athens: flight and suicide of Demosthenes.

321 Perdiccas killed by his troops in Egypt. Antipater regent.

319 Death of Antipater. Polyperchon proclaimed regent. War between Polyperchon and Cassander, Antipater's son. Polyperchon supports the democratic, Cassander the oligarchic factions throughout Greece.

318 Democratic regime seizes power in Athens. Execution of Phocion. Cassander occupies Athens: limits the franchise: installs Demetrius of Phaleron as governor.

317 Cassander expels Polyperchon from Macedonia. Olympias, Alexander's mother, executes Eurydice, queen of Philip Arrhidaeus, and many of Cassander's supporters.

316 Cassander captures and executes Olympias. Antigonus, father of Demetrius, gains control of Asia Minor.

315 Coalition of Cassander, Lysimachus and Ptolemy against Antigonus. Antigonus occupies Syria.

314 Antigonus captures Tyre: proclaims freedom of Greek cities from Cassander.

312 Ptolemy defeats Demetrius at Gaza. Seleucus establishes himself in Babylon. Demetrius defeats Ptolemy's army at Myus.

311 A peace settlement reached: Cassander regent in Greece: Lysimachus in control of Thrace; Ptolemy of Egypt; Antigonus of Asia Minor.

310 Cassander murders Roxane and her son, Alexander IV.
Ptolemy occupies Cyprus.

307 Demetrius expels Demetrius of Phalerum and liberates
Athens.

306 Demetrius defeats Ptolemy's fleet and occupies Cyprus.
Antigonus and Demetrius assume the title of kings.

305-4 Demetrius besieges Rhodes.

303 Demetrius occupies the Peloponnese: re-forms Alexander's
Hellenic League at Corinth and is proclaimed captain-general.
Antigonus plans to subdue his rivals and seize supreme power.

302 Fresh coalition of Cassander, Ptolemy, Seleucus, Lysimachus.

301 'Battle of the Kings' at Ipsus: Antigonus defeated and killed:
Demetrius escapes but finds little support in Athens or Greece:
escapes to the Hellespont to rebuild his forces.

299 Seleucus marries Demetrius' daughter Stratonice: Demetrius'
fortunes revive. Pyrrhus sent to Egypt as hostage.

297 Death of Cassander.

294 Demetrius besieges and captures Athens: enters Macedonia:
kills Alexander, Cassander's successor: assumes the crown.

291 Demetrius captures Thebes.

289 Demetrius campaigns in Aetolia and Epirus against Pyrrhus:
begins to build large fleet and lay plans to recover his father's
dominions.

288 New coalition of Lysimachus, Seleucus, Ptolemy and Pyrrhus
against Demetrius.

287 Pyrrhus invades Macedonia: Demetrius' troops go over to him.
Demetrius raises troops in Greece: crosses to Miletus: attacks
Lysimachus' territories in Caria and Lydia.

285 His guerrilla campaigns terminated by sickness: surrenders to
Seleucus: is kept in open captivity in Syria.

283 Demetrius dies in captivity.

281 Pyrrhus invited to help Tarentum against Rome.

280 Defeats Romans in first battle at Heracleia: advances on Rome
and attempts to negotiate through Cineas: his terms rejected.

279 Romans renew the war: inconclusive and costly battle at
Asculum.

278 Pyrrhus crosses to Sicily at the islanders' invitation to help
them against the Carthaginians.

277-6 Successful at first but later falls out with Sicilians.

275 Returns to Tarentum: (Autumn) defeated by the Romans at Beneventum.

274 Returns to Epirus with barely a third of his original army: invades Macedonia and defeats the king, Demetrius' son Antigonus.

272 Accepts invitation to help Cleonymus regain the throne of Sparta. Repulsed from Sparta, he attempts to capture Argos: engaging the Argives and Antigonus, he is killed in street fighting.

I

AGESILAUS

[444–360 B.C.]

* *
*

ARCHIDAMUS,[1] the son of Zeuxidamas, was one of the most illustrious of the kings of Sparta. When he died, he left a son Agis by Lampido, a woman of noble birth, and a much younger son, Agesilaus, whose mother was Eupolia, the daughter of Melesippidas. Since Agis was the legitimate heir to the throne, it was expected that Agesilaus would spend his life as a private citizen, and he was therefore brought up according to the regular Spartan system of education, which is austere in its way of life, full of hardships, and designed to train young men to obey orders. It was for this reason, we are told, that Simonides applied to Sparta the epithet 'man-taming', because the effect of her customs was above all to make her citizens amenable and obedient to the laws, like horses which are broken in while they are still colts. The law exempts the heir-apparent to the throne from the necessity of undergoing this training, and so Agesilaus was exceptional in this respect, namely that by the time he came to rule he had already been taught to serve. The result was that he was on more harmonious terms with his subjects than any of the other kings of Sparta, because the commanding and regal qualities that he possessed by nature were tempered by a kindliness and a regard for his people which he had acquired through his public training.

2. During the year that he spent in one of the companies of boys who were brought up together under the Spartan system,[2] he had as his lover Lysander, who was especially struck by his natural modesty

1. A friend of Pericles, he was king of Sparta at the time of the beginning of the Peloponnesian war. He died about 427 B.C. For places mentioned in this *Life* see Maps 1 and 4, pp. 433, 437.
2. See *Life of Lycurgus*, ch. 15.

A.A. – 2

and discretion. Agesilaus was more aggressive and hot-tempered than his companions. He longed to be first in all things, and he had in him a vehemence and an impetuosity which were inexhaustible and carried him over all obstacles: yet at the same time he was so gentle and ready to obey authority that he did whatever was demanded of him. He acted in this way from a sense of honour, not of fear, and he was far more sensitive to rebuke than to any amount of hardship. He was lame in one leg, but the beauty of his physique in the prime of his youth made the deformity pass almost unnoticed, and the ease and light-heartedness with which he endured it went far to compensate for the disability, since he was the first to joke and make fun of himself on this subject. In fact his lameness served to reveal his ambition even more clearly, since he never allowed it to deter him from any enterprise, however arduous it might turn out. No likeness of his appearance has come down to us, for he would never agree to sit for a portrait either to a sculptor or to a painter and even when he was dying he forbade the making of a statue or a picture of himself. He is described as having been a small man of a rather insignificant presence. On the other hand his cheerfulness and high spirits at times of crisis and his capacity to raise a laugh, which he did without a trace of harshness or animosity in word or look, made him more agreeable even in his old age than many younger and handsomer men. But it is worth noting that his father Archidamus was fined by the ephors, according to Theophrastus, for having married a small woman. They complained, 'She will bear us a race of kinglets, not of kings.'

3. It was during the reign of Agesilaus' elder brother Agis that Alcibiades, who had been recalled from Sicily, escaped on the way to Athens and came to Sparta, and he had not been long in the city before he was accused of committing adultery with Timaea, Agis' wife. When she bore a child, Agis refused to acknowledge it as his own, and declared that Alcibiades was the father. The historian Douris tells us that Timaea was not at all put out by this, and that when she was at home with her Helot attendants she would under her breath call the child Alcibiades instead of using its given name, Leotychidas: he also reports Alcibiades himself as having said that he had seduced Timaea not out of wanton passion, but because he cherished the ambition that his descendants should reign over the

Spartans. It was for this reason, namely the fear of Agis' anger, that Alcibiades escaped from Sparta. As for the boy himself, he was always regarded by Agis with suspicion, and was never given the honours to which he would have been entitled as a legitimate son. However, when Agis was on his death-bed, Leotychidas besought the king with tears to acknowledge him, and finally prevailed upon him to do so in the presence of many witnesses. But after Agis' death,[1] Lysander, who, as a result of his victory over the Athenians at Aegospotami had advanced to a position of great influence in Sparta, tried to promote Agesilaus' claim to the throne, on the ground that Leotychidas was a bastard and had no lawful title to the succession.[2] Because of his personal virtues and of the fact that he had been brought up as a commoner and had shared the discipline of a Spartan training, many of the citizens welcomed Lysander's plan and gave Agesilaus their support. However, there was a diviner in Sparta named Diopeithes, who had an extraordinary knowledge of ancient prophecies and enjoyed a great reputation for his skill in interpreting religious matters. Diopeithes declared that it was contrary to the will of heaven for a lame man to become king of Sparta, and when the matter came before a court, he cited the following oracle:

Though *you* are sound of limb, proud Sparta, look to your ruler,
Lest from your stock a disabled prince should succeed to the kingdom.
For then unlooked for ordeals and numberless trials shall oppress you
And the stormy billows of man-killing war shall roll down upon you.

Lysander's reply to this was that if the Spartans were really disturbed by the oracle, it was against Leotychidas that they should be on their guard. It did not matter to the God that a man who was literally lame should become king: the real danger was that the succession should fall upon one who was not of legitimate birth at all, nor even a descendant of Heracles, and this was what was meant by the phrase 'a disabled prince'. For his part Agesilaus declared that the Spartans had Poseidon to bear witness that Leotychidas was illegitimate, because Agis had been compelled by an earthquake to run out of his bedroom, and after this more than ten months had elapsed before Leotychidas was born.[3]

1. In 398 B.C.

2. See *The Rise and Fall of Athens*, Penguin Books, 1960, *Life of Alcibiades*. ch. 22.

3. See *The Rise and Fall of Athens*, *Life of Alcibiades*, ch. 23; *Life of Lysander*, ch. 22.

4. These were the circumstances in which Agesilaus had ascended the throne, and he proceeded to expel Leotychidas from the country as a bastard and take possession of Agis' estates. But since his kinsmen on his mother's side, although reputable enough, were all excessively poor, he distributed half of his property among them, and in this way made sure that his inheritance should bring him good-will instead of envy and hostility. As for Xenophon's assertion that by obeying his countrymen's will in everything Agesilaus gained so much power that he could do what he liked, the facts were as follows. At that time the supreme power in the state was exercised by the ephors and the Senate. The ephors held office for a year at a time, while the senators were elected for life, and both these offices had been created to act as a check upon the power of the kings, as I have explained in my *Life of Lycurgus*.[1] This was why a state of perpetual feud and hostility had grown up from the very earliest times between the kings and the magistrates. Agesilaus, however, was determined to break with this tradition. Instead of opposing and thwarting these officials, he made a point of courting their favour: he sought their agreement in every undertaking, and when invited to meet them, almost ran into their presence. If ever the ephors appeared when he was seated on the throne and transacting business, he would rise to greet them, and whenever a new senator was elected, he would send each one a cloak and an ox as a mark of recognition of his membership of the Senate. Thus all the time that he appeared to be honouring and exalting the dignity of their office, he was unobtrusively increasing his own authority and strengthening the power of the crown through the goodwill which he attracted to himself.

5. In his dealings with the rest of the citizens he behaved with more principle towards his enemies than towards his friends. By this I mean that he would never act against the former without just cause, but would sometimes associate himself with injustices committed by the latter. In the same way he was too generous not to give credit to his enemies if they were in the right, but he could not bring himself to condemn his friends if they were in the wrong, indeed he took pleasure in helping them and sharing in their misdeeds. In short he considered that nothing was dishonourable so long as it was done to help a friend. On the other hand, if any of his adversaries fell into

1. *Life of Lycurgus* chs. 5 & 7.

misfortune, he would be the first to sympathize and show himself ready to help if they wished it, and in this way he won the hearts and engaged the loyalty of his whole people. When the ephors saw this they began to be afraid of his power, and fined him on the ground that he had diverted to himself the loyalty which the Spartans properly owed to the state.

Now the natural philosophers believe that if the forces of conflict and discord were eliminated from the universe, the heavenly bodies would stand still, and in the resulting harmony the processes of motion and generation would be brought to a dead stop. In the same way the Spartan law-giver Lycurgus seems to have introduced the spirit of ambition and contention into the country's constitution as an incitement to virtue: evidently he was anxious that good citizens should always be conscious of differences and of an element of rivalry between each other, and he believed that that kind of acquiescence which feebly gives way without contesting the intentions of the other side and avoids any exertion or struggle does not deserve the name of harmony. Some people believe that Homer thought the same, and the fact that he makes Agamemnon rejoice on the occasion when Odysseus and Achilles are so carried away that they fall to abusing one another 'with fearsome words' suggests that he believed that this rivalry and quarrelling between the chieftains would produce some great benefit for the Greeks. However it would be wrong to accept this principle unreservedly, since dissensions of this kind, if they are pushed to extremes, are most harmful to states and carry great dangers with them.

6. Soon after Agesilaus had been raised to the throne, reports arrived from Asia that the Persian king was assembling a great fleet with which he intended to sweep the Lacedaemonians from the sea. Now Lysander was especially anxious to be sent to Asia in order to help his friends there. These protégés were men whom he had left behind as governors and administrators of the Greek cities, but who because of their unjust and violent methods of government were being driven out by the citizens and in some cases put to death. He therefore persuaded Agesilaus to undertake a campaign in Asia and make war on the Persians as the champion of the Greeks, and he advised him to cross the sea so as to carry the war as far as possible away from Greece, and by striking first to anticipate the barbarian's

preparations. At the same time he dispatched letters to his friends urging them to send messengers to Sparta and to invite Agesilaus to be their general. Accordingly Agesilaus appeared before the Spartan assembly and agreed to undertake the campaign if they would give him thirty Spartans to act as commanders and advisers, a picked body of two thousand Helots, and a force of six thousand men drawn from Sparta's allies in Greece. Thanks to Lysander's support, these preparations were quickly approved and Agesilaus was immediately sent out with the thirty Spartans. Lysander assumed the leadership of these advisers, not only because of his great prestige and influence but also because of his friendship with Agesilaus: while for his part the king considered that in securing him this command Lysander had done him an even greater service than in raising him to the throne.

While this expedition was assembling at Geraestus,[1] Agesilaus himself travelled to Aulis, where he spent the night. As he slept, he dreamed that he heard a voice which said to him, 'King of the Lacedaemonians, you must know that no man has ever been chosen as the commander of all Greece save Agamemnon in time past, and now yourself. Since you command the same peoples, are making war against the same enemy and setting out from the same place, it is right that you should offer up to the goddess the same sacrifice as Agamemnon did before he set sail.' Agesilaus at once remembered how Agamemnon had sacrificed his own daughter in obedience to the soothsayers. However he did not allow himself to be disturbed by the vision, but as soon as he rose he told his friends of the dream and said that he intended to honour the goddess with a sacrifice in which she could rightly take pleasure, but that he would not imitate the callous insensibility of Agamemnon. He then had a hind crowned with garlands and gave orders for the sacrifice to be performed by his own diviner, instead of the one who is normally appointed by the Boeotians.[2] When the Boeotarchs heard of this, they were very angry and sent their officials to forbid Agesilaus to offer up a sacrifice in a manner which was contrary to the laws and customs of the Boeotians. Not content with delivering this message, the officers also threw the thigh-pieces of the victim off the altar. This episode caused Agesilaus great distress as he sailed away: he was angry with the Boeotians,

1. A town at the south-eastern end of Euboea. The date was early in 396 B.C.
2. Aulis is in Boeotian territory.

but he was also much disturbed by the ill omen and feared it fore-boded that his enterprise would be frustrated and the expedition fail to achieve its purpose.

7. When he arrived at Ephesus, he found the power and reputation which Lysander had acquired there at first annoying and before long intolerable. There was always a crowd of suitors around Lysander's door, and everybody seemed to follow him about and pay court to him, as if Agesilaus were no more than the nominal commander of the expedition and held this position only as a legal fiction, while the real power, authority, and initiative rested with Lysander. The fact was that none of the Greek generals who had been sent to Asia in the past had ever exercised such autocratic power or made himself so much feared as Lysander: none had conferred greater rewards on their friends or inflicted greater injuries on their enemies. These events were still fresh in men's memories, and when they observed Agesilaus' simple, plain and unassuming character and noted that Lysander's behaviour was as brusque, harsh and overbearing as before, they accepted the latter's authority without question and looked up to him alone as the commander. The immediate result was that the senior Spartans in the expedition were deeply offended when they found themselves treated as subordinates of Lysander rather than advisers to the king. Secondly, although Agesilaus was by no means an envious man, nor one who resented honours being paid to others, still he cherished ambitions of his own and was de-termined to assert himself, and he now began to fear that any brilliant successes which he might achieve in the campaign would be credited by public opinion to Lysander. He therefore adopted the following tactics.

First of all he opposed Lysander's advice. If there was any course of action which Lysander recommended enthusiastically, he made a point of putting it aside or ignoring it and of taking up another in its place. Next any petitioner who he believed had come to him relying upon Lysander's influence he sent away empty-handed, and on the same principle any party to a law-suit who was opposed by Lysander could be sure of winning his case, while those whom Lysander was evidently eager to help, would be hard put to it to avoid being fined. All this was done not casually but deliberately and systematically, and when Lysander understood the reason, he made no attempt to hide it from his friends. He told them that it was on his account that they were being slighted, and he urged them to go and pay their respects to the king and to those who possessed more influence than himself.

8. As these remarks and actions of Lysander's appeared to have been expressly designed to arouse feeling against the king, Agesilaus determined to humble him still further. He appointed him to be his carver, and on one occasion, we are told, remarked in front of a large company, 'Now, let all these petitioners go and pay their court to my carver.' These words touched Lysander to the quick, and he said, 'I see, Agesilaus, that you know very well how to humiliate your friends.' 'Yes, I do,' the king retorted, 'or at any rate those who set themselves up to be more powerful than myself.' Lysander continued, 'Well, perhaps what you have said is wiser than what I have done. In that case, find me some post or some place where I can be of most use to you and cause you least offence.'

After this conversation Lysander was sent to the Hellespont, and there he won over Spithridates, a wealthy Persian who commanded two hundred horsemen and lived in the province that was governed by Pharnabazus. However Lysander could not forgive the king, but continued to nurse his resentment, and for the rest of his life he went on plotting to deprive the two royal families of the crown and throw open the succession to all Spartans alike. In fact he would probably have brought about a great upheaval in his country's affairs in consequence of this quarrel, if he had not been killed on his expedition into Boeotia.[1] We may note that ambitious spirits do far more harm than good in a state, unless they can keep their aspirations within proper limits. Yet even though Lysander behaved with an insufferable arrogance, as he undoubtedly did in pursuing his ambitions without any restraint, Agesilaus could surely have devised some less objectionable way of correcting the faults of a man of his reputation and aspiring disposition. As it was, they both seem to have suffered from a similar obsession, so that the one would not acknowledge the authority of his superior, while the other could not bear being ignored by his comrade.

9. At first Tissaphernes, the governor of the coastal region, was afraid of Agesilaus and concluded a treaty with him in which he

1. See *The Rise and Fall of Athens, Life of Lysander*, chs. 24–8.

undertook to set the Greek cities free and make them independent of the king of Persia. But soon after, when he believed he had gathered a strong enough force, he declared war, and Agesilaus gladly took up the challenge. His expedition to Asia had aroused great hopes throughout Greece, and he thought it would be a disgraceful thing if Xenophon and his Ten Thousand[1] could make their way across Persia to the sea and defeat the king in battle as often as they chose, while he, the leader of the Spartans, who were supreme by land and sea, could achieve no success which would be remembered by the Greeks. So he repaid Tissaphernes' treachery with a justifiable deception of his own, and gave out that he intended to march his army into Caria; but as soon as the barbarian had gathered his forces there, he set out to make a raid on Phrygia. There he captured many cities and seized a huge quantity of treasure: in this way he demonstrated to his friends that to break a solemn covenant shows contempt for the gods, but to outmanoeuvre one's enemy in war at once satisfies justice, earns great glory and combines pleasure with profit. However he knew that his force was weak in cavalry, and since a sacrificial victim – which was found to be without a liver – indicated that the omens were unfavourable, he fell back upon Ephesus. Here he began to recruit a force of cavalry, and gave each member of the richer classes the alternative of furnishing a horse and rider if they did not wish to serve themselves. Many of them preferred to do this, and so Agesilaus quickly built up a force of warlike horsemen instead of useless infantrymen, for those who did not wish to serve at all hired substitutes who were eager to fight, and those who did not wish to serve in the cavalry hired men who could ride. In this Agesilaus was following the example of Agamemnon, who, he thought, had shown great sense in accepting a good mare and exempting from military service a rich man who had no stomach for fighting.[2] On another occasion Agesilaus gave orders that before his prisoners were put up to be auctioned by the dealers in the spoils of war, they should first be stripped of their clothes. The clothes found plenty of buyers, but the spectators burst out laughing at the sight of the men and their naked bodies, for these were white and tender as they had never been exposed to sun or wind, and were regarded as useless and worthless. Agesilaus, who was watching, pointed first to the captives and then

1. See Xenophon, *The Persian Expedition*, Penguin Books, 1949.
2. *Iliad* xxiii, 296ff.

to their clothes and remarked, 'These are the men you fight, and those are the things you will gain by fighting.'

10. When the campaigning season returned[1] and enabled Agesilaus to invade the enemy's territory, he let it be known that he would march into Lydia, and on this occasion he had no intention of misleading Tissaphernes. However, the satrap managed to deceive himself, for he distrusted Agesilaus on account of the trick he had played before. He concluded that this time Agesilaus really would invade Caria, for the country was ill-suited for cavalry operations and he was still weak in cavalry. But Agesilaus did exactly what he had said and marched into the plain of Sardis. Tissaphernes was obliged to hurry to the rescue of the province, and as he advanced over the level country, he cut off many stragglers from the Greek army, who were plundering it. Agesilaus observed that the enemy's infantry had not yet arrived, while he had his whole army at hand, and so he made haste to attack. He distributed some of the light infantry among his cavalry, and ordered them to advance at full speed and charge the enemy, while he himself led forward the infantry. The barbarians were routed, and the Greeks, following hard on their heels, stormed their camp with great slaughter. This victory not only left him free to plunder the king's territory unmolested, but gave him the satisfaction of seeing Tissaphernes punished according to his deserts, for he was a detestable man who had made himself utterly hated by the whole Greek race. Immediately after the battle the king gave orders for him to be arrested by Tithraustes, who had him beheaded. Tithraustes then appealed to Agesilaus to make terms and sail back to Greece, and offered him money to do this. Agesilaus replied that it was only his city that had the authority to make peace, that he took more pleasure in enriching his soldiers than himself, and that as far as their enemies were concerned, the Greeks only considered it honourable to take spoils, not gifts. However, as he wished to oblige Tithraustes for having punished Tissaphernes, that public enemy of the Greeks, he withdrew his army into Phrygia, having first accepted a sum of thirty talents from the Persian to maintain his soldiers on the march.

While he was on his way he received a dispatch from the government in Sparta appointing him to the command of the naval as

1. The spring of 395 B.C.

well as the land forces in Asia, an honour which was never before or after granted to anybody else. He was by general consent at once the most powerful and the most famous man of his time, as Theopompus has noted, but he took more pride in his virtues than in his position. Yet he is considered to have made a mistake at this point in delegating the command of the fleet to Peisander.[1] There were older and more experienced men to choose from, and in making this appointment Agesilaus' real purpose was to please his wife, who was a sister of Peisander: in other words he was acting out of family loyalty rather than in the interests of his country.

11. He had now[2] stationed his troops in the province governed by Pharnabazus: here the food was plentiful and he was able to secure great quantities of treasure. He also advanced as far as the borders of Paphlagonia and entered into an alliance with Cotys, the king of that region: Cotys' confidence had already been won by what he had learned of Agesilaus' virtues and he wished to make friends with the Spartan.

Agesilaus was accompanied on all his journeys and campaigns by Spithridates, the Persian whom Lysander had persuaded to leave Pharnabazus and throw in his lot with the Greeks.[3] He had a son, a very handsome youth named Megabates, to whom Agesilaus was passionately attached, and a beautiful daughter of marriageable age, whom Agesilaus persuaded Cotys to marry. Cotys placed a thousand horsemen and two thousand light infantry under Agesilaus' command, and the king then made another raid on Phrygia and devastated Pharnabazus' territory. The Persian did not dare to meet Agesilaus in the field, nor even to trust to his own fortresses: instead he kept his most valuable and treasured possessions with him and remained continuously on the move, taking refuge in one part of the country after another, and always avoiding a battle. At last Spithridates, who had watched his movements closely, attacked him with the help of Herippidas the Spartan, captured his camp, and seized the whole of his treasure. On this occasion, however, Herippidas behaved with

1. The war at sea was no less important than that on land. The Persians were operating in alliance with the Athenian admiral Conon and in 394 Peisander was decisively defeated and killed at Cnidus. See ch. 17.

2. The autumn of 395 B.C.

3. See ch. 8.

extraordinary severity in supervising the distribution of the spoils: he compelled the Persians to hand over everything they had taken, checked and scrutinized each item, and in the end so annoyed Spithridates that he marched off to Sardis, taking the Paphlagonian contingent with him.

This incident is said to have distressed Agesilaus more than any other in this war. He was grieved at losing a gallant soldier in the person of Spithridates together with a powerful force, and he was ashamed at having incurred the charge of meanness and avarice from which he had always taken pride in keeping himself and his country free. Apart from the public aspect of the affair, he was irritated beyond measure for a more personal reason, namely his love for Megabates which had taken possession of him, although whenever the boy was present, he summoned up all his determination and struggled to master his passion. Indeed on one occasion when Megabates came up and moved as if to embrace and kiss him, Agesilaus turned away. The boy was embarrassed by this and drew back, and afterwards kept his distance when he addressed him, whereupon Agesilaus, who now felt upset and repentant at having rebuffed him, pretended to wonder what was wrong with Megabates and why he no longer greeted him with a kiss. 'It is your fault,' the king's companions told him, 'It was you who refused and took fright and turned away from his kiss, but even now he could be persuaded to come to you again. But this time, see that you do not shrink away.' Agesilaus thought for a while in silence, and then he said, 'There is no harm in your persuading him, for I think I would rather fight that battle of the kiss again, than be master of all the gold I have ever seen.' This was how he acted when Megabates was present, but when the boy was gone, he was so consumed with the fire of his passion for him, that it is hard to say, if he had come back, whether he would have had the strength to refuse his kiss.

12. After this Pharnabazus wished to hold a conference with him, and Apollophanes of Cyzicus, who acted as host to them both, arranged the meeting. Agesilaus arrived first with his friends at the appointed place, and choosing a shady spot where the grass was thick, threw himself down and awaited Pharnabazus. When the Persian arrived, embroidered rugs and soft cushions were at once spread out for him, but seeing Agesilaus reclining there without ceremony, he

felt embarrassed and sat down just as he was beside the king on the grass, in spite of the fact that he was wearing a splendid robe of fine texture and many colours. After they had exchanged civilities, Pharnabazus had a number of just complaints to make. He pointed out that although he had rendered the Spartans many important services in their war against the Athenians, they were now devastating his territory. Agesilaus saw that all the Spartans around him were keeping their eyes fixed on the ground and were at a loss what to say, because they knew that Pharnabazus had been badly treated. He answered: 'While we were on friendly terms with the king in the past, Pharnabazus, we treated all that belongs to him in a friendly fashion; now that we have become enemies, we treat it in a hostile fashion. Since we see that you desire to be numbered among the king's possessions, we naturally injure him through you. But from the day you consider yourself worthy to be called a friend and ally of the Greeks, instead of a slave to the king, you have a right to regard this army, these weapons and ships, and all of us Greeks as the guardians of your possessions and of your liberty, without which nothing in the world is honourable or desirable.' At this Pharnabazus explained his own intentions. 'If the king sends out any other general in my place,' he said, 'I shall be on your side. But if he gives me the command, I shall gladly fight you on his behalf and do you all the mischief in my power.' This answer delighted Agesilaus, and as the two men rose to their feet, he took Pharnabazus by the hand and said, 'Pharnabazus, I hope a man like you will become our friend and not our enemy.'

13. As Pharnabazus and his friends were leaving, his son who was at the rear of the party, ran up to Agesilaus and said with a smile, 'Agesilaus, I make you my guest,'[1] and presented him with a javelin which he was holding in his hand. Agesilaus accepted it, and as he was pleased with the boy's looks and courteous manner, he glanced around among his companions to see whether one of them had something which might serve as a present. His eye fell on a horse ridden by his secretary Idaeus, which was handsomely caparisoned,

1. According to Greek custom, the word 'guest', *xenos*, also signified a person in a foreign city with whom one made a treaty of hospitality for oneself and one's heirs. This arrangement was customarily confirmed by an exchange of gifts and an oath to Zeus as the god of hospitality.

and he had the trappings taken off and gave them to the boy. Agesilaus never forgot this connection, and in later years, when the young man's brothers deprived him of his home and drove him into exile in the Peloponnese, he took him under his protection and even helped him in his love affairs. The Persian was attached to an Athenian boy, an athlete who, because he had outgrown the size and strength of others of his age, was in danger of being debarred from competing at Olympia. So he appealed to Agesilaus to help the boy, and the king, who was anxious to oblige his protégé even in this matter, succeeded after a good deal of trouble in obtaining the concession he was seeking.

For the most part, Agesilaus was a man of strict principles who stood by the letter of the law, but in matters of friendship he considered that to insist on justice was merely an excuse for refusing to do a service. At any rate, it is reported that he wrote a letter to Hidrieus the Carian, which ran as follows: 'As for Nicias, if he is innocent, acquit him: if he is guilty, acquit him for my sake; but in any case, acquit him.' This was how Agesilaus acted in most instances where the interests of his friends were concerned, but sometimes, if the exigencies of the situation demanded it, he allowed expediency to prevail over affection. He gave an example of this once when, after an alarm had been given and he was breaking camp in some confusion, he left behind a favourite companion who was sick. The man entreated him and called after him as he was leaving, whereupon Agesilaus turned and remarked that it was difficult to be compassionate and prudent at the same time. This story has been recorded by Hieronymus the philosopher.

14. Agesilaus was now nearing the end of the second year of his command in Asia. By this time his fame had spread far and wide within the Persian empire, and he had gained an almost legendary reputation for self-discipline, for moderation and for the simplicity of his way of life. Whenever he travelled, he made a point of taking up his quarters in the most sacred precincts by himself, and in this way he made the gods the witnesses of the most private details of his life. Among all the thousands of soldiers in his army, it would have been hard to find one who slept on a harder bed than the king, and in his resistance to the variations of heat and cold he seemed to be constituted as though nature had given him alone the power to endure

whatever seasons or weather the gods might send. In particular it
delighted the Greek inhabitants of Asia to see their former tyrants,
the Persian governors and generals, who had long been intolerably
harsh and who had revelled in wealth and luxury, now bowing and
trembling before a man who walked about in a coarse cloak, and to
watch them obsequiously change their whole bearing and appearance
in response to a single curt and 'laconic' speech from him. For many
of them this sight called to mind the words of the poet Timotheus

> Ares is lord: Greece has no fear of gold.

15. By this time Asia Minor was in a state of ferment, and many
regions were ripe for revolt. Agesilaus now re-established order
among the cities of the coast and restored to them the constitutional
forms of government without resorting to any executions or banish-
ments.[1] Next he determined to advance further into the interior and
to transfer the theatre of the war from the Greek seaboard to the
heart of Persia, to fight for the person of the king and the wealth of
Ecbatana and Susa, and above all to make it impossible for him to sit
on his throne playing the arbitrator between the Greek states in their
wars and corrupting their leaders with gold. But just at this moment[2]
the Spartan Epicydides arrived to report that Sparta had become
embroiled in a great war with Thebes and other states, and to
summon him to return at once and rescue his fellow-countrymen.

> Unhappy Greeks, barbarians to each other [3]

How else can one describe that spirit of envy which now diverted
the attention of the Greeks to forming alliances and conspiracies
against one another, which laid hands on fortune at the very moment
when she was bearing them up on her wings, and which turned
against themselves the very weapons that had been trained on the
barbarians, and brought back to their native land the wars which had
only recently been banished from it? I certainly cannot agree with
Demaratus the Corinthian, who said that those Greeks who did not
live to see Alexander seated on the throne of Darius had been deprived of a great pleasure. On the contrary I believe that they would
have been more likely to weep when they remembered that this

---

1. In particular he brought to an end the misrule which had been practised
by the autocratic governments of ten installed by Lysander after the defeat of
Athens.

2. 394 B.C.   3. Euripides, *Troades*, 766.

triumph was left for Alexander and his Macedonians, while they themselves squandered the lives of Greek generals on the battlefields of Leuctra, Coroneia, Corinth and Arcadia.

At any rate nothing in Agesilaus' life was greater or nobler than his conduct on this occasion, and history has no finer example to show of just obedience to higher authority. Hannibal was in grave difficulties and almost on the point of being driven out of Italy, yet it was only with the greatest reluctance that he obeyed the order to return to the war at home, and Alexander, when he heard of Antipater's battle with Agis merely joked about it and remarked, 'It seems, my friends, that while we have been conquering Darius here, there has been a battle of mice in Arcadia.'[1] Sparta deserves, then, to be congratulated on the honour which Agesilaus paid her and the respect which he showed for her laws. The moment the dispatch roll was delivered to him, although he was then at the height of his power and good fortune, he abandoned these, gave up the great hopes which beckoned him on, and immediately sailed away 'leaving his task unfulfilled'.[2]

He left many regrets behind him among his allies in Asia, and gave the lie to that saying of Erasistratus, the son of Phaeax, who remarked that the Spartans are the better men in public life, but the Athenians in private. Agesilaus proved himself an excellent king and general, but those who knew him most intimately valued him even more highly as a friend and companion.

The gold coins of Persia at this time were stamped with the figure of an archer, and Agesilaus declared that the king was driving him out of Asia with the help of ten thousand archers: this was the sum of money which had been sent to Athens and Thebes and distributed to the demagogues, and it was for this reason that their peoples now went to war with the Spartans.

16. Agesilaus now proceeded to cross the Hellespont and march through Thrace.[3] On his way he made no demands upon any of the barbarians, but merely sent envoys to each people, asking whether he should treat them as friends or as enemies as he passed through their territory. All the tribes of the region received him in friendly

1. The battle of Megalopolis in 331 B.C., at which Agis the Spartan king was killed.
2. *Iliad* iv, 175.
3. He followed the route which had been taken by Xerxes in 480 B.C.

fashion and did everything in their power to help him on his way; the one exception was a tribe known as the Trallians. Even Xerxes, so tradition has it, had given presents to them, and they now demanded of Agesilaus a hundred talents of silver and the same number of women. The king, however, answered them contemptuously, and asked why they did not come and take what they wanted: then he continued his advance, and finding them drawn up to bar his way, attacked them and routed them with great slaughter. He also put the same question as he had done elsewhere to the king of Macedonia, who replied that he would consider the matter. 'Let him consider it then,' retorted Agesilaus, 'but we shall march on.' The king was both amazed and awed by his audacity, and gave orders to let him pass as a friend. When he arrived in Thessaly, he proceeded to ravage the country, since the Thessalians were in alliance with his country's enemies, but he sent Xenocles and Scythes to the city of Larissa in the hope of negotiating a friendly settlement. The Thessalians, however, arrested the two envoys and imprisoned them. Some of Agesilaus' companions were greatly offended at this, and thought that he ought to pitch camp before Larissa and lay siege to it. But the king declared that it mattered more to him to lose one of these men than to conquer the whole of Thessaly, and so he came to terms with the enemy to recover them. And indeed we should not be surprised at this behaviour in Agesilaus. When the news reached him that a great battle had been fought near Corinth,[1] that some of the finest soldiers in Greece were suddenly no more, and that the losses of the Spartans had only been slight, but those of their enemies very heavy, he showed no sign of pleasure or exultation, but sighed deeply and exclaimed, 'Alas for Greece, how many brave men have you killed with your own hands! If these men were still alive, they could have conquered all the barbarians in the world.'

However, when the Pharsalians hung on the flanks of his army and harassed his advance, he ordered a force of five hundred horsemen to attack the enemy, led the charge himself, routed his opponents and set up a trophy at the foot of Mount Narthacium. Agesilaus was especially pleased with this victory, because with a force of cavalry which he had recruited and trained himself, he had defeated quite unaided the Thessalians, who prided themselves on their cavalry more than on any other arm.

1. July 394 B.C.

17. At this point Diphridas, one of the ephors from Sparta, met him and gave him orders to invade Boeotia immediately. His own plan had been to attack the Boeotians later, after gathering reinforcements, but he considered that he was bound to carry out the order of the government, and so he remarked to his friends that the day for which they had returned from Asia was now close at hand. At the same time he sent for two battalions[1] of the army, which were stationed near Corinth. Meanwhile the Spartans at home, who wished to do him honour, issued a proclamation that any young man who wished to volunteer might enlist to serve the king. All the young men who were eligible came forward eagerly, and of these the ephors selected fifty of the finest physique and the most active, and sent them to join him.

Agesilaus now marched through the pass of Thermopylae, crossed the territory of Phocis, which was friendly to him, and pitched his camp near Chaeronea. Here there was a partial eclipse of the sun, and at the same time Agesilaus learned of the death of the Spartan commander Peisander, who had been defeated in a sea-battle off Cnidus by Pharnabazus and Conon the Athenian.[2] Agesilaus was deeply distressed at the news, both because of his feelings for the man, and for the loss that the city had suffered, but in order to avoid spreading alarm or despondency among his troops, he ordered the messengers to report the opposite result and say that the Spartans had been victorious. He himself appeared in public with a garland on his head, offered up sacrifice for the victory, and distributed portions of the victims to his friends.

18. When his advance into Boeotia had taken him as far as Coronea and he had arrived within sight of the enemy, he drew up his troops in battle order, placing the Orchomenians on the left wing while he led the right in person. In the allied army the Thebans occupied the right wing and the Argives the left. Xenophon tells us that this battle was unlike any that had ever been fought before. He was an eye-witness and took part on the side of Agesilaus, whom he had accompanied on the march to Greece from Asia. When the two lines met, the first shock was not very violent, nor was the fighting heavy. The Thebans quickly routed the Orchomenians, and Agesilaus made

1. The Greek word *mora*, which was used to refer to the Spartan army, signifies a formation of between 600 and 900 men.
2. In August 394 B.C. The Athenian and Persian fleets had joined forces.

short work of the Argives; but in both instances the victors turned back when they learned that their respective left wings had been broken and were in full retreat. At this point Agesilaus might easily have won a victory if he had resisted the impulse to make a frontal attack on the Thebans, and had wheeled so as to take them in the rear after they had passed him. Instead, he allowed himself to be carried away by his natural ardour and fighting spirit, and attacked them head on, wishing to drive them back by main force. The Thebans resisted the charge just as fiercely, and a violent action developed all along the line, but the fighting was hottest at the point where the king himself was stationed, guarded by his fifty volunteers. It was these men's courage and the ardent rivalry which they showed in defending their king, which apparently saved his life. They fought furiously and exposed themselves recklessly, and although they could not prevent Agesilaus from being wounded by many thrusts from swords and spears which pierced his armour and entered his body, yet they succeeded with great difficulty in dragging him away alive: they formed a close ring around him and killed great numbers of the enemy, but suffered heavy losses themselves. In the end it proved too difficult to break the Theban front, and the Spartans were obliged to carry out the manoeuvre which they had rejected at the beginning. They parted their ranks and allowed the enemy to pass through, and then, when the Thebans had passed beyond them and were moving in looser formation, the Spartans followed, broke into a run, and attacked them from the flanks. But they failed to put them to rout. The Thebans withdrew in good order to Mount Helicon, proud of their achievement in keeping their own contingent undefeated.

19. Agesilaus was suffering great pain from his many wounds, but he refused to retire to his tent until he had first been carried around his army and had seen all the dead brought into the Spartan lines. Besides this he gave orders that all those of the enemy who had taken refuge in a nearby sanctuary should be allowed to depart. This was the temple of Athena Itonia, and in front of it stood a trophy which the Boeotians had erected many years before, when their army under Sparto had defeated the Athenians and killed their commander Tolmides.[1]

1. In 447 B.C. See *The Rise and Fall of Athens, Life of Pericles*, ch. 18.

'Early the next morning Agesilaus decided to test the spirit of the Thebans to see whether they would resume the fighting, and he gave orders to his soldiers to crown themselves with garlands and for his flute-players to play, while a trophy was set up in honour of the Spartan victory. When the enemy sent messengers to him requesting permission to collect their dead, he granted them a truce, and having in this way formally established his victory, he proceeded to Delphi where the Pythian games were being held. There he took part in the traditional procession in honour of Apollo, and also dedicated to him a tenth part of the spoils of the Asiatic campaigns, which amounted to a hundred talents.

When he returned home his behaviour and his mode of life soon earned him the love and admiration of his fellow-countrymen. In contrast to most of Sparta's generals, Agesilaus came back from foreign countries the same man as he had gone out: he was neither changed nor influenced by foreign customs, nor was he dissatisfied or impatient with those of his own country, but honoured and loved the Spartan traditions just as much as those who had never crossed the Eurotas. He made no changes in his habit of dining at the public table, in his baths, his attendance on his wife, the ornaments of his armour, or the furniture of his house: on the contrary, he made a point of preserving its doors, although they were so ancient that they might appear to have been the very doors originally put there by Aristodemus.[1]

Xenophon also tells us that his daughter's *cannathron* was no more elaborate than any other girl's: the *cannathron* is the wooden carriage carved in the shape of a griffin or a goat-stag, in which the young girls are carried in the sacred processions. Xenophon, it is true, does not mention the girl's name, and Dicaearchus remarks with some indignation that we know neither her name nor that of Epaminondas' mother. However, I have discovered among the annals of the Spartans that Agesilaus' wife was named Cleora and his daughters Eupolia and Proauga. His spear too has been preserved in Sparta: it can still be seen at the present day, but is no different from other men's.

20. Agesilaus had noticed that some of his fellow-countrymen took pride in breeding race-horses and gave themselves great airs in con-

1. The great-great-grandson of Hercules.

sequence, and so he persuaded his sister Cynisca to enter a chariot-team at Olympia: he wanted to prove to the Greeks that to win a prize there was no proof of any particular excellence, but merely of wealth and ostentatious expenditure. At this time Xenophon the philosopher,[1] who had served in Agesilaus' campaign in Asia, was still a member of his entourage, and as the king valued his company, he pressed him to send for his sons and bring them up in Sparta, so that they should learn the most important of all lessons, how to command and how to obey.

Meanwhile Lysander had been killed,[2] and Agesilaus now discovered that a widespread faction was still in existence, which the general had formed against him immediately after his return from Asia. So he set out to expose the true nature of Lysander's character. He discovered a speech which Lysander had left in the form of a pamphlet. This had been written for him by Cleon of Halicarnassus, but Lysander had planned to deliver it before the people in an effort to win them over to his schemes for bringing about a revolution and altering the Spartan constitution. Agesilaus wished to make this document public, but one of the senators who had read the speech and was disturbed by its eloquence and plausibility, urged the king not to bring Lysander back from the grave, but rather to bury the speech with him, and finally Agesilaus decided to accept this advice and say nothing. As for those of the Spartans who he knew were opposed to him, his plan was not to do them any open injury, but to arrange from time to time to send them out of the country as generals or governors of cities. By this means he exposed their faults if they proved themselves unscrupulous or grasping in the exercise of their authority: then, if they were put on trial, he would come to their help, use his influence on their behalf, and thus win them over and make them his partisans instead of his enemies, until in the end there would be no one left to oppose him.

The other king, Agesipolis, was scarcely more than a boy. His father, Pausanias, had been banished,[3] and since he himself was of a

1. Xenophon (c. 430–355 B.C.), the Athenian historian and soldier, best known to posterity as the friend of Socrates and author of *The Anabasis* (*The Persian Expedition*).

2. In 395: the discovery took place about 394–393 B.C.

3. He was blamed for having withdrawn the Spartan forces from Boeotian territory at the battle of Haliartus in which Lysander was killed. See *The Rise and Fall of Athens, Life of Pericles*, chs. 29–30.

gentle and retiring disposition, he played little part in the business of
governing Sparta, and in time Agesilaus succeeded in bringing him
too under his influence. Whenever the kings of Sparta are at home,
it is their custom to eat together in the same *phiditium*, or public mess.
Agesilaus knew that his colleague was prone to form attachments to
boys, just as he was himself, and so he often turned the conversation
to the subject of the boys who were of an age to take part in love
affairs. He would encourage the young king and even share with him
in pursuing these relationships and act as his confidant, for the general
view in Sparta is that there is nothing disgraceful in these attachments,
but that on the contrary such a love inspires modesty, ambition and
a burning desire to excel, as I have described in my *Life of Lycurgus*.

21. Agesilaus had now become the most powerful man in Sparta,
and this enabled him to arrange for the appointment of Teleutias, his
half-brother on his mother's side, to command the Spartan fleet.
Next he made an expedition to attack Corinth, and succeeded in
capturing the Long Walls with his land forces, while Teleutias
seized the enemy's ships and dockyards with his fleet. At that time
Corinth was held by the Argives. At the moment when Agesilaus
appeared with his army, they were celebrating the Isthmian games:[1]
he drove them out just as they had offered up their sacrifice to the
god, and they fled, leaving behind all the material they had brought
for the festival. Thereupon a number of exiles from Corinth, who
happened to be serving in Agesilaus' force, begged him to preside
over the games, but this he refused to do. Instead he remained there
while they celebrated the festival and provided the security for them
to do so without interruption. After his departure the Isthmian games
were again celebrated by the Argives, with the result that some of
the competitors gained victories for the second time, while others
were entered in the records as having won on the first occasion but
been defeated on the second. Agesilaus remarked that the Argives
had proved themselves by this action to be great cowards, since they
regarded the privilege of presiding over the games as a great and
inestimable honour, and yet had not the courage to fight for it.

For his part he thought it best to show only a moderate interest in
such celebrations. He saw to it that the choric and athletic festivals
were carried out with due ceremony in Sparta, he played an ambitious

1. Plutarch is here confusing the expedition of 393 B.C. with that of 390 B.C
when the games were celebrated.

and enthusiastic part in promoting them, and was never absent from any of the contests in which boys or girls competed. But as for some of the festivities which the rest of the world watched with admiration, he seemed scarcely to know what they were about. For example, Callipides, the tragic actor, who was famous throughout the Greek world and was idolized by his public, first met and addressed Agesilaus, and then boastfully thrust himself into the king's entourage: he made it clear that he expected the king to make some courteous gesture of recognition, and finally asked him, 'Sire, do you not recognize me?' Agesilaus stared at him and said, 'Why, are you not Callipides the buffoon?' for this is how the Spartans always refer to actors. On another occasion when he was invited to listen to a man who imitated the nightingale, he declined and remarked, 'But I have heard the bird itself.' Another story concerns Menecrates the physician, who had been given the nickname of Zeus, because of his success in curing a number of cases which had been given up as hopeless. This man had the arrogance to use the nickname on many occasions, and actually had the impertinence to write the king a letter, which began with the words, 'Menecrates, Zeus, to King Agesilaus, greetings,' to which the king replied, 'King Agesilaus to Menecrates, health and sanity.'

22. In the course of this campaign on Corinthian territory Agesilaus seized the temple of Hera,[1] and while he was watching his soldiers lead away the prisoners and carry off the spoils, some envoys arrived from Thebes to negotiate for peace. Agesilaus had always detested that city, and it occurred to him that this was a perfect opportunity to insult the Thebans and not to be missed. He pretended neither to see nor hear the delegation when they presented themselves. However, this action soon brought its retribution, for before the Thebans left news arrived that the battalion of Spartan troops which had been posted at Lechaeum[2] had been cut to pieces by the Athenian general Iphicrates. This was the greatest disaster that the Spartans had suffered for many years, for they lost many brave men, and, worse still, these were Spartan heavy infantry, who had been defeated by lightly armed targeteers and mercenaries.

Agesilaus at once hurried into action and set off to their rescue, but when he learned that the battle was already decided, he returned

1. The Heraeum at Perachora.
2. In 390 B.C. Lechaeum was the port of Corinth on the Corinthian Gulf.

to the temple of Hera, requested the Boeotian ambassadors to meet him, and gave them an audience. It was now their turn to repay his earlier insult, and so they made no mention of any peace negotiations, and merely requested a safe conduct into Corinth. Agesilaus was enraged at this and retorted, 'If you wish to see your friends when they are exulting over their successes, you can go and do so safely enough tomorrow.' The next day he took the ambassadors with him, proceeded to ravage Corinthian territory, and advanced right up to the gates of the city. After this demonstration that the Corinthians did not dare to resist him, he sent the ambassadors away. Then he collected the survivors of the defeated force and led them back to Sparta. On his march he made a point of breaking camp every morning before it was daylight, and not pitching his tents until after dark. His object was to prevent the Arcadians from exulting over his men, for this people hated the Spartans and rejoiced at their humiliation.

Soon afterwards,[1] in order to oblige the Achaeans, he joined them in invading Acarnania, where he secured a great deal of plunder and defeated the Acarnanians in a pitched battle. But when the Achaeans invited him to make his winter quarters there so as to prevent the enemy from sowing their fields, he told them that his tactics would be exactly the opposite, for the enemy would be far more afraid of a war if they had their land all sown when summer arrived. This was exactly what happened, for when the Acarnanians heard that another campaign was threatened, they came to terms with the Achaeans.

23. During the years in which Sparta was at war with Corinth, Conon and Pharnabazus had made themselves masters of the sea with the help of the king of Persia's fleet. They had also begun to ravage the coast of Laconia and the walls of Athens had been rebuilt with money provided by Pharnabazus.[2] In these circumstances the Spartans decided to make peace with the king of Persia and they sent Antalcidas to negotiate with Tiribazus, the satrap of the western provinces of the empire. Antalcidas then arranged in a most shameful and arbitrary fashion to place under the authority of the king all the Greeks then living in Asia, on whose behalf Agesilaus had fought his campaign. Agesilaus had no part in this infamous agreement, for Antalcidas was a bitter enemy of his and did his utmost to secure a peace settlement on any terms because he recognized that war was

1. In the winter of 390–389 B.C.   2. In 393 B.C.

certain to increase Agesilaus' power and reputation. But in spite of this, when someone remarked that the Spartans were 'medizing',[1] Agesilaus remarked that the truth was rather that the Medes were taking the side of the Spartans. What is more, by threatening to make war upon those states which did not wish to accept the settlement, Agesilaus forced all the Greeks to abide by the conditions demanded by the Persians. He chose this course expressly in order to weaken the Thebans by treating the rest of Boeotia as independent of Thebes, and indeed his conduct at a later date made this intention perfectly clear. When Phoebidas committed the outrage of seizing the Cadmeia,[2] the citadel of Thebes, in time of peace, the Greeks were universally indignant, the Spartans were annoyed, and Agesilaus' opponents in particular angrily asked Phoebidas on whose authority he had done this. The question was intended, of course, to cast suspicion on Agesilaus. But the king had no hesitation in defending Phoebidas and replied that what they had to consider was whether the action was advantageous or not: if it served the interests of Sparta, then it was right to act independently, even if nobody actually gave the order. In his talk, however, Agesilaus often declared that justice is the first of all the virtues, for courage is of no use unless it is accompanied by justice, and if all men would only act justly, then there would be no need for courage. Whenever he was told, 'Such and such is the pleasure of the Great King,'[3] Agesilaus would ask, 'How can he be greater than I am, unless he is also more just?' Here he was rightly and nobly expressing the view that justice constitutes as it were a regal standard, which serves to measure the superiority of one ruler to another. After the peace had been concluded, the king of Persia sent Agesilaus a letter in which he proposed that they should guarantee one another friendship and the rights of hospitality.[4] Agesilaus declined this offer and said that the public treaty of friendship between their states was sufficient, and that while this remained in force there was no need for any private agreement. He did not always observe these principles in practice: he was often carried away either by ambition or by personal resentment, as may be seen in particular in his treatment of the Thebans. In this instance he not

1. Collaborating with the Persians: a word which originated in the Persian wars of the early fifth century B.C.
2. In 383 B.C. See *Life of Pelopidas*, ch. 5.   3. i.e. the king of Persia.
4. A similar relationship to the one described in ch. 13 above.

only rescued Phoebidas from punishment, but even persuaded the Spartans to take responsibility for his unjust action and make the occupation of the Cadmeia official; at the same time he entrusted the government of Thebes to Archias and Leontidas, with whose help Phoebidas had made his way into the citadel and seized it.

24. These actions naturally aroused the suspicion that while Phoebidas had been the instrument, the plan had been conceived by Agesilaus, and subsequent events caused this accusation to be generally believed. When the Thebans a few years later[1] drove out the Spartan garrison and liberated their city, Agesilaus charged them with the murder of Archias and Leontidas – who were polemarchs in name but tyrants in reality – and made war against them. By this time Agesilaus' colleague, Agesipolis, was dead, and it was his successor Cleombrotus who was sent into Boeotia in command of an army. Agesilaus declined this appointment, for it was forty years since he had first borne arms and according to the law he was exempted from military service. The real reason, however, was that he had only recently been engaged in a war with the people of Phlia in order to restore the exiled party, and he was ashamed to be seen attacking the Thebans on behalf of their tyrants.

Among the Spartans who opposed Agesilaus, there was a man named Sphodrias, who had been appointed governor of the city of Thespiae. Sphodrias was by no means lacking either in courage or ambition, but his actions were constantly influenced by his hopes rather than by sound judgement. At any rate he longed to make a great name for himself, and when he reflected that Phoebidas had won a reputation throughout the length and breadth of Greece by virtue of his bold exploit at Thebes, he was persuaded that it would be an even finer and more dazzling feat for him to seize the Piraeus on his own initiative. His plan was to cut off the Athenians from access to the sea by launching a surprise attack from the landward side. It is said that the scheme was originally made by Pelopidas and Melo, the Boeotarchs at Thebes, who secretly sent agents to Sphodrias.[2] These men pretended to be supporters of Sparta's interests, and by flattering Sphodrias and giving him a great opinion of himself as the only man who was fit to undertake such an important operation, they encouraged and incited him to attempt an enterprise which was

1. In 379 B.C.   2. See *Life of Pelopidas*, ch. 14.

just as lawless and dishonourable as the seizure of the Cadmeia. The difference was that on this occasion both courage and good fortune were lacking. Sphodrias had hoped to attack the Piraeus by night, but daylight overtook him while he was still crossing the Thriasian plain. The story goes that his soldiers saw a light which appeared to stream out from some of the sanctuaries at Eleusis and were seized with panic. When he saw that he could no longer achieve surprise, Sphodrias lost his nerve, and after ravaging the country for some distance, he ignominiously led his force back to Thespiae. Thereupon the Athenians sent a delegation to Sparta to denounce Sphodrias, but they found that the magistrates had no need of their accusation to enable them to act: they had in fact already indicted him on a capital charge. Sphodrias decided not to stand his trial, for he dreaded the anger of his fellow-citizens who were ashamed of his conduct towards the Athenians: indeed they chose to be regarded as having suffered equally from his treachery rather than as having condoned it.

25. Sphodrias had a son named Cleonymus, a handsome young boy with whom Archidamus, Agesilaus' son, was in love. Archidamus, as was natural, shared the boy's distress for the danger in which his father stood, but it was impossible for him to help Cleonymus or to take his side openly, because Sphodrias was one of Agesilaus' opponents. Cleonymus came to Archidamus and begged him with tears to intercede with the king, since it was he whom they had most reason to fear. For three or four days Archidamus hesitated out of fear and respect for his father, and said nothing as he followed him about. But finally, as the day fixed for the trial drew near, he summoned up the courage to mention that Cleonymus had begged him to appeal on his father's behalf. Agesilaus had long known of his son's attachment to the boy, but he had not put a stop to it, since from his earliest years Cleonymus had shown promise that he would become as estimable a man as any of his fellows. But for the moment he held out no hope to his son that his appeal would produce any concession or act of clemency. All that he said as he went away was that he would consider what was the most honourable and appropriate course. Archidamus was embarrassed at this and stayed away from Cleonymus' company, although before he had been accustomed to see him many times each day. So Sphodrias' friends became even more despondent about his case, until Etymocles, one of Agesilaus'

friends, confided to them the king's opinion of the whole affair: this was that he utterly condemned what Sphodrias had done, but considered him a brave man and recognized that the city needed soldiers of his type. It was in these terms that Agesilaus repeatedly spoke of the trial, and he did so to gratify his son. Then Cleonymus at once understood that Archidamus had made every effort on his behalf, while Sphodrias' friends took heart and rallied to his support. Agesilaus was also, as it happened, extremely fond of his children, and there is a story of how, when they were very small he joined them in their play, sitting astride a stick and playing at riding with them in the house. When one of his friends saw Agesilaus in the midst of this game, the king asked the man not to mention it until he himself had become the father of a family.

26. At any rate Sphodrias was acquitted by the court. As soon as the Athenians heard the news, they prepared to go to war, with the result that Agesilaus became very unpopular. It was considered that he had obstructed the course of justice in a trial and made the city an accessory to outrages against other Greek states, and all this to indulge an absurd impulse and gratify a boy's whims. Besides this, when he saw that his colleague Cleombrotus had little enthusiasm for making war against the Thebans, he disregarded his own exemption from military service, which he had claimed on the occasion of the earlier expedition, and this time led the invading force into Boeotia himself. In this campaign[1] he inflicted some losses on the Thebans, but also suffered several defeats in return. This caused Antalcidas to say on one occasion when the king was wounded, 'The Thebans are paying you well for teaching them to fight, when they had no desire for it in the first place, and no skill either.' In fact, the Thebans, so it is said, became much more formidable opponents at this period than they had ever been before, and this was the result of all the training they had received from the many expeditions sent against them by the Spartans. This was why, centuries before, in one of his three so-called rhetras,[2] Lycurgus had forbidden the Spartans to make frequent expeditions against the same people, his object being to prevent their enemies from learning how to make war.

1. 378 B.C.
2. The pronouncements of Sparta's celebrated legislator: they took the form of unwritten laws.

At the same time Sparta's allies also complained of Agesilaus' conduct. They argued that he was bent on destroying Thebes not on account of any public quarrel, but for some obsessive grudge of his own. They had no wish to be led hither and thither to destruction every year, especially in view of the fact that they supplied so many of the troops, and the Spartans, who gave the orders, so few. It was on this occasion, we are told, that Agesilaus used the following device to disprove their argument about the numbers involved. He ordered all the allies of whatever country to sit down together in one place, and the Spartans by themselves in another. Next he gave orders through a herald for all the potters to stand up, then the smiths, then the carpenters in their turn, then the masons, and so he went through all the crafts. In this way almost all the allies rose to their feet in response to the herald, but not one of the Spartans, since they were forbidden to practise any manual art or craft. Then Agesilaus remarked with a laugh, 'You see, my men, how many more soldiers we send out than you do.'

27. When he was leading the army back from Thebes[1] and was passing through Megara, just as he was going up to the Senate house which stands on the acropolis of that city, he was seized with cramp and suffered intense pain in his sound leg. Soon after the limb swelled up, the blood-vessels appeared to be distended, and there were signs of an acute inflammation. A Syracusan physician opened a vein below the ankle, which at once relieved the pain, but caused a great flow of blood: the doctor could not control this, so that Agesilaus grew faint and his condition became extremely dangerous. At last, however, the haemorrhage was checked and the king was carried to Sparta, where he remained for a long time in a weak condition and could not take the field.

During this period[2] the Spartans suffered a number of reverses both by land and sea. The most important of these was at Tegyra,[3] where for the first time they were defeated in a pitched battle by the Thebans. By this time[4] both sides had come to favour a common peace, and ambassadors from all over Greece assembled in Sparta to negotiate a settlement. One of these was Epaminondas, a man who had already gained a reputation for his culture and learning, but had not yet given

1. From yet another incursion, in 377 B.C.   2. Between 379 and 375 B.C.
3. In 375 B.C. See Life of Pelopidas, chs. 16–17.   4. 371 B.C.

any proof of his military genius. It soon became clear to him that the rest of the delegates were overawed by Agesilaus, and he alone maintained the dignity and confidence to speak out freely. Accordingly he delivered a speech not on behalf of his fellow Thebans but of Greece as a whole: in this he declared that war made the Spartans strong at the expense of all the other states, and insisted that peace should be founded upon terms of justice and equality, and that it would only endure on condition that all the parties concerned were put on an equal footing.

28. Agesilaus noticed that all the Greek delegates listened to Epaminondas with the greatest attention and admiration, and so he asked him whether he thought it just and equitable that the cities of Boeotia should be independent of Thebes.[1] Epaminondas promptly and boldly responded with another question – did Agesilaus think it just and equitable that the cities of Laconia should be independent of Sparta?[2] At this Agesilaus grew angry, jumped to his feet and asked him to state unequivocally whether he intended to make the cities of Boeotia independent, whereupon Epaminondas merely repeated his question as to whether Agesilaus intended to make the cities of Laconia independent. Agesilaus flew into a rage and seized upon this pretext to strike the name of Thebes out of the peace treaty and declare war upon her. He ordered the rest of the Greek delegates to depart now that they had settled most of their disputes. Those differences which were capable of resolution should, he said, be left to the final terms of the peace: those which were not would have to be settled by war, since it was a hard task to remove all the causes of dissension between them.

At this time Cleombrotus, the other Spartan king, was in Phocis

1. Thebes had been deprived of her influence over the other Boeotian cities on account of the support she had given to the Persian cause at the time of the battle of Plataea (479 B.C.) There was a league of autonomous Boeotian cities which had a central federal government and shared Boeotian citizenship. The issue in dispute was whether Thebes could sign the peace treaty on behalf of the rest of Boeotia. The existence of the League enabled the Spartans to argue that the Boeotians were not autonomous, but that their own Peloponnesian allies were. In 386 the Boeotian League had been dissolved after the peace of Antalcidas, but had since re-formed, Agesilaus was anxious to get it dissolved again.

2. A question which struck at the very heart of the Spartan political and class system.

with an army, and the ephors at once sent orders to him to lead his forces against Thebes. They also summoned a meeting of their allies, who considered the campaign a great burden and showed no enthusiasm for it, but did not dare to oppose or disobey the Spartans. A great many threatening portents now appeared, as I have noted in my *Life of Epaminondas*,[1] but although Prothoüs the Laconian opposed the whole enterprise, Agesilaus refused to give way and forced the declaration of war. He calculated that since the Thebans had been barred from the peace and that all the rest of Greece was on his side, this was the right moment to take revenge upon his adversaries. However the timing of this campaign seems to prove that it was undertaken in a spirit of anger rather than of careful calculation. The peace treaty was concluded at Sparta on the fourteenth day of the month Scirophorion, and it was on the fifth day of Hecatombeion, twenty days later, that the Spartans were defeated at Leuctra.[2] In that battle a thousand Spartans fell, among them Cleombrotus the king and the flower of the Spartan army. Cleonymus, the handsome son of Sphodrias, was also killed: it is said that he was struck down three times as he fought in front of the king, and each time got to his feet again, but finally died fighting the Thebans.

29. On this occasion the Spartans had met with an unexpected defeat, while the Thebans, against all probability, had won a victory such as had never been seen in all the wars between Greek peoples, and yet the courage of the vanquished was no less to be envied and admired than that of the conquerors. Xenophon rightly says that the conversation of noble men is always worth remembering even for the casual remarks they let fall when they are joking or drinking, but there are even more valuable lessons to be learned from the dignity and resolution with which such men speak and act in the midst of misfortune. It so happened that Sparta was just then celebrating a festival and was full of foreign visitors – the Gymnopaedia[3] were in progress and the choirs of boys were competing in the theatre. At this moment the messengers arrived with news of the defeat at Leuctra. It was immediately recognized that Sparta had suffered an overwhelming reverse and that her supremacy was lost for ever, but in spite of this the ephors

1. One of the lost *Lives*.   2. In July 371 B.C.
3. An annual festival at which naked boys danced and which commemorated the decisive battle of Thyrea fought between Sparta and Argos about 550 B.C.

would not allow the performances of the choirs to be interrupted or the festal appearance of the city to be changed. They arranged for the names of the fallen to be sent to the homes of their families, while they themselves remained to preside over the spectacle and to see the choral contests carried to their conclusion. On the following morning when the news had circulated and everyone in the city knew who had fallen and who had survived the battle, the fathers, relatives and friends of the slain went down to the market-place and greeted one another, full of pride and exultation. The friends of the survivors, on the other hand, stayed at home with the women, as if they were mourning the dead, and if one of them was obliged to appear out of doors, his dress, his speech and his downcast look all bore witness to his humiliation and dejection. There was an even more striking contrast in the appearance of the women: those who expected their sons back from the battle were silent and dispirited, but the mothers of those who were reported to have been killed at once proceeded to the temples and walked about the city, visiting one another with a proud and cheerful bearing.

30. However, when their allies deserted them and it was expected that the victorious Epaminondas would triumphantly invade the Peloponnese, many of the Spartans remembered the oracles concerning the lameness of Agesilaus[1] and were filled with dismay. They feared that they had incurred the displeasure of the gods and that the city was suffering from its present misfortunes because they had dethroned the king who was sound in limb and preferred the halt and lame one – the very choice which the oracle had warned them to beware of. Yet in other respects Agesilaus wielded so much power in the state and his courage and prestige were so unquestioned that they continued to employ him not only as their king and their general in everything relating to war, but also as their physician and arbiter in all civil disorders and dilemmas. Among the latter was the problem of those who had shown cowardice in the battle and were known as *tresantes* (runaways). The Spartans were reluctant to insist on the loss of rights which is laid down by the laws for such men, since by now they had become so numerous that it was feared they might stir up a revolution. Not only were the offenders disqualified from holding any office, but it was considered a disgrace for a woman to be given

1. See ch. 3.

to any of them in marriage, and anybody who met them was at liberty to strike them if he chose. They were obliged to go about unwashed and unkempt, to wear cloaks which were patched with rags of different colours, and to shave one half of their beards and let the other half grow. The citizens felt that it would be dangerous to allow such a large number of men to remain in the city in this condition when Sparta was desperately short of troops, and Agesilaus was appointed as lawgiver to decide what should be done. He decided neither to pass any new measures nor to abolish any existing ones, nor to alter the laws in any way: instead he came into the assembly and announced that the laws must be allowed to sleep on that day, but that thereafter they must resume their force. By this device he at once preserved the laws for the city and saved the men from disfranchisement. Then, as he was anxious to dispel the atmosphere of dejection which weighed upon the young Spartans, he led a raiding force into Arcadia. He was careful to avoid fighting a battle with the enemy, but he captured a small town belonging to the Mantineans and overran their territory, and in this way he raised his countrymen's spirits, revived their hopes and gave them reason to believe that all was not lost.

31. Soon after this[1] Epaminondas arrived in Laconia with his allies, who comprised a force of forty thousand heavy infantry. Many light-armed troops and unarmed marauders accompanied him hoping to plunder the country, so that the horde which then swarmed into Laconia amounted in all to some seventy thousand men. It was no less than six hundred years since the Dorians had originally settled in Laconia, and throughout these centuries this was the first hostile force ever seen in the country: before this nobody had ever ventured to cross the frontier. Now the invaders burst into an unravaged and inviolate territory, and burned and plundered up to the banks of the Eurotas and the city walls of Sparta, and not a man came out to oppose them. Agesilaus refused to allow the Spartans to resist 'such a raging torrent of war', to borrow Theopompus' phrase. He posted his men to guard the commanding heights of the city and the central quarter, and patiently endured the boasts and threats of the Thebans, who called on him by name and challenged him to come out and fight for his country, since after all he was the firebrand who had

1. In 370 B.C.

kindled the flames of war and had thus been the cause of her misfortunes.

But this was not the greatest of Agesilaus' trials. He was equally
distracted by the commotion within the city caused by the shrieking
and running to and fro of the non-combatants, the old men who were
aggrieved and indignant at what had happened, and the women who
could not keep quiet and were beside themselves when they heard the
battle-cries and saw the camp fires of the enemy. He was also tormented by the thought of how his own reputation would suffer,
since he had begun his reign at the time when Sparta was at the height
of her power and had now lived to see her prestige humbled and her
proud boast given the lie, the boast which he himself had often uttered, that no Spartan woman had ever seen the smoke of an enemy's
fire. There is a story that an Athenian remarked to Antalcidas when
they were arguing about the bravery of their respective nations, 'At
any rate we have often driven you away from the Cephisus,' to which
the Spartan replied, 'Yes, and we have never had to drive you away
from the Eurotas!' This is very like the answer which a less well
known Spartan gave to an Argive who had said, 'Many of you
Spartans lie buried on Argive soil,' to which the Spartan retorted,
'Yes, and not one of you lies buried in Laconia.'

32. This time, however, it is said that Antalcidas, one of the ephors,
was so alarmed at the situation that he secretly sent away his children
to Cythera. As for Agesilaus, when the enemy tried to cross the
Eurotas and fight their way into the capital, he abandoned the rest of
the defences and drew up his troops in front of the high ground in the
centre of the city. At this time the Eurotas was swollen by the snows
which had recently fallen, so that it was in full flood, and the bitter
cold of the water no less than the strength of the current made it very
difficult for the Thebans to cross. When Epaminondas began to ford
the river at the head of his column, some of the Spartans pointed him
out to Agesilaus. The king, we are told, turned to look, and after fix-
ing his gaze on him for a long while, let fall just these words, 'O
ambitious man!' Epaminondas was eager to fight a battle within the
city walls and set up a trophy there, but since he could neither dis-
lodge nor lure Agesilaus from his position, he withdrew his troops
and laid waste the surrounding districts. Meanwhile a body of some
two hundred Spartans, who had long been disaffected and were ready

to betray their country, banded together and seized a building known as the Issorium, which was where the temple of Artemis stood and provided a well-protected and easily defensible position. The rest of the Spartans were anxious to attack them at once, but Agesilaus, who feared that a general uprising might take place, ordered them to stay quiet. Then, dressed in his cloak, and accompanied by only one servant he approached the mutineers and shouted to them that they had mistaken their orders: they had not been told to post themselves there nor to stay all together, but some of them were to take up such and such a position, to which he pointed, and others to go elsewhere in the city. The mutineers were relieved to receive these orders, as they concluded that their plot was still undiscovered, and so they left the Issorium and moved off in separate groups to the places they had been directed to occupy. Agesilaus immediately brought up other troops, seized the Issorium, arrested some fifteen of the conspirators and had them executed the same evening. Soon after this he received information of another and more widespread conspiracy, which consisted of a group of Spartans who met secretly in a house and plotted to change the constitution. At a moment of such crisis it was impossible either to place these men formally on trial or to ignore their intrigues. Accordingly Agesilaus, after consulting the ephors, had these men also executed without trial, despite the fact that up to that time no Spartan had ever been put to death in this way. At this moment the Spartans were also greatly disheartened by the fact that large numbers of the Helots and Perioeci,[1] who had been conscripted into the army, were escaping from the city and deserting to the enemy. Agesilaus ordered his servants to visit these troops' quarters every day, collect any arms they found and hide them so as to conceal the number of desertions.

Various accounts have been given as to why the Thebans left Laconia. Most writers say that it was because of the onset of winter storms and of the fact that the Arcadians began to disperse and melt away in disorderly fashion: others point out that they had already spent three whole months in the country and had laid waste the greater

1. The Dorian conquest of the Peloponnese had established three divisions of the inhabitants: the small military caste of Spartans, the *Perioeci* (dwellers round about) who were freemen but possessed no political rights in the Spartan state, and the *Helots*, the original inhabitants who had been reduced to serfdom. They were the most numerous class.

part of it. However the version given by Theopompus is that after the Boeotian commanders had already decided to withdraw their troops, a Spartan named Phrixus came to them from Agesilaus and offered them ten talents in return for the evacuation of Sparta, so that in fact the Thebans carried out the plans which they had made long before, but were paid to do so by their enemies into the bargain.

33. How Theopompus alone should have come to discover this story while every other authority remains ignorant of it, I do not know, but certainly all writers agree that Sparta owed her salvation at this time to Agesilaus, who laid aside those quarrelsome and ambitious passions to which he was so prone and played only for safety. But it was impossible for him to recover the power and the prestige which Sparta had lost after her defeat at Leuctra. Just as a human body, which is healthy in itself but has followed too strict and severe a diet may be undermined by a single departure from its regime, so one solitary error turned the scale and destroyed the city's strength and prosperity. We should not be surprised by this. The Spartan constitution was admirably designed to promote peace and virtue and harmony within the bounds of the state. But the Spartans had added to it an empire and a sovereignty won by force, something which Lycurgus would have regarded as quite superfluous to the well-being of a city, and it was for this reason that they lost their supremacy.

Agesilaus now declined further military service on account of his age,[1] but his son Archidamus, with the help of a contingent sent him by Dionysius the elder, the tyrant of Syracuse, defeated the Arcadians in an engagement known as 'the tearless battle', in which he lost none of his own men, but killed large numbers of the enemy. And yet it was this victory which gave the clearest proof of Sparta's decline, for in the past the Spartans had always regarded the defeat of their enemies as such a natural and commonplace event that the only sacrifice offered in the city to the gods to celebrate a victory was that of a cock: those who had taken part in the fighting never boasted of it, and those who received the news showed no special elation. Even after the battle of Mantineia,[2] which Thucydides described, the man who brought the first report of the victory received no reward for the good

1. He was seventy-four.
2. In 418 B.C. when the Spartans defeated a combined force of Mantineans, Argives and Athenians.

news but a piece of meat, which the ephors had sent from the public dining tables. But now at the news of this victory over the Arcadians and the approach of Archidamus, nobody could restrain his feelings. Agesilaus went out first to meet his son, weeping for joy, and after him the chief magistrates and public officers: the older men and the women flocked down to the Eurotas, raised their hands to heaven and gave thanks to the gods, as if Sparta had cleared herself of all undeserved reproach and now saw the light shine upon her as of old; for before this battle, we are told, the men had felt so ashamed of the defeats they had suffered that they could not look their womenfolk in the face.

34. Soon afterwards Epaminondas built in the western Peloponnese a new capital for the people of Messene, and its former citizens thronged to it from all quarters. The Spartans did not dare to oppose this plan, nor were they strong enough to hinder it, but they were filled with anger against Agesilaus, because it was during his reign that they had lost a province[1] which they had possessed for many years, a region which was as big as Laconia itself and contained the most fertile land in the whole of Greece. It was for this reason too that Agesilaus refused the peace settlement which the Thebans proposed. He was unwilling to cede the territory to them formally, even though it was actually under their control, and so rejected their terms, with the result that he not only failed to recover Messenia, but was outmanoeuvred by Epaminondas and came near to losing Sparta as well. This happened in the following way. Some years later the people of Mantinea broke away from their alliance with the Thebans,[2] and called in the Spartans to help them. As soon as Epaminondas learned that Agesilaus had marched out from Sparta with his forces and was approaching Mantinea, he made a night march from Tegea, unknown to the Mantineans, and headed for Sparta. He eluded Agesilaus and very nearly succeeded in catching Sparta without defenders.

1. The history of this much contested province goes back several centuries. In the eighth and seventh centuries B.C. the Spartans dispossessed the original inhabitants, reduced them to the status of serfs and distributed their land to their own citizens. About 464 B.C. the Messenians rebelled but the revolt was put down with the help of Athens. The Messenians were allowed to leave the Peloponnese unharmed on condition that they never returned. The Athenians later re-settled them at Naupactus on the Corinthian Gulf.

2. In 362 B.C.

However, Agesilaus was warned by Euthynus, a native of Thespiae, according to Callisthenes – or by a Cretan, as Xenophon reports it: he at once dispatched a courier to take the news to Sparta and soon afterwards arrived himself. It was not long before the Thebans appeared, crossed the Eurotas and began to attack the city, but Agesilaus defended it stoutly and with an energy far beyond his years. He did not consider, as he had in the earlier campaign, that no risks should be run or that caution was the order of the day, but rather that the situation demanded deeds of desperate courage. He had never trusted to such tactics before, nor attempted to apply them, but this time it was only by such means that the danger was averted. In the end he snatched the city from Epaminondas' grasp, set up a trophy of victory, and showed the women and children of Sparta that their menfolk were repaying in the most glorious fashion the upbringing their country had given them. Archidamus was also in the forefront of the fighting and distinguished himself conspicuously both for his impetuous courage and for the speed of his movements, as he ran through the narrow streets to give support wherever the pressure on the defenders was greatest, and repeatedly counter-attacked the enemy with his few followers. But it was Isidas, the son of Phoebidas, who presented the most striking and astonishing sight, both to the enemy and to his fellow-citizens. He was exceptionally tall and handsome and of an age when the human physique reaches the flower of its beauty, as boyhood merges into manhood. He had just anointed his body with oil and dashed out of his house naked, holding a spear in one hand and a sword in the other, but wearing neither armour nor clothing. Then forcing his way through the midst of the combatants, he threw himself at the ranks of the enemy, striking and laying low all who opposed him. He did not receive a single wound, whether it was that some god protected him for his valour, or because his height and his strength made his enemies believe him to be superhuman. It is said that the ephors crowned him with a garland for this feat of arms, and then fined him a thousand drachmae for being so foolhardy as to risk his life by fighting without armour.

35. A few days afterwards[1] another battle was fought near Mantinea. Epaminondas had routed the front ranks of the Spartan force and was eagerly pressing forward in pursuit, when a Spartan named Anti-

1. In August 362 B.C.

crates stepped in front of him and struck him down with a spear, as
Dioscorides tells the story. However the Spartans to this day refer to
Anticrates' descendants as *machaeriones* or swordsmen, because he
struck Epaminondas with a sword. Epaminondas had inspired such
dread in the Spartans while he was alive that they felt an extraordinary
admiration and affection for his slayer: they conferred special honours and rewards upon Anticrates himself, and granted his descendants perpetual exemption from taxes, indeed this privilege is still being
enjoyed in my own time by one of them, named Callicrates.

After the battle and the death of Epaminondas the Greeks concluded
a peace. When the rest of the states took the oath to uphold the peace,
Agesilaus and his supporters tried to exclude the Messenians, on the
ground that they possessed no city and were therefore not a state in
their own right. Then, after all the other Greek cities had admitted
the Messenians to their number and accepted their oaths, the Lacedaemonians refused to be associated with the common peace, and they
alone remained in a state of war in the hope of recovering Messenia. In
this way Agesilaus earned a reputation for being obstinate, headstrong
and insatiably fond of war, because he did everything in his power to
undermine and delay a general settlement and to prolong hostilities.
Worse still, he did this at a time when his treasury was empty, and he
was obliged to burden his friends in Sparta with requisitions, loans
and subscriptions levied from them. It was, after all, his duty to give
the state a respite from these troubles now that there was an opportunity to make peace, instead of which, after losing Sparta's great empire
with its control of land and sea and of many subject cities, he chose to
continue his frantic efforts to recover the goods and revenues of a
petty territory such as Messenia.

36. After this he diminished his reputation still further, because he
actually offered to serve as a commander under an Egyptian prince
named Tachos. It was considered utterly unworthy that a man who
had been regarded as the ablest and bravest soldier in Greece and had
filled the whole world with his renown, should barter his person, his
name and his reputation and put himself into the position of a hired
captain of mercenaries for the gold offered him by a mere barbarian,
who was rebelling against the Great King, his master. And in fact,
now that he had passed his eightieth year and his whole body was
seamed with wounds, even supposing that he had resumed the leader-

ship of his noble undertaking to restore the liberties of the Greeks of Asia, his ambition would still not have been regarded as entirely blameless. Every honourable action has its proper time and season, or rather it is this propriety or observance of a sense of proportion which distinguishes an honourable action from its opposite. Agesilaus, however, ignored these considerations, and indeed he did not regard any public service as beneath his dignity: he took the view that it was even more unworthy of him to live a life of inaction in Sparta and to sit back and wait for a natural death. Accordingly he used the money Tachos had given him to recruit a force of mercenaries, embarked them on transports and set sail. He was accompanied by thirty Spartan advisers, as he had been on his first campaign against the Persians.

When he landed in Egypt[1] Tachos' generals and ministers at once came to greet him and pay their respects. Agesilaus' name and fame had aroused great interest and high expectations among the whole Egyptian people and crowds came thronging to see him. When they found instead of a brilliant and imposing spectacle nothing but a little old man with a deformed body wearing a coarse and shabby cloak and sitting on a patch of grass near the sea, they began to laugh and make fun of him, and remarked that here was the perfect illustration of the mountain being in labour and bringing forth a mouse.[2]

They were still more surprised, however, at Agesilaus' unconventional behaviour when they brought him the gifts which were normally offered to distinguished visitors, and found that he accepted the flour, the calves and the geese, but declined the preserved fruits, pastries and perfumes, and when he was entreated and pressed to accept them, ordered them to be given to his Helots. What especially pleased him, according to Theophrastus, was the neat and simple appearance of the flowering papyrus, which was used for making garlands, and when he left Egypt he asked for some specimens of the plants which were presented to him.

37. However when Agesilaus joined Tachos who was then making preparations for his campaign, he was not offered the leadership of the combined forces of the expedition, as he had expected, but only

1. In 361 B.C.
2. According to Athenaeus it was Tachos who made this remark, to which Agesilaus replied, 'You will find me a lion by and by.'

the command of the mercenaries. Chabrias, the Athenian, was in charge of the fleet, while Tachos reserved the post of commander-in-chief for himself. This was the first check which vexed Agesilaus: next, as time went on, he found the prince's arrogance and empty pretensions intensely provoking, but was obliged to endure them. He went so far as to sail with him on an expedition against the Phoenicians, and setting aside his sense of dignity and his natural feelings, he showed deference and even subservience for a while, until he found his opportunity. This came when Tachos' cousin Nectanabis, who commanded part of the forces, raised a revolt against the prince. He was proclaimed king by the Egyptians and promptly approached Agesilaus for his help: at the same time he appealed to Chabrias and offered both men great rewards if they would join him. Tachos presently learned of this and begged the Greeks to stand by him, whereupon Chabrias tried to appease Agesilaus' resentment and persuade him to uphold Tachos' cause. But Agesilaus answered, 'You, Chabrias, came here on your own account, and so you are free to act as you choose, but I was given by Sparta to the Egyptians as a general. It would be dishonourable for me to fight against the man to whom I was sent as an ally, unless my country gives me different instructions and orders me to do so.' After making this declaration he sent messengers to Sparta whom he had told to denounce Tachos and take the side of Nectanabis. Meanwhile Tachos and Nectanabis also sent envoys of their own to appeal to the Spartans for help, the first pleading that he had long been their friend and ally, and the second arguing that he would be well disposed towards them and more active in furthering their interests. The Spartans received both delegations and made a public answer to the Egyptians that Agesilaus would attend to these matters, while they sent a secret dispatch to Agesilaus ordering him to pursue whichever course was of most advantage to Sparta. Upon this Agesilaus promptly changed sides and took his mercenaries over to Nectanabis: he made his country's interests the screen for this monstrous and unnatural decision, but if we strip away this pretext and judge the matter impartially, his action can only be described as downright treachery. We must remember that the Spartans, whenever any question of honour arises, always give first place to their country's interests; they refuse to learn or to understand any other conception of justice, except for such action as they believe will make Sparta great.

38. When Tachos found himself deserted by his mercenaries, he took to flight, but meanwhile another pretender to the throne appeared in the province of Mendes.[1] He in turn rose against Nectanabis, was proclaimed king, gathered an army of a hundred thousand men, and advanced against his rival. Nectanabis sought to reassure Agesilaus by telling him that although the enemy were strong in numbers, they were no more than a rabble of artisans and tradesmen who possessed no training or experience in war, and that he had nothing to fear from them. 'It is not their numbers that make me anxious,' Agesilaus told him, 'it is just this ignorance and inexperience you speak of, which may make it difficult to outwit them. If your enemy suspects or makes a guess at what you are going to do and tries to prevent you, you may have a chance of outwitting him: but an enemy who makes no attempt to anticipate or even suspect your intentions, gives you no opportunity to catch him unawares. It is the same as in a wrestling-match, where if your opponent stands perfectly still, it is impossible to throw him.' Meanwhile the pretender from Mendes also made overtures to Agesilaus and tried to win him over. Nectanabis took fright at this, but Agesilaus urged him to engage the enemy as soon as possible. He should not, Agesilaus told the Egyptian, try to carry on a war of attrition against an opponent who had little battle experience, but was able through sheer superiority of numbers to encircle him, surround him with entrenchments, anticipate his movements and seize the initiative in a variety of ways. But this advice only confirmed Nectanabis in his fears and suspicions, and he took refuge in a large and strongly fortified town. Agesilaus was angry at this evident lack of confidence in his judgement, but he was ashamed to change sides yet again and return to Sparta without having achieved anything, and so he stayed with Nectanabis and entered the city with him.

39. When the enemy came up and began to surround the city with entrenchments, Nectanabis changed his mind yet again, as he was alarmed at the prospect of a siege and was inclined to risk a battle. The rest of the Greeks welcomed this plan, since the town was very short of provisions, but this time it was Agesilaus who opposed it, where-upon the Egyptians abused him even more insultingly than before and called him a traitor to their king. By this time Agesilaus was able

1. A region in the Nile delta about 100 miles south-east of Alexandria.

to bear these slanders more patiently, and he waited for the right moment to put his plan into effect.

This was as follows. The enemy were digging a deep trench around the city wall, so as to enclose the inhabitants on all sides. When the encirclement was nearly complete, and the two ends of the trench had almost met, Agesilaus towards nightfall ordered the Greeks to get under arms, and then went to Nectanabis and said, 'This is the moment when we can save ourselves, young man. I did not speak of it until the time came, for fear of spoiling our opportunity, but in fact the enemy have rescued us with their own hands. They have dug their trench so far that the part of it which is finished will prevent them from deploying their full strength to attack us, and the gap that still remains gives us the chance of fighting them on fair and equal terms. So prove yourself now to be a man of courage, follow us when we attack, and save yourself and your army.' Nectanabis was filled with admiration at Agesilaus' astuteness, placed himself in the midst of the Greek ranks, attacked with them and easily routed his opponents. Then Agesilaus, having once gained the Egyptian's confidence, proceeded to use the same tactics against the enemy, just as a wrestler sometimes repeats the same throw. By a series of feints, in which he pretended at one moment to fall back and at another to attack on the flanks, he manoeuvred the whole body of the enemy into a space which was enclosed between two deep canals. He then drew up his troops in a line which covered the whole space between the canals, and thus made his front equal to the numbers the enemy could bring against him, since it was impossible for them to outflank or surround him. After a short resistance, the enemy turned and fled: they lost great numbers of their men and the fugitives melted away.

40. After this victory Nectanabis' affairs prospered. He succeeded in establishing himself securely on the throne, and he showed his regard and affection for Agesilaus by pressing him to stay and spend the winter with him. However, Agesilaus was anxious to return and help his country in the war at home, for he knew that the Spartans were short of money, and had been obliged to hire a force of mercenaries. Nectanabis therefore allowed him to go but arranged especial honours and ceremonies for him, at which he presented him with gifts, decorations and a sum of two hundred and thirty talents in silver for the

campaign at home.[1] Since it was by then winter, Agesilaus did not venture out into the open sea, but coasted along the shores of Libya as far as a deserted spot, which was known as the harbour of Menelaus, and there he died at the age of eighty-four. He had been king of Sparta for forty-one years: for more than thirty of these he was the greatest and most powerful man in Greece, and had been regarded as the king and the leader of almost the whole of Hellas, down to the time of the battle of Leuctra.

It was the Spartan custom, whenever commoners died in a foreign country, to give them funeral rites and bury them wherever they happened to be, but to bring back the bodies of their kings to Spartan soil. So the Spartans who accompanied him enclosed his body in melted wax, since they could not obtain honey, and carried it back to Sparta. The succession passed to his son, Archidamus, and remained in his family down to Agis,[2] who was murdered by Leonidas, because he tried to restore the ancient constitution of Sparta. This Agis was the fifth in descent from Agesilaus.

1. The replenishment of Sparta's treasury was her main object in taking part in these mercenary operations.

2. Agis IV, the subject of Plutarch's *Life*.

2

PELOPIDAS[1]

[403–364 B.C.]

* *
*

WHEN the elder Cato once heard some people praising a man who was not merely brave but recklessly daring in war, he observed that there was a difference between valuing courage highly and life cheaply, and his remark was just. At any rate there is a story of one of Antigonus' soldiers, a man who was apparently quite fearless, but who suffered from weak health and a wretched physique. When the king asked him what was the reason for his pallid colour, he admitted that he was afflicted with a little known disease. The king took the matter to heart and gave orders to his physicians that if any remedy could be found, they should give him their utmost skill and care. The result was not only that the man was cured, but that he immediately ceased to risk his life and lost all the fire and dash which had distinguished him on the battlefield, so that even Antigonus reproved him and expressed his amazement at the change. The soldier made no attempt to conceal the reason for his behaviour, but said, 'It is you, sire, who have taken away my courage, because you have freed me from the miseries that made me hold life cheap.' The same point was once made by a citizen of Sybaris, who remarked that it was no great sacrifice for the Spartans to lay down their lives fighting, if this meant an escape from the innumerable hardships and generally wretched existence that they endured. Of course to the Sybarites, a people completely enervated by their soft and luxurious way of living, it was natural to suppose that these men, whose ambition and ardent desire for renown had banished the fear of death, could only feel as they did because they hated life; but the truth was that the

1. For places mentioned in this *Life*, see Map 1, p. 433.

valour of the Spartans gave them happiness both in living and dying, as the following epitaph shows us. These men died, it says

> Not seeing death or life in itself as the object of striving,
> But to accomplish both nobly, this they considered true honour.[1]

There is no disgrace in avoiding death, so long as a man does not cling to life dishonourably; but neither is there any special virtue in meeting it if this is done out of contempt for life. It is for this reason that Homer always brings his bravest and most warlike heroes into battle splendidly and effectively armed, and that the Greek law-givers punish a man for throwing away his shield, but not his sword nor his spear: their object was to teach him that his first duty is to protect himself from harm rather than inflict it on the enemy, and this is most of all true for a man who governs a city or commands an army.

2. The Athenian general Iphicrates[2] once compared the light-armed troops to the hands, the cavalry to the feet, the main body of infantry to the chest and breast-plate, and the general to the head: thus if the commander is over-impetuous and takes undue risks, he endangers not only his own life but those of all the others, whose safety or destruction depend on him. This is why Callicratidas,[3] although in other respects a great man, was wrong in the answer he gave to the diviner who urged him to take care since the sacrificial omens before the battle foretold his death. 'Sparta,' he retorted, 'does not depend on one man!' It is true of course, that when he was fighting, or at sea, or serving under the orders of another, Callicratidas was one man, but as general he combined in his own person the strength of all the rest, so that in this sense he was certainly not one man, when his death involved the destruction of so many others.

A better answer was given by Antigonus in his old age when he was about to engage in a sea-battle off Andros and somebody told him that the enemy's fleet was far stronger than his own, to which he answered, 'How many ships do I count for?' In saying this he was setting a high value on the commander, as is quite right when he combines courage and experience, and it is his first duty to protect the

1. An epigram attributed to Simonides.
2. A commander of this period who was especially expert in training and handling light infantry.
3. The Spartan commander who was defeated and killed by the Athenians at the naval battle of Arginusae, 406 B.C.

man who holds the fate of all the others in his hands. In the same way when Chares was once showing the Athenians his wounds and his shield which had been transfixed by a spear, Timotheus was right in saying, 'For my part I was ashamed at the siege of Samos whenever an arrow passed near me, because I was afraid I was behaving more like an impetuous boy than a general in charge of such a great force.' To sum up we might say that where the whole issue of a battle may turn upon the general's exposing himself, there he must use hand and body unsparingly, and disregard those who say that a general should die in old age, if not of old age. But where the question is of gaining only a minor advantage if he succeeds, and courting total disaster if he fails, no one demands that a general should risk his life fighting like a private soldier.

These remarks seemed to me necessary as an introduction to the *Lives* of Pelopidas and Marcellus, both of them great men who fell in battle through their own rashness. Both of them were gallant fighters, both won honour for their countries in brilliant campaigns, and both were faced with the most formidable opponents of their times. Marcellus, we are told, was the first to rout Hannibal, who had hitherto proved invincible, while Pelopidas defeated the Spartans, who at that time were supreme both on sea and on land, in a pitched battle. Yet both were careless of their own lives, and recklessly threw them away at the very moment when there was the most pressing need that men of their calibre should be alive and hold command. These are the points of resemblance which they share and which have led me to write their *Lives* in parallel.[1]

3. Pelopidas, the son of Hippoclus, was descended, like Epaminondas, from an illustrious Theban family. He grew up surrounded by riches, and having succeeded while he was still a young man to a splendid inheritance, he made it his business to relieve the condition of men who both needed and deserved his help, so as to prove that he was truly the master of his wealth and not its slave. Most rich men, according to Aristotle, either make too little use of their wealth through miserliness, or too much through extravagance, and so live in perpetual slavery, the one class to their business, and the other to their pleasures. At any rate many Thebans were glad to benefit from Pelopidas' kindness and generosity, and of all his friends it was only

1. See Foreword, pp. 13–14.

Epaminondas who could not be persuaded to share his wealth. Instead Pelopidas shared Epaminondas' poverty and took pride in the simplicity of his dress, the austerity of his diet, his readiness to endure hardships, and the thoroughness of his performance of military service. Like Capaneus in Euripides' play he possessed

> Abundant wealth, but in that wealth no pride[1]

and he was ashamed that anyone should suppose that he enjoyed more personal luxury than the poorest citizen of Thebes. Epaminondas, who had been born to poverty and was thus accustomed to it, made it more endurable by his philosophy of life, and by choosing from the beginning to remain single. Pelopidas, on the other hand, married into a noble family and had children born to him, but nevertheless by devoting all his time to public duties, he neglected to make money for himself and suffered losses to his estate. When his friends found fault with him for this and reminded him that money, even though he chose to ignore it, was still a necessity of life, he replied, 'A necessity I dare say – for example, for Nicodemus here!' and he pointed to a man who was both lame and blind.

4. Both men were equally by nature fitted to pursue every kind of excellence, the difference being that Pelopidas took more pleasure in cultivating the body and Epaminondas the mind, so that the one gave his leisure hours to the wrestling arena and the hunting field, and the other to the reading and discussion of philosophy. Both had many claims to renown, but the greatest of these in the opinion of the wise was the unquestioned good faith and friendship which endured between them from first to last throughout a multitude of political crises, campaigns and public actions. For if anyone considers the political careers of Themistocles and Aristides, or of Cimon and Pericles, or of Nicias and Alcibiades and how full they were of mutual dissensions, jealousies and rivalries, and then contrasts these with the honour and consideration with which Pelopidas treated Epaminondas, he will see that they can in the fullest sense be called colleagues in government and in command, which cannot be said of those who were constantly striving to get the better of one another rather than of the enemy. The true reason for the superiority of the two Thebans is to be found in their virtue: because of this their actions were not undertaken to

1. *Supplices*, 863.

obtain personal glory or wealth, which always arouse bitter envy and strife. Instead they were both fired from the beginning by a divine ardour to see their country raised to the heights of power and prestige in their own lifetime and through their own efforts, and to this end each treated the other's successes as if they were his own.

Their close friendship is generally believed to have begun during the campaign at Mantinea,[1] where they served in a contingent sent from Thebes to support the Spartans, who at that time were still their friends and allies. In this battle the two were stationed side by side among the heavy infantry and fought against the Arcadians. When the wing of the Lacedaemonian army where they were posted gave way and most of their companions were put to flight, they locked their shields together and drove back their opponents. Pelopidas received seven wounds in the front of his body, and at last sank down upon a heap of corpses, in which friend and foe lay dead together, but Epaminondas, although he thought his comrade had been killed, stood in front of him to defend his body and his arms and fought desperately, holding a host of attackers at bay single-handed, for he was determined to die rather than leave Pelopidas lying there. It was not long before Epaminondas was in deadly danger himself, for he had received a spear-thrust in the chest and a sword-cut on the arm, but at last Agesipolis, the Spartan king, came to his rescue from the other wing, and when hope was almost gone, saved the lives of both men.

5. After Athens' final defeat in the Peloponnesian War, the Spartans made a show of treating the Thebans as friends and allies, but the truth was that they were suspicious of the city's power and of her ambitious spirit: above all they hated the party which was led by Ismenias and Androcleides and to which Pelopidas belonged, which was believed to be devoted to the cause of liberty and of government by the people. Consequently Archias, Leontidas and Philip, who were rich members of the oligarchic party and whose ambitions were not restrained by any scruples, entered into negotiations with Phoebidas the Spartan as he was passing through Theban territory with a body of troops. They proposed that he should seize the Cadmeia[2] by a surprise attack, banish the party that opposed them, and by establishing

1. In 385 B.C.
2. The acropolis of Thebes. The attack was made in the winter of 382 B.C.

an oligarchy ensure that the regime would be subservient to Sparta. Phoebidas allowed himself to be persuaded, timed his assault upon the Thebans when they were least expecting it in the midst of the festival of the Thesmophoria, and seized the citadel. Ismenias was arrested, carried off to Sparta and soon afterwards executed, while Pelopidas, Pherenicus, Androcleides and many others escaped from the city and were proclaimed outlaws. Epaminondas was allowed to remain, for he was not considered to be a man of action on account of his interest in philosophy, nor to be of any danger to the regime on account of his poverty.

6. The Spartans proceeded to deprive Phoebidas of his command and fined him 100,000 drachmas, but they nevertheless continued to occupy the Cadmeia with a garrison: in this way they made all the rest of Greece marvel at their inconsistency in punishing the offender but approving the offence. As for the Thebans they had lost their ancestral constitution and became enslaved to the party of Archias and Leontidas, nor was there room for any hope of deliverance from this tyranny which they could see was protected by Sparta's military supremacy and could not be unseated, unless Sparta's ascendancy by land and sea could somehow be broken. But in spite of this apparent security, when Leontidas and his supporters learned that the Theban refugees were living in Athens and that they were not only welcomed by the common people but honoured by the nobility, they plotted against their lives. They sent secret agents to Athens, who contrived to assassinate Androcleides by treachery but failed in their attempts against the others. The Spartans sent letters to the authorities in Athens requesting them not to harbour or encourage the exiles, but to banish them on the ground that they had been declared public enemies by the allied cities. The Athenians, however, would do no harm to the Thebans in their city, for apart from their traditional and natural instincts of humanity, they had a debt of gratitude to repay to Thebes, whose people had played a most important part in helping them to restore their own democracy. When Thrasybulus led his band against the tyrants in Athens,[1] Thebes had passed a decree that if any Athenians marched through Boeotia, no Boeotian should see or hear them.

1. In 403 B.C. Thrasybulus had taken refuge with a small group of supporters on Theban territory. It was from here that he launched the invasion which led to the unseating of the oligarchy imposed upon Athens by the Spartans.

7. Although Pelopidas was one of the youngest of the exiles, he took the initiative in encouraging each of his companions privately. Besides this, whenever they met together, he would argue that it was utterly wrong and dishonourable to allow their native city to remain garrisoned and enslaved by foreigners, and for themselves to think of nothing but their personal safety and survival, to depend upon the decrees of the Athenians and to cultivate and fawn upon whichever orators could sway the people in their favour. They should play for the highest stakes, and take the courage and idealism of Thrasybulus as their model, and just as he had started out from Thebes and overthrown the Thirty Tyrants in Athens, so they in their turn should set forth from Athens and deliver Thebes. After a while the exiles were won over by these arguments: they secretly resumed contact with their supporters in Thebes and told them what they had resolved. Their friends approved of these plans and Charon, one of the leading citizens of Thebes, agreed to put his house at their disposal, while Phillidas contrived to have himself appointed secretary to Archias and Philip, the two polemarchs. Meanwhile Epaminondas had already communicated his own ideals to the younger generation of Thebans. He urged them whenever they trained in the gymnasium to challenge the Spartans and wrestle with them. Then when he saw them elated by their victories in these bouts, he would scold them and tell them that such triumphs ought rather to make them feel ashamed; for since they so much excelled their opponents in physical strength, it could only be their cowardice which kept them enslaved to them.

8. When a day had been fixed for the attempt, the exiles decided that the main body led by Pherenicus should wait in the Thriasian plain,[1] while a few of the youngest men undertook the dangerous mission of going on ahead into the city: if these were surprised by their enemies, the rest should see to it that neither their children nor their parents should be left in want. Pelopidas was the first to volunteer for this task, followed by Melon, Damocleides and Theopompus: each of these men belonged to the leading families in Thebes, they were attached to each other by the closest ties of friendship and were rivals only in the pursuit of valour and reputation. A group of twelve volunteers was made up, they embraced those who were to stay behind

1. The plain north-west of Athens on the direct route to Thebes.

and sent a messenger ahead to warn Charon. They set out[1] in short cloaks and took with them hounds and hunting-nets, so that anybody who met them on the road should have no suspicion of their purpose, but should take them for hunters ranging the countryside in search of game.

When the messenger arrived and reported that they were on their way, Charon, although the hour of danger was now at hand, in no way faltered in his determination, but acted as a man of his word and made his house ready to receive them. But there was another conspirator, Hipposthenides, by no means an unprincipled man, indeed a patriot and a sympathizer with the exiles, but one who did not possess the intrepid spirit which the urgency of the moment and the nature of the attempt demanded. The importance of the enterprise, which was now so close at hand, threw him into a panic, especially when he realized that in attempting to overthrow the occupying garrison they were in a sense trying to shake off the hegemony of Sparta, and that for this ambitious purpose they had put their trust in the hopes of refugees who had no resources behind them. Hipposthenides went quietly home and dispatched one of his friends to Melon and Pelopidas urging them to postpone their plans for the present, return to Athens and wait for a more favourable opportunity. The man he sent was called Chlidon, and he hurried to his house, led out his horse and asked for the bridle. His wife was at her wits' end because she could not find it for him, and made the excuse that she had lent it to a neighbour. They began to quarrel, then to curse one another, and finally his wife uttered a prayer that his journey might prove fatal to him and whoever had sent him. By that time Chlidon had wasted a great deal of the day in this squabble: he decided that what had happened was a threatening omen, gave up all idea of the journey and turned his attention to other business. We may reflect how near at the very outset the greatest and most glorious enterprises have sometimes come to missing their opportunity.

9. Meanwhile Pelopidas and his party exchanged clothes with some peasants, separated and entered the city from different directions while it was still daylight. The weather had begun to change, there was a strong wind blowing and some flurries of snow, and it was easy for them to remain unobserved because many people had already gone indoors to shelter from the storm. However, those who were in the

1. In the winter of 379/8 B.C.

plot received them as they arrived and immediately led them to Charon's house: together with the exiles there were forty-eight men in the conspiracy.

As for the tyrants, the situation was as follows. Their secretary Phillidas had for some time been taken into the confidence of the conspirators, as I have mentioned, and was working hand in hand with them. Some while before he had proposed a drinking-party for Archias and his friends to which they were to invite a number of married women: his plan was to get them under the influence of wine and thoroughly relaxed in their pleasures, and then to deliver them into the hands of their attackers. But the drinking had scarcely got under way when a report was brought in which, although true, was unconfirmed and vague in its details, to the effect that the exiles were hidden somewhere in the city. Phillidas did his best to change the subject, but Archias sent one of his attendants to Charon with orders that he should come at once. By then it was evening and Pelopidas and his companions were making themselves ready in Charon's house; they had already buckled on their breast-plates when suddenly a knock was heard at the door. Somebody ran to it, was told by the messenger that he had come from the polemarchs to fetch Charon, and in a state of great agitation gave his news to the rest. All the conspirators at once concluded that the plot had been discovered and that they were lost before they could achieve anything worthy of their courage.

However, they agreed that Charon must obey the summons and appear before the polemarchs as though he suspected nothing. Charon was a man of courage and of stern resolution in the face of danger, but on this occasion he was anxious and his determination was undermined on account of his friends: moreover he feared that if so many brave citizens were to lose their lives, he could scarcely escape the suspicion of treachery. So just before he left the house, he sent for his son, who was still no more than a boy, but handsomer and stronger than others of his age: he fetched the youth from the women's quarters and handed him over to Pelopidas, saying that if they discovered any treachery or deceit in the father, they must treat the son as an enemy and show him no mercy. Many of the conspirators wept at Charon's noble spirit and at the concern which he showed for them, and all were indignant that he should think any of them so demoralized by the present danger and so mean-spirited as to suspect or blame him in any way. They implored him not to involve his son with them, but to send him out of harm's way so that he might escape the tyrants and live to avenge the city and his friends. But Charon refused to take his son away and asked them 'What life or what safety could be more honourable for him than to die a noble death in the company of his father and of so many friends?' Then he offered up a prayer to the gods, embraced and encouraged them all and went off, striving to compose his expression and control his voice so as to yield no hint of the part he was really playing.

10. When he reached the door of the polemarch's house, Archias came out with Phillidas and said to him, 'Charon, I have heard that a number of men have arrived and have hidden themselves in the city, and that some of the citizens are in league with them.' Charon was alarmed at first, but he began by asking who these men were and who was helping to conceal them. He soon saw that Archias had no exact information and that what he had heard did not come from any of those who knew the truth. 'You must take care,' he said, 'not to let yourself be misled by idle rumour. But in any case I will make inquiries. We must not neglect any report of this kind.' Phillidas, who was standing next to him, approved of this answer and thereupon led Archias back into the house, plied him with drink, and did his best to spin out the entertainment with assurances that the women would soon arrive.

When Charon returned to his house he found the conspirators fully prepared: they had given up any hope that they would succeed in their attempt, or even survive it, but they were determined to die gloriously and kill as many of their enemies as possible. And so it was only to Pelopidas that he confided the truth; for the rest he made up a story that Archias had talked about other matters. But even before this first storm had blown over, fortune soon brought another in its train. A messenger arrived from Athens, sent by Archias the priest to his namesake and close friend Archias of Thebes. He brought with him a letter which contained, as was afterwards discovered, no mere vague or imaginary suspicion, but a clear and detailed account of the conspiracy. The messenger was taken to Archias, and handed him the letter saying, 'The man who sent this said that you must read it immediately: it concerns very serious matters.' Archias was by that time so drunk that he merely smiled and answered, 'Serious matters for tomorrow!' Then he took the letter, put it under his pillow, and returned to whatever he had been talking about with Phillidas. This phrase has become a proverb which is current in Greece down to this day.

11. Now that the moment of opportunity seemed to have arrived, the conspirators set out in two parties. One, led by Pelopidas and Damocleides, was to attack Leontidas and Hypates who lived near one another: the other under Charon and Melon went to Archias and Philip. The men had put on women's gowns over their breast-plates and wore thick wreaths of pine and fir which shaded their faces. For this reason when they first came through the door of the dining-room, the company shouted and clapped their hands, imagining that the long-awaited women had at last arrived. The conspirators looked carefully around the party, took note of each one of the guests as they reclined, and then drawing their swords they threw off their disguise and made a rush for Archias and Philip. Phillidas prevailed upon a few of the guests to stay quiet: the rest who staggered to their feet and tried to defend themselves and help the polemarchs were so drunk that they were easily dispatched.

Pelopidas and his party were faced with a harder task, for Leontidas, whom they had marked out as their victim, was a sober man and a formidable adversary, and they found his house shut up, as he was already asleep. They knocked for a long time before anyone answered, but at last one of the attendants heard them, came to the door and drew back the bolt. As soon as the leaves gave way and the door opened, they burst in all together, knocked down the servant and rushed to the bedroom. Leontidas, when he heard the noise and the sound of running feet, guessed what was happening, leaped from his bed and drew his dagger. But he forgot to throw down the lamps so as to make the men stumble over one another in the darkness. The consequence was that when he moved to the door of his bedroom and struck down Cephisodorus, the first man who entered, he came into full view of his attackers. As Cephisodorus fell dead, Leontidas grappled with Pelopidas who was immediately behind. There was a violent struggle between them, in which their movements were hampered by the narrowness of the doorway, and by the dead body of Cephisodorus which lay under their feet. At last Pelopidas got the upper hand and after killing Leontidas, he at once hurried on with his companions to attack Hypates. They broke into his house in the same way, but Hypates instantly guessed why they had come and fled for shelter to his neighbours. The conspirators followed close on his heels, caught him and killed him.

12. Having carried out their mission, they joined Melon's party, and sent a message to the main body of exiles whom they had left in Attica. They also called upon the citizens of Thebes to fight for their liberty, and armed all who came to them, taking down the spoils and trophies of war which hung in the porticoes and breaking open the shops of the spearmakers and swordsmiths in the neighbourhood. Epaminondas and Gorgidas joined them with a band of armed followers consisting of young men and the most active of the veterans. By this time the whole city was in an uproar, the air was filled with shouting, lights came on in the houses, and men ran frantically here and there. The people, however, did not yet gather in a body. They were frightened by the turn which events had taken, but as they had no clear idea of what was happening, they waited for daylight. Here the Spartan commanders seem to have blundered in not making a sortie and attacking them immediately, for their garrison numbered some fifteen hundred men, and many people ran out of the city to take refuge with them. But they too were alarmed at the shouting, the lights and the crowds of people hurrying to and fro, and so they took no action but merely stood to arms on the Cadmeia. At daybreak the exiles from Attica marched into the city fully armed, and a general assembly of the people was summoned. Then Epaminondas and Gorgidas led forward Pelopidas and his companions surrounded by priests who carried garlands in their hands, and called upon the citizens to fight for their country and their gods. At the sight of these men the whole assembly rose and with shouts and loud applause welcomed them as their saviours and benefactors.

13. After this Pelopidas was elected Boeotarch and together with Melon and Charon he at once blockaded the Cadmeia and attacked it on every side, for he was anxious to drive out the Lacedaemonians and free the acropolis before an army could arrive from Sparta. He succeeded in his object, but with so little time to spare that after the Spartans had surrendered on terms and had been allowed to depart, they had gone no further than Megara before they met Cleombrotus

marching against Thebes with a large army. Of the three men who had been harmosts or military governors in Thebes the Spartans condemned and executed Herippidas and Arcissus, while the third, Lysanoridas, was heavily fined and afterwards went into exile.

This exploit so closely resembled the liberation of Athens, not only in the courage displayed and the dangers and ordeals endured by the men who took part in it, but also in the fact that their success was crowned by good fortune, that the Greeks came to refer to it as the sister of Thrasybulus' achievement. It would be hard to find another instance in which so small a group of men with such weak resources overcame so numerous and powerful an enemy by virtue of sheer courage and determination, or conferred greater blessings on their country by so doing. And indeed the change which they brought about in the political situation made their action even more glorious. It can truly be said that the war which destroyed Sparta's prestige and put an end to her supremacy by land and sea began with that night on which Pelopidas, not by surprising any fortress or citadel but simply by entering a private house with eleven other men, loosened and broke in pieces, if we may express the truth in a metaphor, the fetters of Spartan domination which until then had seemed adamantine and indissoluble.

14. The Spartans then invaded Boeotia with a large army,[1] and at this the Athenians took fright and denounced their treaty of alliance with the Thebans. They went on to impeach all those who supported the Boeotian cause, executed some of them and fined or banished others: and as nobody offered to help the Thebans, their situation began to appear desperate. However, Pelopidas who was Boeotarch together with Gorgidas found a way to embroil the Athenians once more with the Spartans by means of the following ruse. There was a Spartan named Sphodrias[2] who enjoyed a high reputation as a soldier, but who lacked judgement and was apt to be misled by vain hopes and reckless ambitions: this officer had been left at Thespiae with a number of troops to help and act as a rallying-point for those Thebans who had been exiled because they favoured the Spartans. Pelopidas and Gorgidas arranged for one of their friends who was a merchant to visit Sphodrias secretly and to unfold a scheme which proved even more attractive to him than money. The idea was that he should

1. In 378 B.C.   2. See also *Life of Agesilaus*, ch. 24.

attempt an ambitious operation and capture the Piraeus by a surprise attack when the Athenians were off their guard. Nothing, the merchant explained to him, would please the Spartans so much as the seizure of the Piraeus, and at that moment the Athenians could expect no help from the Thebans, who were angry with them and regarded them as traitors. At length Sphodrias allowed himself to be persuaded, put his force under arms, and made a night march into Attica. He advanced as far as Eleusis, but there his soldiers lost heart and his attempt was discovered; at this he withdrew to Thespiae, but his action was to involve the Spartans in a serious and difficult war.

15. As a result of this raid the Athenians eagerly renewed their alliance with Thebes and began operations against Sparta by sea; their ships cruised around Greece, encouraged opposition to the Spartans wherever they found it, and accepted the alliance of any Greek cities that were disposed to revolt. Meanwhile the Thebans continually engaged the Spartans in battle on their own account. These actions were no more than skirmishes, but such frequent encounters gave them invaluable training and practice and had the effect of raising their spirits, strengthening their bodies through hardship, and adding to their experience and courage. This is why Antalcidas the Spartan, we are told, when king Agesilaus returned from Boeotia with a wound, remarked to him, 'You taught the Thebans the art of war when they did not want to fight, and now, I see, they have paid you handsomely!' However, the truth was that it was not Agesilaus who had taught them, but those of their own leaders who chose the right time and the right moment, and then unleashed the Thebans against their enemies just like young hounds: they allowed them to get a taste of victory and of the self-confidence which goes with it, and then brought them back again to safety, and of these leaders the chief honour was due to Pelopidas. From the moment when his countrymen first chose him as their commander, there was not a single year in which they did not elect him to office, either as captain of the Sacred Band or more often as Boeotarch, so that he remained continuously on active service until the time of his death.

During these years the Spartans were defeated and routed at Plataea; at Thespiae Phoebidas, the man who had originally seized the Cadmeia, was killed; and at Tanagra a large Spartan force was put to flight, and Panthoidas, the military governor, lost his life. These actions however, although they gave courage and confidence to the victors, by no means broke the spirit of the vanquished. They were not pitched battles, nor were the combatants drawn up in open or in regular formation: the Thebans gained their successes by making well-judged attacks and by adopting flexible tactics, according to which they might retire and break off the action, or pursue and come to close quarters with the enemy.

16. However the battle of Tegyra,[1] which provided as it were a prelude to the Theban victory at Leuctra, greatly increased Pelopidas' reputation, for on this occasion none of his fellow commanders could claim a share in the success, nor had the enemy any excuse for their defeat. The city of Orchomenus had taken the side of Sparta and had received two Spartan battalions[2] to protect it. Pelopidas kept it under observation and watched carefully for his opportunity. When he heard that the Spartan garrison had made an expedition into Locris, he took the Sacred Band and a small detachment of cavalry, and marched against the city, hoping to catch it defenceless. When he approached it he discovered that the garrison had been relieved by fresh troops from Sparta, and so he led his force back to Thebes through the district of Tegyra. This was a roundabout route which skirted the foot of the mountains, but it was the only one he could take, for the river Melas which spreads out from its source into marshes and quagmires, made the centre of the plain completely impassable.

A little below the marshes stands the temple of Apollo of Tegyra, whose oracle was only abandoned comparatively recently. It flourished down to the time of the Persian wars, when Echecrates served as priest and prophet there. According to the legend it was here that the god was born, and the mountain which overlooks the temple bears the name of Delos: at its foot the river Melas contracts into its channel, while behind the temple flow two springs, whose water is much praised for its sweetness, coolness and abundance. One of these is called the Palm and the other the Olive to this day, as though the goddess Leto had borne her children not between two trees[3] but

1. 375 B.C.
2. Plutarch uses the word *mora*, which denoted one of the formations, originally six in number, in which all Spartans were enrolled. Its strength might vary between 400 and 900 men.
3. As in the story of the birth of Apollo and Artemis on the island of Delos.

between two fountains. Close by is the mountain range known as the Ptöum, from which it is said that a wild boar suddenly appeared and terrified the goddess, and in the same way the legends of the dragon Python and the giant Tityus which belong to this locality also lend some support to the tradition that the god was born here. However I shall pass over most of the evidence on this subject, since according to our ancestral tradition Apollo is not to be ranked among those deities who were born in a mortal and later changed into an immortal state, as for example Hercules and Dionysus, who through their virtues were enabled to cast off mortality and suffering. Apollo is one of those deities who are eternal and unbegotten, if we may be guided by the testimony which the oldest and wisest men have uttered on these matters.

17. It was in the neighbourhood of Tegyra, then, that the Thebans met the Spartans, as they were returning in the opposite direction from Locris. As soon as the Thebans caught sight of the Spartans emerging from the narrow defiles in the hills, one of them ran to Pelopidas and cried out, 'We have fallen into our enemy's hands!' 'Why not the enemy into our hands?' retorted Pelopidas. He immediately ordered his whole cavalry force to ride up from the rear and to prepare for a charge, and he drew up his infantry, who numbered three hundred, in close formation: his hope was that wherever the cavalry charged, this point would offer him the best chance to break through the enemy who outnumbered him. There were two battalions of Spartans, each consisting of five hundred men according to Ephorus, although Callisthenes gives their strength as seven hundred, and other writers, Polybius among them, put it at nine hundred. The Spartan polemarchs Gorgoleon and Theopompus felt certain of victory, and advanced against the Thebans. There was a furious clash as the two lines met, the fighting being fiercest at the point in the line where the two commanders were stationed, and it was there that the Spartan polemarchs engaged Pelopidas and were both killed. Then when the Spartans around them were also cut down, panic began to spread through the army, and they parted their ranks to make a passage for the Thebans, supposing that they wanted to force their way to the rear and escape. However, Pelopidas used the corridor which was thus opened to attack the formations which were still holding their ground, and he cut his way through them with great slaughter,

until finally the entire Spartan force turned and fled. The Thebans did not press the pursuit far, because they were afraid of being counter-attacked by the Orchomenians, whose city was close at hand, or by the relieving force from Sparta. Nevertheless they had succeeded in defeating the enemy outright and forcing their way through the whole of the beaten army; so they set up a trophy, stripped the Spartan dead, and returned home in triumph. In all the wars that had been fought between Greeks and barbarians, the Lacedaemonians, it appears, had never been beaten by an army smaller than their own, nor for that matter in a pitched battle in which the numbers were equal. For this reason they possessed an invincible spirit and when they came to close quarters their mere reputation was enough to give them an ascendancy over their enemies, since other men could not believe that they were a match for the same number of Spartans. So it was this battle which first proved to the rest of Greece that it was not only the Eurotas, nor the country between Babyce and Cnacion[1] which bred brave and warlike soldiers. The truth is that if the youth of a nation is ashamed of disgrace, is ready to dare anything in a noble cause and shrink from dishonour rather than from danger, these soldiers prove the most terrible to their enemies.

18. The Sacred Band, we are told, was originally founded by Gorgidas. It consisted of three hundred picked men, who were given their training and lodging by the city and were quartered on the Cadmeia. This was why they were called the city regiment, because at that time the acropolis was known as the city. But according to some accounts, this force was composed of lovers and beloved, and a joke of Pammenes has come down to us in which he remarks that Homer's Nestor was paying little attention to tactics when he urged the Greeks to arrange their military formations by clans and tribes

That clans should stand shoulder to shoulder with clans, and tribes aid one another,[2]

and that he ought instead to have posted lovers side by side. Tribesmen or clansmen do not feel any great concern for their kinsfolk in time of danger, but a band which is united by the ties of love is truly indissoluble and unbreakable, since both lovers and beloved are ashamed to be disgraced in the presence of the other, and each stands

1. Tributaries of the Eurotas, the principal river of Sparta.
2. *Iliad* ii, 363.

his ground at a moment of danger to protect the other. We need not be surprised at this, since men are more anxious to earn the good opinion of their lovers, even when these are absent, than that of others who are present: there is the case of a man who when his enemy was about to kill him as he lay on the ground, implored the other to run him through the breast, 'so that my beloved may not see me lying dead with a wound in my back and be ashamed of me'. The legend has it too that Iolaus, who was beloved by Hercules, accompanied him during his labours and shared them with him, and Aristotle says that even down to his own times the tomb of Iolaus was a place where lovers exchanged their vows.

It was natural, therefore, that the Band was termed Sacred for the same reason that Plato describes the lover as a friend 'inspired by God',[1] and it is said that it was never defeated until the battle of Chaeronea. The story goes that when king Philip of Macedon was inspecting the dead after the fighting, he stood at the place where the three hundred had faced the long pikes of his phalanx, and lay dead in their armour, their bodies piled one upon the other. He was amazed at the sight, and when he learned that this was the band of lovers and beloved, he wept and exclaimed, 'A curse on those who imagine that these men ever did or suffered anything shameful!'

19. Speaking generally of love between men, it was not, as the poets have reported, the passion of Laius for the young Chrysippus which first set the fashion for this kind of relationship in Thebes. Its origins are rather to be traced to their law-givers who wished to soften and tone down the hot-tempered and violent element in the Theban character, beginning from earliest boyhood, and for this reason they paid great attention to the flute, both in their education and their recreation. They gave this instrument especial prominence and value, and at the same time gave the emotions of love a place of honour in the wrestling-school and the gymnasium, and in this way they tempered, like steel, the characters of their young men. It was for the same reason that they established in their city the worship of the goddess Harmony, who is said to have been the child of Ares and Aphrodite: they believed that where the courage and aggressive qualities of the soldier are blended and mingled with eloquence and the social

1. *Symposium*, 179 A.

graces, there all the elements of communal life are harmonized, so that they produce the most perfect consonance and order.

When Gorgidas founded the Sacred Band, he originally distributed its members among the front ranks of the entire Theban phalanx. The result was that their exceptional courage was made inconspicuous, and their striking power was not exploited in any way which could benefit the whole army, because it was dissipated and diluted with that of a large body of inferior troops. But after the Band had distinguished themselves so brilliantly at Tegyra where they had fought as an individual formation around Pelopidas' own person, he saw to it that they were never afterwards separated from one another or broken up: instead he treated them as a single unit and gave them the place of danger in his greatest battles. Just as horses gallop faster when they are harnessed to a chariot than when they are ridden singly – not because they travel through the air more rapidly as a result of their combined weight, but because their mutual rivalry and competition kindles their spirits – so Pelopidas believed that brave men are at their most ardent in a common cause and give of their best when they strive to outdo one another in valour.

20. The Spartans now concluded a common peace with the rest of Greece,[1] but continued to wage war against Thebes alone, and Cleombrotus their king invaded Boeotia with a force of two thousand infantry and a thousand cavalry. The Thebans found that they had to face a new danger, that of being completely displaced from their native land, and a fear such as they had never experienced before now spread through the whole of Boeotia. It was at this time, just as Pelopidas was leaving his house, that his wife followed him on his way, weeping and entreating him to take care of his life. 'My dear,' he said to her, 'this is very good advice for private soldiers, but generals need to be told to take care of the lives of others.' When he reached the camp, he found that the Boeotarchs disagreed as to what should be done: he at once gave his support to Epaminondas and voted in favour of engaging the enemy. Pelopidas did not hold the office of Boeotarch, but he enjoyed great confidence as the commander of the Sacred Band, as was only right for a man who had given his country such proofs of his devotion to liberty.

Accordingly the decision was taken to risk a battle, and the Thebans

1. 371 B.C. See *Life of Agesilaus*, ch. 28.

pitched camp opposite the Spartan army at Leuctra. Here Pelopidas had a dream which disturbed him deeply. In the plain of Leuctra
are the tombs of the daughters of Scedasus. These girls are known as
the Leuctridae, because it was here that they were buried after they
had been raped by some Spartan strangers and had later committed
suicide. Their father could obtain no satisfaction from the Spartans for
this brutal and lawless outrage, and so, after solemnly cursing the
Spartan race, he killed himself on the tombs of his daughters, and
hence for ever after prophecies and oracles continually warned the
Spartans to beware of the vengeance of Leuctra. Most of them, however, did not fully understand the allusion and were also uncertain as
to the place it concerned, since there is a small town in Laconia near
the sea which is also named Leuctra, and another near Megalopolis in
Arcadia. This atrocity, of course, took place long before the battle.

21. As Pelopidas slept in the camp, he dreamed that he saw the girls
weeping over their tombs and calling down curses on the Spartans,
and also that Scedasus urged him to sacrifice a red-haired virgin to his
daughters if he wished to conquer his enemies. Pelopidas thought this
a terrible and impious command, but nevertheless he rose and described his dream to the diviners and the generals. Some of these insisted that he must not neglect or disobey the order, and they quoted a
number of precedents for human sacrifice in ancient times – for example, Menoeceus the son of Creon; Macaria the daughter of Hercules; then, coming nearer to the present, the case of Pherecydes the
philosopher, who was put to death by the Spartans and whose skin
was preserved by their kings on the instructions of some oracle; of
Leonidas, the Spartan king, who, in a sense, was obeying the command of the oracle when he sacrificed his life at Thermopylae to save
the rest of Greece; and of the Persian youths, who were sacrificed by
Themistocles to Dionysus the eater of flesh before the sea-battle at
Salamis.[1] In all these instances the sacrifices were vindicated by the
successes that followed. On the other hand, when Agesilaus was setting out on an expedition from the same place and against the same
enemies as Agamemnon, he had the same vision as he lay asleep at
Aulis, in which the goddess Artemis demanded his daughter as a sacrifice, but he was too tender-hearted to give her up, and thus ruined his
expedition, which ended unsuccessfully and ingloriously. Others took

1. See *The Rise and Fall of Athens, Life of Themistocles*, ch. 13.

the opposite view, and argued that such a barbarous and impious sacrifice could not be pleasing to the powers above, because it is not the Typhons or Giants or other monsters who rule in heaven, but the Father of gods and men. They argued that it is probably foolish in any case to believe that there are deities who delight in bloodshed and in the slaughter of men, but that if they exist, we should disregard them and treat them as powerless, since it is only weak and depraved minds that could conceive or harbour such cruel and unnatural desires.

22. While the Theban leaders debated this problem and Pelopidas in particular was at a loss what to do, a filly suddenly broke away from a herd of horses, galloped through the camp and stopped at the very spot where the conference was taking place. The other spectators admired above all the colour of her glossy mane, which was a fiery chestnut, the vigour of her movements and the strength and boldness of her neighing, but Theocritus the prophet, with a sudden flash of understanding, cried out to Pelopidas, 'The gods are with you! Here is your victim. Let us not wait for any other virgin, but take the gift the god has provided for you.' At this they caught the filly and led her to the tombs of the girls. There they crowned her with garlands, consecrated her with prayers and joyfully offered up the sacrifice. Then they explained to the whole army the details of Pelopidas' dream and the reasons for the sacrifice.

23. During the battle Epaminondas kept edging his phalanx to the left so as to form an oblique angle to the front. His object was to draw away the right wing of the Spartans as far as possible from the rest of the Greeks, and to drive back Cleombrotus, who commanded the Spartan right, by launching an attack in which the main strength of the Theban infantry was concentrated in column on that wing. The enemy perceived his intention and began to change their formation, extending their right wing and starting an encircling movement so as to outflank and envelop Epaminondas. But at this point Pelopidas dashed forward from his position, and advancing with his band of three hundred at the run, attacked the Spartans before Cleombrotus could either deploy his wing or bring it back to its previous position and close up his ranks. His charge caught the Spartans out of position: they had not yet formed their line and were still moving about indecisively. And yet the Spartans were the most skilled and experienced

soldiers in the world, and in their training they paid special attention to the problem of changing formation without falling into disorder or confusion; each man was accustomed to take any one of his comrades as his right-hand or rear-rank man, and, wherever danger might threaten, to concentrate on that point, knit their ranks, and fight as effectively as ever. But now when Epaminondas' main phalanx bore down on them alone and ignored the rest of their army, and Pelopidas with a charge of extraordinary speed and daring had already hurled himself upon them, their spirit faltered, their courage deserted them, and there followed a rout and a slaughter of the Spartans such as had never before been seen. In this battle Pelopidas, although he was not one of the generals and commanded only a few men, won as much fame for the victory and the triumph of Theban arms as Epaminondas, who was the Boeotarch in command of the whole army.

24. However, when the Thebans invaded the Peloponnese,[1] both men held the office of Boeotarch. In this campaign they won over most of the peoples of the region and detached from the Lacedaemonian alliance the states of Elis, Argos, the whole of Arcadia and most of Laconia itself. By this time the winter solstice was approaching, so that only a few days of the latter part of the last month of the year remained. The law ordained that as soon as the first month of the new year began, other officials must take their places, and that those who refused to give up their offices could incur the death penalty. The other Boeotarchs were in a hurry to withdraw the army and march home, not only because they feared the law, but also because they wished to escape the hardships of winter. But Pelopidas was the first to support Epaminondas in urging a contrary resolution: he joined him in appealing to the Thebans to follow them, and led the army into Sparta and across the Eurotas. He captured many of the enemy's cities and ravaged their territory as far as the coast. The army he led numbered seventy thousand, of whom the Thebans formed less than a twelfth part. Yet the reputation of the two men was such that they did not need a formal decree, but were able to persuade all the allies to follow wherever they led without a murmur. The first and supreme law, it would seem, which is a law of nature, makes the man who wishes to be saved submit to the authority of the man who can save him; in the same way men sailing on a calm sea or lying at anchor

1. In 370 B.C.

near the shore may treat their captains insolently or rebelliously, but as soon as a storm blows up or danger threatens, they look up to him and place all their hopes in him. Similarly the Argives and Eleans and Arcadians would argue and dispute with the Thebans in their joint assemblies as to who should lead the allies, but at times of crisis and when battles had to be fought, they obeyed the Theban generals and followed them of their own free will. In this campaign the allies united the whole of Arcadia into one state, freed the territory of Messenia from the Spartans who had annexed it, recalled the former inhabitants of Messenia, and established them in their ancient capital of Ithome. On their way home, as they marched through Cenchreae, they defeated the Athenians when they tried to hinder their passage in a series of skirmishes in the passes.

25. After these achievements the rest of the Greeks idolized the two men for their valour and marvelled at their success. But as their fame grew, so did the envy of their compatriots, who now prepared for them a reception as disgraceful as it was undeserved. On their return both Pelopidas and Epaminondas were put on trial for their lives, the charge being that they had not resigned the office of Boeotarch, as the law required, in the first month of the new year (which the Thebans call Boucation), but had extended their terms by four months, during which time they had carried out their campaign in Messenia, Arcadia and Laconia. It was Pelopidas who was tried first, and so ran the greater risk of being condemned, but both men were acquitted.

Epaminondas bore this attempt to slander him with patience, for he believed that a man of true courage and magnanimity should be forbearing when he comes under political attack. But Pelopidas who was more hot-tempered by nature and was encouraged by friends to avenge himself upon his enemies, seized the opportunity to retaliate, and he did it as follows. The orator Menecleidas had been one of the conspirators who had accompanied Pelopidas and Melon from Athenian territory to Charon's house in Thebes. After the liberation of Thebes from the Spartans he was not held in so much honour as the other conspirators, and since he was an able speaker but a man of little self-control and of a malevolent disposition, he employed his eloquence in slandering and attacking the reputations of those who were in power, and he continued to do this even after the trial.

In this way Menecleidas succeeded in preventing Epaminondas

from being elected to the office of Boeotarch and in weakening his influence in affairs for a long while. But he was not strong enough to damage Pelopidas' reputation in the eyes of the people, and so he attempted to stir up trouble between him and Charon. It is often a comfort to the envious to make out those whom they cannot surpass to be in some way inferior to others, and so in all his speeches to the people Menecleidas made a point of magnifying Charon's achievements and lavishing praise on his campaigns and victories. In particular he tried to have a public monument set up to commemorate the victory which the Theban cavalry had won at Plataea under Charon's command, some time before the battle of Leuctra. Androcydes of Cyzicus had been commissioned by the city to paint a picture of another battle and had been engaged on the work at Thebes. Before he could complete the painting, the city had revolted from Sparta, and the Thebans were left with the unfinished work on their hands. It was this picture which Menecleidas persuaded the people to dedicate with Charon's name inscribed on it as the victor, and he hoped in this way to overshadow the fame of Pelopidas and Epaminondas. It was an absurd piece of pretension to single out for praise one action and one victory – in which we are told that an obscure Spartan named Gerandas and forty other soldiers were killed, but nothing else of any importance was accomplished – and to ignore the many great battles won by the other two men. At any rate Pelopidas attacked this decree as unconstitutional and contended that it was against the traditions of the Thebans to honour any man individually, but that the whole city should share equally in the glory of a victory. All through the trial which followed, he paid generous tribute to Charon, but he argued that Menecleidas was an unscrupulous slanderer, and repeatedly asked the Thebans whether they had never before done anything worthy of note themselves. The outcome was that Menecleidas was heavily fined, and as he could not pay because the amount was so large, he tried at a later date to overthrow the government and bring about a revolution. These events, then, throw some light on Pelopidas' life.

26. At this time Alexander the tyrant of Pherae[1] was openly at war with many of the Thessalian cities and was plotting against all of

1. A city in eastern Thessaly, not far from the modern Volos. It had been the seat of Jason, who had established his dominion over the area. His assassination in 370 and the subsequent seizure of power by Alexander of Pherae had thrown the region into chaos.

them. These communities therefore sent a delegation to Thebes to ask for a body of troops and a general. Pelopidas knew that Epaminondas was fully occupied in the Peloponnese[1] and so he offered his services to the Thessalians, partly because he could not bear to let his military skill and talents remain unused, and partly because he believed that wherever Epaminondas was, there could be no need for another general. He therefore led the expedition into Thessaly and immediately captured Larissa; then when Alexander came to him and begged for peace, he tried to convert him from a tyrant into a mild ruler and to persuade him to govern the Thessalians according to their laws. But on closer acquaintance Alexander turned out to be incorrigibly brutal and given to savage cruelty, and so, since he received frequent complaints of the man's insolence and greed, Pelopidas treated him harshly and severely, whereupon Alexander departed in a rage taking his bodyguard with him.

Pelopidas left the Thessalians secure against the threat of the tyrant, and after he had united them in harmony, he set out for Macedonia. Here Ptolemy was at war with Alexander, the king of Macedon, and on this occasion both parties had invited Pelopidas to act as arbitrator, judge between their claims, and then give his help and support to whichever party proved to have been wronged. He came and settled their dispute, and after he had restored the exiles to their homes, he took Philip,[2] the king's brother, and thirty other sons of the leading men in the state and brought them to Thebes as hostages. He did this to show the Greeks how far the prestige of Thebes had advanced: his action not only demonstrated her power but also the confidence which men placed in the justice of her decisions.

This was the same Philip who was later to make war upon the Greeks and deprive them of their freedom, but at this time he was no more than a boy and was quartered in Thebes with Pammenes. It was for this reason that he was believed to have become a devoted disciple of Epaminondas. It may be that Philip was quick to appreciate the Theban's efficiency in the art of war and generalship, which represented no more than one of his virtues: as for the qualities of moderation, justice, magnanimity and clemency which constituted the true greatness of his character, Philip had no share of these by nature, nor did he choose to imitate them.

1. In 369 B.C.
2. Philip of Macedon, the father of Alexander the Great.

27. In the following year[1] the Thessalians again appealed for help because Alexander of Pherae was threatening their cities. Pelopidas and Ismenias were sent to them as ambassadors, but as no fighting was expected, they brought no troops with them from Boeotia and so Pelopidas was forced to make use of the Thessalians to deal with the emergency. It so happened that at this moment Macedonia was also in a state of disorder. King Alexander had been murdered by Ptolemy, who had then seized power, and the dead ruler's friends had appealed to Pelopidas to intervene. Pelopidas wished to support their cause, and as he had no troops of his own, he recruited some mercenaries on the spot and took the field against Ptolemy. As the two forces converged Ptolemy was able to subvert the mercenaries and bribe them to come over to his side, but as he was afraid of Pelopidas' mere name and reputation, he went to pay his respects to him. At their meeting he greeted Pelopidas as his superior, begged for his favour, and agreed to act as regent for the brothers of the dead king and to conclude an alliance with the Thebans: to confirm these undertakings he handed over as hostages his own son Philoxenus and fifty of his followers. Pelopidas sent this party off to Thebes. But he was also angry at the treachery of his mercenaries, and he now discovered that their wives and children and most of their possessions had been sent to Pharsalus for safety; he decided to punish them for their affront to him, and so he gathered a number of Thessalian troops and marched upon the town. But he had hardly arrived when Alexander the tyrant of Pherae appeared before the city with his own forces. Pelopidas and Ismenias supposed that he had come to justify his conduct, and so they went of their own accord to meet him. They knew that he was a depraved creature, who had often been guilty of bloodshed, but they expected that their own dignity and reputation and the prestige of Thebes would protect them. However, when the tyrant saw them approaching unattended and unarmed, he at once arrested them and took possession of Pharsalus. This step aroused horror and dismay among his subjects, who concluded that after committing an act of such flagrant injustice he would spare nobody, but would behave on all occasions and to all persons like a man who had by now given up all hope for his own life.

28. The Thebans were enraged when they heard the news and at once dispatched an army, but Epaminondas was temporarily out of favour

and they appointed other commanders. As for Pelopidas, the tyrant
brought him back to Pherae, and at first allowed him to be visited by
anyone who wished to speak to him, imagining that he had been crushed by his misfortunes, and would become an object of pity. But when
the Pheraeans visited him to lament his plight, Pelopidas urged them
to take heart, since they could now be sure that the tyrant would be
punished for his crimes. He also sent a message to Alexander himself
telling him that it made no sense to torture and murder unhappy and
innocent citizens every day but to spare him, the man whom he knew
would surely take his revenge if he escaped. Alexander was amazed at
his fearless spirit and asked, 'Why is Pelopidas in such haste to die?'
to which the Theban replied, 'So that you may become even more
hateful to the gods than you are now, and die all the sooner.' After
this the tyrant forbade anybody but his personal attendants to visit
the prisoner.

Alexander's wife Thebe, who was a daughter of Jason of Pherae,
had heard from Pelopidas' gaolers of his courageous and noble conduct and was seized with an impulse to see him and speak to him.
When she visited him she did not at once recognize the greatness of his
nature in the midst of his misfortunes, but at the sight of his hair, his
ragged clothes and his meagre diet, she supposed, as was natural for a
woman, that he was suffering anguish from these indignities which
were hard to bear for a man of his position, and she burst into tears.
Pelopidas, who at first did not know who she was, watched with
amazement, but when he understood, he addressed her as a daughter
of Jason, since he knew her father well. When she said 'I pity your
wife', he replied, 'So do I pity you, for you are not a prisoner, and yet
you are compelled to endure Alexander.' Thebe was touched by this
speech, since she detested Alexander not only for his cruelty and arrogance, but also for the fact that he had seduced her youngest brother.
She came to see Pelopidas frequently, and during these visits she spoke
openly of her sufferings: the result was that these conversations filled
her at once with courage and with a burning hatred of Alexander.

29. The Theban generals invaded Thessaly but accomplished nothing,
and finally either through inexperience or misfortune they beat an
ignominious retreat. The state fined each of them 10,000 drachmae
and then dispatched Epaminondas with another army.[1] This news

1. In 367 B.C.

immediately aroused great excitement among the Thessalians, and their hopes rose high because of Epaminondas' reputation. Alexander's generals and supporters, on the other hand, were so overcome by fear, and his subjects were so eager to revolt and so overjoyed by the prospect of his impending punishment, that the tyrant's cause seemed to be tottering at the very brink of destruction. Epaminondas, however, was more concerned for Pelopidas' safety than for his own fame. He was afraid that if the country were allowed to fall into disorder, Alexander would be driven to despair and would then turn upon his prisoner like a wild beast, and so he played a waiting game and advanced only in a roundabout fashion. He hampered and circumscribed the tyrant's movements by his own preparations and apparent intentions in such a way that he neither encouraged him to take reckless or precipitate action, nor provoked the harsh and malignant element in his disposition. Epaminondas had heard of his cruelty and his contempt for right and justice, and of how he sometimes had men buried alive or sewn into the skins of wild boars or bears and then set his hunting-dogs upon them, or shot at them for sport; and how in the case of Meliboea and Scotusa, two cities which were on friendly terms with him, he had surrounded them with his guards while the popular assembly was in session and slaughtered the inhabitants from the youths upward. He had also consecrated the spear with which he had killed Polyphron, his uncle, hung garlands on the weapon, offered sacrifice to it as a god, and named it 'Tycho', signifying Luck. On another occasion when he was watching a tragedian perform Euripides' *Trojan Women*, he left the theatre suddenly and sent a message to the actor telling him not to lose heart or to relax his efforts because of his departure: it was not out of contempt for his acting that he had left the theatre, but rather because he was ashamed to let the citizens see him, who had never pitied any of the men he had done to death, shedding tears over the sufferings of Hecuba and Andromache. But it was this same tyrant who was so terrified by the name and fame of Epaminondas and the very appearance of an expedition led by him that

> He cowered slave-like, as a beaten cock
> That lets its feathers droop.[1]

1. The author of this iambic trimeter is unknown. It is also quoted in *The Rise and Fall of Athens*, *Life of Alcibiades*, ch. 4.

and hurriedly sent a deputation to excuse his actions. However Epaminondas would not tolerate the suggestion of making a treaty of peace and friendship with such a man: he merely concluded a truce of thirty days, and after Pelopidas and Ismenias had been handed over he returned home.

30. Soon after this the Thebans discovered that Sparta and Athens had both sent ambassadors to the king of Persia to negotiate an alliance. They therefore dispatched Pelopidas on a similar mission,[1] a choice which proved well justified because of the great prestige he had won. In the first place his reputation had already preceded him: as he travelled through the provinces of the Persian empire he attracted universal attention, for the fame of his battles against the Spartans had by no means been muted nor had it been slow to circulate among the Persians, and no sooner had the report of the battle of Leuctra become known abroad than it was echoed time and again by the news of some fresh exploit which penetrated to the remotest parts of the interior. All the satraps, generals and officers who met him at the king's court spoke of him with wonder as the man who had routed the Lacedaemonians by land and sea, and had shut up between the bounds of Mount Taygetus and the Eurotas those same Spartans who only a few years before had made war upon the great King under the leadership of Agesilaus and fought the Persians for the possession of Susa and Ecbatana. King Artaxerxes was naturally pleased on this account: he admired Pelopidas for his reputation and paid him exceptional honours, since he wished to create the impression that he was courted and highly regarded by the greatest men of every country. But when he saw Pelopidas face to face and understood his proposals, which were more trustworthy than those of the Athenians and more straightforward than those of the Spartans, his pleasure was even greater, and using his kingly prerogative to display his sentiments, he made no secret of the admiration he felt for Pelopidas, and allowed the ambassadors to see that he stood the highest in his favour. However, it was to Antalcidas[2] that he ostensibly showed the greatest honour, when he took off the garland which he had worn at a banquet, had it steeped in perfume and presented it to him. He did not favour Pelopidas with refinements of this kind, but sent him the richest and most magnificent of the gifts which were customary on such occasions, and granted

1. In the winter of 367/6 B.C.   2. The chief Spartan envoy.

his requests. These were that the Greeks[1] should be left independent, that Messene[2] should continue as an independent city, and that the Thebans should be regarded as the king's hereditary friends. With these answers, but without accepting any of the gifts save those which were simply intended as pledges of friendship and goodwill, Pelopidas set out for home, and it was this action which more than anything else brought the other ambassadors into discredit. At any rate Timagoras was condemned and executed by the Athenians, and if this was on account of the vast quantity of gifts which he accepted, then the sentence was just: these had included not merely gold and silver, but an expensive bed, complete with slaves to make it up, since, according to him, Greeks were not capable of doing this, and also eighty cows with their herdsmen since, as he claimed, he needed cows' milk for some ailment. Finally he was carried down to the coast in a litter, and the king gave him four talents to pay the bearers. However it was apparently not so much the fact that he accepted these gifts which enraged the Athenians. His shield-bearer Epicrates at once admitted that his master had received gifts from the king, and had spoken of putting forward a proposal to the assembly that instead of electing nine archons, they should choose nine of the poorest citizens as ambassadors to the king so that they could benefit from his bounty and become rich men, and at this suggestion the people burst out laughing. The real cause of the Athenians' anger was that the Thebans should have been granted all their requests. They did not stop to think that in the eyes of a ruler who had always shown most regard for a militarily strong people, Pelopidas' reputation counted for far more than any amount of skill in oratory.

31. The success of Pelopidas' mission, and his achievement in ensuring the re-settlement of Messenia[3] and the independence of the rest of the Greeks, earned him much goodwill on his return. Meanwhile, how-

1. This meant the Greeks of the Greek mainland and islands, not those of Asia Minor. This settlement in effect renewed that of Antalcidas (387 B.C.). See *Life of Agesilaus*, ch. 23. According to this, the Greeks in Asia were the King's subjects: those outside were autonomous, i.e. not subject to any dominant Greek state, whether Sparta or Athens. The Thebans had originally refused to ratify these terms.

2. See ch. 24.

3. The recognition of the independence of Messenia was a crippling diplomatic defeat for Sparta. Antalcidas, their so-called 'Persian expert', was so disgraced that he anticipated his condemnation by committing suicide.

ever, Alexander of Pherae had reverted to his former ways. He had destroyed several of the cities of Thessaly and had installed garrisons in the territory of the Achaeans of Phthiotis and of the people of Magnesia. So when the cities learned that Pelopidas had returned, they at once sent ambassadors to Thebes to ask for an army to be dispatched to them and for him to command it. The Thebans enthusiastically passed a decree to this effect, preparations were quickly made, and the commander was about to set out when there was an eclipse of the sun and darkness descended on the city in the middle of the day. Pelopidas saw that all the Thebans were dismayed by this phenomenon, and decided that it would be wrong to coerce men whose courage and hopes had deserted them or to risk the lives of seven thousand citizens. So he offered his own services to the Thessalians, took with him a detachment of three hundred cavalry who belonged to other cities and had volunteered for the expedition, and set out: in this he was defying the advice of the seers and the wishes of the rest of the people, who considered that the eclipse must be a portent sent from heaven and must refer to some great man. For his own part he was enraged against Alexander when he remembered the humiliations he had suffered, and his earlier conversations with Thebe led him to hope that the tyrant's family was already divided within itself and hostile to its head. But above all else it was the glory of the enterprise which spurred him on. At this moment the Spartans were sending out generals and governors to help Dionysius the tyrant of Syracuse, while the Athenians who were in Alexander's pay, were setting up a bronze statue of him as a benefactor, and so Pelopidas was eager to show the Greeks that it was only the men of Thebes who took up arms for the cause of the oppressed, and who dethroned those dynasties in Greece which relied on violence and defied the rule of law.

32. Accordingly when he arrived at Pharsalus he combined his foreign contingent with a Thessalian force and marched at once against Alexander. The tyrant saw that there were only a few Thebans with Pelopidas and that his own infantry outnumbered his opponent's by more than two to one, and met him near the shrine of Thetis. When Pelopidas was told that Alexander was advancing against him with a large force, he remarked, 'All the better, there will be more for us to conquer.'

At the place which is known as Cynoscephalae, or the Dogs' Heads, a number of steep and lofty hills project into the middle of the plain, and both sides advanced to occupy these with their infantry. Pelopidas, who possessed a large force of cavalry of excellent quality, ordered them to attack and they routed the enemy's horsemen and pursued them into the plain. But in the meanwhile Alexander had secured the high ground, and when the Thessalian cavalry went forward and tried to force their way up the steep slopes, he attacked and killed the leading files, and the rest were so harassed by missiles that the assault was thrown back. When Pelopidas saw this, he recalled the cavalry and ordered it to attack the enemy's infantry where they still held together on the plain, while he himself took up his shield and ran to join the fighting in the hills. He forced his way through the rear and quickly inspired the front ranks with such courage and vigour that the enemy imagined they were being attacked by reinforcements who were fresh in body and spirit. They succeeded in resisting two or three attacks, but when they saw that the enemy came on resolutely and that the cavalry were now returning to support them, they began to give ground and fell back step by step. Pelopidas had now reached the heights and saw as he looked down that the enemy, although not yet routed, was beginning to waver and fall into disorder, and he cast his eyes around searching for Alexander. At last he saw him on the right wing encouraging and rallying his mercenaries. All his hatred instantly flared up at the sight, his rage overwhelmed his judgement, and sacrificing both his own safety and his responsibility as a general to his passion, he ran out far in front of his own men and rushed towards the tyrant, shouting and challenging him to fight. Alexander did not stand his ground and await his adversary's attack, but turned and took refuge in the ranks of his bodyguard. Pelopidas threw himself upon the mercenaries, cut down the foremost of them and even killed a few of the main body, but most of them kept their distance and attacked him with their javelins, which pierced his armour and riddled his body with wounds. Then the Thessalians, in great anxiety for his safety, rushed down the hill to rescue him, but by then he had already fallen. Meanwhile the cavalry launched another charge in which they routed the whole of the enemy's phalanx. They pursued the infantry to a great distance, cut down more than three thousand of them, and left the countryside strewn with corpses.

33. It was no wonder that those of the Thebans who were present at Pelopidas' death should have been plunged into grief and called him

their father, their saviour and their teacher of all that was best and noblest. But the Thessalians too and their allies went further than this: not only did they surpass in their decrees the highest honours that are rightly paid to human valour, but by their sorrow they demonstrated even more conspicuously the gratitude which they felt for their deliverer. It is said that the soldiers who took part in the battle neither took off their breast-plates, nor unbridled their horses, nor even bound up their wounds when they heard of his death, but still wearing their armour and hot from the fighting they came first to Pelopidas' body, as if he were still conscious: then they piled around it the arms of their slain enemies, sheared their horses' manes and cut off their own hair. After they had dispersed to their tents, many of them neither lit a fire, nor ate any supper: instead a melancholy silence reigned throughout the camp, as if they had been defeated and enslaved by the tyrant instead of having won a great and glorious victory over him. In the same way when the news reached the cities of Thessaly, the magistrates, accompanied by priests, young men and boys came out in procession to take up the body, and they carried trophies, wreaths and suits of golden armour in its honour. Then when the body was to be taken out for burial, the leading citizens of Thessaly begged the Thebans to grant them the privilege of burying it themselves, and one of them spoke as follows: 'Friends and allies, we ask of you a favour which we shall consider an honour to us in our great misfortune and a comfort in our grief. We Thessalians can never escort a living Pelopidas again, nor render him honours which he can see and hear. But if we may have his body to touch, to adorn and bury, we shall be able to show you, we believe, that this is an even greater loss for Thessaly than it is for Thebes. For you have lost only a good commander, but we both a commander and our freedom. For how can we dare to ask of you another general when we have failed to give you back Pelopidas?' This request the Thebans granted.

34. There has never been a more splendid funeral, at least in the estimation of those who do not believe that splendour necessarily demands a profusion of ivory, gold and purple: such was the kind of display of which Philistus gives a rapturous description at the funeral of Dionysius, which rang down the curtain in grandiose style upon the great tragedy of his tyranny. In the same fashion Alexander the Great, when Hephaestion died, not only cut off the manes of his

horses and mules, but even demolished the battlements of city walls in order to show the cities in mourning and make them present a shorn and dishevelled appearance in place of their former beauty. But these tributes represented the commands of despots, they were carried out under duress, and they excited envy against those who received them and hatred against those who enforced them: they were not prompted either by gratitude or by true regard for the dead, and they expressed only a barbaric pomp and an arrogant luxury which was characteristic of men who squandered their superfluous wealth on vain and paltry ostentation. The fact that a mere commoner dying in a strange country far from his wife and children should be borne forth and escorted and crowned, with so many peoples and cities vying with one another to show him honour, and yet with nobody demanding or compelling this, surely demonstrates that he attained the height of good fortune. To die in the hour of triumph is not, as Aesop calls it, a most cruel stroke of fate, but a most happy one, since it secures beyond all mischance the enjoyment of the blessings a man has earned and places them beyond the reach of fortune. The Spartan's advice was better than this, when he greeted Diagoras who had not only won victories at Olympia, but had lived to see his sons and daughters crowned there besides. 'Die now, Diagoras,' he said, 'You cannot climb Olympus and become a god!'

Yet I do not suppose that anyone would compare all the Olympian and Pythian victories put together with a single one of Pelopidas' achievements. He accomplished many of these and every one successfully, he spent the greater part of his life surrounded with honour and renown, and finally, after being appointed Boeotarch for the thirteenth time and while engaged in a heroic action aimed at the destruction of a tyrant, he sacrificed his life for the freedom of Thessaly.

35. Pelopidas' death caused great sorrow to his allies, but it brought them even greater advantages. When the Thebans learned the news they made immediate preparations to avenge his fate, and at once dispatched an army consisting of seven thousand infantry and seven hundred horsemen under the command of Malcitas and Diogeiton. They found that Alexander was weakened and that his forces had suffered heavy losses, and they forced him to restore the cities he had taken from the Thessalians, to set free the Magnesians and the Achaeans of Phthiotis and withdraw his garrisons from those territories,

and to guarantee to the Thebans that he would proceed against any enemy they might require him to attack. The Thebans were satisfied with these terms, but soon after this the gods took their own revenge for Pelopidas' death in a manner which I shall now describe.

As I mentioned in an earlier chapter, Pelopidas had taught Thebe the tyrant's wife not to be afraid of Alexander's display of outward pomp and splendour, since these depended entirely on force and the security of his bodyguards. For her own sake she feared his untrustworthiness and dreaded his cruelty, and she now entered into a plot with her three brothers Tisiphonus, Pytholaus and Lycophron, to kill him in the following way. The rest of the palace was patrolled by sentries who were on duty all night, but the bedchamber in which she and Alexander slept was on an upper floor and was guarded on the outside by a chained dog, which would attack anyone except his master and mistress and the one servant who fed him. When Thebe was ready to make the attempt, she kept her brothers hidden in a nearby room all through the day, and at night went into Alexander alone, as was her custom. She found him already asleep, and soon afterwards came out and ordered the servant to take the dog outside, explaining that his master wished to sleep undisturbed. Next she covered the stairs with wool to prevent them creaking as the young men climbed them, brought up her brothers safely with their swords drawn, and posted them outside the bedroom door. Then she went inside herself, took down the sword which hung over her husband's head and showed it to them as a sign that he was fast asleep. When she found that the young men were terrified and could not bring themselves to strike, she scolded them and swore in a rage that she would waken Alexander and tell him of the plot. After this she led them into the room, still unnerved, but by now filled with shame, placed them round the bed and brought the lamp. Then one of them seized the tyrant's feet and held them down, another dragged his head back by the hair and the third ran him through with his sword. The swiftness of the killing gave him a more painless death then he perhaps deserved. Nevertheless he was the first and perhaps the only tyrant to die at the hands of his own wife, and since his body was outraged after his death, thrown out of doors and trampled underfoot by the Pheraeans, it may be judged that he suffered a fate to match his own lawless crimes.

3

DION[1]

[408–354 B.C.]

* *
*

THE poet Simonides tells us, Sosius Senecio, that Troy bears no grudge against the men of Corinth for having fought against her on the side of the Greeks, since Glaucus, one of the very staunchest of her allies, was also, as it happened, a Corinthian. In the same way it is unlikely that either the Romans or the Greeks will find fault with the Academy, since in this book, which presents the *Lives* of Dion and of Brutus,[2] each nation receives very similar treatment. Dion was a disciple of Plato who knew the philosopher personally, while Brutus was nurtured on his doctrines, so that both men were trained in the same wrestling school, one might say, to take part in the struggle for supreme power. There is a remarkable similarity in many of their actions, and so we should not be surprised that they often illustrate a particular conviction of their teacher in virtue, namely that power and good fortune must be accompanied by wisdom and justice if a man's political actions are to be seen as noble as well as great. Hippomachus the trainer used to say that he could always pick out one of his pupils from afar off by the way he carried himself, even if he was only taking home some meat from the market-place, and in the same way it follows that where men have been trained in a particular school of philosophy, its principles should guide their conduct and confer a certain grace, harmony and fitness upon all their actions.

2. These two men's lives resemble each other in their fortunes, that is in those events which were the result of chance rather than of deliberate choice. Both of them were cut off in the prime of life and so failed

1. For places mentioned in this *Life* see Maps 1 and 3, pp. 433, 436.
2. See Introduction, p. 10.

to accomplish the purposes to which they had devoted such long and arduous efforts. But the strangest thing of all is that both of them were warned by the gods of their approaching death in the form of a malevolent and threatening spectre which appeared to each of them alike. Those who utterly deny the existence of such phenomena maintain that no man in his right senses has ever set eyes on a ghost or apparition sent by the gods. They insist that it is only little children or women or men under the stress of sickness or of some bodily disorder or mental aberration who have indulged in such extravagant imaginings, and that these really arise from an evil spirit or superstition within themselves. But Dion and Brutus were men of solid understanding and intellectual training, whose judgement was not easily deceived nor their composure shaken, and yet each of them was so affected by an apparition that they actually described what they had seen to others. So in the light of their experience we may be compelled to give credit to one of the strangest theories of ancient times, namely that there exist certain mean and malevolent spirits who envy good men. They strive to frustrate their actions, to confuse and terrify them, and thus to weaken their allegiance to virtue: all this is done to hinder them from continuing their upright and blameless progress along the path of honour, which would enable them to win a happier lot after death than the envious spirits themselves. However, this subject I must leave for discussion elsewhere, and in this, the twelfth book of my *Parallel Lives*, I begin with the life of the elder of the two.

3. Dionysius the elder, as soon as he had made himself master of Syracuse,[1] married the daughter of Hermocrates the Syracusan. But before the tyranny had been securely established, the people of Syracuse rose in revolt and violated her in such a cruel and barbarous fashion that she took her own life. Dionysius then recovered control, and once he had asserted his supremacy, he married two wives. One of these was a woman of Locris named Doris; the other, Aristomache, was the daughter of Hipparinus, one of the most prominent citizens of Syracuse, who had been a colleague of Dionysius when he had been appointed commander-in-chief of the army with unlimited powers to carry on the war against Carthage. It is said that he married both these women on the same day, and that nobody ever knew with which one he first consummated the marriage, but that after-

1. 405 B.C.

wards for the rest of his life he spent an equal share of his time with
each: it was his custom to dine with both of them together, and at
night they shared his bed in turn. The Syracusans, however, were
anxious that their own countrywoman should take precedence over
the foreigner, but it was Doris' good fortune to be the first to become
a mother, and thus by presenting Dionysius with his eldest son[1] she
was able to offset her foreign birth. Aristomache, on the other hand,
remained barren for a long time, although Dionysius passionately
desired that she should bear him children, and he even went so far as
to accuse the mother of his Locrian wife of giving her drugs to
prevent conception, and had her put to death.

4. Dion was a brother of Aristomache, and at first he was treated with
honour because of his sister's position; but after a while he was able
to give proof of his ability and earned the tyrant's regard on his own
account. Besides the other privileges which Dion enjoyed, Dionysius
instructed his treasurers to give the young man anything he asked for,
but to inform him of the amounts on the same day. Now from the
very beginning Dion had shown a high-principled, generous and
manly character, and these qualities became even more strongly
developed in him when by a providential accident Plato arrived in
Sicily.[2] This event was certainly not the work of any human agency,
but it seems that some supernatural power was already preparing far
in advance of the time the means to liberate the Syracusans and overthrow the tyranny, and to this end brought Plato to Syracuse and
introduced him to Dion. Dion was then a young man of twenty, but
of all Plato's followers he was by far the quickest to learn and the most
ready to respond to the call of the virtuous life. Plato himself wrote
of him in these terms and events bore out his judgement. Although
Dion had been brought up to accept the habit of submission to
tyrannical rule and had been steeped in an atmosphere of servility
and intimidation on the one hand, and of ostentatious adulation and
tasteless luxury on the other – a way of life which has no higher aspirations than pleasure and the love of gain – yet at the first taste of philo-
sophic reason and of a doctrine which requires obedience to virtue,
his spirit was instantly fired with enthusiasm. Then because he
himself was so quickly won over by these ideals, he assumed with all

1. Dionysius II, who succeeded to the tyranny, see ch. 6.
2. About 388 B.C.

the innocence of youth that Dionysius would respond just as readily to the same arguments, and so he set to work and finally persuaded the tyrant that when he was at leisure he should meet Plato and listen to his ideas.

5. At this encounter the general theme of the conversation was human virtue, and most of the discussion centred upon the topic of courage. Here Plato took the line that of all mankind the tyrant possesses the smallest share of this quality, and then turning to the subject of justice, he maintained that the life of the just is happy, while the life of the unjust is full of misery. Dionysius would not hear out this argument, since it implied a direct reproach to himself, and he grew exasperated with the audience when he saw how much they admired the speaker and were charmed by his doctrines. At last he lost his temper and angrily demanded of Plato why he had come to Sicily. Plato replied that he had come in search of a man of virtue, whereupon Dionysius retorted, 'Indeed! Then, by the gods, you do not seem to have found one yet!'

Dion and his friends supposed that this was the end of the tyrant's anger and that nothing more would come of it. Accordingly, as Plato was by then anxious to leave Sicily, they arranged passage for him on a trireme which was taking Pollis the Spartan envoy back to Greece. But Dionysius secretly approached Pollis and asked him to have Plato killed on the voyage if this could be arranged, or, if not, at least to sell him into slavery. This, he argued, would not do Plato any harm, since according to his own doctrines he would, as a just man, be equally happy even if he became a slave. Pollis, therefore, took Plato to Aegina, so we are told, and sold him into slavery, for the people of Aegina were at war with Athens at that time and had passed a decree that any Athenian who was caught on the island should be sold as a slave.

In spite of this Dion enjoyed the same honour and confidence in the eyes of the tyrant as before, and he was entrusted with the most important diplomatic missions: in particular he was sent to Carthage, where his achievements won great admiration. Dionysius even tolerated his habit of frank speech, and indeed, Dion was almost the only man who was left free to express his opinions, as for example when he reproved Dionysius for what he had said about Gelon.[1]

1. One of the most illustrious of Siceliot rulers (485–479 B.C.): he was the conqueror of the Carthaginians at Himera in 480.

The tyrant was sneering at Gelon's government, and when he said that Gelon had become the laughing-stock of Sicily,[1] the other courtiers pretended to admire the joke, but Dion was indignant and retorted, 'You might remember that the reason why you are our tyrant today is that people trusted you because of the example that Gelon set. After what you have said, nobody will be trusted because of *your* example.' The truth is that Gelon seems to have succeeded in making the spectacle of a city under absolute rule appear admirable, whereas Dionysius could only make it appear detestable.

6. Dionysius had three children by his Locrian wife Doris, and four by Aristomache: two of the latter were girls, Sophrosyne and Arete. Sophrosyne married her half-brother, Dionysius the younger, and Arete the tyrant's brother Thearides. Then after Thearides died, Arete married Dion, who was her uncle. When the elder Dionysius fell sick and it was considered certain that he would die, Dion tried to speak to him on behalf of Aristomache's children, but the physicians who were anxious to ingratiate themselves with the heir to the throne refused to allow this. Indeed, according to Timaeus, when Dionysius asked for a sleeping-draught, they gave him a drug which made him completely insensible, so that he died without ever regaining consciousness.[2]

At the first council which the young Dionysius held with his friends, Dion summed up the political situation and the immediate needs of the state with such authority that the rest of the company gave the impression of being mere children, while his frankness of speech made them appear by comparison the merest slaves of the tyranny, who could only offer in the most timorous and servile fashion the kind of advice which was calculated to please the young man. But what impressed the council most of all – since they were greatly disturbed by the danger which threatened the kingdom from Carthage – was Dion's undertaking that if Dionysius wanted peace, he would sail at once to Africa and put an end to the war on the best terms he could obtain; but that if he was set on war, Dion would supply fifty fast triremes and maintain them at his own expense.

7. Dionysius was greatly astonished at his magnanimity and delighted at his public spirit. But the other members of the council felt that this

1. A pun on the word *gelos* (laughter).   2. In 367 B.C.

display of generosity reflected on them and that they were humiliated by Dion's power, and so they at once began a campaign in which they seized every opportunity to turn the young ruler against Dion. They accused him of trying to manoeuvre himself into the position of tyrant through the authority which he exercised over the fleet, and of using the ships to place the control of the state in the hands of Aristomache's children, who were his own nephews and nieces. However the strongest and most obvious reasons for their hatred of him lay in the difference between his way of life and their own, and in his refusal to mingle with others. From the very beginning they made it their business to cultivate the friendship of the young and ill-educated tyrant and to become intimate with him by devising all kinds of flatteries and pandering to his amusements. They continually drew him into love affairs, crowded his leisure with entertainments, complete with wine and women, and contrived many other dissipations for him. In this way the tyranny was gradually softened like iron in the fire. To its subjects it may have seemed to have become more benevolent and its inhumanity to have abated, but if the edge of cruelty had been blunted, this was really due to the tyrant's indolence rather than to any genuine clemency. Thus little by little the laxity of the young ruler increased, until those adamantine chains by which the elder Dionysius had claimed to have left the monarchy secured, were dissolved and destroyed. The story goes that the young man once kept a drinking party going for ninety days in succession, and that during the whole of this time no person of consequence was admitted or business discussed, while the court was given over to carousing, scurrilous humour, singing, dancing and every kind of buffoonery.

8. It was only natural that the courtiers should detest Dion, since he never indulged in any pleasure or youthful folly, and so they tried to destroy his reputation. In particular they excelled at finding plausible ways of misrepresenting his virtues as vices; for example, they described his dignity as arrogance and his frankness of speech as presumption. When he gave good advice, they made out that he was denouncing them, and when he refused to join in their misdemeanours that he was looking down on them. And indeed it was true that there was a certain haughtiness in his character together with an austerity which made him difficult to approach and unsociable in conversation. In

fact it was not only a young man like Dionysius whose ears had been corrupted by flattery who found him a disagreeable and tiresome companion: many of his closest friends who loved the simplicity and nobility of his disposition still blamed him for his manner, because he behaved with unnecessary harshness or discourtesy towards those who sought his help in public life. Later on Plato also wrote to him on this subject, with a foresight that was to prove prophetic, and warned him to guard against self-will, as the inevitable concomitant of a solitary life. And yet even at this time, although through force of circumstances he was regarded as the most important man in the state and the only, or at least the principal bulwark of the storm-tossed tyranny, he knew very well that his prominence owed nothing to the tyrant's goodwill, but was actually contrary to his wishes and rested simply on the fact that he was indispensable.

9. Dion believed that this situation resulted from the tyrant's lack of education, and so he tried to interest him in liberal studies and to give him a taste of literature and science in the hope of forming his character, delivering him from the fear of virtue, and accustoming him to take pleasure in high ideals. Dionysius did not belong by nature to the worst class of tyrants. He had suffered from his father's fear that if he acquired a judgement of his own and associated with men of good sense, he would plot against him and deprive him of his power. In consequence he had been kept closely shut up at home, and there because of the lack of company and his ignorance of affairs, he had spent his time making little waggons and lamp-stands and wooden chairs and tables. Indeed, the elder Dionysius had been so obsessed by his fears and so distrustful and suspicious of all and sundry that he would not even allow his hair to be cut with a barber's instruments, but arranged for one of his workmen to come and singe his hair with a live coal. Neither his brother nor his son were admitted to his apartment in the dress they happened to be wearing, but everyone was obliged to strip, to be inspected naked by the guard, and to put on other clothes before entering.

On one occasion when his brother Leptines was describing to him the nature of some place, he took a spear from one of the guards and drew a sketch on the floor; Dionysius immediately flew into a rage against his brother and had the man who had given him the spear put to death. He used to say that he was on his guard against all those of his friends who were intelligent, because he felt sure that they would rather be tyrants themselves than a tyrant's subjects. He also executed a Sicilian named Marsyas whom he had himself promoted to a position of authority, because the man had had a dream in which he saw himself killing the tyrant. He could only have experienced the dream, Dionysius argued, because he had conceived and planned the action in his waking hours. So much had he become the prey of his own fears and the victim of all the miseries brought on by cowardice, and yet it was he who had been angry with Plato because Plato did not consider him to be the bravest man alive.

10. Dion, as I have already mentioned, recognized that the son's character had been warped and stunted by lack of education, and so he urged him to apply himself to study and to use every means to persuade Plato, the most eminent of living philosophers, to visit Sicily. With Plato in Syracuse, Dionysius should submit himself to his teaching, and so aided, his character might accept the discipline imposed by virtue and form itself upon the fairest and most divine of models, in obedience to whose direction the universe moves from chaos towards order. In this way he would not only win great happiness for himself, but would also ensure it for his people. He would find that the spirit of indifference in which they now obeyed him under compulsion would change to one of goodwill in response to his own justice and moderation, once these qualities were expressed in a benevolent and fatherly mode of government. In short, he would become a king instead of a tyrant. The celebrated adamantine chains which secured the state were not, as his father used to say, forged out of fear and force, a great fleet and a host of barbarian bodyguards, but rather out of the goodwill, the loyalty and the gratitude which are engendered by the exercise of virtue and justice. These forces, although they are more pliant than the stiff, harsh bonds of absolute rule, are the ties which prove the strongest in enabling the leadership of one man to endure. And apart from these considerations, so Dion argued, it showed a mean and ignoble spirit in a ruler to clothe his body magnificently and decorate his home with fine and luxurious furniture but to achieve no greater dignity in his conversation and in his dealings with others than any ordinary man, and to neglect to adorn the royal palace of his soul in a manner worthy of a king.

11. Dion repeatedly pressed this advice on the young man and skil-fully introduced some of Plato's own ideas into his arguments, until Dionysius became impatient, indeed almost obsessed with the desire to acquaint himself with Plato's teachings and to enjoy his company. Before long he was writing letter after letter to Athens, while at the same time Plato received further advice from Dion as well as from a number of Pythagorean philosophers in Italy. All of these last urged him to make the journey, establish his influence over this youthful soul, which was now being tossed and buffeted about as it were on the seas of great power and absolute rule, and steady it with his balanced reasonings. So Plato yielded to these requests, though he did so rather out of a sense of shame, as he has written,[1] so as to dispel the impression that he was only interested in theory and was unwilling to put it to the test of action.[2] At the same time he hoped that if he could purify the mind of this ruler, who seemed to dominate all the Sicilians, he might be able to cure the disorders of the whole island.

Dion's enemies, however, became alarmed at the prospect that Dionysius' character might be transformed, and they persuaded him to recall Philistus[3] from exile. This man was both a distinguished writer and a politician who possessed long experience of the ways of tyrants, and by this move the courtiers hoped to offset the influence of Plato and his philosophy. Philistus had played a most active part in establishing the tyranny from the beginning, and for a long time he had commanded the garrison which guarded the citadel. There was also a story that he had been the lover of the mother of the elder Dionysius and that the tyrant had known of this, or so at least it might be supposed judging by his treatment of Philistus. There was a Sicilian named Leptines, who had two daughters by a woman whom he had seduced while she was living with another man. Leptines later married her, and gave one of his daughters in marriage to Philistus, but kept this arrangement secret from Dionysius. Dionysius had Leptines' wife put in chains, imprisoned Philistus, and later

1. Letter VII (see Plato: *Phaedrus and Letters VII & VIII*, Penguin Books, 1973.

2. Plato's ideal state was not a democracy, but a community governed by a king or autocrat who was also a philosopher. In Dionysius he had the authori-tarian ruler required for the experiment. It was his task, an impossible one, in the event, to transform the prince into a philosopher.

3. Philistus (432–356 B.C.), wrote a history of Sicily in eleven books down to 363 B.C. He was recalled in the same year that Plato arrived (367 B.C.).

banished him. He took refuge in Adria and there, as it seems, wrote the greater part of his history during his enforced leisure. He remained in exile for the rest of the tyrant's lifetime, but after the latter's death, as I have explained, the envy which the other courtiers felt towards Dion, prompted them to arrange his recall, since they saw in Philistus a man whom they could count on to serve their purposes and to be a staunch supporter of autocratic rule.

12. Accordingly, as soon as Philistus returned, he began to work closely with the supporters of the tyranny. At the same time others began to lodge accusations and slanders against Dion, and in particular they charged him with having plotted with Theodotus and Heraclides to overthrow the government. It seems he had hopes that with the help of Plato's presence the autocratic and arbitrary nature of the tyranny could gradually be relaxed, and Dionysius transformed into a moderate and constitutional ruler. On the other hand he had made up his mind that if Dionysius resisted his efforts and refused to be softened, he would depose him and restore power to the hands of the Syracusan people. This was not because he was in favour of democracy in itself, but because he considered it in every way preferable to a tyranny in the absence of a stable aristocracy.

13. This was the state of affairs when Plato arrived in Sicily, and at first he was received with wonderful demonstrations of kindness and respect. One of the royal chariots, magnificently decked out, was waiting to receive him as he stepped ashore, and the tyrant offered up a sacrifice of thanksgiving for the great blessing which had been granted to his government. The sobriety of the royal banquets, the decorous tone of the court, and the tolerance displayed by Dionysius himself in his dealings with the public, all combined to inspire the citizens with wondrous hopes of change. The study of letters and philosophy became all the fashion, and it is said that so many people began to study geometry that the very palace was filled with dust.[1] There is a story that a few days later one of the customary sacrifices was held in the grounds of the palace and that the herald, according to the usual formula, intoned a prayer that the tyranny might remain unshaken for many years, whereupon Dionysius cried out, 'Stop cursing us!' This greatly disturbed Philistus and his party, who

1. Geometrical figures were traced in sand on the floor.

concluded that if Plato had already brought about such a change in the young man's ideas even after this brief association, his influence would become irresistible if he were allowed the time to get to know Dionysius intimately.

14. And so the courtiers no longer abused Dion singly and in secrecy, but attacked him all together and quite openly. They declared that he had caused the tyrant to be charmed and bewitched by Plato's doctrines, and that his motives for doing so were now transparent: his plan was to persuade Dionysius to give up his authority of his own accord, after which Dion would assume power and hand it over to Aristomache's children, whose uncle he was. Some of them pretended to be deeply indignant at the idea that the Athenians, who had once invaded Sicily with a great military and naval expedition and had perished utterly before they could take Syracuse, should now succeed in overthrowing the tyranny of Dionysius[1] through the efforts of a single sophist. Plato would persuade the young man to disband his ten thousand bodyguards, dismiss his fleet of four hundred triremes and his ten thousand horsemen and countless hosts of infantry, and all this in order to pursue the ineffable good in the schools of the Academy, to make geometry his guide to happiness, and to hand over the blessings of power, of wealth and of luxury so that they could be enjoyed by Dion's nephews and nieces. The result of these tactics was that Dionysius at first became suspicious, and then began to show his displeasure and anger more openly. At this point a letter was secretly brought to him which Dion had written to the representatives of Carthage. In it he advised them that whenever they opened their negotiations for peace with Dionysius, they should not hold their conference without his being present: he assured them that with his help there would be no possibility of mishap in obtaining a settlement. According to Timaeus, Dionysius read this letter over to Philistus, and after taking his advice deceived Dion by pretending to be reconciled with him. He made out that he harboured no extreme feelings and that their differences were at an end, and then after he had led Dion alone down to the sea below the acropolis,

1. Dionysius had greatly extended the dominions of Syracuse during his reign. He controlled most of Sicily except for the small Carthaginian enclave in the west: he dominated much of the heel and south-eastern coast of Italy and planted colonies in Dalmatia.

he showed him the letter and accused him of plotting with the Carthaginians against himself. When Dion tried to defend himself, the tyrant refused to listen, but immediately forced him to board a small boat just as he was, and ordered the sailors to put him ashore on the Italian coast.[1]

15. When this became known, Dionysius was considered to have acted very harshly, and the women of his household went into mourning. But the spirits of the rest of the Syracusans rose and they began to look forward to a revolution and a speedy change of government, partly because the treatment of Dion had caused such a stir, and partly because others would now feel distrustful of the tyrant. Dionysius took fright at this, and he tried to pacify Dion's friends and the women of his own household by making out that he had not banished him, but merely sent him out of harm's way, for fear that he himself might be provoked by the man's independent conduct into doing him some mischief if he remained at home. He also put two ships at the disposal of Dion's family and told his kinsmen to embark any servants or possessions of his that they might choose, and have them sent to the Peloponnese. Now Dion was very rich, and his house and style of living were kept up on an almost royal scale, and so his friends collected his valuables and sent them to him. Besides his own property, the women of the court and his supporters also sent him many gifts: in this way, so far as wealth and possessions were concerned, he cut a brilliant figure among the Greeks and the riches he displayed, even as an exile, gave some hint of the power and resources of the tyrant.

16. At the same time Dionysius at once transferred Plato to the acropolis, and here as a mark of hospitality he arranged to give him a guard of honour: the object of this was to prevent him from sailing away to join Dion and revealing to the world how badly he had been treated. Meanwhile as time passed and their association continued, Dionysius learned to tolerate Plato's company and conversation, much as a wild animal becomes accustomed to the presence of a human being, and he developed a passion for him which was characteristic of a tyrant: he demanded that Plato should respond to his love alone and admire him above all others, and he even offered

1. Late in 366 B.C.

to hand over the tyranny to him on condition that Plato would not prefer Dion's friendship to his. This passion of Dionysius' was a great misfortune for Plato, since like most lovers, the tyrant was violently jealous, would often fly into a rage, and then soon afterwards beg to be forgiven. He was also extravagantly eager to listen to Plato's theories and take part in his philosophical discussions, but he felt ashamed of them when he was in the company of those who wanted him to break off his studies on the grounds that they would corrupt him.

At this point a war broke out, and Dionysius sent Plato away, promising that he would recall Dion in the following summer. He promptly broke his promise, but he continued to send Dion the revenues from his property and asked Plato to excuse his change of plan concerning Dion's return, which was occasioned by the war. As soon as peace was concluded, he would send for Dion: meanwhile he asked Plato to appeal to him to stay quiet and to refrain from making any revolutionary attempts or speaking ill of him among the Greeks.

17. Plato tried to carry out these requests by keeping Dion with him in the Academy, where he turned his attention to philosophy. Dion was living in Athens at the house of Callippus,[1] one of his friends, but he also bought a house in the country for pleasure, and later when he sailed for Sicily he gave it to Speusippus,[2] who was his closest friend and most frequent companion in Athens. Plato was anxious that Dion's austere disposition should be mellowed and sweetened by the company of men who possessed some social charm and whose wit was good-natured and well-timed. Speusippus was a man of this kind: he is referred to in Timon's *Silloi*[3] as being good at making jokes. Besides this, when Plato himself was called upon to provide a chorus of boys for a public festival, Dion undertook both the training and the expense. Plato encouraged him to earn this distinction in the eyes of the Athenians, because he was more concerned to create goodwill for Dion than fame for himself.

1. Who was later to murder him: see chs. 54-8.
2. Plato's nephew, who later succeeded his uncle as head of the Academy.
3. Timon of Phlius, a Sceptic philosopher and satirical poet of the 3rd century B.C. He taught at Chalcedon near Byzantium and later retired to Athens. His *Silloi* were satirical poems in hexameters directed against the Greek philosophers.

Dion also travelled to a number of other cities in Greece, where he visited their nobility and political leaders and took part in their recreations and festivities. During these visits he never showed himself in any way boorish, arrogant or effeminate: his behaviour was always conspicuous for its moderation, virtue, courage, and a becoming devotion to literature and philosophy. By this means he earned the goodwill and admiration of all he met, and many cities decreed him public honours. The Lacedaemonians even made him a citizen of Sparta and disregarded any offence which this might cause to Dionysius, who was at that time their staunch ally against the Thebans. On another occasion it is said that Dion was invited to visit Ptoedorus the Megarian and went to his house. This man, it appears, was one of the most wealthy and influential citizens of Megara, and so when Dion saw that there was a crowd of people at his door and that the number of visitors made it difficult to approach him, he turned to his friends who seemed indignant at this hindrance, and asked them, 'Why should we blame this man? We ourselves used to do exactly the same thing in Syracuse.'

18. As time went on Dionysius began to grow jealous of Dion, and to fear the popularity which he was creating for himself among the Greeks. He stopped remitting the revenues from his property and handed over Dion's estates to his own officials. On the other hand he was anxious to efface the bad reputation he had earned among the philosophers because of his treatment of Plato, and he therefore gathered at his court a number of men with some pretensions to learning. But as he was ambitious to outshine them all in discussion, he was obliged to make use, often incorrectly, of ideas he had picked up from Plato but had only half digested. So he began once more to long for Plato's company, and reproached himself for not having made the best use of him when he was in Sicily or paid more attention to his admirable lessons. And since, like so many tyrants, he was erratic in his impulses and impatient to obtain whatever he desired, he at once set his heart on bringing Plato back. He was ready to try anything to get his way, and so he persuaded Archytas and his fellow Pythagoreans to send the invitation to Plato and to guarantee his offer, for it was through Plato that he had first entered into friendly dealings with these philosophers. They sent Archedemus to Plato, and Dionysius also dispatched a trireme and several of his friends to

beg Plato to return. The tyrant also wrote to Plato in clear and
explicit terms telling him that there would be no concessions or
favours for Dion unless the philosopher agreed to come to Sicily,
but that much could be expected if he did. Dion was also pressed by
his wife and sister to urge Plato to let the tyrant have his way and
not provide any excuse for treating him still more harshly. It was in
this way that Plato ventured for the third time, as he describes it,
into the straits of Scylla and

Shaped his course yet again within reach of the deadly Charybdis.[1]

19. Dion was delighted at his coming, and once more the hopes of
the Sicilians rose. They all agreed in praying and hoping that Plato
should prevail over Philistus and philosophy prove stronger than
tyranny. The women too, especially Aristomache and Arete, gave
Plato their support, and Dionysius bestowed on him a special mark
of confidence which nobody else enjoyed – the privilege of coming
into his presence without being searched. The tyrant also pressed
gifts of money on him, repeatedly offering him large sums, but Plato
would accept none of them. At this Aristippus of Cyrene,[2] who was
present on one of these occasions, remarked that Dionysius' generosity
was of the safest kind: he offered small sums to men such as himself who wanted more, and large ones to Plato, who refused
everything.

After the first formal courtesies had been exchanged, Plato raised
the subject of Dion. Dionysius first put off the discussion, and later
there were reproaches and quarrels. Nobody else knew of these,
since Dionysius was careful to conceal them, and by paying honours
and assiduous attentions to Plato he tried to detach him from his
friendship for Dion. Plato at first kept silent about the tyrant's
treachery and double dealing, endured it as best he could, and played
the part that was required of him. Then while they were on these terms
and imagined that nobody else knew of this situation, Helicon of
Cyzicus, one of Plato's close friends, predicted an eclipse of the sun.
This duly took place, as he had forecast, whereupon the tyrant expressed his admiration and presented him with a talent of silver. At
this Aristippus put on a bantering tone towards the other philosophers

1. *Odyssey* xii, 428. He arrived in 361 B.C.
2. A former close companion of Socrates who had gone to seek his fortune
at Dionysius' court and was jealous of Plato's success and prestige there.

and declared that he too had a remarkable event to predict. When they pressed him to tell them what it was, he replied, 'Well then, I predict that in a short while Dionysius will fall out with Plato.'

Finally Dionysius sold Dion's property and kept the money for himself. He then removed Plato from his quarters in the gardens of the palace and lodged him among his mercenaries. The soldiers hated him and wanted to kill him because they believed that he was trying to persuade Dionysius to give up the tyranny and live without a bodyguard.

20. As soon as Archytas and his friends learned that Plato was in such danger, they immediately sent a galley with messengers to demand that Dionysius should send him back, and they reminded the tyrant that they had guaranteed Plato's safety when he had agreed to sail to Syracuse. Dionysius did his best to disguise his hostility towards Plato by giving banquets in his honour and doing him various kindnesses before his departure, but he could not resist letting fall a remark to this effect: 'I dare say, Plato, that you will have many things to say against me to your fellow philosophers,' to which Plato answered with a smile, 'God forbid that we should have so little to talk about in the Academy that we need mention your name at all.' It was on these terms, so it is said, that they parted, but Plato's own version does not entirely agree with this account.[1]

21. Dion had already been angered by these events, but it was the treatment of his wife that soon afterwards turned him into an open enemy of Dionysius. Plato also referred enigmatically to this subject in a letter to Dionysius. What had happened was the following. After Dion's banishment and at the time when Dionysius was sending Plato back to Athens for the first time, he asked Plato to sound Dion as to whether he would object to his wife being married to another man. There had been rumours, which may have been true or may have been fabricated by Dion's enemies, that his marriage had not been happy and that he did not live harmoniously with his wife. After Plato had returned to Athens and had discussed the subject at length with Dion, he sent a letter to Dionysius. Part of this concerned other matters and was phrased in a manner which would be clear to every-

1. Plato: Letter VII. Plato left Syracuse in 360 B.C.

body, but on this particular topic he used allusive language, which only Dionysius could understand: he mentioned that he had spoken about the affair with Dion, who, it was clear, would be furious if Dionysius carried out any such plan. For a time, then, as there were still hopes that a reconciliation was possible, Dionysius did nothing to change his sister's situation, but allowed her to continue to live with Dion's young son. But when it became clear that the breach between the two men was irreparable and Plato's second visit had ended in his incurring the tyrant's displeasure and being sent away, then Dionysius compelled Arete against her will to marry one of his friends named Timocrates.

Certainly in this action Dionysius fell short of the tolerance shown by his father. The elder Dionysius had, as it happened, made an enemy of Polyxenus, the husband of his sister Theste. Polyxenus feared for his life, escaped from Sicily and fled into exile, whereupon Dionysius sent for his sister and reproached her because she had known of her husband's plan to escape, but had told her brother nothing about it. Theste was quite undismayed and answered him confidently, 'Do you think, Dionysius, that I am such a mean and cowardly wife that if I had known beforehand that my husband was planning to escape I would not have sailed away with him and shared his fortunes? The truth is that I knew nothing of it. If I had, it would have been more honourable for me to have been called the wife of Polyxenus the exile than the sister of Dionysius the tyrant.' It is said that Dionysius admired her for speaking out so boldly, and the Syracusans also greatly respected her for her courage, so much so that even after the tyranny had been overthrown, they continued to treat her with the honour and deference that they paid to royalty, and when she died, the citizens by public consent walked in procession at her funeral. This is a digression, but the story is relevant to my subject.

22. From this point onwards Dion began to prepare for war.[1] Plato himself refused to take any part in such an attempt, partly out of respect for the bond of hospitality between Dionysius and himself, and partly because of his age. However, Speusippus and Dion's other friends rallied to his support and urged him to liberate Sicily,

1. 360 B.C. The expedition took three years to assemble.

which they said beckoned to him and was ready to receive him with open arms. It seems that during Plato's stay in Syracuse Speusippus and his friends had circulated among the people and made it their business to discover their feelings. At first the Syracusans had been alarmed by the frankness of Speusippus' talk and suspected that this was a trap set by the tyrant to test their loyalty, but after a time they came to trust him. On every side Speusippus heard the same story: they all begged and entreated Dion to come, not to bring ships or cavalry or soldiers, but simply to step into an open boat and lend the Syracusans his name and his person in their struggle against Dionysius. Dion was heartened by this news from Speusippus, and through the agency of others he began secretly to recruit mercenaries, taking care to conceal his plans. Many statesmen and philosophers gave him their help, including Timonides of Leucas and Eudemus of Cyprus, concerning whom after his death Aristotle wrote his dialogue *On the Soul*. They also engaged Miltas of Thessaly, a soothsayer who had studied in the Academy. Yet of all the Syracusans who had been exiled by the tyrant – and there were no less than a thousand of them – only twenty-five joined the expedition: the remainder played the coward and shrank from it. The starting point was the island of Zacynthus, and here the soldiers assembled. Their total strength was less than eight hundred, but these were all men of some note who had gained a reputation from their service in many great campaigns. They were in superb physical condition, for experience and daring they had no equals in the world, and they were fully capable of rousing and inspiring to action the thousands whom Dion expected to rally to him in Sicily.

23. When these men learned that the expedition was directed against Dionysius and Sicily, they were at first dismayed and condemned the whole enterprise. They could only suppose either than Dion was being driven on like a madman in some wild fit of rage, or else that he had lost all rational hopes of success. There seemed to be no other reason to throw himself into such a desperate undertaking, and they were furious with their commanders and recruiting officers for not having warned them of the object of the war at the very beginning. But then Dion addressed them, explained in detail the weakness and rottenness of Dionysius' regime, and announced that he was taking them not merely as fighting troops but as leaders of the Syracusans

and the rest of the Sicilians who had long been ripe for rebellion. He was followed by Alcimenes, one of the most influential and distinguished of the Achaeans serving with the expedition, who spoke to the same effect, and finally the men were convinced and their doubts set at rest.

It was now midsummer,[1] the Etesian winds[2] were blowing steadily at sea and the moon was at the full. Dion prepared a magnificent sacrifice to Apollo and marched in solemn procession to the temple with his troops, who paraded in full armour. After the ceremony he entertained them to a banquet at the stadium of the Zacynthians. Here as they reclined on their couches, they marvelled at the splendour of the gold and silver drinking-vessels and of the tables which far exceeded the means of a private citizen, and no doubt they reflected that a man who possessed such wealth and was by then past middle life, as in Dion's case,[3] would never attempt such a risky undertaking, unless he had solid hopes of success and could count upon friends on the spot who could offer him unlimited resources.

24. No sooner had the libations and the customary prayers been offered than there followed an eclipse of the moon. Dion and his friends found nothing surprising in this, since they knew that eclipses recurred at regular intervals, and also that the shadow which is projected upon the moon is produced by the interposition of the earth between it and the sun. But as the soldiers were dismayed at the portent and needed to be reassured, Miltas the diviner rose to his feet in the midst of the company and urged them to take heart. He assured them that the expedition would succeed, since through this portent the gods were foretelling that something which was then at the height of its splendour would be eclipsed. There was no regime whose splendour exceeded that of Dionysius' tyranny, and it was its light that they would extinguish as soon as they arrived in Sicily. Miltas made public his interpretation of the eclipse to all and sundry. But as for the phenomenon of the bees, which were seen to be settling in swarms on the sterns of the ships, he told Dion and his friends privately he feared this might signify that their expedition would

1. 357 B.C.
2. A prevailing wind which blows from the north in the summer.
3. He was by then fifty-one.

prosper at the start, but that after flourishing for a short while, it would wither away. It is said that Dionysius also witnessed a number of prodigies at this time. An eagle snatched up a spear from one of his guards, flew up into the air with it, and then let it fall into the sea. Besides this the sea-water which washes against the walls of the citadel of Syracuse became sweet and drinkable for a whole day, as all those who tasted it could perceive. Also a number of pigs were born within his realm, which were perfectly formed in other respects but possessed no ears. This was interpreted by the diviners as a sign of rebellion, since it indicated that the people would no longer obey the tyrant's commands. The sweetness of the sea-water, so they said, heralded a change from harsh and oppressive times to more agreeable circumstances. As for the eagle, this bird, they said, is a servant of Zeus, while the spear is the symbol of power and sovereignty, and hence the portent indicated that the greatest of the gods intended to remove and annihilate the tyranny. This at any rate is the account which we have from Theopompus.

25. It required no more than two merchant vessels to accommodate Dion's troops, and they were accompanied by a third small transport and two thirty-oared galleys. Besides the arms which the soldiers carried, Dion took with him two thousand shields, great quantities of spears and other missiles, and ample stocks of provisions, so that there should be no risk of running short during the voyage. Their intention was to put themselves at the mercy of wind and waves and sail across the open sea: they were afraid to hug the coast, because they had learned that Philistus was lying in wait for them with a fleet off Iapygia.[1] For twelve days they sailed with a light and gentle breeze and on the thirteenth reached the cape of Pachynus, a headland at the south-eastern extremity of Sicily. Here Protus their pilot urged them to disembark without any delay, since if they were once driven off shore and did not take advantage of this landfall, they would be tossed about in the open sea for many days and nights while they waited for a southerly wind in the summer season. Dion was afraid to disembark so near the enemy and wished to land further along the coast, and so he sailed past Pachynus. Soon afterwards a violent northerly gale swept down on them, whipped up the sea and drove the squadron away from Sicily: at the same time the sky was

1. Philistus' fleet was patrolling the heel of Italy.

filled with flashes of lightning, peals of thunder, and sheets of torrential rain, the storm coinciding with the rising of Arcturus. The sailors were dismayed and had quite lost their reckoning, until they discovered that their ships were being driven by the waves upon the island of Cercina[1] off the coast of Libya, at a point where the cliffs present a craggy, precipitous face that falls sheer to the water. After they had narrowly escaped being driven ashore and dashed to pieces against the rocks, they heaved and thrust their way along with great difficulty using their punting-poles until the storm gradually abated, when they learned from a vessel they hailed that they had arrived at what were known as the 'heads' of the Great Syrtes. They were by now disheartened to find themselves becalmed and were drifting helplessly up and down the coast when a gentle breeze sprang up from the south, which was so little expected that they could scarcely believe in the change. Gradually the wind freshened and gathered strength, and so they set all the sail they could, offered up prayers to the gods, and skimmed across the open sea from Africa towards Sicily. For five days, they ran on at full speed and finally dropped anchor at Minoa, a small coastal town in the western part of Sicily, which was controlled by the Carthaginians. It so happened that Synalus, the Carthaginian commander of the region, was a guest-friend[2] of Dion's, but as he knew nothing of the expedition nor of Dion's presence there, he tried to prevent the troops from landing. The Greeks charged ashore fully armed, and although in obedience to Dion's orders they did not kill a single man, they routed their opponents, entered the town on their heels and seized possession of it. But as soon as the two commanders had met and greeted one another, Dion handed back the town to the Carthaginian without any damage having been done, while for his part Synalus treated the soldiers hospitably and supplied Dion with all the stores he needed.

26. What gave them the greatest encouragement of all was the lucky accident of Dionysius' absence from Syracuse at that moment, for it so happened that he had just set off for Italy with a fleet of eighty ships. So although Dion urged his men to rest and recover after the hardships of their long voyage, they would have none of it, but were

1. Situated off the coast of Tunisia, opposite the modern Sfax.
2. See p. 37, n. 1.

eager to seize the opportunity and clamoured for him to lead them on to Syracuse. He therefore stored his surplus arms and baggage at Minoa, asked Synalus to send them on to him when opportunity offered, and set out for Syracuse. As he marched, he was joined first by two hundred horsemen from Agrigentum who lived near Ecnomum, and then by a contingent from Gela.

The news of his movements was quickly brought to Timocrates, who had married Dion's wife, the sister of Dionysius. He was the most prominent of Dionysius' friends who had remained in Syracuse, and he at once sent off a messenger with letters reporting Dion's arrival. At the same time he took measures to forestall any disturbances or uprisings in the city. All the Syracusans were excited at the news of the invasion, but they remained quiet because they were as yet uncertain what to believe and were afraid of the outcome. But in the meanwhile an extraordinary mischance befell the bearer of the letters. After crossing the straits to Italy he passed through the territory of Rhegium, but as he was hurrying on to Dionysius at Caulonia, he fell in with an acquaintance who was carrying a victim which had just been slaughtered. His friend gave him a piece of the meat and he continued his journey with all speed. Then after he had walked for part of the night, he was obliged by sheer exhaustion to take a little sleep, and lay down just as he was in a wood by the roadside. As he slept, a prowling wolf, attracted by the scent, came up, seized the meat which had been fastened to the wallet containing the letters, and made off with both. When the man awoke and saw what had happened, he spent a long time wandering about and searching in vain for the lost wallet, but as he could not find it, he decided not to go to the tyrant without the letters, but to run off and stay out of harm's way.

27. So Dionysius was fated to learn that war had broken out in Sicily from other sources and only after some time had passed. Meanwhile, as Dion advanced, the people of Camarina came over to him, and large numbers of the peasants in the districts surrounding Syracuse rose in revolt and attached themselves to him. Next Dion sent a false report to the Leontines and Campanians who were garrisoning the plateau west of Syracuse, which is known as Epipolae: he informed them that he intended to attack their cities first, with the result that they deserted Timocrates and went off to help their com-

patriots. When the news of their movements was brought to Dion at his camp at Acrae, he roused his troops while it was still dark and advanced to the river Anapus, which flows a little over a mile from the city. There he halted, offered sacrifice by the river, and addressed his prayers to the rising sun. Immediately the diviners announced that the gods would grant him victory. His followers had noticed that Dion was wearing a wreath on his head while he was sacrificing, and straightaway with a single impulse they all crowned their heads with garlands. No fewer than five thousand men had joined him on the march, and although these were wretchedly equipped and carried only such improvised weapons as they could find, their spirit made up for their lack of arms, so that when Dion ordered the advance, they ran forward with shouts of joy, encouraging one another to regain their freedom.

28. As for the townsfolk of Syracuse, the most prominent and best educated of the citizens put on clean clothes and went to meet the invaders at the gates, while the populace set upon the tyrant's supporters and seized the informers. These were an abominable race, detested by gods and men alike, who made it their business to circulate among the citizens and report on their opinions and conversations to the tyrant. They were the first to suffer for their misdeeds, and were beaten to death by any of the townspeople who found them. Timocrates was unable to join the garrison within the citadel, and so took horse and galloped out of the city: in his flight he created panic and confusion by spreading exaggerated reports of Dion's strength, for he was anxious to avoid the suspicion of having surrendered the city to an insignificant force. Meanwhile Dion was close at hand and presently came into view, marching at the head of his troops, clad in splendid armour, and flanked by his brother Megacles on one side and Callippus the Athenian on the other, both of them crowned with garlands. After them came a bodyguard of a hundred mercenaries, and next the officers leading the rest of the army in good order. The Syracusans looked on and welcomed the troops as if this were a sacred and religious procession to celebrate the return to the city of liberty and popular government after an absence of forty-eight years.

29. Dion entered the city by the gate which is close to the sacred

enclosure and statue of Apollo Temenites, and here he ordered his trumpets to be sounded so as to quieten the shouting. Then his herald proclaimed that Dion and Megacles had come to overthrow the tyranny, and that they declared the Syracusans and the rest of the Sicilians to be free of the rule of Dionysius. Next, as he wished to address the people himself, he marched through the quarter of Achradina, while on each side of the street the Syracusans set out tables, sacrificial victims, and bowls of wine, and each group as he passed strewed flowers before him and hailed him with prayers and vows as if he were a god. Below the citadel in the space encircled by five gates, there stood a tall and conspicuous sun-dial, built by Dionysius. Dion sprang up on this, addressed the citizens, and urged them to defend their liberty. Then the people in an ecstasy of joy and gratitude appointed Dion and Megacles generals with absolute powers, and besides this, at the two men's own request, they elected twenty colleagues, half of whom were chosen from the exiles who had returned with Dion. The diviners found it a most happy omen that Dion, while he was addressing the people, should have placed his feet on the tyrant's pretentious monument; but because it was a sun-dial on which he was standing at the moment when he was elected general, they were afraid that his cause might suffer some swift change of fortune.

After this Dion went on to capture Epipolae and release the citizens who were imprisoned there, and he cut off the citadel by building a palisade.[1] Then on the seventh day after his arrival Dionysius sailed into the harbour with his fleet and entered the citadel, and at the same time a convoy of waggons arrived bringing Dion the arms and armour he had left with Synalus. He distributed these among the Syracusans, while the rest armed themselves as best they could and eagerly offered to serve under him.

30. At first Dionysius sent emissaries privately to Dion in the hope of making terms with him. Dion's reply was that any negotiations with the Syracusans must be carried out publicly, because they were a free people. The tyrant's envoys then returned with a generous offer, in which he promised a reduction of taxes and an easing of the

---

1. The citadel was built upon Ortygia, which was virtually an island: it could easily be isolated by walling off the narrow isthmus which connected it to the mainland.

burden of military service, subject to the people's vote of consent. But the Syracusans only laughed at these proposals, and Dion told the envoys that Dionysius was not to continue negotiations with the people unless he formally renounced his sovereignty: if he agreed to this, Dion would guarantee his personal safety and obtain any other reasonable concession that was in his power, bearing in mind the close association they had had in the past. Dionysius accepted these conditions and again sent his representatives to invite some of the Syracusans to come to the citadel: he proposed to discuss with them a general settlement for the common benefit with concessions to be made by both sides. Dion chose the delegates, who were at once sent to meet the tyrant, and rumours began to reach the Syracusans from the acropolis that Dionysius really intended to abdicate, and would do this to claim the credit for himself, rather than let Dion enjoy it.

All this, however, was nothing but a treacherous pretence on Dionysius' part, which had been carefully devised to trick the Syracusans. He promptly arrested the delegates who came to him from the city, issued a ration of neat wine to his mercenaries, and ordered them to make a sortie at dawn to attack the siege works which Dion had erected so as to cut off the citadel. The manoeuvre achieved complete surprise. The barbarians set to work boldly and with loud shouts to demolish the wall; then they attacked the Syracusans so fiercely that no one had the courage to stand his ground, except for a number of Dion's mercenaries who were the first to hear the commotion and ran to the rescue. Even these troops were at first uncertain as to how they could help, and unable to hear what was being said to them, for the Syracusans were shouting wildly, running back in panic through the midst of the mercenaries and breaking their ranks. In the end Dion, when he saw that he could not make his orders heard, determined to show by his own example what ought to be done, and charged into the midst of the enemy. A fierce and bloody battle raged around him, since he was as well known to the enemy as he was to his own troops, and both sides converged on him at the same moment, shouting at the top of their voices. He had reached an age at which he was no longer agile enough for this kind fo hand-to-hand fighting, but his courage and vigour enabled him to stand his ground and cut down all his attackers, until he was wounded in the hand by a spear. By then too his breastplate had been so battered that it could hardly give protection against the thrusts and missiles which rained upon him; finally he was wounded by a number of spears and lances which had pierced his shield, and when these were broken off, he fell to the ground. His soldiers carried him away and he ordered Timonides to take command of the front line, while he himself mounted his horse and rode round the city, rallying the Syracusans who had fled. Then he ordered up a detachment of his mercenaries who had been posted to guard the quarter of Achradina, and launched these troops who were fresh and full of spirit against the flagging barbarians, who had already begun to despair of victory. Dionysius' troops had counted on overrunning and capturing the whole city at their first onslaught, but now that they had unexpectedly come up against men who knew how to fight and counter-attack, they fell back towards the citadel. As soon as they gave ground, the Greeks pressed them all the harder, and finally they turned tail and took refuge within the walls of the citadel. They had killed seventy-four of Dion's men, and lost many of their own.

31. This was a brilliant victory for Dion, and the Syracusans presented his mercenaries with a hundred minas, while the mercenaries honoured Dion with a crown of gold. Soon after some heralds arrived from Dionysius bringing letters to Dion from the women of his family. One of these was addressed 'To his father from Hipparinus', which was the name of Dion's son, although according to Timaeus he was named Aretaeus after his mother Arete; but for these details I think we should accept the evidence of Timonides, since he was a friend and comrade of Dion. At any rate the letters from the women, which were full of supplications and entreaties, were read aloud to the Syracusans, but they did not wish the letter which purported to be from Dion's son to be opened in public. However, Dion overruled them, and insisted on reading it aloud. It turned out to be from Dionysius, who was nominally addressing himself to Dion, but in reality was appealing to the Syracusan people. On the face of it, the writer was pleading his case and justifying his actions, but the letter was really intended to bring discredit on Dion. It recalled how devotedly Dion had worked for the tyranny, and at the same time it threatened the persons of those dearest to him, his sister, his child and his wife. It combined importunate demands with lamentations, and, what angered him most of all, with the proposal that so far

from abolishing the tyranny, he should carry it on himself. The writer urged him not to set free a people who hated him and would never forget their wrongs, but to seize power himself and so ensure the safety of his friends and his family.

32. When these letters had been read aloud, it did not occur to the Syracusans, as it should have done, to admire Dion's altruism and magnanimity in upholding the ideals of honour and justice against the claims of his personal loyalties. Instead they became alarmed that he might come under strong pressure to spare the tyrant, and so they at once began to look round for other leaders, and they were particularly excited at the news that Heraclides was just putting into the harbour. This man was one of those who had been exiled by Dionysius. He possessed some experience as a soldier, and had gained a reputation through the commands he had held under the tyrants, but he was a man of erratic and unstable disposition and not at all reliable as a colleague in an enterprise in which power and prestige were at stake. He had already fallen out with Dion in the Peloponnese and had determined to sail against the tyrant with an expedition under his own command. But when he arrived in Syracuse with a squadron of seven triremes and three transports, he found Dionysius once more blockaded and the Syracusans elated at their victory. He therefore immediately set out to ingratiate himself with the masses. He possessed a natural facility for winning over and swaying the emotions of the populace, which loved to be courted, and he was able to gain his ends and draw the people to his side all the more easily because they were repelled by Dion's grave and serious manner. They found this too austere and quite out of place in a public man: the power they had suddenly acquired had made them careless and arrogant, and they expected to be flattered by their leaders before they had been knit together as a people.

33. Accordingly, they first summoned the assembly on their own initiative and elected Heraclides admiral. At this Dion came forward and protested that by conferring this appointment upon Heraclides they had abolished the command which they had previously entrusted to him, for it was impossible to regard himself as a commander-in-chief with absolute powers if another officer wielded authority over the fleet. The Syracusans then reluctantly cancelled Heraclides' appointment. Dion afterwards summoned him to his

house and mildly reproved him, pointing out that he was acting neither honourably nor even sensibly in starting a quarrel concerning a matter of prestige at a moment of crisis when the least false step might ruin their cause. He then summoned a fresh assembly, nominated Heraclides as admiral[1] and prevailed upon the citizens to allow him a bodyguard, such as he possessed himself. Heraclides then professed great respect for Dion, so far as his words and his manner went, acknowledged his indebtedness and obeyed his orders with a great show of humility, but in secret he undermined the loyalty of the populace, stirred up the revolutionaries, and by distracting him with disturbances on every side, manoeuvred him into a most difficult position. If he were to urge the people to let Dionysius leave the citadel under a truce, he would be accused of sparing and protecting the despot: while if he took care not to give offence in this way and merely continued the siege, he would appear to be deliberately prolonging the war in order to keep himself in command and overawe the citizens.

34. Now there was a man named Sosis who simply through his audacity and lack of principle had gained a certain reputation in Syracuse, where people imagined that liberty was inseparable from the kind of licence of speech which he enjoyed. This man, who was secretly plotting against Dion, first of all stood up one day in the assembly and abused the Syracusans for failing to understand the fact that they had merely exchanged an imbecile and drunken tyrant for a vigilant and sober one; then having thus openly shown himself an enemy of Dion's, he left the assembly. The next day he was seen running through the city naked, with his head and face covered with blood, as though he were fleeing from some pursuers. He rushed into the market-place in this condition, cried out that he had been attacked by Dion's mercenaries, and showed his wounded head to the spectators. He found many who were ready to share his grievances and take his side, and who declared that Dion was guilty of a monstrous act of tyranny if he was attempting to deprive the citizens of freedom of speech by acts of murder or threats against their lives. A noisy and disorderly meeting of the assembly then gathered, but in spite of their riotous mood Dion came before them

1. A necessary concession on Dion's part. Heraclides had after all brought the ships and they were under his orders.

and spoke in his own defence. He pointed out that Sosis was a brother of one of Dionysius' guards and had been set on by him to stir up dissensions and disturbances, since Dionysius' only hope of safety now lay in the chance of making the citizens distrust and quarrel with one another. Meanwhile some physicians examined Sosis' wound and discovered that it had been made by a glancing rather than a vertical stroke. A blow dealt by a sword leaves a wound which is deepest in the middle, because of the weight of the blade, but the gash on Sosis' head was shallow throughout its length: besides this it was not one continuous cut, as it would be had it been inflicted with a single stroke, but there were a number of incisions, as one would expect if he had left off because of the pain and begun again. Apart from this evidence a number of well known citizens brought a razor to the assembly and testified that as they were walking along the street, Sosis had met them all covered in blood and explained that he was running away from Dion's mercenaries who had just wounded him: the witnesses at once ran after the alleged attackers, but could find nobody. What they did find, however, was a razor lying under a hollow stone near the place where Sosis had been seen coming out.

35. By this time Sosis' case had been almost completely discredited, and when in addition to all these proofs his servants gave evidence that he had left his house while it was still dark, alone and carrying a razor, Dion's accusers dropped their charges and the people condemned Sosis to death and were reconciled with Dion.

They continued to be as suspicious as ever of the mercenaries, all the more so since most of the operations against Dionysius were now carried on by sea: this was because of the arrival of Philistus, who had sailed over from Iapygia with a large fleet of triremes to help Dionysius. As the mercenaries were infantrymen, the Syracusans concluded that there would be no further need for them in the war: indeed, they actually imagined that these troops depended to some extent upon the citizens for their protection, since the Syracusans themselves were seamen and their power lay in their fleet. Their spirits rose still higher after a successful action at sea: here they defeated Philistus[1] and then proceeded to treat him in a most inhuman fashion. Ephorus, it is true, says that Philistus killed himself when his ship was captured,

1. Early summer, 356 B.C.

but Timonides, who was present with Dion throughout these events from the very beginning, describes in a letter to Speusippus how Philistus was taken alive when his trireme ran aground. The Syracusans then stripped off his breastplate and humiliated him in his old age by exposing his naked body. After this they beheaded him and handed over his corpse to the boys of the city, with orders to drag it through the quarter of Achradina and throw it into the stone quarries. Timaeus gives more details of these outrages, and says that when Philistus was dead the boys tied a rope to his lame leg and hauled his body through the streets, while all the Syracusans looked on and jeered. They laughed at the spectacle of this man being dragged about by the leg, since it was he who had once told Dionysius that he must not try to escape from his tyranny with a swift horse, but must wait until he was pulled down from it by the leg. Philistus, however, has said that this advice was given to Dionysius by someone else, not by him.

36. Certainly Philistus was to blame for the fervour and devotion he showed on behalf of the tyranny, but Timaeus takes advantage of this by fabricating slanders against him. It was perhaps excusable for those who were actually wronged by Philistus in his lifetime to express their hatred of him, even to the point of maltreating his lifeless body. But those who came to write the history of the period many years afterwards and who suffered nothing from his actions while he lived but have made use of his writings, owe it to his reputation not to attack him with vulgar and insolent abuse for his misfortunes, which fate may inflict upon even the best of men. On the other hand, Ephorus is also at fault in showering praises on Philistus; for although Philistus shows infinite resource in inventing flattering motives for unjust actions and unscrupulous characters and finding decorous names for both, the fact remains that for all his ingenuity, he cannot escape the charge of having been the most devoted supporter of tyrants alive and, more than any other man, a fervent admirer of the luxury they enjoyed, their power, their wealth, and their marriage alliances. In my opinion the man who neither praises Philistus' conduct, nor exults over his misfortunes, is the one who shows the best judgement.

37. After Philistus' death Dionysius approached Dion with an offer

to hand over the citadel, all the weapons it contained and the mercenaries, for whom he provided five months' pay. In return he asked that he should be allowed to depart unharmed to Italy, and that while he lived there he should enjoy the revenues of Gyarta, a large and fertile area of Syracusan territory which stretches from the sea to the interior of the island. Dion refused these terms, but told him that he must address himself to the Syracusans, and as they hoped to capture Dionysius alive, they dismissed the envoys. At this the tyrant handed over the citadel to Apollocrates, his eldest son: meanwhile he embarked all the persons and possessions that he valued most dearly, and watching his opportunity for a fair wind, managed to elude the blockade of Heraclides the admiral, and make his escape.

The Syracusans angrily blamed Heraclides for this blunder; he thereupon persuaded Hippo, one of the popular leaders, to lay before the people a scheme for the distribution of land, using the argument that equality is the source of freedom, while poverty reduces those who have no possessions to a state of slavery. Heraclides spoke in support of his motion, placed himself at the head of a faction which overruled Dion's opposition, and prevailed upon the Syracusans to pass this measure, and not only this but others to deprive the mercenaries of their pay, to elect other generals, and thus to rid themselves of Dion's allegedly oppressive authority. After such a long period of tyranny, the Syracusans were in the position of a man who tries at the end of a long illness to stand immediately on his feet, and so in attempting to act the part of a free people before they were ready for it, they stumbled in their efforts. At the same time they resented the attentions of Dion, who, like a good physician, tried to impose a strict and temperate course of treatment.

38. When the Syracusans summoned their assembly to elect new commanders it was midsummer, and there occurred a succession of extraordinary thunderstorms and other ominous portents which continued for fifteen days consecutively: these prodigies were enough to disperse the people, and their superstitious fears prevented them from electing any other generals. The popular leaders, however, bided their time, at last found a fine, clear day, and proceeded to hold the elections. But on this occasion a draught-ox, which was quite tame and accustomed to crowds, for some reason became enraged with its driver, broke away from its yoke and made a dash towards

the theatre. The people immediately scattered and took to their
heels in a disorderly rout, and the beast then ran on, leaping and throwing everything into confusion, and it traversed just that quarter of
the city which the enemy afterwards occupied. However, the Syracusans paid no attention to all this, but elected twenty-five generals,
one of whom was Heraclides. They also secretly approached Dion's
mercenaries, and tried to persuade them to desert him and transfer
their allegiance to the Syracusans, in return for which they offered
them equal rights with the rest of the citizens. The mercenaries refused to listen to these proposals. Instead they showed their courage
and their loyalty to Dion by taking up their arms, placing him in
their midst and escorting him out of the city. They did no harm to
anyone on their march, but reproached the citizens they met for
their shameful and ungrateful behaviour. The Syracusans treated
them with contempt because they were so few in number and had
shown no disposition to attack, and so when a crowd had gathered
together which outnumbered the mercenaries, they set upon them,
expecting that they would easily be able to overpower them and
kill them all before they could escape from the city.

39. Dion thus found himself compelled by fortune to make a most
painful choice, either to fight against his fellow-citizens or to die
with his mercenaries. He pleaded with the Syracusans, stretched out
his hands to them and pointed to the citadel, crammed as it was with
their enemies, who were looking down from the battlements to
watch the spectacle below. But the mob was in no mood to respond
to entreaty, and the speeches of the demagogues seemed to have
stirred up the whole city, just as the wind whips up the waves of the
sea, and so at last Dion ordered his mercenaries not to charge the
crowd but to advance towards them brandishing their weapons.
When this was done, not one of the Syracusans stood his
ground: they took to their heels and fled through the streets,
although nobody followed them in pursuit, for Dion immediately
ordered his men to turn about and led them in the direction of
Leontini.

This affair made the newly elected Syracusan generals a laughing-
stock in the eyes of the women of the city, and so in an effort to wipe
out their disgrace they armed the citizens again and set out in pursuit
of Dion. They came up with him just as he was crossing a river, and

some of their horsemen rode up to his troops in skirmishing order. But the moment they saw that Dion would no longer treat their provocations indulgently and in a paternal fashion, but was angrily ordering his men to turn about and drawing them up in battle-order, they beat a hasty and even more ignominious retreat, and returned to the city with the loss of a few men.

40. The people of Leontini welcomed Dion and accorded him exceptional honours. They engaged his mercenaries on full pay, granted them civil rights, and also sent a delegation to the Syracusans demanding that they should do justice to these men, to which the Syracusans replied by sending envoys to denounce Dion. Later, when all the allied Sicilian states had assembled at Leontini and discussed the question, it was decided that the Syracusans were in the wrong. For their part the Syracusans repudiated this verdict: they had become arrogant and full of their own importance because they had no one to rule them, and also because they employed generals who acted like slaves and lived in perpetual fear of the people.

41. After this a squadron of triremes arrived at Syracuse under the command of Nypsius the Neapolitan.[1] It had been sent by Dionysius, and brought food and pay for the besieged troops in the citadel. There followed a naval battle in which the Syracusans gained the day and captured four of the tyrant's ships. The victory quite turned their heads, so that casting aside all sense of discipline, they fell to celebrating their triumph with banquets and carousals. In this mood they became so oblivious of their real interests that at the very moment when they imagined that the citadel was within their grasp, they lost it and the city besides. Nypsius had taken note that there was no sign of order or control to be found among his opponents, that the masses had abandoned themselves to music-making and drinking from dawn till midnight, and that their generals actually welcomed these revels and shrank from using force to recall the drunken troops to their duty. He therefore seized his opportunity and attacked the siege-works which walled off the citadel. Then having captured and demolished these, he let loose his barbarians into the city, giving them leave to deal as they chose with everyone

1. A soldier of fortune from Neapolis (Naples), the capital of Campania.

they met. The Syracusans quickly perceived their plight, but they had been so much taken by surprise that it was only slowly and with difficulty that they could organize any resistance. What was now happening was nothing less than the sack of their city. The men were being slaughtered, the walls torn down, the women and children dragged screaming into the citadel, while the generals gave up all for lost and were helpless to rally the citizens against the enemy, who by then were everywhere in their midst and inextricably mingled with them.

42. With the city in this plight and the quarter of Achradina in imminent danger of being captured, there remained one man alone upon whom the entire population's hopes were fixed: Dion's name was in everyone's thoughts, but nobody dared to mention it, because they were ashamed of the folly and ingratitude with which they had treated him. But sheer necessity left them no choice, and at last some of their Sicilian allies and their horsemen raised the cry to send for Dion and his Peloponnesians from Leontini. As soon as someone had nerved himself to do this and Dion's name was again heard, the Syracusans shouted aloud and wept for joy. They prayed for Dion to appear before them and longed for the sight of him, for they remembered the courage and strength which he had shown in time of danger, and how he was not only undaunted in himself, but could make them share his fearless confidence when they engaged their enemies. So they immediately dispatched a party to his camp consisting of Archonides and Telesides to represent the allies, and Hellanicus with four others from the cavalry corps. They set off at full gallop and arrived at Leontini just as the sun was setting. Their first action was to leap from their horses and throw themselves at Dion's feet, and then with tears in their eyes they told him of the disasters the Syracusans had suffered. Presently some of the Leontines came up and a crowd of the Peloponnesians gathered around Dion, for they had guessed from the speed of the men's arrival and the imploring tone of their voices that something extraordinary had happened. Dion immediately led the messengers to the place of assembly, and the people eagerly gathered there. Then Archonides and Hellanicus briefly described to them the catastrophe which had befallen the city, and begged the mercenaries to forget the wrongs that had been done to them and to come to the rescue of the Syra-

cusans, since those who had committed the injustice had suffered a punishment even harsher than their victims would have expected to inflict on them.

43. As soon as the envoys had finished their appeal, a dead silence fell upon the theatre. As Dion rose to speak his voice was choked with sobs, but his mercenaries who shared his feelings urged him to take heart. So when he had mastered his emotions somewhat, he said to them, 'Men of the Peloponnese and allies of Syracuse, I have brought you here to decide how you should now act. For myself I cannot think of my own interests while Syracuse is on the brink of destruction, but if I cannot save her, I shall return to bury myself in her ruins and make the flames that consume her my funeral pyre. As for you, if you can find it in your hearts after all that has passed to come to the rescue of us Syracusans, who are the most ill-advised and ill-fated of mankind, then I beg you to rescue once more this city of ours which was founded by your own fellow countrymen.[1] But if you condemn the Syracusans and decide to abandon them to their fate, I pray that at least the gods will grant you a just reward for the courage and the loyalty you have shown towards me, and that you will remember Dion as a man who did not desert you when you were wronged, nor his own fellow-citizens in their hour of misfortune.'

While Dion was still speaking, the mercenaries leaped to their feet, interrupted him with shouts, and clamoured for him to lead them immediately to the rescue. The envoys from Syracuse threw their arms around the soldiers and embraced them with joy, calling upon the gods to bless Dion and his men. Then when the uproar had subsided, Dion dismissed his troops to their quarters and ordered them to make ready to march, take their supper, and reassemble with their arms in the same place, for he was determined to march to the relief of Syracuse that very night.

44. Meanwhile Dionysius' troops continued to make havoc in the city so long as daylight lasted; then as soon as it was dark, they withdrew to the citadel, having lost a few of their men. At this point the demagogues again recovered their spirits: their hope was that the enemy would rest content with what they had achieved, and so they

1. Syracuse was originally a colony of Corinth: hence the Peloponnesian association.

once more urged the people to have nothing to do with Dion. If he approached with his mercenaries, they should not let him in: they must not regard his troops as superior to themselves in courage, but should make up their minds to save the city and defend their liberty by their own efforts. In consequence further emissaries were sent out to Dion, some from the generals forbidding his advance, and others from the cavalry corps and the more prominent citizens exhorting him to hasten it, and these contradictory messages caused him to proceed more slowly but with more determination. As the night wore on, Dion's opponents seized possession of the gates to prevent him from entering the city, but at the same time Nypsius led a sortie from the citadel. This time he attacked in greater strength and with still more confidence, with the result that he at once demolished the whole of the siege wall and overran and pillaged the city. He went on to massacre not only numbers of the male citizens but also women and children; few prisoners were taken and the Syracusans were slaughtered without discrimination. Dionysius had evidently come to despair of his prospects, and as he was consumed with hatred of the Syracusans, he had resolved to bury his falling tyranny in the ruins of the city. His soldiers were determined to forestall Dion's arrival and so sought out the quickest way to annihilate everything before them, that is by reducing the city to ashes: anything that was close at hand they set alight with the torches and firebrands they carried, and anything further away they shot at with blazing arrows. As the Syracusans fled from the destruction, some of them were overtaken and butchered in the streets, while those who sought refuge in the houses were forced out by the flames, for many buildings were now ablaze and collapsed upon the fugitives as they ran past.

45. It was this catastrophe above all which caused the citizens to unite in opening the gates to Dion. When he had first received the news that the enemy had retreated into the citadel, he had slackened the pace of his march. But as the day went on, first some of the cavalrymen met him with the news that the city had been captured a second time; then not long after, even some of those who had opposed his coming arrived to beg him to hasten his advance. Next, as the situation grew desperate, Heraclides dispatched his brother and finally Theodotes his uncle to entreat Dion to help them:

the report said that resistance was at an end, that Heraclides was wounded and that almost the whole of the city was in ruins or in flames. When this terrible news reached Dion he was still more than seven miles from the city gates. He at once explained to his troops the danger in which the city stood, spoke encouragingly to them and then led them forward, no longer marching but at the double, while one messenger after another met him and implored him to hasten. The mercenaries responded with a sudden burst of speed, and advancing with tremendous ardour Dion broke through the gates into the open space which is known as the Hecatompedon. From there he ordered his light-armed troops to charge the enemy, so that the Syracusans might take heart from their presence. Next he drew up his heavy infantry in order of battle and included with them those of the citizens who kept running up to join him: he divided these formations into separate commands and grouped them in columns, so as to create greater alarm among the enemy by attacking from several points at once.

46. When he had made these preparations and offered up a prayer to the gods, the sight of him leading his troops through the city to attack the enemy caused the Syracusans to raise a great shout of joy: in the clamour that then arose were mingled battle-cries, prayers and supplications as the citizens hailed Dion as their saviour and their god and his mercenaries as their brothers and fellow-citizens. Certainly at that moment of crisis there was not a man so selfish or so cowardly that he did not value Dion's life more dearly than his own or all the rest, as he marched at their head to meet the danger, forcing his way through blood and fire and the heaps of corpses which littered the streets.

As for the enemy, they presented a terrifying appearance, for the fighting had made them savage, and they had posted themselves along the demolished siege-wall in a position which was awkward to approach and hard to force: at the same time the dangers caused by the fire distracted Dion's troops and created further obstacles to their advance. They were surrounded on all sides by the glare of the flames as the conflagration spread from house to house. Every step they took was upon burning ruins and whenever they ran forward they risked their lives, as great fragments of buildings came crashing down: they struggled on through clouds of dust and smoke, always striving to keep together and not break their formation. When they

came to grips with the enemy, the approach was so narrow and uneven that only a few men could engage at a time, but the Syracusans
urged them on with shouts of encouragement, and at last Nypsius
and his men were overcome. Most of them managed to save themselves by escaping into the citadel which was close by, but those who
were left outside and scattered in different directions were hunted
down and killed by the mercenaries. However, in the city's desperate
situation the Syracusans had no time to relax and enjoy their victory,
or to indulge in the rejoicing and congratulations which such an
achievement deserved. Instead they devoted their efforts to saving
their houses, and by dint of toiling all night they succeeded in putting
out the fires.

47. When daylight came, not one of the popular leaders dared to
remain in the city: all of them in effect condemned themselves by
taking to flight. Heraclides and Theodotes came of their own accord
and surrendered themselves to Dion. They openly admitted that they
had done wrong and implored him to treat them more justly than
they had treated him. But it was only right, they pleaded, that Dion
who surpassed them in every other good quality, should also show
that he was more capable of controlling his anger than these ungrateful men who had now come to confess that he excelled them in the
very quality in which they had disputed his superiority, that is in
virtue. Heraclides and Theodotes pleaded with Dion in this way, but
his friends urged him not to spare such unprincipled and envious
rascals: instead he should hand over Heraclides to the soldiers and
deliver the state from the habit of pandering to the mob, a disease
scarcely less pernicious than tyranny itself. Dion did his best to appease
their anger and pointed out that while other generals devoted most of
their training to the handling of weapons and the fighting of battles,
he had spent a long time in the Academy studying how to overcome
anger, envy and the spirit of rivalry. To show kindness only to one's
friends and benefactors is no proof of having acquired such self-
control: the real test is for a man who has been wronged to be able
to show compassion and moderation to the evil-doers: besides he
wished it to be seen that he excelled Heraclides not so much in power
or in statesmanship as in virtue and justice, for these are the qualities
in which true superiority resides. After all, fortune can always claim
some of the credit for successes in war, even when no other man has

a share in them. And if Heraclides had been led by envy into base and treacherous conduct, that was no reason for Dion to sully his virtue by giving way to anger, for although taking revenge for a wrong is more justifiable in the eyes of the law than committing the wrong without provocation, yet in the nature of things both actions spring from the same weakness. What is more, although baseness is a deplorable thing in a man, yet it is not so savage and intractable a defect that it cannot be overcome by repeated kindness and transformed by a sense of gratitude.

48. On the strength of arguments such as these, Dion released Heraclides and Theodotes. Next he turned his attention to the siege-wall facing the citadel. He ordered every Syracusan citizen to cut a stake and lay it down near the siegeworks. Then he set the mercenaries to work all night while the citizens were resting and fenced off the acropolis with a palisade, so that when day dawned both the Syracusans and the enemy were amazed to see how quickly the work had been finished. He also buried the Syracusans who had been killed in the fighting, ransomed those who had been captured – although there were at least two thousand of these – and summoned a meeting of the assembly. On this occasion Heraclides put forward a motion that Dion should be elected general with absolute powers both by land and sea. The wealthier citizens supported the proposals and urged that it should be put to the vote, but the majority, the working-classes and the sailors, raised an uproar and rejected it. They were angry that Heraclides should lose his position as admiral, and even though he was worthless in other respects, they regarded him as more of a friend of the people than Dion. On this issue Dion gave way and reinstated Heraclides in command of the fleet, but when the people pressed for the redistribution of land and houses, he incurred great unpopularity by opposing them and annulling the earlier decrees. Seeing this, Heraclides promptly resumed his intrigues. When he was stationed at Messana, he addressed the soldiers and sailors who had sailed there with him and tried to rouse them against Dion, whom he accused of plotting to make himself tyrant: at the same time he entered into secret negotiations with Dionysius with the help of Pharax the Spartan. The nobility of Syracuse suspected that these moves were in progress and violent dissensions broke out in his camp, which led to a severe shortage of provisions and much

distress in the city. Dion was at his wits' end what to do and was bitterly reproached by his friends for having allowed a man so unprincipled and so corrupted by envy to build up a position of strength against him.[1]

49. Pharax the Spartan was at this time encamped at Neapolis in the territory of Agrigentum, and Dion, who led out the Syracusan forces against him, did not wish to engage him on this occasion but to bide his opportunity. However Heraclides and his sailors raised a clamour against these tactics, and made out that Dion had no wish to finish the campaign by a battle but was content to make it last indefinitely so as to keep himself in command. He was therefore forced to fight and suffered a defeat. However since this was by no means a serious reverse, but was due to the confusion created by his men's lack of discipline rather than to the enemy's efforts, Dion once more prepared to engage, drew up his order of battle and spoke to his men to raise their spirits. But that evening he received a report that Heraclides had weighed anchor and was making for Syracuse with the fleet, intending to seize possession of the city and shut out Dion and his troops. He at once gathered together the most active and devoted of his men, rode all through the night and was at the gates of the city by about nine o'clock the next morning, having covered some ninety miles. Heraclides, although he had made the best speed he could, arrived too late and stood out to sea again. For a while he was at a loss as to what to do next, and then by chance he fell in with Gaesylus the Spartan, who informed him that he was sailing from Sparta to take command of the Sicilians, just as Gylippus had done before him.[2] Heraclides gladly took up with this man; he displayed him to his allies, attached him to himself as it were like a talisman against the influence of Dion, and secretly dispatched a herald to Syracuse with orders that the citizens should accept the Spartan as their commander. Dion sent back the answer that the Syracusans had quite enough commanders, and that if the situation demanded the presence of a Spartan, then he himself was the man, since he had been created a citizen of Sparta. When Gaesylus learned this, he gave up any claim to command, sailed to meet

1. It is possible that the crews of the triremes held the whip-hand and would accept no other commander but Heraclides.

2. Against the Athenian expedition in the Peloponnesian war. See *The Rise and Fall of Athens*, *Life of Nicias*, chs. 19ff.

Dion, and arranged a reconciliation between him and Heraclides. He made Heraclides swear oaths and give the most solemn pledges, and he himself vowed that he would avenge Dion and punish Heraclides if the latter broke his word.

50. After this the Syracusans disbanded their fleet; by then it was of no further use to them, required large outlays to pay the crews, and was a constant cause of dissension among the generals. But at the same time they tightened the blockade of the citadel and completed the encircling wall that enclosed it. No attempt was made from any quarter to raise the siege, the garrison's provisions were running out and the mercenaries were on the verge of mutiny; in these circumstances Dionysius' son Apollocrates gave up all hope and came to terms with Dion.[1] He surrendered the citadel together with all the arms and warlike stores it contained, and then after embarking his mother and sisters and taking five warships, he sailed away to his father. Dion allowed him to depart unmolested, and the spectacle of his departure was watched by every Syracusan in the city, in fact they even invoked those of their fellow-countrymen who were absent and pitied them because they could not witness that day and see the sun rise upon a free Syracuse. Even to this day the expulsion of Dionysius is still cited as one of the most spectacular examples of the vicissitudes of fortune, and so we may imagine what joy and pride the Syracusans must then have felt at having overthrown with the most meagre resources the greatest tyranny that had ever been established.

51. After Apollocrates had sailed off and Dion was on his way to the citadel, the women could no longer bear to wait for him to enter the fortress, but ran out to the gates. Aristomache was leading Dion's son, while Arete came behind her in tears, quite unsure as to how she should greet and address her husband after she had lived with another man. Dion first embraced his sister, and next his young son, and then Aristomache led Arete forward and said, 'We lived in misery, Dion, all through the years when you were in exile. But now that you have come back to us, your victory has taken away our sorrows – for all of us except Arete, whom I had the misfortune to see forced to take another husband while you were still alive. Now that fate has made you our lord and master, how will you judge what she was compelled

1. In 355 B.C.

to do? How is she to greet you, as her uncle or as her husband?'
These words of Aristomache's made Dion weep, and he threw his
arms around his wife fondly, put his son's hand in hers and bade her
come to his house; there he continued to live after he had handed over
the citadel to the people of Syracuse.

52. Now that all his plans had been successfully accomplished, Dion
did not think it right to enjoy his good fortune before he had first
shown his gratitude to his friends, rewarded his allies – especially those
with whom he had been associated in Athens – and bestowed some
special mark of honour and recognition upon his mercenaries; but
here his generosity outran his resources. For his own part, he continued to live in a modest and frugal style using only his own private
means, and this was a matter for wonder to the whole world. His
successes had captured the attention not only of Sicily and of Carthage
but of all Greece: all these peoples considered his achievements the
greatest of his age and himself a commander who combined a degree
of courage and good fortune which none could rival, and yet he was
so unassuming in the style of his dress, his household and his table that
he might have been dining with Plato in the Academy, not sitting
down with commanders and mercenaries and hired soldiers, who
compensate themselves for the toils and dangers of their profession by
keeping up a lavish standard of eating and drinking and other pleasures. Plato indeed once wrote to remind him that the eyes of the whole
world were now fixed upon him, but Dion himself, it would seem,
kept his eyes fixed upon that one spot in one city, namely the Academy. He believed that those who watched him from there were not
so much impressed by feats of arms or courage or battles won, but
judged his conduct only according to whether he had used his good
fortune with moderation and wisdom and behaved with due restraint
after he had reached the heights of power. He also made a point of
maintaining the same gravity in his bearing and the same formality of
manner in dealing with the people, even though the times called for a
more gracious demeanour: he did this in spite of the fact, as I have
mentioned earlier, that Plato wrote and warned him that 'self-will
keeps house with solitude'. However Dion possessed the kind of
temperament which finds it difficult to unbend, and besides this he
thought it important to curb the behaviour of the Syracusans,
who were accustomed to too much luxury and too little self-
discipline.

53. It was not long before Heraclides began to oppose him again. First of all, when Dion invited him to become a member of the council he declined to come, declaring that as a private citizen he would only go to the public assembly with his fellow-citizens. Next he publicly attacked Dion for not having demolished the citadel, for having prevented the people from breaking open the tomb of Dionysius the elder and casting out his body, and for having insulted his fellow-countrymen by sending a request to Corinth to provide a number of advisers and officials for the government. It was quite true that he had appealed to the Corinthians, but this was precisely because he hoped that their participation in the government would make it easier to establish the constitution he had planned. Through this plan he intended to put a curb upon unrestrained democracy, which he did not regard as a constitution at all, but rather as a kind of supermarket of constitutions – to use Plato's phrase – and to introduce a blend of democracy and monarchy on the Spartan and Cretan model. According to this system it is an oligarchy which is in control of affairs and decides the most important issues: at any rate Dion had noticed that the government of Corinth is inclined towards oligarchy, and that very little public business is handled in the popular assembly.

At this point, since he expected that Heraclides would take the lead in opposing these measures, and since the man was unstable and a born trouble-maker and rabble-rouser, Dion at last gave way to those who had long ago wished to kill him but whom he had hitherto restrained, and so they forced their way into Heraclides' house and murdered him. The Syracusans were deeply indignant at his death, but when Dion gave him a spectacular funeral and escorted his body to the grave with his troops and afterwards made a speech to them, they recognized that the city would never be at peace so long as Dion and Heraclides were both engaged in political life.

54. One of Dion's companions was a man named Callippus, an Athenian who according to Plato had been an intimate friend of his, not as a fellow student of philosophy, but because he happened to have initiated him into certain of the mysteries and was therefore regularly in his company. He had taken part in the expedition from the beginning and had distinguished himself brilliantly in action. Dion accorded him special honours, and at their entry into Syracuse had placed him by his side at the head of their companions wearing a

wreath on his head. By this time many of the noblest and best of Dion's friends had died on the battlefield, and since Heraclides was also now dead, Callippus perceived that the Syracusans were without a leader, and that he himself had more influence than anyone else with Dion's troops. So like the detestable creature that he was, Callippus calculated that he could make Sicily his prize in return for killing his friend, while some writers say that he accepted twenty talents from Dion's enemies as his reward for the murder. At any rate he bribed a number of Dion's mercenaries to form a conspiracy against him, and he set his plot working in a peculiarly mean and treacherous manner. He made a practice of reporting to Dion any seditious remarks uttered by the soldiers against him, sometimes using words he had actually heard and sometimes making them up, and in this way he won Dion's confidence and was authorized to hold clandestine meetings and talk freely with the men against him, in order that none of those who were secretly disaffected should remain undiscovered. In this way Callippus quickly succeeded in identifying and bringing together all the most unscrupulous and discontented of the mercenaries: at the same time, if any man refused his overtures and reported them, Dion was not at all disturbed and showed no anger, but simply assumed that Callippus was carrying out his orders.

55. While this conspiracy was being hatched, Dion saw a phantom of gigantic size and terrible appearance. As he was sitting late in the day in the portico of his house by himself and lost in thought, he suddenly heard a noise at the far end of the colonnade. He looked up and in the twilight he saw a tall woman, whose face and dress were exactly like those of one of the Furies on the stage, sweeping the house with a kind of broom. He started violently, and finding himself shaking with terror, he sent for his friends, described to them what he had seen, and begged them to stay and spend the night with him, for he was almost beside himself with fear and was afraid that if he were left alone, the apparition might return. This did not happen, but a few days later his only son, who was by then almost grown up, flew into a passion on account of some trivial grievance, threw himself head-long from the roof and was killed.

56. While Dion was in this state of distress, Callippus made all the more progress with his conspiracy and spread a rumour among the

Syracusans that Dion, now that he was childless, had decided to send for Dionysius' son Apollocrates, who happened to be at once his wife's nephew and his sister's grandson, to make him his successor. By this time both Dion and his sister had begun to suspect what was afoot, and information about the plot reached them from all sides. But it seems that Dion was tormented by the death of Heraclides, and the memory of his murder continually weighed upon and depressed his mind, since he regarded it as a stain upon his own life and actions. He declared that he was ready to die many times over, and that he would let any man cut his throat if he were to be obliged to live in perpetual fear not only of his enemies but even of his friends.

At this point Callippus, who had noticed that the women were becoming very inquisitive to discover what was going on, took fright and came to them in tears: he denied vehemently that there was any plot, and offered to give any pledge of his loyalty they might demand. At this they demanded that he should swear the great oath, which was done in the following manner. The giver of the pledge goes down into the precinct of Demeter and Persephone and there, after certain ceremonies have been performed, he puts on the purple robe of the goddess, takes a lighted torch in his hand and recites the oath. Callippus performed all these ceremonies and repeated the oath, but treated the gods with such contempt that he actually waited for the festival of the goddess by whom he had sworn, and on that day committed the murder.[1] But it may be that he paid no attention to the day, for he must have known that he was committing just as outrageous a sacrilege when he, as an initiating priest, shed the blood of an initiate, no matter which day he chose to do it.

57. There were many people in the plot, and as Dion was sitting with his friends in a room furnished with several couches, some of the conspirators surrounded the house outside, while others guarded the doors and the windows. The murderers, who were all from Zacynthus, entered the room in their tunics and without swords. Then at the same moment those outside shut the doors and held them fast, while those in the room threw themselves upon Dion and tried to strangle and crush him. When they could not succeed in this, they called for a sword, but nobody dared to open the door. There were many of Dion's friends in the room, but each of them seemed to imagine that

1. In June 354 B.C.

if he left Dion to his fate, he could save his own skin, and so no man had the courage to help him. After a long delay Lycon the Syracusan handed a short sword through the window and with this they cut his throat, like a victim at a sacrifice: he had for a long while been overpowered and was trembling as he waited for the blow. The conspirators at once took away his wife, who was pregnant, and threw her into prison. She endured a most wretched confinement and gave birth to a boy in the gaol: the women ventured to rear the child and found it easy to obtain the permission of the gaolers, because Callippus was already embroiled in troubles of his own.

58. At first after the murder of Dion Callippus enjoyed great prestige and was in complete control of Syracuse. He even sent a dispatch to the city of Athens, the place for which he should have felt most dread, second only to that which he felt for the gods, since he had brought such a terrible pollution on himself. But it seems to have been truly said of Athens that the good men she breeds are the best of their kind, and the worst the most abominable, just as her soil brings forth the sweetest honey and the deadliest hemlock. At any rate, Callippus did not long survive as a living reproach to fortune and the gods, as though they could overlook the impiety of a man who had won position and power by committing such an outrage: instead he very soon paid the penalty. First, when he made an expedition to capture Catana, he at once lost Syracuse, after which he is said to have remarked that he had lost a city and gained a cheese-grater. Next he attacked Messana, and here many of his soldiers were killed, among them the murderers of Dion. Then, as no city in Sicily would admit him, but all showed how they hated and abhorred him, he seized possession of Rhegium. There he found his resources so much reduced that he could not pay his mercenaries and was murdered by Leptines and Polyperchon, who, by a twist of fate, used the same short-sword as the one with which Dion is said to have been killed. It was recognized by its size, which was very short, after the Spartan fashion, and also by the style of its workmanship, for it was finely and elaborately chased.

Such was the retribution which overtook Callippus. As for Aristomache and Arete, when they were released from prison, they were received by Hicetas the Syracusan, who had been a friend of Dion's and who had at first seemed to treat them loyally and honourably.

But later, at the instigation of some of Dion's enemies, he provided a ship for them and made out that they were to be sent to the Peloponnese: then once they were at sea he ordered the sailors to cut their throats and throw their bodies overboard. According to another version, however, they were thrown into the sea alive and their little boy with them. In the end Hicetas also suffered a fitting punishment for his crimes. He was captured by Timoleon and put to death, and the Syracusans killed his two daughters in revenge for the murder of Dion. These events I have described at length in my *Life of Timoleon*.

4

TIMOLEON[1]

[c. 411–c. 337 B.C.]

* *
*

WHEN I first took up the writing of these *Lives* I did it for the sake of others, but now I find that I have grown fond of the task and continue it for my own pleasure. The reason is that it allows me to treat history as a mirror, with the help of which I can adorn my own life by imitating the virtues of the men whose actions I have described. It is as though I could talk with the subjects of my *Lives* and enjoy their company every day, since I receive each one in turn, welcome him as my guest, observe with admiration as Priam did of Achilles

What was his stature, what his qualities[2]

and select from his career those events which are the most important and the most inspiring to record. As Sophocles has written

What greater joy could you attain than this?[3]

and what could do more to raise the standards by which we live?

Democritus[4] tells us we should pray that we may be visited by spirits which are propitious, and that of those phantoms which materialize from the surrounding atmosphere we may encounter only those which are benevolent and in harmony with our natures, not those which are evilly disposed and can work us harm. In saying this he foists upon philosophy a theory which is untrue in itself and points the way towards unlimited superstition. But in my own case the study

---

1. For places mentioned in this *Life* see Maps 1 and 3, pp. 433, 436.
2. *Iliad* xxiv, 630.
3. From Sophocles' lost play *The Tympanistae*.
4. The great physical philosopher of the fifth century B.C., the pioneer of the theory that the universe is composed of atoms.

of history and the familiarity with it which I gain from my writing accustoms me to keep always before me the memory of the noblest and most admirable characters: by the same process I can reject and dismiss from my thoughts any base, ignoble and vicious suggestion which such enforced association may have introduced, and turn my attention calmly and dispassionately to the finest of my examples. Among these I have selected for my readers the lives of Timoleon and of Aemilius Paulus.[1] These men resemble one another not only in the principles which they followed, but also in the good fortune which they enjoyed in their conduct of affairs, and thus their biographies raise the question of whether the greatest of their achievements were due to their wisdom or their good luck.[2]

1. The situation in Syracuse before Timoleon's expedition arrived in Sicily was as follows. Soon after Dion had driven out the tyrant Dionysius he was treacherously murdered, and the men who had joined him to free the Syracusans were divided amongst themselves. The city had passed through a period during which it repeatedly exchanged one tyrant for another,[3] and as a result of all the misfortunes it had suffered, was in an almost derelict condition. As for the rest of Sicily, some districts had been ravaged and had become almost completely depopulated through incessant warfare. Most of the cities were in the hands of barbarians of various races and of disbanded soldiers, who because they had no regular pay were ready to accept any change of ruler. At last Dionysius the younger, after spending ten years in exile, recruited a force of mercenaries, drove out Nisaeus who was at that time the ruler of Syracuse, recovered control of affairs and reestablished himself as tyrant. He had unexpectedly been dislodged by a very small force[4] from the most powerful tyranny that ever existed and now, more unexpectedly still, he had raised himself from the con-

1. See Introduction, pp. 10–11.
2. In the MS this introduction stands as the first chapter of the *Life of Aemilius Paulus*. It is included here for the light which it throws upon Plutarch's conception of biography.
3. The tyrant Dionysius II was expelled by Dion in 356 B.C. After Dion's murder his assassin, the Athenian Callippus, held power from 354–353, when he was ousted by Dionysius II's half-brother Hipparinus. He in turn was assassinated in 351 and succeeded by his brother Nisaeus, who was driven out when Dionysius II returned to power in 347.
4. i.e. by Dion's expedition.

dition of a lowly exile to become the master of those who had banished him. Those of the Syracusans who remained in the city found themselves the slaves of a tyrant who had always been oppressive and had now become even more inhuman as a result of the misfortunes he had suffered. But the most prominent and influential of the citizens turned to Hicetas, the ruler of Leontini, placed themselves under his protection and elected him their general for the war. This man was no better than any other of the acknowledged tyrants, but the citizens had no other refuge, and they were prepared to trust a man who belonged to a Syracusan family and commanded a force which could match that of Dionysius.

2. Meanwhile the Carthaginians appeared with a powerful fleet and hovered off the coasts of Sicily, awaiting their opportunity to invade the island. Their approach struck terror into the Sicilians, and they resolved to send a delegation to Greece and appeal for help to Corinth. This was not only on account of their kinship with the Corinthians[1] and of the many services they had received from them in the past, but because they knew that Corinth had always upheld the cause of freedom, that she detested tyranny, and that she had fought most of her wars – and the greatest ones at that – not to acquire an empire or make herself more powerful, but to defend the liberty of Greece. Hicetas, on the other hand, when he accepted the command had no intention of freeing the Syracusans but rather of bringing them under his own tyranny, and he had already entered into secret negotiations with the Carthaginians. But in public he praised the Syracusan plan and supported the decision to send a delegation to the Peloponnese. He was not at all anxious to see an allied army arrive from that quarter. He hoped that if, as seemed likely, the Corinthians refused to send help on account of the troubled state of Greece and of their own commitments at home, he could more easily sway the course of events so as to favour the Carthaginians: he planned to use them as allies and auxiliaries either against the Syracusans or against Dionysius. These intentions were revealed not long afterwards.

3. When the delegation from Syracuse arrived, the Corinthians eagerly voted in favour of sending help. They were always concerned for the interests of their colonies overseas and especially for those of

1. Syracuse had originally been founded by Corinth in 735 B.C.

Syracuse, and by a happy chance there were no distractions to divert their attention either in Greece or within their own frontiers, where they were enjoying peace and leisure. Then, when the question arose of choosing a commander for the expedition, and while the magistrates were writing down the names of those citizens who wished to be considered for this honour and nominating them for election, a man from the crowd rose to his feet and proposed Timoleon the son of Timodemus. Timoleon was not at this time active in politics and had no intention of standing for the command or expectation that he would be appointed to it. But some god, it would seem, inspired the proposer to put forward his name, because fortune immediately revealed herself to be on his side; this became evident not only in the ease with which he was elected, but also in a peculiar grace which attended all his subsequent actions and enhanced his personal virtues.

Timoleon's parents, Timodemus and Demariste, both belonged to noble families, and he himself was an ardent patriot and a man of gentle disposition, except only for his hatred of tyrants and of base behaviour in any form. As a soldier his abilities were so finely and evenly balanced that he proved himself exceptionally astute in the exploits of his youth, and no less daring in those of his old age. He had a brother named Timophanes who was older but possessed a completely different temperament. Timophanes was headstrong and was dominated by a fatal passion for absolute power, which was encouraged by a circle of worthless friends and foreign military adventurers with whom he spent all his time. He enjoyed the reputation of being a fire-eater in war and of having a positive craving for danger: for this reason many of the Corinthians thought highly of him as a soldier and man of action and he was appointed to senior commands. Timoleon helped him to obtain these and did his best to cover up or extenuate his faults, while at the same time he praised and made the most of those virtues which nature had given him.

4. In the battle which the Corinthians fought against the Argives and the people of Cleone[1] Timoleon was serving with the infantry, but Timophanes, who was in command of the cavalry, suddenly found himself in great danger. His horse was wounded and threw him while he was surrounded by the enemy. Some of his companions scattered and fled in panic, and the few who stood fast were fighting against

1. About 368 B.C.

greatly superior numbers and could scarcely hold their ground. When Timoleon saw what was happening, he ran to the rescue and covered Timophanes with his shield as he lay on the ground. He received a hail of blows on his body and armour both from the spears and darts that were hurled at him and in the hand-to-hand fighting, but he succeeded at last in driving back the enemy and in saving his brother.

Some two years later the Corinthians became alarmed that their city might once more be captured because of the treachery of their allies,[1] and so they passed a decree to maintain a force of four hundred mercenaries and placed Timophanes in command of it. The immediate result was that Timophanes put aside all considerations of justice and honour, took steps to seize power, executed a large number of the leading citizens without trial, and proclaimed himself tyrant. Timoleon was outraged by these actions, but since he regarded his brother's crimes as his own misfortune, he tried to reason with him and begged him to abandon his insane and ill-starred ambition and make amends for the wrong he had done to his fellow citizens. Timophanes contemptuously rejected all his appeals, whereupon Timoleon called together his kinsman Aeschylus, who was Timophanes' brother-in-law, and his friend the diviner Satyrus: at least this was his name according to Theopompus, but Ephorus and Timaeus refer to him as Orthagoras. Timoleon waited a few days and then went up to the citadel. Here the three men surrounded Timophanes and made a final appeal, urging him even now to listen to reason and change his mind. Timophanes at first laughed at them, but then flew into a violent rage. At this Timoleon stepped a little way aside, covered his face and wept, while the other two drew their swords and straightaway killed him.

5. When the news became known, the leading Corinthians praised Timoleon for his hatred of wrongdoing and his greatness of soul. They saw that although he was a kindly man who loved his family, he had nevertheless placed his country before his own flesh and blood, and the cause of honour and justice before expediency. When his brother was fighting valiantly for his country Timoleon had saved his life, but after he had plotted against her and enslaved her, Timoleon had killed him. On the other hand those who could not bear to live in a democracy and were accustomed to pay court to whoever was in power, pretended to rejoice at Timophanes' death but nevertheless reviled

1. In 393 the Argives had seized Corinth in this way.

Timoleon for having committed an impious and detestable action, and their abuse reduced him to a state of deep dejection. When he heard that his mother's grief had turned to hatred and that she had uttered the most terrible denunciations and curses against his name, he went to try to console her; but she could not bear to see his face and shut him out of her house. Then his grief overcame him completely, he became distracted and determined to starve himself to death. His friends, however, would not stand by and allow this, and brought every kind of pressure and entreaty to bear on him, until finally he resolved to live by himself apart from the world. He withdrew completely from public life and for the first years of his retirement did not even return to the city, but spent his time wandering in great agony of mind in the most deserted parts of the country.

6. From this we may see that men's minds are unstable, and may easily be swayed by casual praise or blame and forced away from their natural train of thought, unless they acquire strength and steadiness of purpose from the practice of philosophy and rational reflection. It is not enough, it seems, that our actions should be noble and just: the conviction from which they spring must be permanent and irrevocable, if our conduct is to earn our full approval. Otherwise we may find ourselves becoming a prey to despondency, or to sheer weakness when the vision of the ideal which inspired us fades away, just as a glutton who devours cloying delicacies with too keen a pleasure soon loses his appetite and becomes disgusted with them. Remorse may cast a sense of shame over even the noblest of actions, but the determination which is founded upon reason and understanding is not shaken even if the outcome is unsuccessful. The case of Phocion the Athenian is a good example. Phocion had opposed the course of action taken by Leosthenes, and when Leosthenes' policy seemed to have triumphed, and the Athenians were seen to be sacrificing and exulting over their victory, Phocion remarked that he could have wished the success had been his, but that he was glad to have given the advice that he did.[1] And Aristides the Locrian, who was one of Plato's companions, put the matter even more cogently, when he was asked by Dionysius the elder for the hand of one of his daughters in marriage: he said that he would rather see the girl dead than the wife of a tyrant. Some while later Dionysius put Aristides' sons to death, and then asked him scorn-

1. See *Life of Phocion*, ch. 23.

fully whether he had changed his opinion about giving his daughters in marriage, whereupon Aristides replied that he was grieved at what Dionysius had done, but did not repent of what he had said: such sayings as these are the mark of a greater, a more perfect virtue than is found in ordinary men.

7. In the case of Timoleon his grief, whether it arose out of pity for his dead brother or the reverence which he bore his mother, so crushed and overwhelmed his spirit that it was almost twenty years before he could again engage in any important public enterprise.[1] So when he had been named as the commander of the expedition and the people had gladly accepted him and given him their votes, Telecleides, who was at that time the most distinguished and influential man in Corinth rose and appealed to Timoleon to show all his valour in the enterprise he was undertaking. 'If you fight bravely,' he said, 'we shall think of you as the man who destroyed a tyrant, but otherwise as the man who killed his brother.'

While Timoleon was making ready for his voyage and collecting his troops, letters from Hicetas were brought to the Corinthians which clearly revealed that he had changed sides and betrayed them. As soon as he had sent off his ambassadors to Corinth, he openly attached himself to the Carthaginians and joined forces with them so as to expel Dionysius from Syracuse and make himself tyrant instead. Meanwhile he became alarmed that he might miss his opportunity if a general and an army were to arrive from Corinth too soon, and so he sent a letter to the Corinthians pointing out that there was no need for them to incur the trouble, the expense and the danger of sending a force to Sicily. Because of their delay he had been obliged to make an alliance with the Carthaginians against the tyrant, and his new allies forbade the Corinthians to send an expedition and were on the watch to intercept it with a large fleet. These letters were read out in public, and if any of the Corinthians had previously been lukewarm about the operation, they were now roused to fury against Hicetas and eagerly contributed to support the expedition and help Timoleon prepare for his voyage.

8. After the fleet had been made ready and the soldiers completely equipped, the priestesses of Persephone dreamed that they saw the

1. He stayed out of public life from 366 till 346 B.C., when he was sixty-five years old.

goddess and her mother preparing for a journey and heard them say that they intended to sail with Timoleon to Sicily. Thereupon the Corinthians fitted out a sacred trireme and named it after the two goddesses. Moreover Timoleon himself travelled to Delphi and offered sacrifice to Apollo there. As he descended into the chamber where the oracular responses were delivered, he was the witness of a portent. Among the votive offerings which were hung up there, a wreath, which had crowns and figures of victory embroidered on it, slipped down and fell directly on his head, and thus gave the impression that he was being sent forth upon his enterprise crowned with success by the god.

So Timoleon set sail[1] with seven ships from Corinth, two from Corcyra, and a tenth supplied by the people of Leucas. That night when he had reached the open sea and was sailing with a fair wind, suddenly the heavens seemed to burst open above his ship and pour down a flood of brilliant light. Then a torch, like one of those which are carried in the procession of the Mysteries, rose up before them, and moving in the same direction as his vessel, descended upon exactly that part of Italy towards which the pilots were shaping their course. The diviners declared that this apparition confirmed the dreams of the priestesses, and that the goddesses were displaying this light from heaven to show that they were taking part in the expedition, for Sicily is sacred to Persephone: it is the scene of her mythical rape by Hades, and the island was presented to her as a wedding gift.

9. These divine portents greatly encouraged the expedition; the fleet made its best speed across the open sea and sailed down the coast of Italy. However, the news which they then received from Sicily perplexed Timoleon and disheartened his men. Hicetas, they learned, had defeated Dionysius in battle, and captured most of the outlying districts of Syracuse; he had then driven the tyrant into the acropolis and the quarter which is known as 'the island'[2] and was blockading him there. At the same time he had ordered the Carthaginians to prevent Timoleon from landing in Sicily. The Corinthian expedition was to be driven off, so that Hicetas and the Carthaginians could then divide

---

1. In the winter of 344 B.C.
2. Ortygia: this may originally have been an island, but had certainly become a peninsula by Thucydides' time. Syracuse was divided at this date into five fortified zones: Ortygia was separate from the acropolis.

the island between them at their leisure. Accordingly the Carthaginians despatched twenty triremes to Rhegium carrying envoys from Hicetas to Timoleon. The proposals they brought with them were as deceitful as the rest of his actions: they consisted of specious overtures and declarations which concealed treacherous designs. The envoys requested that Timoleon should, if he wished, join Hicetas, who would treat him as his adviser and partner in all his successes, but that he should send his ships and his soldiers back to Corinth. They claimed that the campaign against Dionysius was virtually finished, and that the Carthaginians were prepared to oppose his passage and fight him if he attempted to force the issue. So when the Corinthians arrived at Rhegium, they met the ambassadors and saw the Carthaginian fleet riding at anchor close by. They were filled with indignation at the insult they had suffered,[1] with rage against Hicetas, and with fear for the people of Sicily, since it was evident that they were being handed over to Hicetas as a prize for his treachery and to the Carthaginians for their help in making him tyrant. It seemed to the Corinthians quite impossible that they could overcome both the barbarians, who faced them with a fleet twice the size of their own, and Hicetas' army in Syracuse, of which they had expected to take command.

10. However, after Timoleon had met the envoys and the Carthaginian commanders, he calmly informed them that he would comply with their demands – for what would he achieve by refusing? He added that he wished to have their proposals and his answer discussed before they parted in the presence of the people of the city of Rhegium, since this was a city which was friendly to both parties. This arrangement, he pointed out, would help to justify his action before his own countrymen, while for their part the envoys and commanders would be the more bound to carry out their promises concerning the Syracusans if the people of Rhegium were made the witnesses to the agreement. This proposal was in fact a trick to enable him to cross the straits, and the people of Rhegium gave him their help because they were anxious that the Sicilian Greeks should come under the protection of Corinth and were afraid of having the barbarians as neighbours. They therefore summoned an assembly of the people and

1. There was a law recorded by Diodorus, which enabled the Syracusans in the event of war to send to Corinth or Sparta for a general. The Corinthians felt that this agreement had been invoked and was now being flouted.

closed the gates to ensure that the citizens should not engage in any other business. Then they came forward and addressed the populace with lengthy speeches, one man handing on the same topic to his successor: they took care not to reach any conclusion but spun out the time, apparently to no purpose, until the Corinthian triremes had put to sea. Meanwhile the Carthaginians were kept in the assembly; they suspected nothing because Timoleon was present and gave the impression that he was on the point of rising to address the people. Then somebody unobtrusively brought him word that the rest of the Corinthian triremes were under way, and that his ship alone remained behind and was waiting for him. The Rhegians who were standing around the platform helped to screen him so that he could slip through the crowd unnoticed, and he hurried down to the sea and sailed away at full speed.

The squadron put in at Tauromenium[1] in Sicily. They had been invited some while before and were now warmly received by Andromachus, the ruler of the city. This man was the father of Timaeus the historian. He had made himself by far the most powerful[2] of the rulers of Sicily of that time, and he not only observed the principles of law and justice in governing his people, but made no secret of the fact that he was constantly and implacably hostile to tyrants. For this reason he allowed Timoleon to make Tauromenium his base of operations, and prevailed upon the citizens to join the Corinthians in their campaign to liberate Sicily.

11. Meanwhile when the assembly at Rhegium was dissolved and Timoleon's escape was discovered, the Carthaginians were beside themselves with rage. The people of Rhegium were greatly amused not only to have defeated them in this battle of wits, but also to hear Phoenicians complaining bitterly of deceit.[3] The Carthaginians then sent a trireme to Tauromenium with an envoy on board. This man held a long conversation with Andromachus in which he threatened the Greek in insulting and barbaric fashion if he did not immediately send the Corinthians away. Finally he stretched out his hand with the

1. The modern Taormina.
2. It has been conjectured that Plutarch wrote *aristos*, meaning the best (which is certainly nearer the truth), not *kratistos*, the most powerful.
3. Evidently to the Greeks, as well as to the Romans, *perfidia Punica* was a by-word.

palm upwards, and then, turning it downwards, declared that he would overturn the city in the same way. Andromachus merely laughed and made no reply, except to hold out his hand and repeat the gesture, showing his palm first upwards and then downwards. Then he ordered him to sail off at once, if he did not want to see his ship capsized in the same fashion.

As soon as Hicetas heard that Timoleon had crossed the straits of Messina, he became alarmed and sent for a strong fleet of Carthaginian ships, but for their part the Syracusans were in despair that they could ever be rescued. They saw their harbour controlled by the Carthaginians, their city in the hands of Hicetas, and their citadel occupied by Dionysius. Timoleon, on the other hand, seemed to have no more than a foothold on the edge of Sicily in the little city of Tauromenium, with few hopes of success and only a slender force to support him. Apart from his thousand soldiers, for whom he had barely enough supplies, he possessed no resources whatever. The cities of Sicily showed little confidence in him, for they were beset with troubles of their own, and were particularly exasperated against all those who claimed to lead armies to liberate them. These feelings were the result of the treachery of Callippus[1] and of Pharax,[2] the first an Athenian and the second a Spartan. Both of these men had declared that they had come to fight for the freedom of Sicily and overthrow her despots, but in fact they had caused the rule of the tyrants to appear like a golden age compared to their own, and led the people to believe that those who had died in slavery were happier than those who had survived to witness her so-called independence.

12. The cities therefore did not expect that the Corinthian liberator would turn out to be any better than his predecessors. They feared that the same enticements and sophistries would be held out, and that they would be offered fair hopes and generous promises to make them docile enough to accept a new master. In consequence all the cities were suspicious of the overtures made by the Corinthians and rejected them, with the exception of the little city of Adranum.[3] This

---

1. See *Life of Dion*, chs. 54–7.   2. See *Life of Dion*, chs. 48–9.
3. The city had been founded in the late fifth century B.C. by Dionysius the elder. It was situated on the south-westerly slope of Mount Etna, and was sacred to Adranus, a god of fire and war of Oriental origin, whose temple was guarded by a hundred dogs.

people lived in a small town dedicated to Adranus, a god who is held in the highest honour throughout Sicily. At this time the people were divided: one party had called in Hicetas and the Carthaginians, while another had sent an invitation to Timoleon. As fortune would have it, both generals hurried to answer the summons and arrived at the same moment, with the difference that while Hicetas came with five thousand soldiers, Timoleon's force numbered no more than twelve hundred. He started with these from Tauromenium, which is forty-two miles from Adranum, and on the first day covered only a short distance before pitching camp for the night. On the second he quickened his march, and after passing through difficult country, received news late in the day that Hicetas had just reached the little town and was pitching his camp. Thereupon Timoleon's officers halted the vanguard in order to rest and feed the men and make them ready and eager for battle. But when Timoleon arrived, he begged them not to wait but to press on as fast as they could so as to fall upon the enemy while they were in disorder, as they were likely to be when they had just finished their march and were engaged in pitching their tents and preparing a meal. With these words he snatched up his shield, put himself at the head of the column, and marched on as if he were leading his troops to certain victory. Inspired by his example, the men followed him and quickly covered the four miles which separated them from Hicetas. Their attack achieved complete surprise, and the enemy fled as soon as they saw the Corinthians advancing upon them. For this reason no more than three hundred of them were killed, but twice as many were taken prisoner and their camp was captured. Thereupon the people of Adranum opened their gates to Timoleon and gave him their allegiance. They also told him with awe and wonder that at the very beginning of the battle the sacred doors of the temple had flown open of their own accord, the spear of the god was seen to quiver at its point, and drops of sweat ran down the face of his image.

13. These portents, it seems, foretold not only Timoleon's immediate victory, but also a number of future successes to which this battle was an auspicious prelude. Other cities immediately sent envoys to Timoleon and began to attach themselves to his cause, and in particular Mamercus, the tyrant of Catana, a warlike and wealthy ruler, came forward as an ally. But most important was the fact that Dionysius himself had by now lost all hope of success and was almost at the end

of his resistance. He despised Hicetas for his shameful defeat, but was full of admiration for Timoleon, and now offered to surrender both himself and the citadel to the Corinthians.[1]

Timoleon welcomed this unexpected stroke of good fortune, and sent a detachment of four hundred soldiers to the acropolis under two Corinthian officers, Eucleides and Telemachus. He could not send them openly nor all together, since the Carthaginian fleet was block-ading the harbour, but infiltrated them in small groups. These soldiers then took possession of the acropolis and of the tyrant's fortress, to-gether with all its equipment and military stores, for the place con-tained many horses, all kinds of artillery and siege weapons, great quantities of missiles, and arms and armour for seventy thousand men, all of which had been kept there for many years. Dionysius also had with him two thousand soldiers, whom he handed over to Timoleon with the stores. Then gathering together a few friends and his treasure, he put to sea and passed through Hicetas' lines unnoticed. After this he was brought to Timoleon's camp, where he was seen for the first time in the humble dress of a private citizen, and as such he was sent with a single ship and a small allowance of money to Corinth. Dionysius had been born and bred under a tyranny which was the greatest and most celebrated of all tyrannies. He had wielded this power for ten years, but then for the next twelve, ever since the time of Dion's expedition against him, he had been continually harassed by wars and political struggles, during which his personal sufferings had far outweighed all his acts of tyranny. He had lived to see his sons die in their early manhood, his daughters violated, and his wife, who was also his sister, subjected to the brutal lusts of his enemies and finally murdered with her children and thrown into the sea. These episodes have been fully described in my Life of Dion.[2]

14. When Dionysius arrived in Corinth there was hardly a man in Greece who did not feel the desire to see and speak to him. Some, who rejoiced in his misfortunes, came for the pleasure of trampling on a man who had been cast down by fate; others, who were more inter-

1. Dionysius may well have realized that his only hope of safety lay in escap-ing to Greece. Hicetas could not and the Carthaginians would not provide him with a ship: hence his readiness to deal with Timoleon.
2. These outrages were committed by the people of Locri in southern Italy but they are not mentioned in the Life of Dion.

ested in the change in his situation and who sympathized with him, saw in his destiny a convincing proof of the potency with which divine and invisible causes operate in the midst of human and visible circumstances. Certainly that age produced no example either in nature or in art which was so striking as this change of fortune – namely the sight of the man who had not long before been tyrant of Sicily whiling away his time at Corinth in the food market, sitting in a perfumer's shop, drinking diluted wine in the taverns, bandying jokes in public with prostitutes, correcting music-girls in their singing, or earnestly arguing with them about songs for the theatre or the melodies of hymns. Some people thought that Dionysius indulged in these undignified pastimes out of sheer idleness, or because he was naturally easy-going and fond of pleasure, but others considered that he acted deliberately so that the Corinthians should despise him rather than fear him: they believed that he wished to dispel any suspicion that he was oppressed by the change in his way of living or that he still hankered after power, and that by making a parade of these trivial amusements he was acting out a part that was foreign to his nature.

15. For all that, some of his sayings have come down to us, from which it appears that there was nothing ignoble about the way in which he adapted himself to his changed situation. When he arrived at Leucas which, like Syracuse, had originally been colonized by the Corinthians, he said that he had the same feelings as young men who had managed to disgrace themselves. They pass their time gaily with their brothers, but are ashamed to meet their fathers, and in the same way he would gladly settle in Leucas, but felt ashamed to live in her mother-city, Corinth. Again, when in Corinth some stranger made a cheap joke about the conversations with philosophers in which he used to take pleasure during the days of his power, and finally asked him what good was Plato's wisdom to him now, he replied, 'Do you really think that I gained nothing from Plato, when I can bear the changes of fortune that I have suffered as I do?' On another occasion when Aristoxenus the musician and others asked him what fault he had found with Plato and for what reason, Dionysius replied that there were many evils inherent in absolute power but by far the greatest was the fact that of all a tyrant's so-called friends not one will speak his mind, and that it was through such people that he had lost Plato's goodwill. Another man who thought himself witty tried to

make fun of Dionysius by shaking out his cloak when he came into his presence, as is the custom before a tyrant: Dionysius turned the joke against him by asking him to do the same thing before leaving, to make sure that he had not taken anything from the house away with him. On another occasion when Philip of Macedon at a banquet began to sneer at the lyrics and tragedies which Dionysius had left behind him, and expressed surprise as to how a ruler could find so much time for writing, Dionysius smartly retorted, 'He can do it in the hours which you and I and all those whom we call happy fritter away over the wine-bowl.'[1]

Plato had already died by the time that Dionysius arrived in Corinth.[2] But when another famous philosopher,[3] Diogenes of Sinope, met Dionysius for the first time, he remarked, 'How little you deserve to live in this way, Dionysius.' The former tyrant stopped and answered, 'It is kind of you, Diogenes, to sympathize with me in my misfortunes.' 'What do you mean?', retorted Diogenes, 'You surely do not suppose that I am sympathizing with you. I am only angry that a slave such as you, a man who deserved to have grown old and died surrounded by tyranny, as your father did, should now be sharing the luxury and the wit of our society.' When I compare these sayings of Dionysius with the lamentations which Philistus poured out about the daughters of Leptines and how they had fallen from the splendours of tyrannical power to a humble station in life, they sound to me like the complaints of a woman who pines for her alabaster caskets, purple dresses and golden trinkets. At any rate these details have a bearing, it seems to me, upon the design of my biography, and may appeal to readers who are not in too much haste or absorbed in other concerns.

16. If Dionysius' misfortunes appeared extraordinary, Timoleon's good fortune had something almost miraculous about it. Fewer than

1. Philip was notorious for his fondness for drinking.

2. Plato died in 348 B.C. Diogenes came to Corinth in 343 B.C.

3. Diogenes (412–323 B.C.) emigrated from Sinope to Athens where he attached himself to Antisthenes, the founder of the Cynic school of philosophy, and became famous for his practice of its ascetic doctrines. He abjured all possessions, even a roof over his head, and made his home in a large receptacle outside the temple of Cybele. While on a voyage to Aegina he was captured by pirates and sold as a slave to Xeniades, a Corinthian citizen. He arrived in Corinth in 343 B.C. and spent the rest of his life there, preaching his doctrines and tutoring Xeniades' sons.

fifty days had passed since his first landing in Sicily before he had accepted the surrender of the acropolis of Syracuse and had dispatched Dionysius to the Peloponnese. The Corinthians were so encouraged by this success that they sent him a reinforcement of two thousand infantry and two hundred horsemen.[1] This expedition reached Thurii, but found it impossible to cross into Sicily, as the straits were patrolled by a strong Carthaginian fleet. They were therefore obliged to remain there quietly and await their opportunity, but they took advantage of this enforced idleness to perform a most noble action. When the Thurians left their country on an expedition against the neighbouring people of Bruttium, the Corinthians took charge of their city and guarded it as faithfully and scrupulously as if it had been their own.

Meanwhile Hicetas was blockading the acropolis of Syracuse and preventing any food from reaching the Corinthians by sea. He also engaged two foreigners to assassinate Timoleon and sent them to Adranum. Timoleon had never kept a bodyguard about him, and at this time in particular he felt so much confidence in the protection of the god Adranus that he spent his time there in a carefree fashion without fear for his security. The two agents learned by chance that he was about to offer a sacrifice, and so they made their way into the sacred precinct with daggers concealed under their cloaks, mingled with the crowd that stood round the altar, and gradually edged nearer to Timoleon. Then at the very moment that they were about to give the signal to attack, a man struck one of them on the head with his sword and cut him down. Neither the assailant nor the surviving assassin stood his ground. The first fled to a lofty rock and sprang on to it still clutching his sword, while the other laid hold of the altar and begged for Timoleon's pardon on condition that he revealed the plot. When he had been promised his safety, he confessed that he and his dead accomplice had been sent to assassinate Timoleon. In the meanwhile others dragged down the man who had climbed the rock, who kept crying out that he had done no wrong, but had taken a just revenge for the death of his father, whom the other had murdered some while before at Leontini. Several of the bystanders confirmed the truth of his story, and they marvelled at the ingenious workings of fortune, how she makes one thing the cause of another, brings the most incongruous elements into conjunction, interweaves events

1. In the spring of 343 B.C.

which appear to have no relation or connection with one another, and so makes use of their respective beginnings and endings to serve her purpose.

The Corinthians gave this man a reward of ten minas because he had put his just resentment at the service of the deity who was guarding Timoleon. Besides this he had not, on an immediate impulse, expended the wrath which had long burned within him, but for personal reasons had bided his time and put off the desire to avenge his injury until fortune availed herself of it to preserve the general's life. This stroke of fortune had consequences which stretched beyond the present, since it raised the Corinthians' hopes for the future: they believed that men would revere and protect Timoleon and regard him as a minister of the gods who had come with a divinely appointed mission to avenge the wrongs of Sicily.

17. When Hicetas had failed in this attempt on Timoleon's life and saw that more and more Sicilians were going over to him, he began to blame himself for not having taken full advantage of the strong Carthaginian forces which were at hand. Hitherto he had only used them secretly and in small detachments, introducing the troops of his allies by stealth as though he were ashamed of their presence, but now he appealed to the Carthaginian commander Mago to join him with all the forces at his disposal. So Mago with a formidable fleet of a hundred and fifty ships sailed in and took possession of the harbour. At the same time he landed sixty thousand of his infantry and quartered them in the city, so that it seemed to everyone that the subjugation of Sicily by the barbarians which had so long been talked of and expected had finally come to pass. For never before in all their many campaigns in Sicily had the Carthaginians actually captured Syracuse, but now Hicetas had opened the gates and handed over the city, and men could see that it had been transformed into a barbarian camp. In the meanwhile the Corinthian troops who were holding out in the acropolis were in a position of great difficulty and danger: their food was running short because the harbours were blockaded, and they were constantly obliged to divide their forces to beat off skirmishes and assaults upon the walls and to repel all kinds of siege weapons and storming tactics employed by the attacking army.

18. Timoleon came to their rescue by sending them grain from Catana, which was carried in small fishing smacks and light skiffs.

These vessels could run the gauntlet of the Carthaginian fleet, especially in heavy weather, by stealing in between the barbarian triremes, which could not keep together because of the roughness of the sea. Mago and Hicetas soon became aware of these operations and determined to capture the Corinthians' source of supply at Catana, and so they sailed out of Syracuse with the best of their troops. Meanwhile Neon, the Corinthian officer in command of the garrison, noticed from the citadel that the enemy's forces left behind had relaxed their attention and were off their guard. He launched a sudden attack, caught them dispersed, killed a number of them, routed others, and then stormed and occupied the district known as Achradina. This was the strongest and most impregnable part of Syracuse, which is a city consisting of several townships joined together. Neon was now in possession of large supplies of grain and of money. Accordingly he did not withdraw or go back to the citadel but fortified the perimeter of Achradina, and by linking it to the defences of the acropolis succeeded in holding both areas at once. Meanwhile Mago and Hicetas had almost arrived at Catana when a courier from Syracuse overtook them and reported the capture of Achradina. They were alarmed at the news and returned at full speed, so that in the end they not only failed to capture the objective for which they had set out, but lost the position they had originally held.

19. In these successes foresight and courage might very well claim to have played as important a part as fortune, but the one which followed must be entirely credited to good luck. The Corinthian reinforcements had all this time been waiting at Thurii, partly for fear of the Carthaginian warships which were lying in wait for them under the command of Hanno, and partly because of a storm which had lasted for many days and had made the sea too rough for them to attempt the crossing: they now set out to travel over land through Bruttium. They used a combination of force and persuasion to make their way through this barbarian territory, and finally arrived at Rhegium, where a violent storm was still raging at sea. Meanwhile the Carthaginian admiral had formed the conclusion that the Corinthians would never venture out and that there was thus no object in his continuing to keep watch for them. So he devised, as he imagined, a masterly ruse. He ordered his sailors to crown themselves with garlands, decked out his triremes with scarlet battle-flags and Greek shields, and sailed

off towards Syracuse. As he sailed past the acropolis at full speed, his crews clapped their hands and laughed, and he shouted out that he had just defeated and captured the Corinthian reinforcements as they were attempting to cross the straits, imagining that in this way he would make the besieged garrison despair of relief. But while he was playing the fool and trying to impose on his opponents, the Corinthians had already arrived in Rhegium. There they found nobody to bar their passage, and as the gale had unexpectedly died down and left the sea completely calm and smooth, they quickly embarked in the ferry boats and fishing craft which they found at hand and crossed to Sicily; indeed, there was such a dead calm that they were able to make their horses swim alongside and tow them by the reins.

20. As soon as they had all crossed, Timoleon came to meet them and immediately took possession of Messana. There the reinforcements were united with his other troops and the whole army marched on Syracuse. In taking the offensive in this way he was relying more on the good fortune and success he had so far enjoyed than on the strength of his army, for his entire force numbered no more than four thousand. However, when Mago learned of his approach he became alarmed and perplexed, and his suspicions were increased by the following circumstance. In the marshes around the city which receive much fresh water from springs and rivers flowing to the sea, there lived great numbers of eels which could always be caught by anybody who cared to fish for them, and whenever there was a pause in the fighting, the mercenary soldiers of both sides used to meet and fish there. As they were all Greeks and had no reason to hate each other personally, these men would bravely risk their lives in battle, but at times of truce they would meet and converse in the friendliest fashion. So on this occasion, as they fished, they spoke enthusiastically of how rich the sea was in fish and of the character of the city and the neighbourhood. Then one of the Corinthian garrison said, 'You are Greeks like us. Can it be that you really want to hand over a great city such as this with all its riches and amenities to the barbarians? Do you really want to plant the Carthaginians, who are the cruellest and wickedest people on earth, so much nearer to our country? You ought to pray that there were many more Sicilies to stand between them and Greece. Or do you imagine that these men have gathered an army from the Pillars of Hercules and the Atlantic to risk their lives for the sake of

Hicetas and his family? If Hicetas possessed the judgement of a real ruler, he would not be trying to drive out the founders of his city, or leading his country's enemies against her, when he could be enjoying the honour and authority which would be his by right if he allied himself to Timoleon and the Corinthians.' The news of these talks quickly spread through the mercenaries' camp, and implanted in Mago's mind the suspicion that a plot was being hatched against him; he was all the more ready to believe this because he had long been searching for a pretext to leave the island. So although Hicetas begged him to remain and tried to convince him how far superior his forces were to the enemy's, Mago preferred to believe that Timoleon's courage and good fortune more than compensated for his weakness in numbers. And so he weighed anchor at once and sailed for Libya, thus allowing Sicily to slip out of his hands to his own discredit and for no reason that anyone could satisfactorily explain.

21. On the day after Mago's departure Timoleon drew up his troops to attack. But when the Corinthians learned of his flight and saw the docks completely empty of ships, they could not help laughing at his cowardice, and sent a crier round the city to offer a reward for anyone who could tell them where the Carthaginian fleet had gone. In spite of this Hicetas still put on a bold front and showed no sign of relaxing his grip on the city: instead he held on tenaciously to those quarters which were well fortified and difficult to attack. Accordingly Timoleon divided his forces. He himself led the assault along the river Anapus, where the fighting was likely to be fiercest, and ordered another force under Isias the Corinthian to advance on the city from Achradina. A third assault was directed against Epipolae by Deinarchus and Demaretus, the officers who had brought the reinforcements from Corinth. The attack was launched from all three quarters at once, and Hicetas' troops were soon overwhelmed and routed. To have captured the city by storm and gained control of it so quickly once the enemy had been driven out was undoubtedly due to the valour of the soldiers and the skill of their general, but the fact that not a single Corinthian was killed or even wounded can only be ascribed to Timoleon's luck: this good fortune of his seemed to rival even his personal courage, so as to make those who read his story marvel even more at the providence which smiled on all his undertakings than at his own achievements. His fame now spread not only

over Sicily and Italy, but within a few days the news of his success
was echoing through every state in Greece, and in Corinth, where the
people were still in doubt as to whether the second expedition had
arrived in Sicily, the news of its safe crossing and of its victory
arrived at the same moment. The triumph of his campaign was
complete and fortune added a special lustre to his achievements
because of the extraordinary speed with which they were accomplished.

22. When Timoleon had captured the citadel, he did not repeat
Dion's mistake of sparing the building because of the beauty of its
architecture, or the money it had cost to build. He was determined
not to arouse the suspicions which had brought first discredit and
finally disaster upon his predecessor, and so he had it proclaimed that
any Syracusan who wished could come with a crowbar and help to
cast down the bulwarks of tyranny. Thereupon the whole population
went up to the fortress, and taking that day and its proclamation to
mark a truly secure foundation for their freedom, they overthrew and
demolished not only the citadel but also the palaces and tombs of the
tyrants. Timoleon immediately had the site levelled and built the
courts of justice over it, thus delighting the Syracusans by displaying
the supremacy of the rule of the people over tyranny.

But once he had captured the city, Timoleon found it empty of
citizens. Many of the Syracusans had perished in the various wars and
uprisings, while others had escaped from the rule of the tyrants into
exile. The population had declined so rapidly that the market-place of
Syracuse had become thickly overgrown, and horses were pastured in
the midst of it, while their grooms stretched out beside them on the
grass. In the other cities almost without exception deer and wild boar
roamed at large, and those who had leisure could hunt them in the
streets and around the walls. Those citizens who had established
themselves in castles and strongholds were unwilling to obey any
summons or venture down to the city, and they had come to regard
the market-place, political activity and public speaking with fear and
horror, because they had so often proved the breeding ground for
their tyrants. Accordingly Timoleon and the Syracusans decided to
write to the Corinthians and urge them to send settlers from Greece.
One reason for this was that the land would otherwise be doomed to
lie uncultivated, and another was that they expected a great invasion

from Africa. They had learned that Mago had committed suicide, that the Carthaginians in their rage at his mishandling of the expedition had impaled his dead body, and that they were gathering a great force with the intention of crossing into Sicily in the following summer.

23. When these letters from Timoleon were delivered at Corinth, they were accompanied by delegates from Syracuse who begged the Corinthians to take the city under their protection and become its founders once again. For their part the Corinthians would not take any advantage of this opportunity to enrich themselves, nor did they annex the city. Instead they first visited the sacred games in Greece and the principal religious festivals, and sent heralds to proclaim that they had overthrown the tyranny in Syracuse and driven out the tyrant: they now invited former citizens of Syracuse and any other Sicilian Greeks who wished to settle in the city to go and live there as free and independent men and divided the land among them on just and equal terms. Secondly they dispatched messages to Asia Minor and to the islands, where they had learned that most of the scattered groups of exiles were living. These men they invited to come to Corinth, and they promised that the Corinthians would at their own expense provide them with leaders, ships and a safe passage to Syracuse. Through these proclamations the city of Corinth won for herself the most well-deserved praise and the noblest fame for her actions in liberating the country from its tyrants, rescuing it from the barbarians, and restoring it to its legitimate citizens.

However even when all the exiles had assembled at Corinth their numbers were still too few, and so they begged to be allowed to invite colonists from Corinth and from the rest of Greece. Then after they had raised their numbers to as many as ten thousand, they sailed for Syracuse. In the meanwhile multitudes of people from Italy and Sicily had flocked to Timoleon, and when he found that the total of immigrants had risen to sixty thousand, he sold the houses in the city for a thousand talents. This measure secured for the original owners the right to buy back their houses and at the same time raised a large sum of money for the benefit of the community. Before this the public funds had sunk so low, not only for any civil requirements but also for the financing of the war, that the community had been obliged to put up the public statues for auction. A meeting of the assembly had been held, and a vote taken on the case of each statue, as if they had been officials submitting their accounts. It was on this occasion, so the story goes, that the Syracusans voted to save the statue of Gelon, their former tyrant – although they condemned all the rest to be sold – because they admired and honoured him for the victory he had won over the Carthaginians at Himera.[1]

24. Now that the life of the city was beginning to revive and its population to be replenished as citizens poured in from every quarter, Timoleon resolved to set the other Sicilian cities free, and to root out every tyrant in the island. He therefore invaded the territory of these rulers[2] and compelled Hicetas to abandon his alliance with the Carthaginians and to agree to pull down his fortresses and live as a private citizen in Leontini. Soon afterwards Leptines, the tyrant who ruled Apollonia and a number of other small towns, saw that he was in danger of being captured and surrendered voluntarily, whereupon Timoleon spared his life and sent him to Corinth. He considered that it would be an admirable lesson for the tyrants to live in the mother-city which had colonized Sicily and where all the rest of the Greeks could see them leading the humble life of exiles. Besides this he was anxious that his own mercenaries should not remain idle, but should have the opportunity to enrich themselves by plundering enemy territory. He then returned to Syracuse in order to supervise the remodelling of the constitution and to help Cephalus and Dionysius, the law-givers who had come from Corinth, to embody its most important provisions in the most satisfactory form. But at the same time he sent out an expedition under Deinarchus and Demaretus into the western districts of Sicily, which were still controlled by the Carthaginians. Here they persuaded many cities to revolt against the barbarians and not only secured great quantities of plunder for themselves, but succeeded in raising money from the spoils to finance the impending war.

25. Meanwhile[3] the Carthaginians landed at Lilybaeum[4] with an army of seventy thousand men, two hundred warships and a thousand transports. These ships carried artillery, four-horse chariots, abundant supplies of food and other military stores. The Carthaginians had had

enough of the minor operations of earlier campaigns and were deter-mined to drive the Greeks out of Sicily in a single offensive, and in-deed their force was quite enough to overwhelm all the Sicilian Greeks, even if the latter had not been disunited and weakened by their own internal quarrels. When the Carthaginians learned that the territory they controlled was being ravaged by the Corinthians, they were enraged and immediately sent an expedition against them under the command of Hasdrubal and Hamilcar. The news quickly reached Syracuse and the people were so alarmed by the reports of the size of the enemy's forces that Timoleon could only with difficulty prevail upon three thousand men out of the many tens of thousands of able-bodied Syracusans to take up arms and march out with him. His force of mercenaries was only four thousand strong, and of these about a thousand lost heart as they neared the Carthaginians, and slunk back to Syracuse. They protested that Timoleon must be out of his wits, and that the judgement one should expect of a general of his years had obviously deserted him. Not only was he advancing with five thous-and infantry and a thousand cavalry against an enemy force of seventy thousand, but he was leading his troops on a march of eight days away from Syracuse. This would make it impossible for any fugitives from the battle to escape, and those who fell on the battlefield could expect no burial. For his part Timoleon thought it an advantage that these men had revealed their cowardice before the fighting began. As for the rest he encouraged them and led them by forced marches to the banks of the river Crimesus,[1] where he had heard that the Carthagin-ians were concentrating their forces.

26. Timoleon was climbing a hill, from the crest of which he expected to gain a view of the enemy's troops and their camp, when quite by chance he met a convoy of mules laden with parsley. The soldiers thought that this was an unlucky omen, because it is the custom to place wreaths of this herb upon tombs – hence the saying concerning anyone who is dangerously ill, 'He needs nothing but his parsley.' Timoleon was anxious to get rid of their superstitious fears and raise

1. Timoleon had decided to meet the Carthaginians in their own territory. They were on their way to Entella, one of the towns which had been incited by Deinarchus and Demaretus to revolt. The Crimesus which is less than thirty miles from Lilybaeum was the only stream between the Carthaginians and Entella when they were intercepted by Timoleon.

their spirits, and so he ordered a halt and made a short speech to meet the occasion. He ended it by telling them that the crown of victory had of its own accord fallen into their hands before the battle. He was referring to the fact that it is this very herb which the Corinthians use to crown their victors at the Isthmian games[1] since they regard parsley as the sacred wreath of their country. Certainly at that date parsley was still used at the Isthmian, as it is now at the Nemean games, for it was only quite recently that the pine was introduced at Corinth. So when Timoleon had finished speaking, he took some parsley and crowned himself with it, whereupon the officers and soldiers around him all followed his example. Besides this the diviners noticed two eagles flying towards them, one of which was clutching a snake in its talons, while the other uttered a loud and inspiring cry as it flew. The diviners pointed these out to the soldiers, and the whole army with one accord began to pray and call upon the gods.

27. The time of year was the early summer:[2] the month of Thargelion was nearing its end and the summer solstice was approaching. A thick mist hung over the river, which at first completely enveloped the plain, so that nothing could be seen of the enemy: a confused and indistinguishable noise which echoed up to the brow of the hill was the only indication that their huge army was on the move. When the Corinthians had reached the summit, they halted, laid down their shields and rested. Meanwhile the sun was climbing towards the meridian and drawing the mist into the upper air. The thick haze began to gather together and drift towards the heights, so that it hung in clouds over the mountain crests, while the lower parts of the valley became clear and open: the river Crimesus came into view and the enemy could be seen crossing it. First came the four-horse chariots formidably arrayed for battle, and next a body of ten thousand heavy infantry carrying white shields.[3] These the Corin-

1. The Isthmian games were held every other year, and the Nemean games in the first and fourth years of each Olympiad: the Pythian games were mainly musical contests. The prize for the last-named, which were held at Delphi, was a wreath of bay; at Olympia the prize was a wreath of wild olive.

2. June 341 B.C.

3. This was the Sacred Band, a crack formation of the Carthaginian army: they were equipped with large shields covered with elephant hides. According to Diodorus they numbered two thousand five hundred, so that the remaining seven thousand five hundred may have been ordinary Libyans.

thians supposed to be Carthaginians, judging by the brilliance of their armour and the slow pace and strict discipline of their advance. After them the troops of other nationalities straggled along making the crossing in a confused and disorderly fashion. Timoleon at once grasped the fact that it was the river which controlled the speed of the enemy's advance and gave the Greeks the opportunity of cutting off and engaging whatever numbers of the enemy they chose. He pointed out to his men how the enemy's main body had been divided by the river, so that some had already crossed, while others were still awaiting their turn. Next, he ordered Demaretus to take the cavalry and charge the picked troops consisting of Carthaginians, so as to throw their ranks into confusion before they could take up their battle formation. He then marched down into the plain and drew up his own order of battle, for which he placed the Sicilian Greeks on the wings, distributed a few of his mercenaries among them, and massed the Syracusans and the best of his mercenary troops in the centre. Then he waited a little to watch the effect of the cavalry charge. He saw that the horsemen could not get to close quarters with the Carthaginians, because the chariots drove up and down and protected their front. The horsemen were compelled to wheel about continually so as to prevent their own formation from being broken up, and to charge in short rushes whenever the opportunity offered. At last Timoleon snatched up his shield and called upon the infantry to take heart and follow him. His voice seemed to them to have taken on a superhuman strength and volume, whether it was from emotion that he raised it so high because of the intensity of the fighting and the enthusiasm which it inspired, or whether, as most of his men felt at the time, some god were speaking through his lips. His troops instantly responded with encouraging shouts, and urged him to lead them on and not wait a moment longer. Thereupon he ordered the cavalry to ride round the line of chariots and attack the enemy from the flank; at the same time he made his own front ranks close up and lock their shields, and then with the trumpet sounding the charge he bore down upon the Carthaginians.

28. The enemy resisted his first attack courageously, and thanks to the protection of their iron breastplates and helmets and the great shields which they held in front of them, they were able to ward off

the spear-thrusts of the Greeks. But when they closed to sword-fighting and the struggle became a matter of skill no less than of strength, suddenly a tremendous storm burst upon them from the hills with deafening peals of thunder and brilliant flashes of lightning. The dark clouds which until then had hovered over the mountain peaks descended upon the battlefield mingled with sudden gusts of wind, rain and hail. The tempest enveloped the Greeks from behind and beat upon their backs, but it struck the barbarians in the face, while the lightning dazzled their eyes as the storm swept violently along with torrents of rain and continual flashes darting out from the clouds. These were terrible disadvantages, especially to inexperienced troops, and above all, it seems, the roar of the thunder and the beating of the rain and hail upon the men's armour prevented them from hearing their officers' commands. Besides this the mud also proved a great hindrance to the Carthaginians – who were not lightly equipped, but clad in full armour, as I have described – and so did the water which filled the bosoms of their tunics and made them heavy and unwieldy in their movements. It was easy for the Greeks to fell them, and once on the ground it was impossible for them to rise again from the mud because they were encumbered by their armour. The Crimesus, which had already been swollen to a torrent by the rain, overflowed its banks because the great numbers who were crossing it impeded its course. At the same time the surrounding plain, into which many ravines and hollows ran down from the hills, was flooded with rivulets which poured over the ground unconfined to any channels, and among these the Carthaginians floundered and could only move with great difficulty. At last as the storm still beat upon them and the Greeks had broken their front line of four hundred men, the main body turned and fled. Many were overtaken in the plain and cut down as they ran, many were caught by the river and swept away as they became entangled with those who were trying to cross, but most of the slaughter was done by the Greek light-armed troops who intercepted the fugitives and dispatched them as they made for the hills. At any rate it is said that of the ten thousand who fell on the battlefield three thousand were Carthaginians, a fearful loss to the city, for these men had no superiors in birth, in wealth or in military prowess. Nor is there any record of so many Carthaginians ever having fallen in a single engagement before; this was because they generally employed Libyans, Iberians and Numidians to fight their battles, so that when they were defeated the loss was borne by other nations.[1]

29. The Greeks discovered the exalted rank of those who had fallen through the richness of the spoils. They crossed the river and seized the Carthaginian camp, and those who stripped the bodies paid little attention to bronze or iron, so great was the abundance of silver and gold. A great many prisoners were stolen and hidden by the soldiers and later privately sold,[2] but even so five thousand were delivered into the public stock, and two hundred of the four-horsed chariots were also captured. But the most glorious and magnificent spectacle of all was Timoleon's tent, which was surrounded by piles of booty of every kind, among them being a thousand breastplates of particularly fine workmanship, and ten thousand shields. There was only a small number of men to strip so many bodies, and the quantities of plunder which they found were so immense that it was not until the third day after the battle that they erected a trophy.

Timoleon sent home to Corinth the handsomest pieces of the captured armour, together with the dispatch announcing his success, for he wished his native city to be the envy of the whole world. His ambition was that in Corinth, alone of Greek cities, men should see the most conspicuous temples adorned not with the spoils taken from Greek states, melancholy offerings obtained by the slaughter of men of their own race and blood, but decked with ornaments won from the barbarians and bearing honourable inscriptions which testified to the justice as well as the courage of the victors: in this instance the memorial proclaimed that the Corinthians and their general Timoleon freed the Greeks living in Sicily from the yoke of Carthage and thus dedicated these thank-offerings to the gods.

30. After the battle Timoleon left his mercenaries to plunder the Carthaginian dominions in the west of the island and returned to Syracuse. There he expelled from Sicily the thousand mercenaries who had deserted him before the battle, and compelled them to leave Syracuse before sunset. These men crossed into Italy and were

1. According to Diodorus the Carthaginians lost twelve thousand five hundred men in this battle, including the whole of the Sacred Band.

2. The same fate befell many of the Athenian prisoners captured after the Sicilian expedition.

there treacherously massacred by the Bruttians: such was the vengeance that the gods took upon them for their betrayal of Timoleon. But now Mamercus of Catana and Hicetas – either because they were jealous of Timoleon's successes or because they feared him as an implacable enemy who would never trust a tyrant – once more formed an alliance with the Carthaginians and urged them to send a general and an army, if they did not wish to be driven out of Sicily altogether. Accordingly Gisco sailed across with a fleet of seventy ships.[1] His force also included a contingent of Greek mercenaries: the Carthaginians had never recruited Greek soldiers before,[2] but by now they had come to admire them as irresistible troops and the most warlike to be found anywhere. Mamercus and Hicetas joined forces in the territory of Messana and there killed four hundred of Timoleon's mercenaries who had been sent to reinforce the local inhabitants: next they laid an ambush near the town named Ietae,[3] which was situated in the part of the island controlled by Carthage, and annihilated the force of mercenaries commanded by Euthymus of Leucas. These apparent reverses, however, made Timoleon's good fortune appear even more remarkable. For this band of mercenaries included some of the men who, under the command of Philomelus the Phocian and Onomarchus, had seized Delphi and taken part in the plundering of the sacred treasures.[4] This act of sacrilege caused them to be universally detested and shunned as men who had put themselves under a curse. For some time they roamed about the Peloponnese, and there they were recruited by Timoleon, who at that time was unable to enlist any other troops. Since they had come to Sicily they had been victorious in every action they had entered under his command, but after his greatest battles had been fought, he had sent them out to help the other Sicilian peoples and there they had perished to a man, not all at once but in a succession of engagements. Thus justice exacted her penalty, while at the same time Timoleon's good fortune was sustained through a stroke of retribu-

1. In the summer of 340 B.C.
2. This statement seems quite inconsistent with ch. 20.
3. Some ten miles south of Palermo.
4. The so-called Sacred War of 356–346 B.C. originated with the refusal of the Phocians to pay a fine imposed by the Delphic authorities on the ground that they had tilled sacred territory. The Phocians who were allied with the Athenians and Spartans against the Thebans, Locrians and Thessalians supported the expenses of the war by plundering the sacred treasures.

tion which ensured that no harm should come to the good through the punishment of the wicked. In short the favour which the gods showed towards Timoleon was a cause for wonder just as much in his apparent reverses as in his successes.

31. However, the people of Syracuse were angry at the insults which the tyrants heaped upon them after these defeats. Mamercus who had a high opinion of himself as a writer of poems and tragedies boasted of his victory over the mercenaries, and when he dedicated their shields to the gods, he composed the following insulting inscription

> These gilded bucklers of purple with amber and ivory inlaid
> Proved no match in the field for our cheap little, plain little shields.

Not long afterwards, while Timoleon was engaged in an expedition against the town of Calauria,[1] Hicetas made a raid on Syracusan territory, carried off much plunder and caused a great deal of wanton damage. On his return he marched close by the walls of Calauria to show his contempt for Timoleon, who only had a small force with him. Timoleon allowed him to pass, but then pursued him with cavalry and light-armed troops. When Hicetas learned that he was being followed, he crossed the river Damurias and halted on the far side to receive the enemy: he was encouraged to do this by the difficulty of the crossing and the steepness of the river banks. This caused an astonishing outburst of rivalry among the officers of Timoleon's cavalry, which delayed the attack. Not one of them was willing to follow behind his comrades, but each demanded the honour of leading the charge himself. As it was certain that their crossing would be disorderly if they crowded and tried to push their way past one another, Timoleon decided to settle the order of precedence by lot. He therefore took a seal-ring from each of the commanders, dropped them all into his cloak, mixed them up, and held up to them the first one that came out, which, as luck would have it, displayed as its device a trophy of victory. When the young officers saw this, they gave a shout of delight and, without waiting for the other rings to be drawn, all made their way across the river-bed and closed with the enemy. Their charge proved irresistible and Hicetas' troops fled: they all threw away their arms and left a thousand dead upon the field.

1. Some fifteen miles north of Syracuse.

32. A little later Timoleon invaded the territory of the Leontines and captured Hicetas alive, together with his son Eupolemus, and Euthymus the commander of his cavalry. The soldiers bound the three and led them into Timoleon's presence. Hicetas and his young son were put to death as tyrants and traitors, and Euthymus, although he was a man of exceptional courage, who had shown great daring in battle, was likewise executed without mercy, because of an insult which he was accused of having uttered against the Corinthians. It was alleged that when the Corinthians were marching against Leontini, Euthymus had made a speech to the people telling them that they had nothing to fear if

> Corinthian women came out from their homes.[1]

The truth is that the great majority of mankind are more offended by a contemptuous word than by a hostile action, and find it easier to put up with an injury than an insult. An act of self-defence is tolerated from an enemy as a matter of necessity, while insults are regarded as springing from an excess of hatred or spite.

33. On Timoleon's return from Leontini the Syracusans brought the wives and daughters of Hicetas and his friends before the assembly to be tried in public and later put them to death. This seems to have been the most cruel and repellent action in the whole of Timoleon's career, for if he had opposed the sentence it would not have been carried out. But apparently he chose not to interfere, and abandoned the victims to the fury of the citizens and their desire to avenge the wrongs done to Dion, who had driven out Dionysius. On that occasion it had been Hicetas who had had Dion's wife Arete thrown into the sea alive, together with her son, who was still a young boy and her sister Aristomache, as I have related in my Life of Dion.[2]

34. After this Timoleon marched to Catana against Mamercus, defeated and routed his army in a pitched battle near the river Abolus, and killed over two thousand of his troops, many of whom were Carthaginian auxiliaries sent him by Gisco. The result of this

1. The line is a parody of Euripides' Medea, 215, where the heroine says to the chorus

> Women of Corinth, I have left my home.

2. See Life of Dion, ch. 58.

victory was that the Carthaginians sued for peace and a treaty was negotiated. The terms were that they should keep the territory west of the river Lycus;[1] that any of the inhabitants of this region who so wished should be allowed to emigrate to Syracusan territory with their families and property, and that they should renounce their alliances with the tyrants. This agreement reduced Mamercus to despair, and he sailed to Italy to try to form an alliance with the Lucanians against Timoleon and the Syracusans. But he was deserted by his followers who put their triremes about, sailed back to Sicily, and handed over Catana to Timoleon, so that Mamercus was obliged to seek refuge with Hippo, the tyrant of Messana. Timoleon followed him and blockaded Messana by land and sea, and Hippo was captured as he tried to escape by ship. The people of Messana brought him to the public theatre and summoned their children from the schools to witness that most exemplary of spectacles, the punishment of a tyrant: they then tortured him and put him to death. As for Mamercus, he surrendered to Timoleon on condition that he should be put on trial before the people of Syracuse and that Timoleon should not be his accuser. He was taken to Syracuse, and when he was brought before the assembly, he tried to deliver a speech which he had prepared a long while before. But he was continually shouted down, and when he saw that the assembly was inexorably hostile to him, he threw away his cloak, rushed across the theatre, and dashed his head against one of the stone steps in an effort to kill himself. He did not enjoy the good fortune of dying in this way, but was taken away while he was still alive and crucified like a common thief.

35. In this way Timoleon rooted out all the tyrannies in Sicily and put an end to the wars between her rulers. When he had first arrived, he found that the island had been reduced almost to a wilderness by its troubles and had grown hateful to its inhabitants. He transformed it into a country so civilized and so desirable in the eyes of the rest of the world that foreigners came from across the sea to settle in the places from which the native inhabitants had fled before. Acragas and Gela, for example, two great cities which had been sacked and left desolate by the Carthaginians after the war with Athens, were now repopulated, the first by Megellus and Pharistus from Elea, and the

1. No such river is known. Plutarch may have mistaken it for the R. Helycus, the Carthaginian boundary fixed in a treaty with Dionysius I.

second by Gorgus who sailed from Ceos and brought back with him a number of the original citizens. To all these colonists Timoleon offered not only security and tranquillity while they were establishing themselves after many years of war, but also supplied their wants and took especial pleasure in assisting them, so that they cherished him as a founder. These feelings were shared by every other city in the island, so that no peace could be concluded, no laws laid down, no land divided between colonists, and no constitutional changes made to the general satisfaction, unless Timoleon took a hand in them: he was, as it were, the master-craftsman who, when a building is nearing completion, adds a final touch of his artistry which makes the work pleasing to gods and men.

36. Although in Timoleon's lifetime there were many Greeks, such as Timotheus,[1] Agesilaus, Pelopidas and Epaminondas (Timoleon's especial model), who rose to positions of great power and accomplished great things, yet there was in these men's achievements an element of violence and of laborious effort which detracts from their lustre, and which in some instances caused their authors to be blamed or to regret what they had done. But in the whole career of Timoleon, if we set aside his treatment of his brother, which was forced upon him by circumstances, there is not a single action to which we could not fitly, as Timaeus says, apply the words of Sophocles

> Ye gods, what Cypris, or what love divine
> Took part in this?[2]

The poetry of Antimachus[3] and the paintings of Dionysius[4] (both of them men of Colophon), for all their strength and energy, leave us with an impression of something strained and forced about them; on the other hand the paintings of Nicomachus[5] and the verses of Homer, in addition to the power and grace which they possess, strike us as having been executed with an extraordinary ease and spontaneity. In the same way if we contrast the generalship of Epaminondas and

1. A distinguished Athenian commander of the first half of the fourth century B.C.

2. Nauck, Tragoedia Graeca Fragmenta, p. 316.

3. A contemporary of Plato and an epic poet, author of a poem on the battle of the Seven against Thebes.

4. A portrait painter mentioned by Aristotle.

5. A famous portrait painter of the time of Alexander the Great.

of Agesilaus – both of whom faced great difficulties and had to overcome tremendous odds – with that of Timoleon, the glories of whose achievements seem to have been accomplished almost without effort, it strikes us not merely as the product of good fortune, if we consider the matter justly and carefully, but of courage reinforced by fortune. Timoleon himself put down all his successes to fortune, for in his letters to his friends in Corinth and in his public speeches to the Syracusans he often remarked that he was grateful to the divine power which had evidently determined to save Sicily and had designated him as its liberator. It is significant that he built in his house a shrine to Automatia, the goddess of Chance and dedicated the whole building to the divine spirit of Fortune. The house he lived in had been chosen for him by the Syracusans as a prize for his achievements in the field, and they presented him with the pleasantest and most beautiful estate in their territory: here he spent most of his leisure with his wife and children after he had brought them from Corinth. He never returned to his native land, nor did he play any part in the troubles of Greece at this time, nor expose himself to political factions, the rock upon which so many generals have been wrecked because of their insatiable pursuit of honours and power. Instead he remained in Sicily enjoying the blessings which he himself had brought about, the greatest of which was the spectacle of so many cities and tens of thousands of people whose happiness was due to his efforts.

37. However, every lark, as Simonides tells us, must grow a crest, and every democracy must produce, it seems, a false accuser, and so even Timoleon found himself attacked by two of the Syracusan demagogues, Laphystius and Demaenetus. Laphystius on one occasion tried to make him give bail and appear at a trial, and Timoleon refused to allow the people to shout the man down or prevent his action: he told them that he had willingly endured all the trials and dangers of his campaigns for just this object, that any Syracusan who wished could have recourse to the laws. When the other demagogue, Demaenetus, repeatedly attacked Timoleon's generalship in the assembly, he offered no reply except to say that he owed thanks to the gods for having granted his prayer that he might live to see the Syracusans in possession of the right of free speech. Timoleon had accomplished what were universally regarded as the greatest and

most glorious achievements of any Greek of his time: he was indeed the only man who had actually performed those exploits which the orators of the various national assemblies were constantly exhorting his countrymen to attempt. His usual good fortune had removed him from the troubles which befell his native land, and saved him from staining his hands with the blood of his compatriots. He had shown courage and resourcefulness against barbarians and tyrants, and justice and moderation towards the Greeks and his friends; he had set up most of his trophies without causing tears to be shed or mourning to be worn by his fellow-citizens of Syracuse or of Corinth, and in less than eight years he had restored Sicily to its inhabitants, delivered from the strife and disorders which had constantly plagued it in the past.

Now at last as he grew old his sight began to fail him, and then after a little while he became completely blind. He had done nothing himself to bring on this condition, nor was he the victim of any wanton trick of fortune, but this impairment of his vision was hereditary, it seems, and came upon him with advancing years: it is said that several of his kindred lost their sight in the same way after it had been weakened by old age. Athanis records that Timoleon was already suffering from a cataract when he was in his camp at Mylae at the time of his campaign against Hippo and Mamercus, and says that it was clear to everybody that he was going blind: however he did not abandon the siege for this reason, but persevered until he had taken the tyrants prisoner. Then, as soon as he returned to Syracuse, he laid down his post of commander-in-chief and begged the Syracusans to relieve him of it, since the war had been successfully concluded.

38. It was to be expected that Timoleon would endure his misfortune without complaint, but what was more remarkable was the honour and gratitude which the Syracusans showed him in his affliction. They frequently visited him in person, and would often bring to his town or country house any strangers who might be staying in the city, so as to let them set eyes on the benefactor of Syracuse. They were delighted and intensely proud of the fact that he had chosen to spend the rest of his life among them, and had disregarded the brilliant reception which had been prepared for him in Greece in consequence of his successes. And of all the many decrees that were passed and

ceremonials enacted in his honour, none is more impressive than the resolution voted by the Syracusans that whenever they engaged in a war against a foreign enemy, they would employ a Corinthian as their commander. They also honoured Timoleon in the procedure which they adopted in the meetings of their assembly, for whereas they would discuss ordinary business among themselves, as soon as any important debate was impending, they would send for Timoleon. On these occasions he would drive through the market-place in a carriage drawn by mules to the theatre, where their assemblies were held. The carriage would then be ushered in and the people would greet him all in unison and call upon him by name. He would return their greeting and allow a short pause for their salutations and applause, after which he would listen carefully to the subject of the debate and finally give his own opinion. When this had been confirmed by a vote, his attendants would escort his carriage out of the theatre, the citizens would cheer and applaud him on his way, and would then proceed at once to dispatch the rest of their business by themselves.

39. Such was the honour and affection with which Timoleon was cherished in his last years. He had come to be regarded as the father of the whole people, and at last a mild illness combined with old age to end his life.[1] A period of several days was decreed for the city to prepare his funeral, and for the inhabitants of the country districts and foreign visitors to assemble. The ceremony was performed with great splendour and the bier, superbly decorated, was carried by a group of young men chosen by lot over the ground where the palace of Dionysius had stood before Timoleon had had it pulled down. The bier was followed by many thousands of men and women, all of them crowned with garlands and dressed in white, so that their appearance suggested a festival rather than a funeral. Their tears and their lamentations which mingled with their praises of the dead man clearly showed that this was no merely formal tribute nor a ceremony enacted in obedience to a decree, but a true expression of their sorrow and gratitude. At last when the bier was placed upon the funeral pyre, a man named Demetrius, who possessed the most powerful voice of any herald of his time, read out the following ordinance:

1. In 337 or 336 B.C.

The people of Syracuse have decreed the burial of Timoleon the Corinthian, son of Timodemus, at public cost of two hundred minas. They resolve to honour his memory for all time to come with annual contests of music, horse-racing and gymnastics, because he overthrew the tyrants, subdued the barbarians, repopulated the largest of the devastated cities, and then restored their laws to the people of Sicily.

They buried him in the market-place, and later surrounded the precinct with a colonnade, built wrestling-schools, set it apart as a gymnasium for young men, and named it the Timoleonteum. They continued to apply the laws and the constitution which Timoleon had established, and lived for many years[1] in happiness and prosperity.

1. For about twenty years, after which Agathocles set up another autocracy in 317 B.C.

5

DEMOSTHENES[1]

[384–322 B.C.]

* *

*

THE famous ode, Sosius, which celebrates Alcibiades' victory in the chariot race at Olympia,[2] tells us that the first necessity for a happy life is to be born a native of a famous city. But in my opinion if a man is to enjoy true happiness, this will depend most of all upon his character and disposition, and consequently it will make no difference if he happens to belong to an obscure and humble city, any more than it need do if he is born the son of a small or a plain-looking woman. It would be absurd to suppose that Iulis,[3] which is no more than a small town on the little island of Ceos, or Aegina,[4] which a famous Athenian[5] appealed to his countrymen to subdue because it was 'the eyesore of Piraeus', should be capable of producing a fine actor or poet but not a man who was just, independent, wise and magnanimous. It is true, certainly, that the arts, since one of their objects is to bring fame and employment to the men who practise them, are likely to wither in cities which are poor and undistinguished: but virtue, on the other hand, like a tough and hardy plant, will take root and flourish in any place where it can lay hold upon a noble nature and a persevering spirit. In the same way, if we fall below the standards which we ought to attain in thought and action, we must not blame the insignificance of our native city, but rather our own shortcomings.

1. For places mentioned in this *Life*, see Maps 1 and 2, pp. 433–5.
2. Plutarch remarks here, in parenthesis, that the ode may be the work of Euripides or of some other poet. In his *Life of Alcibiades*, ch. 11 where he quotes from the poem, he attributes it to Euripides.
3. Birthplace of Simonides, the lyric poet.
4. Birthplace of Polus a famous actor.
5. See *Life of Pericles*, ch. 5.

2. However, when a man has undertaken to compose a history, the sources for which are not easily available in his own country, or do not even exist there, the case is quite different. Because most of his material must be sought abroad or may be scattered among different owners, his first concern must be to base himself upon a city which is famous, well populated and favourable to the arts. Here he may not only have access to all kinds of books, but through hearsay and personal inquiry he may succeed in uncovering facts which often escape the chroniclers and are preserved in more reliable form in human memory, and with these advantages he can avoid the danger of publishing a work which is defective in many or even the most essential details. For my part I belong to a small city and I choose to live there to prevent its becoming even smaller. When I lived in Rome and other parts of Italy, my public duties and the number of pupils who came to me to study philosophy took up so much of my time that I had no leisure to practise speaking the Latin tongue, and so it was not until quite late in life that I began to study Roman literature. When I did I made a surprising discovery, which was nevertheless a genuine one. I found that it was not so much through words that I was enabled to grasp the meaning of things, but rather that it was my knowledge of things which helped me to understand the words that denoted them. To be able to appreciate the beauty and the pithiness of the Roman style, the figures of speech, the oratorical rhythms and the other embellishments of the language would be a most graceful and enjoyable accomplishment. But the study and practice required would be formidable for a man of my age, and I must leave such ambitions to those who have the youth and the leisure to pursue them.

3. Accordingly in this fifth book of my *Parallel Lives* which is devoted to Demosthenes and Cicero,[1] I shall examine the character and the disposition of each in the light of their respective actions and political conduct, but I shall make no critical comparison of their speeches, nor attempt to determine which was the more agreeable or powerful orator. As Ion[2] puts it

The dolphin's strength deserts him on dry land.

1. See Introduction, p. 9.
2. A contemporary of Sophocles, Ion of Chios, a lyric, elegiac and tragic poet who died in 422 B.C.

In other words, do not venture out of your element – a proverb which that unbalanced critic Caecilius[1] forgot, when he published with youthful presumption his comparison of Demosthenes and Cicero. But enough of this: if it came easily to every man to practise the famous imperative 'Know thyself', we should not think of it as a divine commandment.

Demosthenes and Cicero resemble each other so closely that the gods might almost be thought to have fashioned them out of the same mould. There are many similarities in their characters, notably the same personal ambition, the same love of liberty and the same lack of courage in the face of war or physical danger – and many similarities in their fortunes. History offers us no other parallel, in my opinion, of two orators who raised themselves from small beginnings to positions of authority and power, who opposed kings and tyrants, who each lost their daughters, who were exiled from their native cities, recalled with honour, forced to seek refuge again, were finally captured by their enemies, and lost their lives at the same time as their fellow-countrymen lost their liberty. In short if there were to be a contest between nature and fortune, as it might be between two sculptors, it would be difficult to decide which had produced the more complete resemblance, the one in shaping their characters and the other their destinies. I shall begin with the one who comes first chronologically.

4. Demosthenes' father, who bore the same name, was of a good family, as Theopompus tells us, and was surnamed Cutler, because he owned a large factory and employed slaves who were skilled in this type of manufacture. As for the charge made by Aeschines against Demosthenes' mother, that she was the daughter of a barbarian woman and that her father was a certain Gylon[2] who was exiled from Athens for treason, I cannot say whether this is true or a malicious slander. Demosthenes' father died when he was seven and left him a considerable inheritance, the estate being valued at a little less than

1. A Greek rhetorician of Calacte in Sicily, contemporary with Virgil and Horace.

2. Aeschines' story was that Gylon had betrayed Nymphaeum, a Milesian colony in the Crimea which paid tribute to Athens, and that the Athenians charged him with treason and sentenced him to death in his absence. Gylon settled in the Chersonese and married a Scythian whose daughter was Demosthenes' mother.

fifteen talents, but he was disgracefully treated by his guardians, who appropriated part of his patrimony to their own uses, neglected the rest and even failed to pay the boy's tutors. It was for this reason that he did not receive the education which a boy of good family should have had. Besides, because he was delicate and physically under-developed, his mother discouraged him from training in the wrestling-school and his tutors did not press him to attend it. He was a skinny and sickly child from the beginning and his companions made fun of his puny physique by christening him Batalus.[1] According to one account Batalus was an effeminate flute-player, who was caricatured in a farce by the poet Antiphanes. Another story has it that Batalus was a poet who wrote voluptuous lyrics and drinking songs, and yet another that the word was used as slang at that time for the anus. We are told that Demosthenes was also nicknamed Argas: the name may have been given him on account of his manners, which were boorish and surly: in some of the poets the word signifies a snake, or it may have referred to the impediment in his speech which offended the ears of his listeners – Argas was also the name of a composer of scurrilous and disagreeable songs.

5. His desire to become a public speaker is said to have originated as follows. Callistratus the orator was due to speak in court on the question of Oropus,[2] and the lawsuit was eagerly awaited, partly because of the eloquence of Callistratus, who was then at the height of his powers, and partly because of the importance of the issue, which was in the forefront of everyone's minds. So when Demosthenes heard several of his teachers and schoolmasters discussing their plans for attending the trial, he begged and implored his own tutor to take him to the hearing. As it happened this man knew some of the

1. There is yet another tradition that Batalus was a nickname given to Demosthenes on account of his stammer.

2. Oropus was situated near the north-east frontier of Attica facing Euboea and was a port of consequence because it commanded the communications between Decelea and Euboea. The Athenians lost it to the Spartans during the Peloponnesian war (411 B.C.). It was captured by the Thebans in 402, and although later restored to Athens was constantly threatened by Thebes, and in 366 was taken over by Oropian supporters of the Thebans. The date of the trial is uncertain and so is Callistratus' role. He was impeached in 365 for having acquiesced in Thebes' retention of the city, but if Plutarch's statements about Demosthenes' age are correct, this trial would have taken place in 369-8, before Callistratus could have been involved in this way.

officials who were on duty at the doors of the courts, and secured a seat where the boy could sit and listen without being seen.[1] Callistratus gained the verdict and was extravagantly praised, and when Demosthenes saw him being escorted by a large following and congratulated on all sides, he was seized with the desire to emulate his fame. But what won his admiration and appealed to his intellect even more strongly was the power of Callistratus' eloquence, which, as he saw, could engage and subdue all opposition. From this moment he abandoned all other studies and all the normal pastimes of boyhood, and threw himself wholeheartedly into the practice of declamation, in the hope that he would one day take his place among the orators. He employed Isaeus as his teacher in the art of speaking, even though Isocrates was also lecturing at this time; one tradition has it that because he was an orphan, he could not pay Isocrates the required fee of ten minas, but according to another account he preferred Isaeus' style as being more vigorous and effective in actual use. On the other hand, Hermippus tells us that he discovered an anonymous book of memoirs, according to which Demosthenes was a pupil of Plato and owed his instruction in the art of speaking chiefly to him. He also says that, according to Cte.ibius, Demosthenes secretly obtained from Callias the Syracusan and others the treatises on rhetoric of Isocrates and Alcidamas, and learned these thoroughly.

6. However this may be, once Demosthenes had come of age,[2] he began to prosecute his guardians and to compose speeches attacking them. They resorted to various legal evasions and procured re-trials, but Demosthenes gained some hard-won experience 'by running risks and sparing no effort', as Thucydides puts it, and finally won his case, though he did not succeed in recovering even the smallest fraction of his inheritance. However in this way he acquired some practice and assurance in public speaking and got a foretaste of the distinction and power which forensic eloquence can bring, and so he ventured to come forward and engage in debate. We are told that Laomedon of Orchomenus originally took up long-distance running on the advice of his doctors to protect him against some disease of

1. An Athenian youth was not entitled to be present at public assemblies until he became an *ephebos* (at 18). Hence this trial must have taken place before 366, as it is implied that Demosthenes was not entitled to be there.
2. i.e. when he reached his eighteenth year.

the spleen, and that once he was obliged to go into training in the first place to recover his health, he soon afterwards entered the Olympic games and became one of the best long distance athletes of his time. Similarly Demosthenes was obliged to make his first appearance in the courts in the effort to recover his property; thereafter he developed such skill and power in pleading and later in public debate, that in the political championships, so to speak, he outstripped all his rivals among the orators in the public assembly.

And yet when he first came before the people he was interrupted by heckling and laughed at for his inexperience: this was because his manner of speaking appeared confused and overloaded with long periods, and his expression contorted by a formality which his audience found harsh and wearisome. It appears too that his voice was weak and his utterance indistinct and that he suffered from a shortness of breath, which had the effect of breaking up his sentences and making his meaning difficult to follow. At last, when he had left the assembly, and was wandering about the Piraeus in despair, he met another orator named Eunomus[1] of Thriasia, who was by then a very old man. Eunomus reproved him and said: 'You have a style of speaking which is very like Pericles', and yet out of sheer timidity and cowardice you are throwing away your talents. You will neither stand up to the rough and tumble of the assembly, nor train your body to develop the stamina that you need for the law-courts. It is through your own sheer feebleness that you are letting your gifts wither away.'

7. On another occasion, it is said, when he had again been rebuffed by the people and was going home in a state of bewilderment and depression, Satyrus[2] the actor, who knew him well, followed him and accompanied him indoors. Demosthenes then told him with tears in his eyes that although he took more trouble than any other orator to prepare his speeches and had almost ruined his health in his efforts to train himself, he never succeeded in gaining the ear of the people: drunken sailors and illiterate louts were listened to with respect and could hold the platform, but he was always ignored. 'What you say is true,' Satyrus told him, 'but I will soon put that

---

1. Eunomus was one of the earliest pupils of Isocrates. It is implied that he had heard Pericles speak when he was a boy, some seventy years before.

2. Satyrus was a famous comic actor.

right if you will just recite to me a longish speech from Sophocles or
Euripides.' Demosthenes did this, whereupon Satyrus repeated the
same passage and so enhanced its effect by speaking it with the
appropriate characterization and tone of voice that the words seemed
to Demosthenes to be quite transformed. Now that he could see how
much grace and dignity an orator gains from a good delivery, he
understood that it is of little or no use for a man to practise declamation if he does not also attend to the arrangement and delivery of
what he has to say. After this, we are told, he built an underground
study, which, in fact, was preserved intact up to my lifetime. Every
day without fail he would go down to work at his delivery and to
train his voice, and he would often remain there for two or three
months on end, and would shave only one side of his face, to prevent
himself from going out, even if he wanted to.

8. Besides these formal exercises, he took advantage of his interviews,
conversations and other dealings with the outside world to give himself further training. As soon as his acquaintances had left, he would
review in due order everything that had been discussed and the
arguments used for and against each course of action. Any speeches
that he happened to have heard delivered he would afterwards
analyse by himself and work them up into regular propositions and
periods, and he would introduce all kinds of corrections or para-
phrases into speeches that had been made against him by others, or
into his own replies to them. It was this habit which created the
impression that he was not really an eloquent speaker, but that the
skill and the power of his oratory had been acquired by hard work.
There is strong evidence for this in the fact that Demosthenes was
very seldom heard to make an impromptu speech. The people often
called on him by name as he sat in the assembly to speak to the subject under debate, but he would not come forward unless he had
given thought to the question and could deliver a prepared speech.
For this reason many of the popular leaders used to sneer at him, and
Pytheas in particular told him mockingly that his arguments smelled
of the lamp. Demosthenes had a sharp retort for this. 'I am sure that
your lamp, Pytheas,' he told him, 'sees a very different kind of night
life from mine.' However to other people he did not trouble to deny
the facts: he admitted that his speeches were prepared, but said that
he did not write them out word for word. But he also declared that

the man who prepares what he is going to say is the true democrat, for the fact that he takes this amount of trouble indicates respect for the people, whereas to speak without caring what they will think of one's words is the sign of a man who favours oligarchy and is inclined to rely on force rather than persuasion. Another fact often cited as a proof that Demosthenes lacked the confidence to speak on the spur of the moment is that when he was being shouted down by the people, Demades would often take his place and make an impromptu speech in his support, but that Demosthenes never did this for Demades.

9. How was it then, we may ask, that Aeschines could refer to him as a man of astounding audacity in his speeches? Or that Demosthenes was the only man to stand up and refute Python[1] of Byzantium when he confidently attacked the Athenians and let loose a torrent of eloquence against them? Or again, when Lamachus of Myrrhine had composed a panegyric on Philip and Alexander, which was also full of abuse of Thebes and Olynthus and which was being read out aloud at Olympia, how was it that Demosthenes came forward and marshalled a complete array of historical facts to remind the audience of the benefits which the peoples of Thebes and Chalcidice had conferred on Greece and of the misfortunes for which the flatterers of Macedonia had been responsible? With these arguments he worked upon the feelings of his audience so powerfully that the sophist took fright at the uproar which arose against him and slunk away from the festival. The fact is that while Demosthenes did not wish to model himself upon Pericles in every respect, he especially admired and sought to imitate the modulation of his speech and the dignity of his bearing, and also his determination not to speak on impulse or on any subject which might present itself, and he seems to have been persuaded that it was to these qualities that Pericles owed his greatness. For the same reasons Demosthenes did not aspire to the kind of reputation which is won in a sudden crisis, and he was very seldom willing to expose his oratorical power to the

    1. In 343 B.C. Python headed a diplomatic mission backed by Philip of Macedon, which tried to persuade the Athenians to become truly reconciled to Philip's position in Greece. He assured them that Philip was animated only by the most benevolent sentiments, and attacked the anti-Macedonian party for their unwillingness to negotiate.

mercy of fortune. However those speeches which he delivered
impromptu displayed more courage and spirit than those which he
wrote out, if we are to believe the evidence of Eratosthenes, Demetrius of Phaleron and the comic poets. Eratosthenes tells us that often
in his speeches he seemed to be transported into a kind of ecstasy, and
Demetrius says that on one occasion he pronounced to the people
the well-known metrical oath which runs

> By earth, by all her fountains, streams and floods

as if he were possessed by some god. As for the comic poets, one of
them calls him a dealer in petty bombast, and another makes fun of
his fondness for the antithesis:

1ST CITIZEN   All this my master felt belonged to him,
              So taking it, he was only taking back
              His own.
2ND CITIZEN   Now that's a phrase Demosthenes
              Would love to take up . . .

Antiphanes may also have intended this as a dig at the passage in
one of Demosthenes' speeches which concerns Halonesus, where he
urges the Athenians not to accept the island as a gift from Philip, but
to recover it as a right.

10. At any rate, it was universally agreed that Demades, when he
used his natural gifts, was invincible as an orator, and that when he
spoke on the spur of the moment, he far excelled Demosthenes'
carefully prepared efforts. Ariston of Chios has given us Theophrastus' verdict on these two orators. When he was asked what kind
of orator he considered Demosthenes to be, he replied, 'An orator
worthy of Athens,' but of Demades he said 'He is too good for
Athens.' According to the same philosopher, Polyeuctus of Sphettus,
one of the leading Athenian politicians, declared that Demosthenes
was the greatest orator, but Phocion the most effective, because his
speeches packed the greatest proportion of sense into the fewest
words. In fact we are told that Demosthenes himself, whenever
Phocion rose to answer him, would mutter to his friends 'Here comes
the chopper of my speeches.' It is not clear from the phrase whether
Demosthenes felt like this towards Phocion because of his oratory, or
because of his life and character, and so was implying that even a

single word from a man in whom the people felt so much confidence carries more weight than any number of lengthy perorations.

11. Demetrius of Phaleron has described the various exercises which Demosthenes took up to overcome his physical deficiencies, and he says that he learned of these from the orator himself when he was an old man. He corrected his lisp and his indistinct articulation by holding pebbles in his mouth while he recited long speeches, and he strengthened his voice by running or walking uphill discoursing as he went, and by reciting speeches or verses in a single breath. Besides this he kept a large mirror in his house and would stand in front of it while he went through his exercises in declamation.

There is a story that a man once came to Demosthenes, asked him to represent him in court, and explained to him at length how he had been physically assaulted. 'But you did not suffer this ill-treatment you are telling me about,' said Demosthenes. At this the man raised his voice, and shouted, 'What do you mean, I did not suffer it?' 'Ah, now,' said Demosthenes, 'I can hear the voice of a man who has been attacked and beaten.' So important did he consider the tone and the bearing of a speaker in convincing his audience.

His own manner of speaking was very popular with the general public, but men of sensibility, such as Demetrius of Phaleron, thought it mean, vulgar and weak. On the other hand Hermippus tells us that when Aesion, a contemporary of Demosthenes, was asked his opinion of the ancient orators as compared with the moderns, he said that anyone who heard the orators of the past must admire the decorum and the dignity of their manner, but that when we read Demosthenes' speeches, we must admit that they are superior in their construction and more powerful in their effect. It goes without saying that his written speeches contain many harsh and bitter judgements, but in his extempore replies he could also be humorous. For example when Demades exclaimed, 'Demosthenes teach *me*? Athena might as well take lessons from a sow!', Demosthenes retorted, 'That was the Athena who was seen the other day in a brothel in Collytus.' When a well-known thief who was nicknamed 'brazen' tried to make fun of the orator's late hours and midnight studies, Demosthenes answered, 'I know my lighted lamp must be a nuisance to you. But you Athenians should not be surprised at the number of thefts that are committed, when we have thieves of brass, while the walls of our houses are only made of clay.' There are many more stories of this kind, but here I must stop and consider Demosthenes' other qualities and characteristics in the light of his achievements as a statesman.

12. It was after the outbreak of the Phocian war[1] that he first began to take an active part in affairs: we know this partly from his own statements and partly from the speeches he made against Philip. Some of these were delivered after the war had ended, and the earliest of them touch upon matters which were closely connected with it. It is evident that when he was preparing his speech for the prosecution of Meidias he had reached the age of thirty-two, but had not yet acquired any influence or reputation in the political arena. It was his lack of confidence on this score, so it seems to me, which was the principal reason for his dropping the case in return for a sum of money, in spite of his personal animosity towards Meidias. For, as Homer says of Achilles[2]

He was not a sweet-tempered man, nor kindly towards his opponents,

and Demosthenes was sharp and even forceful in avenging any wrongs done to him. However he recognized that it was no easy task, indeed scarcely within his power, to destroy a man such as Meidias, who was well protected not only by his oratory but by his friends and his wealth, and so he gave way to those who pleaded on his enemy's behalf. I doubt very much whether the three thousand drachmae he was paid would have appeased the hatred he felt towards Meidias, if he had hoped or felt able to get the better of his enemy.

However once he had found a noble cause to engage his political activity, that is the defence of the Greeks against Philip, he fought for it with admirable spirit. He quickly became famous and his reputation was enhanced by the courage of his speeches, so that he was admired in Greece and treated with respect by the king of Persia. King Philip took more notice of him than of any other Athenian statesman, and even his enemies were forced to agree that they were dealing with a man of distinction: both Aeschines and Hypereides admit as much, even in their denunciations of him.

1. This lasted from 356–346 B.C.   2. *Iliad* xx, 467.

13. For this reason I do not know what evidence Theopompus had for his statement that Demosthenes was of a fickle and unstable disposition and incapable of remaining faithful for any length of time either to the same policies or the same men – on the contrary it is clear that he remained loyal to the same party and the same line of policy that he had chosen from the beginning, and indeed he was so far from forsaking these principles during his lifetime that he deliberately sacrificed his life to uphold them. Demades, when he wanted to excuse his change of policy, would plead that he had often said things that were contrary to his former opinions, but never contrary to the interests of the state. Melanopus,[1] who belonged to the opposite party to Callistratus was often bribed by him to change sides, and he would then say to the people, 'This man is my personal opponent, but the essential thing is that the public interest should prevail.' Nicodemus the Messenian, who first took the side of Cassander[2] and later supported Demetrius of Phalerum, declared that there was no inconsistency in this, because it is always best to obey whoever is in power. We cannot bring any of these charges against Demosthenes, nor accuse him of being a man who ever wavered or deviated from his course in word or deed. He maintained a single unchangeable harmony throughout, and continued, to use a musical metaphor, in the same key that he had chosen from the start. Panaetius the philosopher remarks that in most of his speeches, for example *On The Crown*, *Against Aristocrates*, in the one on those who should be exempted from taxation, and in the *Philippics*, we can trace the conviction that honour ought to be pursued for its own sake. In all these orations Demosthenes does not try to persuade his fellow-citizens to do what is most agreeable, or easy, or profitable, but time and again he argues that they ought to place their honour and their obligations before their safety or self-preservation. In short if only the nobility of his aspirations and the dignity of his words had been matched by an equivalent courage in war and integrity in his other dealings, he would have deserved to be ranked not with orators such as Moerocles,

1. A politician who took part in various embassies sent by the Athenians to Sparta, Egypt and Caria.

2. The son of Antipater – the latter governed Macedon as regent during Alexander's Asiatic campaigns. Cassander became master of Athens from 311 to 307 B.C., when he left the city under the governorship of Demetrius of Phalerum. It was then taken over by Demetrius Poliorcetes, to whom Nicodemus transferred his allegiance.

Polyeuctus[1] and Hypereides,[2] but with the men of Athens' greatest days, such as Cimon,[3] Thucydides[4] and Pericles.

14. Among Demosthenes' contemporaries we may say that Phocion, although he championed an unpopular policy and had the reputation of favouring the Macedonians, was considered by virtue of his courage and integrity to be a statesman of the calibre of Ephialtes and Aristides and Cimon. Demosthenes, on the other hand, could not be relied on when it came to fighting, nor was he altogether proof against bribes. He could resist any number of offers from Philip or from Macedon, but he not only yielded to but was finally overwhelmed by the Persian gold, which poured down from Susa and Ecbatana in a torrent. And so while he was admirably fitted to extol the virtues of former generations, he was not so good at imitating them. Yet in spite of these shortcomings he led a more exemplary life than the other orators of his time, always excepting Phocion. It is undeniable, for example, that he went further than any of them in speaking frankly to the people, and that he often opposed the desires of the majority and continually criticized their faults, as we may see from his speeches. Even his enemy Theopompus had recorded that when the Athenians called upon him to impeach a man, and, finding that he refused, began to create an uproar, he rose and declared, 'Men of Athens, I shall continue to give you advice, whether you ask for it or not, but I refuse to become a false accuser, even if you insist on it.' His conduct in the case of Antiphon was not at all that of a man who courts the favour of the people. Antiphon had been acquitted by the assembly, but Demosthenes had him arrested and brought before the Council of the Areopagus, and disregarding the affront to the sovereignty of the people which his action implied, he succeeded in proving him guilty of having promised Philip to set fire to the dock-yards. As a result Antiphon was handed over to justice by the Areopagus and later executed. Demosthenes also accused the priestess Theoris of a number of misdemeanours, and amongst others of teaching slaves to cheat their masters. As one of the parties before the court, he was allowed to propose her sentence, and caused her to be put to death.

1. A native of Salamis who, like Demosthenes, opposed the ambitions of Macedon, but had a doubtful reputation in financial matters.
2. A politician of similar reputation.
3. The son of Miltiades: see *The Rise and Fall of Athens*.
4. Not the historian, but the aristocratic statesman and opponent of Pericles.

15. Demosthenes is said to have written the speech which was used by Apollodorus to obtain judgement against Timotheus the general, whom he was suing for debt, and likewise the speeches which Apollodorus used against Stephanus and Phormio. In this instance Demosthenes was rightly considered to have acted dishonourably, for he had also written Phormio's defence, and was thus, as it were, selling the two adversaries weapons from the same shop with which they could fight one another.[1]

Among his public speeches he wrote those against Androtion, Timocrates and Aristocrates to be delivered by others;[2] he must have composed these before he had begun his political career, for it appears that these speeches were made public when he was only twenty-seven or twenty-eight years of age. But he himself delivered the speech against Aristogeiton, as well as the one concerning tax-exemptions.[3] He says that he took up the latter case at the request of Ctesippus, the son of Chabrias, but according to other accounts, he did so because he was wooing the young man's mother. This match did not materialize, but he later married a Samian woman, as Demetrius of Magnesia tells us in his treatise *On Persons of the Same Name*. As for the speech which was made against Aeschines for his misconduct as ambassador, it is not certain that this was ever delivered, although Idomeneus has recorded that Aeschines was acquitted by a bare thirty votes. But this is contradicted by the speeches of both Demosthenes and Aeschines *On The Crown*, for neither of them refers to the case of the embassy as ever having come into court. This is a question I shall leave others to decide.

16. Demosthenes' political position was clear enough even while peace still prevailed, for he allowed no act of Philip's to pass un-criticized, and seized upon every occasion to incite and inflame the Athenians against him. In consequence nobody was more talked of

1. Lawsuits which involved public issues as distinct from the private ones previously mentioned.

2. Apparently this is true only of the first of the three.

3. A politician named Leptinus had passed a law to the effect that nobody should enjoy exemption from the ordinary state burdens except the descendants of the tyrannicides Harmodius and Aristogeiton. Chabrias, the famous admiral, had been granted exemption on account of his public services, and this privilege had been inherited by his effete son, Ctesippus, who challenged the repeal of his exemption.

at Philip's court, and when Demosthenes visited Macedonia as one of a delegation of ten, Philip listened to all their speeches, but took most trouble to answer Demosthenes. As regards other official courtesies or marks of honour, Philip did not pay him so much attention, but singled out the party of Aeschines and Philocrates for his especial favour. So when they complimented Philip as the most eloquent speaker, the handsomest man and the drinker with the biggest capacity in the company, Demosthenes could not refrain from belittling these tributes and retorting sarcastically that the first of these qualities was excellent for a sophist, the second for a woman, and the third for a sponge, but none of them for a king.

17. At length the course of events began to move inexorably towards war, since Philip was incapable of sitting quietly at home, and the Athenians were constantly being stirred up against him by Demosthenes. First of all he urged his countrymen to invade Euboea,[1] which had been subdued and handed over to Philip by its local tyrants, and as the result of a resolution passed in his name the Athenians crossed over to the island and drove out the Macedonians. Next,[2] when Macedonia was at war with the citizens of Byzantium and Perinthus, Demosthenes persuaded the Athenians to lay aside their grievances and forget the wrongs they had suffered from these peoples in the Social War,[3] and to dispatch a force which succeeded in relieving both cities. After this he set off on a diplomatic mission, which was designed to kindle the spirit of resistance to Philip and which took him all over Greece. Finally he succeeded in uniting almost all the states into a confederation against Philip. The result of these efforts was to raise a mercenary army of fifteen thousand infantry and two thousand cavalry besides the local forces of each city, and the allies readily agreed to pay these soldiers. It was on this occasion, according to Theophrastus, when the Greek states requested that a quota should be fixed, that the Athenian demagogue Hegesippus, who was nicknamed Crobylus ('top-knot'), remarked, 'War has an appetite that cannot be satisfied by quotas.'

Greece was now wrought up to a high pitch of expectation at the thought of her future, and her peoples and cities all drew together,

1. In 341 B.C.   2. In 340 B.C.
3. 357–355 B.C. when Chios, Cos, Rhodes and Byzantium revolted against Athens.

Euboeans, Achaeans, Corinthians, Megarians, Leucadians and Corcyraeans. But there remained the most important task of all for Demosthenes to accomplish, namely to persuade Thebes to join the alliance. The Thebans had a common frontier with the Athenians and an army ready to take the field, and at that time they were regarded as the finest soldiers in Greece.[1] But it was no easy matter to persuade them to change sides: moreover during the recent Phocian war Philip had rendered them a number of services and cultivated their goodwill, and the various petty quarrels which arose because of their proximity to Athens were continually breaking out afresh and exacerbated the relations between the two cities.

18. Meanwhile Philip, encouraged by his success in dealing with Amphissa,[2] marched on to take Elateia[3] by surprise and proceeded to occupy Phocis. The news stunned the Athenians. No speaker dared to mount the rostrum, nobody knew what advice should be given, the assembly was struck dumb and appeared to be completely at a loss. It was at this moment that Demosthenes alone came forward and urged the people to stand by the Thebans. Then in his usual manner he put heart into his compatriots and inspired them with fresh hopes, and he was then sent off with others as an ambassador to Thebes. At the same time Philip, as we learn from Marsyas the historian, sent Amyntas and Clearchus of Macedonia, Daochus of Thessaly, and Thrasydaeus to oppose the Athenians and put the case for Macedon. For their part the Thebans could see clearly enough where their interests lay, but each of them could also visualize the horrors of war, for the sufferings they had endured in the Phocian conflict[4] were still fresh in their memories. Yet in spite of this Demosthenes' eloquence, so Theopompus tells us, stirred their courage, kindled their desire to win glory and threw every other consideration into the

1. Demosthenes' strategy for the defence of Athens against landward attack depended on securing the alliance of Thebes.

2. Amphissa, a few miles from Delphi, had given offence to the Amphictyonic Council by sacrilegiously cultivating the plain below Delphi. When the inhabitants ignored orders made by the Council, the authority which governed the sacred precincts, Philip was delegated to use force against Amphissa.

3. Elateia, the principal town of Phocis, commanded the paths from Mount Oeta into central Greece and was therefore a position of great military importance.

4. In this war, 357–346 B.C., Macedon had sided with the Thebans and Athens with the Phocians.

shade. As if transported by his words, they cast off all fear, self-interest or thought of obligation towards Macedon and chose the path of honour. So complete and so glorious was the transformation wrought by his oratory that Philip promptly dispatched an embassy to ask for terms of peace: just then all Greece seemed to have recovered her confidence and was up in arms to support Demosthenes for the future – so much so that not only did the Athenian generals take their orders from him, but also the Boeotarchs. At this moment he could control all the meetings of the Theban assembly as effectively as those of the Athenian, he was beloved by both nations, and exercised supreme authority; moreover he never used his position unconstitutionally nor did he go beyond his powers, so Theopompus tells us, but acted with complete propriety.

19. However, it seems that at that very moment some divinely ordained power was shaping the course of events so as to put an end to the freedom of the Greeks: this fatal destiny opposed all their efforts in the common cause and produced many portents of what was to come. Among these were the ominous prophecies uttered by the Pythian priestess and an ancient oracle which was quoted from the Sibylline books

Let me fly far from the battle at Thermodon, let me take refuge
Watching from high in the clouds, as I soar with the wings of an eagle.

Now the Thermodon is said to be a small stream near my native town of Chaeronea, which flows into the river Cephisus. I know of no stream which bears this name today, but my guess is that the one which is now called Haemon was then known as Thermodon. It flows past the Heracleum, where the Greeks pitched their camp, and I imagine that after the battle this river was filled with blood and corpses, and that its present name of Haemon was substituted for the original one. However the historian Duris writes that the Thermodon was not a river at all, but that some soldiers who were pitching a tent and digging a trench around it, found a small stone image with an inscription on it, signifying that this was Thermodon[1] carrying a wounded Amazon in his arms: he also reports that there was another oracle current about it, which ran as follows

1. The statue represented the god of the river Thermodon in Cappadocia: the river flowed through the territory in which the Amazons were reputed to dwell.

Bide your time for the battle of Thermodon, bird of black pinions;
There you shall find the flesh of mankind to devour in abundance.

20. It is difficult to discover the exact truth about these prophecies,
but certainly Demosthenes is said to have had complete confidence
in the Greek forces and to have been elated by the strength and spirit
of so many men, all of them eager to engage the enemy: in consequence he would not allow his countrymen to pay attention to the
oracles or listen to the prophecies. Indeed he even suspected that the
Pythian priestess was on the side of Philip, and he reminded the
Thebans of the example of Epaminondas and the Athenians of
Pericles, both of whom acted only on the promptings of reason and
regarded prophecies of this kind as mere pretexts for faint-hearted-
ness. Up to this point, then, Demosthenes acted like a brave man, but
in the battle of Chaeronea which followed, so far from achieving
anything honourable, he completely failed to suit his actions to his
words. He left his place in the ranks and took to his heels in the most
shameful fashion, throwing away his arms in order to run faster, and
he did not hesitate to disgrace the inscription on his shield, on which,
according to Pytheas, were engraved in letters of gold the words
'With good fortune'.

In the first flush of victory Philip felt insolently exultant at his
success. He went out with a party of companions to look at the bodies
of the dead, and drunkenly sang the opening words of the decree
which had been passed on Demosthenes' initiative, dividing it according to the metre, and beating the time

Demosthenes, son of Demosthenes, of Paeania, moves as follows:

But when he came to himself and understood the magnitude of the
dangers that had surrounded him, he trembled to think of the power
and skill of the orator who had forced him to risk his empire and his
life on the outcome of a few hours in a single day. For the fame of this
speaker had travelled even to the Persian king, who had sent letters
to the satraps on the coast ordering them to offer money to Demosthenes and to pay more attention to him than to any other Greek,
since he could create a diversion and keep the king of Macedon busy
at home by means of the troubles he stirred up in Greece. This intelligence was discovered long afterwards by Alexander, who found
in Sardis letters from Demosthenes and papers belonging to the king's

generals and containing details of the sums of money which had been given to him.

21. However, at this moment when the news of the disaster to Greece became known, the orators who opposed Demosthenes attacked him and prepared indictments and impeachments against him. But the people not only acquitted him of these charges, but continued to honour him and appealed to him as a loyal citizen to remain in public life. Consequently when the bones of those who had fallen at Chaeronea were brought home to be buried, they chose him to deliver the panegyric in honour of the dead.[1] So far from displaying a cowardly or ignoble spirit in the hour of disaster (as Theopompus implies in his exaggerated description of the scene) they made it clear by the special honour and respect which they paid their counsellor that they did not regret the advice he had given them. So Demosthenes delivered the funeral oration, but henceforth he would not put his own name to any of the decrees he proposed in the assembly: instead he used those of his friends, one after the other, and avoided his own as being ill-omened, until he once more took courage after Philip's death. And in fact Philip died soon afterwards and survived his victory at Chaeronea by less than two years, and this it would seem was foretold in the last verse of the oracle

Tears there shall be for the vanquished, and the victor shall meet his destruction.

22. Now Demosthenes had obtained secret intelligence of Philip's death, and in order to inspire the Athenians with hope for the future, he appeared before the senate with an air of high spirits and told them he had had a dream which seemed to presage that some great stroke of good fortune was in store for Athens. Not long afterwards the messengers arrived with the report of Philip's death. The Athenians immediately offered up sacrifices for the good news and voted a crown for Pausanias, the king's assassin, while Demosthenes appeared in public dressed in magnificent attire and wearing a garland on his head, although his daughter had died only six days before. These details are reported by Aeschines, who attacked him for his action and reviled him as an unnatural father. This only proves the weakness

1. An exceptional honour which the Athenians would hardly have paid if they had been convinced of his cowardice.

and vulgarity of his own nature, if he considers that the wearing of mourning and an extravagant display of grief are the signs of a tender heart, but finds fault with a man who bears his loss in a serene and resolute fashion.

For my part I cannot say that the Athenians did themselves any credit in putting on garlands and offering sacrifices to celebrate the death of a king who, when he was the conqueror and they the conquered had treated them with such tolerance and humanity.[1] For apart from provoking the anger of the gods, it was a contemptible action to make Philip a citizen of Athens and pay him honours while he was alive, and then, as soon as he had fallen by another's hand, to be beside themselves with joy, trample on his body, and sing paeans of victory, as though they themselves had accomplished some great feat of arms. On the other hand I praise the behaviour of Demosthenes for leaving his personal misfortunes to be lamented over by the women, and devoting himself to the action he thought necessary for his country. I believe it is the duty of a man of courage and one who wishes to be considered fit to govern never to lose sight of the common good, to find consolation for his private griefs and troubles in the well-being of the state, and to conduct himself with a dignity far greater than actors show when they play the part of kings or tyrants; for these men as we see them in the theatres do not laugh or weep as their feelings dictate, but as the subject of the drama demands.

Apart from these considerations it is our duty not to leave our neighbour without any consolation in his misfortune, but to find words which will relieve his sorrow and turn his thoughts to less distressing subjects, just as those who are suffering from sore eyes, are advised to look away from brilliant or dazzling colours and towards softer or more verdant shades. And I believe that a man can find no better consolation for his private griefs than to balance them against the well-being of his fellow-citizens, when his country's fortunes are prospering, thus making the happier circumstances of the majority outweigh the misfortunes of the individual. I have been led to offer these reflections because I have noticed how this speech of Aeschines has melted the hearts of many people and encouraged them to indulge an unmanly tenderness.

1. After his victory Philip had freed his Athenian prisoners without ransom and had offered the city generous peace terms.

23. It was not long before Demosthenes again took the initiative in rebuilding the confederacy of Greek states. He helped to provide the Thebans with arms, whereupon they attacked the Macedonian garrison in their city and killed many of them, and the Athenians began to prepare to go to war in their support. Demosthenes now completely dominated the assembly and he wrote letters to the Persian generals in Asia inciting them to declare war on Alexander, whom he referred to as a boy, and compared to Margites.[1] But as soon as Alexander had established his authority in his own kingdom and led his army to Boeotia, the Athenians' courage wilted, Demosthenes' ardour was extinguished, and the Thebans, betrayed by their allies, fought alone and lost their city. Panic reigned in Athens, and Demosthenes was chosen with a number of others to form a delegation to visit Alexander, but he dreaded the king's anger so much that he turned back at Cithaeron and abandoned his mission. Alexander at once sent to Athens to demand that ten of the popular leaders should be surrendered to him. This is the account given by Idomeneus and Douris, but, according to most of the more reliable authorities, he only specified eight, namely Demosthenes, Polyeuctus, Ephialtes, Lycurgus, Moerocles, Damon, Callisthenes and Charidemus.[2] It was on this occasion that Demosthenes reminded the Athenians of the fable of the sheep who gave up their watch-dogs to the wolves, and he compared himself and his colleagues to sheep-dogs who fought to defend the people, and referred to Alexander as the lone wolf of Macedonia.[3] He added, 'You know how corn-merchants sell whole consignments of their stock by showing a few grains of wheat which they carry around with them in a bowl as a sample. In the same way, if you deliver us up, you are delivering up yourselves, every one of you.' These details we have from Aristobulus of Cassandreia.[4]

1. The principal character in a comic epic attributed to Homer; Margites was a boy who, though grown up, had never attained the maturity of a man, who knew many things, but nothing properly.

2. The best-known of these to posterity were Lycurgus the famous orator, Charidemus and Ephialtes, both soldiers who were banished from Athens and later took service under Darius: the latter was killed at the siege of Halicarnassus, the former executed by Darius before the battle of Ipsus for opposing offensive operations.

3. The Greek word *monolycus* denotes a particularly rapacious wolf, which hunted alone and preyed upon men.

4. Aristobulus accompanied Alexander on his campaign in India and later wrote a history of him.

The Athenians debated these demands in the assembly, but could not decide how to reply to them. Then Demades in return for five talents which he had been offered by the eight men, volunteered to go to the king and plead on their behalf: he may have trusted to his personal friendship with Alexander, or he may have counted on finding him sated with blood, like a lion that has been glutted with slaughter. At any rate Demades persuaded the king to pardon the eight men, and arranged terms of peace for the city.

24. In consequence when Alexander returned to Macedonia, Demades and his party were all powerful and Demosthenes was completely humbled. Later when Agis the Spartan organized a revolt against Macedonia,[1] Demosthenes made a feeble effort to support him, but his attempt collapsed ignominiously, because the Athenians refused to take part in the uprising. Agis was killed in battle and the resistance of the Spartans was crushed.

It was at this time that the indictment against Ctesiphon on the subject of the crown finally came up for trial.[2] The case had originally been prepared in the archonship of Chaerendas, shortly before the battle of Chaeronea, but it did not come into court until ten years later in the archonship of Aristophon. Although this was a private suit, no public action ever attracted more attention, not only on account of the fame of the orators, but also because of the admirable conduct of the jurors. Demosthenes' accusers were then at the height of their power and enjoyed the favour of Macedon, yet the jurors would not bring in a verdict against him, but acquitted him so decisively that Aeschines did not obtain a fifth of their votes.[3] The result was that Aeschines immediately left Athens and spent the rest of his life in Rhodes and Ionia as a teacher of rhetoric.

1. Agis III, the king of Sparta, carried on a campaign against Macedonia, which was supported by Persia, from 333 to 330 B.C. when he was defeated by Antipater and killed at Megalopolis in the Peloponnese.
2. In 336 B.C. Ctesiphon had proposed that Demosthenes should be awarded a golden crown for public services. Aeschines had denounced the proposal on a technicality as unconstitutional and instituted a prosecution. This had remained in abeyance for over six years, and it was possibly the defeat of Agis which encouraged Demosthenes' enemies to proceed. The trial was the occasion for one of Demosthenes' most famous orations, On the Crown. Plutarch's dating of the indictment is incorrect.
3. Aeschines was in consequence condemned to pay a fine of 1000 drachmae and was debarred from bringing any future action.

25. Several years later Harpalus, Alexander's treasurer arrived in Athens from Asia.[1] He had fled from the king's service because he knew that he was guilty of many misdeeds committed through his love of extravagance, and because he dreaded his master, who had by then become an object of terror even to his friends. He therefore sought refuge in Athens and placed himself, his ships, and his treasure in the people's hands. The other orators at once rallied to his support and urged the Athenians to receive him as a suppliant and protect him, while at the same time they cast longing eyes upon his wealth. Demosthenes, on the other hand, began by advising the Athenians to turn him away and urged them to beware of involving the city in a war by taking such an unnecessary and unjustifiable action. But a few days later when an inventory was being made of the treasure, Harpalus noticed that Demosthenes was admiring a cup of Persian manufacture and was examining closely the style and the workmanship of the moulding. He then invited him to balance it in his hand and feel the weight of the gold. Demosthenes was astonished at this and asked how much it would fetch, at which Harpalus smiled and replied, 'It would fetch *you* twenty talents.' Then as soon as it was dark, he sent the cup and the twenty talents to Demosthenes' house. Harpalus was exceptionally shrewd at discerning the character of a man who had a passion for gold, which he recognized from the expression which passed over his face and the gleam that lit up his eyes. And he was not deceived in this instance, for Demosthenes could not resist the bait, and having once, as it were admitted a garrison into his house, immediately went over to Harpalus' side. The next day he appeared in the assembly, having first carefully swathed his throat with woollen bandages: then when he was called upon to

1. Harpalus, prince of Elymiotus, was a friend of Alexander's boyhood at the Macedonian court. He accompanied the expedition to Asia and after the battle of Gaugamela was head of the financial superintendence of the empire. He shared the widespread belief that Alexander would never come back from India and during his chief's absence behaved as though he were king and treated his various mistresses as queens. In 325, on the news of Alexander's return he absconded with a large sum of treasure. The next year he appeared off the coast of Attica with thirty ships and 6000 mercenaries and offered the aid of his forces against Alexander. On Demosthenes' proposal the Athenians decided to sequester the treasure until Alexander should demand it. After being imprisoned in Athens, Harpalus made his way to Crete, where he was killed by his own troops. After Alexander's death the Athenians used the treasure to finance their revolt against Macedon.

rise and speak, he made gestures to signify that he had lost his voice. The wits of the day made fun of him by remarking that the orator had been seized overnight not with a common quinsy, but with a silver quinsy. Afterwards it became clear to the whole assembly that he had been bribed, and when he tried to get a hearing to explain his conduct, the people showed their indignation by raising an uproar and shouting him down. At this another speaker rose and shouted sarcastically, 'Men of Athens, won't you give a hearing to the man who has the cup in his hand?'[1]

The Athenians then expelled Harpalus from the city and as they were afraid that they might have to account for the money which the orators had received, they organized a thorough search and ransacked all the speakers' houses, except for that of Callicles, the son of Arrhenides. His was the only house which they exempted, because he was newly married and his bride was living there, so Theopompus tells us.

26. Demosthenes decided to meet the issue squarely and put forward a motion that the matter should be referred for investigation to the Council of the Areopagus, and those against whom the Council found there was a case should be put on trial. However he himself was one of the first to be brought to court, and when the case was heard, he was found guilty, sentenced to a fine of fifty talents, and committed to prison in default of payment.

He tells us that he was overcome with shame at these accusations and that since his weak health made it impossible for him to endure imprisonment, he escaped thanks to the negligence of some of his gaolers, and the active assistance of others. At any rate the story goes that he had not fled far from Athens before he discovered that he was being pursued by some of his opponents, and so he tried to hide himself. Presently they caught up with him, called out to him by name, and begged him to accept some help for his journey. They explained that they had brought money from home for this very purpose, and were only pursuing him to put it into his hands, and they urged him to take heart and not let himself be cast down by what had happened. At this Demosthenes broke out into even more

1. The joke alludes to Demosthenes' cup and to the custom at Greek feasts whereby the cup was passed from hand to hand, and the person holding it had the right to speak or sing a song without interruption.

anguished cries of grief and exclaimed, 'What comfort can I have at leaving a city where even my enemies treat me with a generosity I shall hardly find among friends anywhere else?'

He showed little strength of character during his exile, but spent much of his time in Aegina or Troezen looking towards Attica with tears in his eyes. The only sayings of his which have come down to us from this period are quite unworthy of him and quite inconsistent with the bold actions for which he was responsible when he was active in politics.

We are told that as he was leaving the city, he stretched out his hands towards the Acropolis and exclaimed, 'Athena, goddess and guardian of Athens, how can you take pleasure in these three savage and intractable creatures, the owl, the snake and the people?' And when young men came to visit and converse with him, he would try to dissuade them from having anything to do with politics. He told them that if at the beginning of his political career, he had been offered two roads, the one leading to the rostrum and the assembly, and the other to certain death, and if he could have foreseen the innumerable evils which lie in wait for the politician – the fears, the jealousies, the slanders and the struggles – he would have chosen the path which led directly to destruction.

27. While Demosthenes was still in exile, Alexander died in Babylon,[1] and the Greek states combined yet again to form a league against Macedon. They were encouraged in this action by the gallant exploits of the Athenian general Leosthenes,[2] who had succeeded in driving Antipater, the regent of Macedonia, into the city of Lamia, where he held him besieged. At this the orators Pytheas and Callimedon, who was nicknamed 'the crab', fled from Athens, joined Antipater, and travelled about with the regent's supporters and ambassadors, urging the rest of the Greeks not to rebel against Macedon or to ally themselves with Athens. Demosthenes, on the other hand, attached himself to the Athenian envoys, and threw all his energies into helping them incite the various states to attack the Macedonians and drive them out of Greece. Phylarchus tells us that in Arcadia Pytheas and Demosthenes actually met face to face and abused one another in the assembly, the one speaking for Macedon

1. In June 323 B.C.
2. Leosthenes was killed during the siege towards the end of 322 B.C.

and the other for Greece. Pytheas, so the story goes, argued that just as we can always expect to find sickness in a house when we see asses' milk being carried into it, so a city must be in a state of decay if it receives an embassy from Athens. Demosthenes then turned his illustration against him, by pointing out that asses' milk is given to restore health, and that the Athenians only came to benefit the sick.

At any rate the people of Athens were so pleased with Demosthenes' efforts that they voted for him to be recalled from exile. The decree was introduced by Demon of Paeania, who was a cousin of Demosthenes, and a trireme was dispatched to Aegina to bring him home. When he landed at Piraeus every archon and priest was present and the entire citizen body gathered to watch his arrival and give him an enthusiastic welcome. On this occasion, according to Demetrius of Magnesia, Demosthenes lifted up his hands to heaven and congratulated himself, because he was returning on that day more honourably than Alcibiades had done, for his fellow-citizens had been persuaded, not compelled, to welcome him back. The fine, which had been inflicted on him, however, still remained in force, for it was unconstitutional for the people to abolish a penalty by an act of grace, and so they devised a means to evade the law. It was the custom at the festival of Zeus the Preserver to pay a sum of money to those who prepared and decorated the altar, and so they appointed Demosthenes to make these arrangements for the sum of fifty talents, which had been the amount of his fine.

28. However, Demosthenes did not have long to enjoy his return to his native land, for in the month of Metageitnion of the following year[1] the Greek cause went down to defeat at the battle of Crannon. In the following month of Boedromion a Macedonian garrison entered Munychia, and in the next, Pyanepsion, Demosthenes met his death in the following way.

When reports came in that Antipater and Craterus were marching upon Athens, Demosthenes and his supporters escaped secretly from the city, and the people condemned them to death on the motion of Demades. Meanwhile they had split up and fled in different directions, and Antipater sent out troops to scour the country and arrest them: these detachments were under the command of Archias, who was

1. August 322 B.C. The Greeks were decisively defeated in Thessaly by the Macedonian generals Antipater and Craterus.

known as 'the exile-hunter'. This man was a citizen of the colony of
Thurii in Italy, and it was said that he had at one time been a tragic
actor, and that Polus of Aegina, the finest actor of his time, had been
a pupil of his. According to Hermippus, however, Archias had been
one of the pupils of Lacritus the rhetorician, while Demetrius of
Phalerum says that he was a pupil of Anaximenes the historian.[1] At
any rate Archias discovered that Hypereides the orator, Aristonicus
of Marathon, and Himeraeus the brother of Demetrius of Phalerum
had all taken refuge in the sanctuary of Aeacus at Aegina. He then
had them dragged out by force and sent to Antipater at Cleonae.[2]
There they were put to death, and it is said that Hypereides also had
his tongue cut out.

29. When Archias learned that Demosthenes had taken sanctuary in
the temple of Poseidon at Calauria,[3] he crossed over in some small
boats with a detachment of Thracian spearmen, and tried to persuade
Demosthenes to leave the sanctuary and go with him to Antipater,
assuring him that he would not be harshly treated. It so happened
that Demosthenes had experienced a strange dream the night before,
in which he had seen himself acting in a tragedy and competing with
Archias. But although he acted well and won the applause of the
audience, the verdict went against him, because of the lack of stage
decorations and costumes and the poverty of the production. So
when Archias offered him this string of assurances, Demosthenes
remained seated where he was, looked him full in the face and said,
'Archias, I was never convinced by your acting, and I am no more
convinced by your promises.' Then when Archias became angry and
began to threaten him, he said, 'Ah, before this you were acting a
part, but now you are speaking like the genuine Macedonian oracle.[4]
Give me a few moments to write a letter to my family.' With these
words he retired into the inner part of the temple. There he picked
up his tablets as if he were about to write, put his pen to his mouth,
and bit it, as was his habit when he was thinking out what to say.

1. Anaximenes of Lampsacus, on the Hellespont, was a rhetorician and historian: he is believed to have accompanied Alexander on some of his Asiatic
campaigns.

2. A small city between Corinth and Argos.

3. An island near Troezen: the temple was famous as a supposedly inviolable
sanctuary for the persecuted.

4. i.e. expressing your real sentiments.

He kept the reed between his lips for some while, then covered his head with his cloak and bent down. The soldiers who stood at the door jeered at him, because they supposed that he was afraid to die and called him a faint-hearted weakling, while Archias came near, urged him to get up, and began to repeat his assurances about reconciling him to Antipater. By this time Demosthenes recognized from his sensations that the poison was beginning to work upon him and overcome him, and he uncovered his head, looked steadfastly at Archias and said, 'Now you can play the part of Creon as soon as you wish, and throw my body to the dogs without burying it.[1] I, good Poseidon, will leave your sanctuary while I am still alive, although Antipater and his Macedonians would have been ready to defile it with murder.' With these words he asked to be supported, since by now he was trembling and could scarcely stand, and as they were helping him to walk past the altar, he fell, and with a groan gave up the ghost.

30. As for the poison, Ariston says that he sucked it from the reed as I have described, but a man named Pappus, from whom Hermippus took his account of the scene says that when Demosthenes had fallen by the side of the altar, the opening words of a letter were found on his tablets, beginning 'Demosthenes to Antipater' and nothing more. The speed and suddenness of his death astonished everybody, and the Thracian guards who had been standing at the door said that he took the poison into his hand from a cloth, put it to his mouth and swallowed it. They themselves had supposed that what he had swallowed was gold, but the young girl who waited on him told Archias, in answer to his questions, that Demosthenes had long carried this cloth girdle with him as a last resort to protect him against his enemies. Eratosthenes says that Demosthenes carried the poison in a hollow bracelet, which he wore as an ornament upon his arm. There is no need for me to list all the different versions of this scene which have been given by the many authors who have described it. I will mention only that of Demochares one of his kinsmen, who says that in his opinion Demosthenes did not die from poison, but thanks to the honour and benevolence shown him by the gods, he was delivered from the cruelty of the Macedonians by a swift and painless

1. The allusion is to Sophocles' *Antigone*, in which Creon decrees that the body of Polyneices, Antigone's brother is to be left unburied.

death. He died on the sixteenth of the month Pyanepsion, the most solemn day of the festival of the Thesmophoria,[1] which the women observe by fasting in the temple of the goddess.

Soon after his death the people of Athens paid him fitting honours by erecting his statue in bronze,[2] and by decreeing that the eldest member of his family should be maintained in the *prytaneum*[3] at the public expense. On the base of his statue was carved this famous inscription.

If only your strength had been equal, Demosthenes, to your wisdom
Never would Greece have been ruled by a Macedonian Ares.

It is of course absurd to say, as some writers have done, that Demosthenes himself composed these lines in Calauria just before he took the poison.

31. A little while before I paid my first visit to Athens, the following episode is said to have occurred. A soldier who had been summoned by his commanding officer to be tried for some offence, put what little money he had between the hands of this statue which are represented as clasped together. Beside the statue grew a small plane-tree, and the leaves from the tree, whether they were blown there by chance or placed there on purpose by the soldier, piled up over the gold and hid it for a long time. Finally the soldier returned and found his treasure intact, and later the story spread abroad and became a theme to inspire the wits of the city to compete with one another in their epigrams celebrating the incorruptibility of Demosthenes.

As for Demades, he did not live long to enjoy his growing prestige. The vengeance of the gods for the part he had played in the death of Demosthenes took him to Macedonia, where he justly met his death at the hands of the people he had so basely flattered. He had for some time already been disliked by the Macedonians, but he now incurred an accusation which it was impossible for him to evade. A letter of his was intercepted in which he had urged Perdiccas to seize the throne of Macedonia and rescue the Greeks, who he said were attached to it

1. An annual festival, which lasted three days, dedicated to the goddesses Demeter and Persephone: it was observed by the women of the noblest families in Athens.

2. The statue was the work of Polyeuctus and was erected in 280 B.C.

3. The city hall, in which citizens who had performed notable public services and distinguished foreigners were privileged to dine.

only by the old and rotten thread, by which he meant Antipater. Deinarchus of Corinth accused him of treason and Cassander was so enraged at his treachery that he killed Demades' son as he stood by his father's side, and then ordered Demades himself to be put to death. Through this terrible fate he learned that traitors always betray themselves first, a truth which Demosthenes had often prophesied to him, but which he would not believe.

And so, Sosius, you have the life of Demosthenes, which I have drawn from all that I have read or heard about him.

6

PHOCION[1]

[402–318 B.C.]

* *
*

DEMADES the orator, who rose to power in Athens by serving the interests of Antipater and the Macedonians, was in consequence obliged to propose and support many measures which were contrary to the city's dignity and traditions. He often made the excuse that by the time he came to the helm, the ship of state was already a wreck. It was surely an exaggeration for Demades to say this; but it has more of the ring of truth if it is applied to the career of Phocion. Indeed one might say that Demades himself was the mere flotsam of public life: his course of conduct both in personal and in public life was so outrageous as to make Antipater remark of him that in his old age he had become like a victim which has been dismembered for sacrifice – there was nothing left but the tongue and the guts. Phocion, on the other hand, was fated to carry on an unequal struggle against the violent and distressing events through which he lived, when the misfortunes suffered by Greece caused his virtues to be overshadowed and undervalued. We need not agree with Sophocles' description of how virtue may be rendered ineffectual when he says

> Reason, my lord, may dwell within a man
> And yet abandon him, when troubles come.

but we must admit that when Fortune is ranged against good men, she prevails to the extent that she often brings upon them slanders and false accusations instead of the honour and gratitude which they deserve, and in this way undermines the world's belief in their virtue.

2. On the other hand it is often held that a people is more inclined to insult and humiliate its best men when the nation's affairs are going

1. For places mentioned in this *Life*, see Maps 1 and 2, pp. 433–5.

well, because it then feels buoyed up by a sense of ascendancy and power: but equally the opposite has been known to happen. Misfortunes cause men's dispositions to become bitter, intolerant and ready to take offence at trifles, they grow peevish and unwilling to listen, and are angry with any counsellor who gives them forthright advice. If he makes criticisms, they think he is insulting them on account of their misfortunes, and if he speaks his mind freely they feel that he is despising them. Just as honey can irritate wounded and ulcerated parts of the body, so also does truthful and reasoned advice sting and provoke people who are in trouble, unless it is offered in a kindly and soothing manner. It is no doubt for this reason that Homer uses the word *menoeikes* to signify that which is pleasant because it yields (*hypeikon*) to that part of the soul which experiences pleasure, and does not fight with or oppose it. Just as an eye that is inflamed finds most relief in colours which are subdued and lack lustre, and turns away from those which are brilliant and dazzling, so too a city which is passing through a crisis in its fortunes becomes too timid and sensitive to endure plain speaking at the very moment that it needs it most badly, because the situation may offer no chance of retrieving the mistakes that have been made. It is in a state of this kind that political life is most dangerous: here the man who speaks only to please the people may be involved in their ruin, but the man who refuses to indulge them may be destroyed even sooner.

Now the sun, so the mathematicians tell us, does not move in the same path as the rest of the heavenly bodies, nor yet in a completely opposite direction, but pursues an oblique course at a slight angle to theirs: it follows a spiral progression with gentle and easy curves, and by this means all created things are kept in their place and the most suitable blending of the elements is maintained. So too in political affairs, a method of government which is too rigid and opposes the popular will on every occasion will be resented as harsh and overbearing, but on the other hand, to acquiesce in all the demands of the people and share in their mistakes, is a dangerous, sometimes a catastrophic policy. The art of wise administration consists in making certain concessions and granting that which will please the people, while demanding in return an obedience and cooperation which will benefit the whole community – and men will cooperate readily and usefully in many ways provided they are not treated harshly and despotically all the time. This is the style of government which ensures the security of the state, but its practice is arduous and beset with difficulties, and it must combine those elements of severity and benevolence which are so hard to balance. But if such a happy mixture can be achieved, it provides the most complete and perfect blending of all rhythms and all harmonies. It is in this fashion, we are told, that God governs the universe, introducing his ultimate purpose not by force but by reason and persuasion.

3. We find a parallel to Phocion's situation in the life of the younger Cato.[1] He lacked the power of persuasion, his manner did not endear him to the people, and he never attained much popularity in his political career. Cicero tells us that he was defeated when he stood for the consulship, because he conducted his campaign as if he had been living in Plato's republic, not among the dregs of the descendants of Romulus, but I should rather say that he suffered in the same way as certain kinds of fruit do when they appear out of season: people gaze at them with wonder and delight, but do not eat them. In the same way when the old style of virtue which had vanished for many years was reincarnated in the person of Cato amid a general climate of depraved lives and corrupted manners, it won great fame and estimation. But it proved quite unsuited to men's needs: its nature was grand but ponderous, and therefore out of harmony with the age in which he lived. Cato did not find the ship of state on her beam-ends, as Phocion did, but beset by storms and heavy seas. In politics he could only serve her by lending a hand with the sails and the shrouds, so to speak, and by giving his support to those with greater influence, since he himself was kept away from the helm, but nevertheless he gave Fortune a hard struggle. In the end the Roman constitution was violated and overthrown, but this was the work of others and only came about slowly, with difficulty, and after a long struggle in which the cause of the Republic almost prevailed through Cato and his virtue. It is because of this quality – not because of general resemblances between the two – that I make this comparison with Phocion, in the sense that both were good men and devoted to the public interest. My point is that two men may possess the same attribute in different forms. For example the courage of Alcibiades is quite distinct from that of Epaminondas, the wisdom of Themistocles from that of Aristides, and the justice of Numa from that of Agesilaus. But in the case of

1. See Introduction, p. 9.

Cato and Phocion it is clear that their virtues bore the same stamp, shape and colour down to the most minute particulars. Both alike displayed the same blend of kindness and severity, of caution and daring, of solicitude for the safety of others and disregard for their own: both alike abhorred dishonour, but were indefatigable in the pursuit of justice. We shall therefore need a most finely adjusted instrument, so to speak, to discover and define the points of difference between them.

4. It is generally agreed that Cato's origins which I shall describe later, were noble, but Phocion's too, so far as I can judge, were by no means lowly or undistinguished. If his father had really been a pestle-maker, as Idomeneus makes out, we may be sure that Glaucippus, the son of Phocion's opponent Hypereides, would not have missed the opportunity of mentioning his humble birth in the speech he composed which cast so many aspersions on Phocion's character. Nor, in that case, would Phocion have enjoyed a life of leisure or the excellent education which enabled him to become a pupil of Plato's when he was only a boy, in later life a disciple of Xenocrates in the Academy, and to devote himself to the noblest pursuits from the very beginning of his career. Hardly any Athenian ever saw him laugh or shed tears, so Douris tells us, nor did he make use of the public bath, or take his hand from under his cloak – that is when he wore a cloak. Indeed whenever he was in the country or on active service, he wore neither shoes nor an outer garment, unless the cold was unendurably bitter, and after a while his soldiers used to make a joke of this habit and say that when Phocion put on his cloak it was the sign of a hard winter.

5. By nature he was one of the kindest and most considerate of men, but his appearance was stern and forbidding, so that those who did not know him intimately were discouraged from talking to him alone. Chares raised a laugh at Phocion's expense in one of his speeches by referring to his lowering brow, whereupon Phocion retorted, 'At least this brow of mine has never caused you any harm, but the laughter of those who are now sneering at me has given the city plenty to cry about.'

In the same way Phocion's choice of words brought great benefit to his listeners, since it was full of keen insight which often led to successful action, but it also had a brevity which made his expression peremptory, severe and altogether lacking in charm. Zeno used to say that a philosopher should steep his words in meaning before he utters them, and Phocion's speeches followed this principle, in that they used the fewest possible words to convey the strongest concentration of meaning. This characteristic of his is probably what Polyeuctus the Sphettian had in mind when he said that Demosthenes was the best orator, but Phocion the most effective speaker, for just as the coins which are very small in bulk are those which are very great in value, so effectiveness of speech may be judged by the ability to communicate the maximum of meaning within the smallest possible compass. There is a story that once, when the audience was beginning to fill up the theatre, Phocion was seen walking about behind the stage lost in thought. One of his friends remarked, 'You seem to be pondering something, Phocion.' 'Yes,' he said, 'I am thinking out whether I can shorten the speech I am going to make to the Athenians.' Demosthenes himself, who had a very low opinion of the other orators, used to say quietly to his friends whenever Phocion rose to speak, 'Here comes the chopper of my speeches.' But this remark should perhaps be taken as referring to Phocion's character since a mere word or a nod from a good man carries more weight than any number of elaborate pieces of reasoning or flowery periods.

6. As a young man Phocion attached himself to Chabrias, the general, and followed him on his campaigns. In these operations he gained plenty of experience of action, and also on occasion he was able to check the irregularities of Chabrias' temperament, which was both inconsistent and liable to fly to extremes. Normally Chabrias was phlegmatic and difficult to move, but once in action his spirits would be roused and kindled, and he would rush into the thick of the battle and expose himself unnecessarily. This was in fact what happened at Chios,[1] where he undoubtedly sacrificed his life by being the first to run his trireme on shore in the effort to force a landing in the face of the enemy. On these occasions Phocion, who knew how to temper courage and initiative with prudence, would urge on Chabrias when he was slow to act, but would restrain his impetuosity when this was out of place. The result was that Chabrias, who was a good-natured and upright man, became much attached to Phocion and promoted him to a number of enterprises and commands. In

this way he was employed in most of the important military operations of the time and his name became known throughout Greece.
In particular, on the occasion of the sea battle off Naxos, he gave
Phocion the opportunity to distinguish himself and enhance his
reputation: he placed him in command of the left wing, and it was
here that the fighting raged most fiercely and the issue was quickly
decided. This was the first sea battle[1] in which the Athenians had
fought against Greek opponents since the capture of their city at the
end of the Peloponnesian war,[2] and as they won it without allies they
were overjoyed at Chabrias' triumph and came to regard Phocion as
a commander of great potential. The battle was won at the time when
the Great Mysteries were being celebrated at Eleusis, and to commemorate this Chabrias made it his custom to provide the Athenians
with wine for the festival every year on the sixteenth day of the month
Boedromion.[3]

7. After this Chabrias sent out Phocion to collect the contributions
which were due from a number of islands and gave him an escort of
twenty warships. Phocion's comment was that if he was being sent to
fight the islanders he would need a larger force, but that if he was visiting them as allies, one ship was enough. He sailed in his own trireme,
discussed the purpose of his mission with the cities, dealt in a frank yet
considerate manner with their leading men, and returned home with a
large fleet which the allies themselves dispatched to carry the tribute
to Athens. Phocion not only honoured and showed his regard for
Chabrias as long as the older man was alive, but when he died he took
good care of his family. He paid particular attention to Chabrias' son
Ctesippus, whom he tried to make into a good man, and although he
found the youth stupid and intractable, he persevered in trying to
correct and cover up his faults. But on one occasion when the young
man was serving on an expedition, he continually vexed Phocion by
asking him tiresome questions and offering him ill-timed advice, as
though he were in a position to criticize the general and share in his
command. Then at last Phocion exclaimed, 'O Chabrias, Chabrias,
did ever a man show so much gratitude for your friendship as I do in
putting up with your son?'

Phocion recognized that the politicians of his time had divided between themselves the duties of the general and of the orator, almost as

I. 376 B.C.   2. 404 B.C.   3. August.

if they had cast lots for them. Thus some men such as Eubulus, Aristophon, Demosthenes, Lycurgus and Hypereides did nothing but make speeches before the people and introduce measures, while others such as Diopeithes, Menestheus, Leosthenes and Chabrias pursued their careers by holding the office of general and directing campaigns. Phocion wished to revive the kind of public service which had been rendered by Pericles, Aristides and Solon, which was at once comprehensive and well-balanced, so that it included both political and military service to the state. For each of these men had proved himself in the words of Archilochus

> Equally fitted to follow the stern commands of the War-God
> Or to promote the arts of peace, the delights of the Muses,

and Phocion did not forget that Athena, the city's patron deity, presided over the arts both of war and of peace.

8. Having adopted this principle, Phocion's policies were always aimed at preserving a state of peace; yet in spite of this he held the office of general more frequently not only than any of his contemporaries, but even than any of his predecessors. He never sought nor campaigned for the post, but neither did he shun or decline it when his city called upon him. It is generally agreed that he held the office of general forty-five times, yet he never once attended the election, but was always absent when the people sent for him and chose him. Those who did not understand the situation were constantly amazed at the Athenians' behaviour, since Phocion opposed their wishes more often than any other leader, and never said or did anything to win their favour. The truth is that just as kings are supposed to call in their flatterers after dinner has been served, so the Athenians would listen to the most sprightly and sophisticated of their demagogues by way of entertainment; but when they wanted a commander, they would switch to a more sober and serious mood and would call upon the wisest and most austere of their citizens, the man who alone, or at least more than all the rest, stood fast in opposing their impulses and wishes. Indeed when an oracle from Delphi was read out one day in the assembly, which declared that the rest of the Athenians were unanimous in their opinions and that there was only one man who dissented from them, Phocion came forward and told them that they need look no further: he himself was the man in question, for it was

only he who disapproved of everything that they did. And on another occasion when he uttered some sentiment which was greeted with applause and saw that the whole assembly had accepted his argument, he turned to his friends and asked them, 'Can it be that I have been arguing on the wrong side without knowing it?'

9. One day the Athenians were collecting money for a public sacrifice. Everybody else put in their contribution, but Phocion after he had several times been invited to follow suit, remarked, 'I suggest you appeal to these rich men. I should be ashamed to give you anything before I have paid my debt to this man here,' and he pointed to Callicles, the money-lender. On another occasion when his listeners would not stop clamouring and trying to shout him down, he told them this fable: 'Once upon a time, there was a cowardly man who was setting out for a war. Some ravens began to croak around him, whereupon he laid down his arms and sat still. After a while he picked them up and started again. Then, when the ravens croaked once more, he stopped and said, "You may croak to your hearts' content, but you shall never make a meal of me."' On another occasion when the Athenians urged him to lead them out against the enemy and called him a coward and a man of no spirit because he refused, he retorted, 'You cannot make me bold, and I cannot make you cowards. But we know very well what each of us really is.' Then at a time of crisis for Athens, when the people were showing great hostility towards him and demanding an inquiry into his generalship, Phocion's advice was, 'My friends, first of all make sure of your own safety.' Again when the people had been humble and submissive during a war, but as soon as peace had been proclaimed became overbearing and denounced him for having robbed them of victory, he told them, 'You are lucky to have a general who knows you – otherwise you would have been ruined long ago.' When there was a territorial dispute with Boeotia, about which the Athenians refused to negotiate but insisted on going to war, he recommended them to fight by using words, in which they had the advantage, not weapons, in which they were inferior. When he was addressing the assembly and the people refused to take his advice or even to give him a hearing, he told them, 'You can make me act against my wishes, but you shall never make me speak against my judgement.'

Demosthenes, one of the orators who opposed his policies, said to him, 'One of these days, Phocion, the Athenians will kill you, if they lose their heads,' to which Phocion replied, 'Yes, but they will kill you, if they get them back again.' Once on a very hot day he saw Polyeuctus the Sphettian urging the Athenians to declare war on Philip of Macedon. The speaker was gasping as he was a very fat man, the sweat was pouring off him, and he was gulping down great draughts of water, whereupon Phocion remarked, 'It is most fitting that you should vote for war on the strength of this man's advice. What sort of figure do you think he will cut when the enemy are close at hand and he is carrying a shield and a breastplate? Even the effort of making a prepared speech to you is enough to suffocate him!' On another occasion Lycurgus showered abuse on him in the public assembly, and was particularly bitter because, when Alexander of Macedon had demanded that ten orators should be surrendered to him, Phocion had supported the request.[1] Phocion's reply was, 'I have often given this people good advice, but they will not listen to me.'

10. There was a certain Archibiades who was nicknamed Laconistes, because he aped the Spartans by growing a huge beard, wearing a short cloak, and going about with a permanent scowl on his face. At a meeting of the Council, Phocion was greeted with a stormy reception, and so he appealed to this man to testify in his favour. However when Archibiades rose to speak, he merely gave the advice which he thought would please the Athenians, whereupon Phocion seized him by the beard and exclaimed, 'Archibiades, you might just as well have shaved this off!' Aristogeiton, the common informer, was well known in the assembly as a fire-eater who was always trying to urge the people into warlike action, but when the lists of those to be selected for military service had to be drawn up, he arrived hobbling with the aid of a staff and with both legs bandaged. Phocion, who was on the rostrum, caught sight of him in the distance and cried out, 'Put down Aristogeiton as lame and unfit for service.' All these sayings of his make it astonishing that a man who created such a harsh and austere impression should ever have earned the nickname of the Good.

It is certainly difficult, though not, I think, impossible for the same man to be at once sweet and sharp, as a wine can be. In the same way other men and other wines may at first appear agreeable, but in the end prove both unpleasant and harmful to those who use them. And

1. See ch. 17. The episode took place in 335 B.C. after the capture of Thebes.

yet we are told that Hypereides once said to the people. 'Men of
Athens, do not ask yourself whether I am harsh, but whether I am
paid to be harsh.' In other words his question implied that the populace would only fear or attack men because they were avaricious, and
not because they used their power to gratify their insolence, their
envy, their anger, or their ambition. Phocion, then, never harmed
any of his fellow-citizens out of personal spite, nor did he regard a
single one of them as his enemy: if he ever showed himself to be
harsh or stubborn or inexorable, it was only to the extent that he was
forced to struggle against those who opposed his efforts to save his
country. In all his other dealings, he was benevolent, accessible and
considerate to everyone, indeed he even came to the rescue of his
opponents when they were in trouble or in danger of being put on
trial for their actions. Once when his friends reproached him for
appearing on behalf of some worthless individual who had been
accused, he retorted that good men need no defenders. Again when
Aristogeiton the public informer had been condemned and begged
Phocion to visit him, he responded to the appeal and set out for the
prison. His friends tried to prevent him, whereupon he said to them,
'Let me go, my friends: after all, where would one rather meet
Aristogeiton than in prison?'

11. Certainly if the Athenians sent out emissaries under the command
of any general other than Phocion, the allies and inhabitants of the
islands would always treat them as enemies. They would bar their
gates, close their harbours, and bring back their herds, their slaves,
their wives and their children from the countryside to shelter behind
the city walls. But whenever Phocion was in command, they would
come far out to sea to meet him in their ships, put garlands on their
heads and welcome him into their homes with joy.

12. King Philip of Macedon planned to make himself master of
Euboea by stealth.[1] He brought over an army from Macedonia and
began to take control of the cities by installing tyrants there. Plutarch
of Eretria appealed to the Athenians and begged them to save the
island from falling under the rule of Macedon: in consequence
Phocion was sent out in command of a small expedition on the assumption that the people of the island would rally enthusiastically to his

1. In 348 B.C.

support. But when he arrived, he found that Euboea was full of traitors; the people were disaffected, their patriotism had been undermined by Philip's bribes, and in consequence his own situation was
extremely dangerous. Accordingly Phocion occupied a ridge which
was separated by a deep ravine from the plains which surrounded the
city of Tamynae, and there he established himself and concentrated
the best of his troops. As for the disorderly, argumentative and un-
trustworthy soldiers in his force who were apt to steal out of his lines
and desert, he told his officers to make no effort to keep them: he calculated that if they remained in his camp, they would be useless
because of their lack of discipline and would only demoralize those soldiers who were reliable, while if they returned to Athens the memory
of their cowardice would make them less likely to denounce him, and
would deter them from making false accusations.

13. When the enemy advanced against him, he ordered his men to
stand to arms, but to remain quiet until he had finished sacrificing. In
this way a long time elapsed, possibly because the omens were unfavourable, but alternatively because he wanted to draw the enemy
closer to his position. At this Plutarch the Eretrian, who imagined
that Phocion's backwardness in engaging was due to cowardice, began the action by charging the enemy at the head of his mercenaries:
then when the cavalry saw him advance, they could not bear to remain idle but at once rode at their opponents, galloping out of the
camp in scattered groups and without formation. The result was that
first the leading ranks were repulsed, then the whole body of troops
broke, and Plutarch himself took to his heels. The enemy surged forward up to the palisade of Phocion's camp and, imagining that they
were masters of the field, tried to tear up the stakes of which it was
built. But at this moment the sacrifices were completed, the Athenians burst out of their camp, routed the attackers and cut down most
of them as they strove to escape among the entrenchments. Phocion
then ordered his phalanx to halt and hold its ground, so that the soldiers who had been scattered in the earlier action could rally to it and
re-form: meanwhile he himself with his picked troops launched a fresh
attack on the enemy. There followed a fierce engagement in which all
the Athenians fought with great courage and gallantry: on this occasion Thallus the son of Cineas and Glaucus the son of Polymedes who
fought side by side with Phocion distinguished themselves most con-

spicuously. Cleophanes also made a name for himself in the battle. It
was he who halted the cavalry in their headlong flight, and by shouting at them to rally to their general who was in great danger, he
made them ride back and complete the victory which had been won
by the infantry. After this battle Phocion had Plutarch banished from
Eretria, and he also captured a fortress named Zaretra, which commands the narrowest part of the island where the sea reduces it to a
mere neck of land. He also released all his Greek prisoners, for he was
afraid that the demagogues at Athens might give way to a fit of anger
and persuade the people to pass some cruel sentence on them.

14. After these successes Phocion sailed home, but all too soon the
allies were to feel the absence of his high principles and just conduct,
and the Athenians the loss of the experience and vigour he had just
shown. His successor Molossus carried on the war so ineptly that he
was actually captured by the enemy.

Several years later[1] Philip invaded the Hellespont with all his
forces: he had great hopes of subduing the Chersonese and making
himself master of Perinthus and Byzantium at the same time. The
Athenians were anxious to help these cities, but thanks to the efforts
of the demagogues it was Chares who was appointed to command the
expedition. When he arrived there he achieved nothing worthy of the
size of his force, and the cities even refused to allow his fleet to enter
their harbours. They all regarded him with suspicion and he was reduced to roaming about the country, where he extorted money from
the Athenians' allies and was treated with contempt by their enemies.
At length the people in Athens, urged on by the demagogues, became exasperated with him and began to regret that they had ever sent
help to the Byzantines. But then Phocion rose in the assembly and
declared that they had no right to blame the allies for withholding
their trust: the fault lay with their own generals who had failed to
inspire it. 'These men,' he declared, 'make you feared even by those
who need your help to save them.'

The people were so impressed by this speech that they again
changed their minds. They ordered Phocion to raise another army
and set out to help the allies on the Hellespont. It was this decision
above all which saved Byzantium. Phocion's credit already stood high
there, but more important still Leon, one of their leading citizens who

1. In 340 B.C.

was well known among the Byzantines for his courage and who had
been a close friend of Phocion's at the Academy, personally guaranteed the Athenian's good faith. The citizens would not let Phocion
encamp outside their walls as he had intended, but opened their gates,
welcomed the Athenians into their homes and fraternized with them.
After this gesture of confidence the Athenians not only behaved with
exemplary discipline and courtesy inside the city, but fought with
great spirit to defend it. The result was that in this campaign Philip
was driven out of the Hellespont and his previous reputation as an
unbeatable commander suffered a severe setback. Besides this Phocion
captured several of Philip's ships and recaptured some cities which the
Macedonian king had garrisoned. He also made landings at a number
of points on Philip's territory, plundered and overran it: finally when
an enemy force was mustered for its defence, he was wounded and
sailed back home.

15. On one occasion the people of Megara appealed secretly to Athens
for help.[1] Phocion was afraid that the Boeotians might discover this
and prevent the Athenians from sending help, and so he summoned a
meeting of the assembly early in the morning and explained the communication from Megara. Then as soon as the necessary decree had
been approved, he had the trumpet sounded, ordered his men to leave
the assembly and immediately marched them away under arms. The
Megarians received him with enthusiasm, and he proceeded to fortify
their harbour at Nisaea and to build two long walls running down to
it from the city: in this way he made Megara's communications with
the sea so secure that she had no need to fear her enemies by land and
could be connected with Athens by sea.

16. A few years later Athens was on the brink of war with Philip,[2] and
in Phocion's absence other generals were elected to take charge of the
expected campaign. However when Phocion returned with his fleet
from the islands, he at first tried to persuade the people not to go to
war and to accept Philip's terms, in view of the fact that the king was
peaceably inclined and greatly feared the dangers which were likely
to ensue from a war. One of the Athenians who made his living by

1. About 344 B.C. The Megarians wished to resist a pro-Macedonian faction
inside the city.
2. 340 B.C.

hanging about the law-courts and acting as a public informer opposed Phocion and asked, 'Do you dare to try to dissuade the Athenians from going to war when they are already under arms?' 'Certainly I do,' retorted Phocion, 'and I am not forgetting that if we go to war, it is I who will be in charge, while if we remain at peace, it will be you.' In the event Phocion could not make his point of view prevail. It was Demosthenes who carried the day and urged the Athenians to engage Philip as far away from Athens as possible. At this Phocion declared, 'The problem is not where we are going to fight, my good sir, but how we are to win the battle. If we can do that, we shall keep the war at a distance anyhow, but it is the loser who finds that the horrors of war are on his very doorstep.' But when Athens was defeated[1] and the most discontented and revolutionary elements among the people dragged Charidemus to the public platform and clamoured for him to be appointed general, the more reputable citizens were filled with alarm. They appealed to the Council of the Areopagus, and after its members had implored the people with tears and entreaties, they prevailed upon them at last to allow Phocion to take charge of the city.

Phocion considered that the terms which Philip was offering to Athens were generous and humane and that the Athenians should accept them. But when Demades proposed a motion that the city should associate herself with the common peace and take part in the congress for all the states,[2] Phocion would not support it until he had first discovered what demands Philip would make upon the Greeks. His advice was overruled because of the critical situation in which Athens stood, but as soon as he saw that the Athenians were beginning to regret their choice, because they were being called upon to supply Philip with cavalry and warships, he said to them, 'This is exactly what I was afraid of when I resisted your proposals, but since you made the choice, you must not allow yourselves to become disappointed or cast down. You must remember that your ancestors sometimes gave the orders, and at other times had to submit to them: but because they acted with honour in both situations, they saved their city and the rest of the Greeks.' A little later, when Philip was assassinated, the people's first impulse was to offer up sacrifice for the good news, but Phocion opposed this. He said it would show an ignoble

1. At Chaeronea in 338 B.C.
2. The League of Corinth, the alliance into which Philip organized the Greek states after Chaeronea.

spirit to rejoice at what had happened, and reminded them that the army which had opposed them at Chaeronea had been weakened by the loss of no more than one man.

17. Again when Demosthenes was speaking abusively of Alexander even while the king was already advancing upon Thebes, Phocion quoted to him the line from the *Odyssey*

Foolhardy man, why provoke one whose temper is savage already?[1]

'Why provoke one who is also a man of limitless ambition? Or do you wish, when there is already a fearful holocaust on our borders, to make the flames spread to our city too? My whole object in taking up the burden of office was to prevent this, and I shall not allow my fellow-citizens to destroy themselves, even if they wish it.'

A little later, after Thebes had been destroyed,[2] Alexander demanded that Demosthenes, Lycurgus, Hypereides, Charidemus and several others should be handed over to him. When the people heard this proposal, the whole assembly turned their gaze upon Phocion and called upon him repeatedly by name. Phocion then rose to his feet. He beckoned to his side one of his closest friends, whom he loved and confided in above all others and said, 'These men, whom Alexander has demanded, have brought our city to such a pass that for my part, even if the king were to ask for my friend Nicocles, I should urge you to give him up. And if I myself could sacrifice my life to save you all, I should count this a happy fate. I feel pity too, men of Athens, for the Thebans who have fled here for shelter, but it is enough for Greece to have to mourn the destruction of Thebes. For this reason it is better to ask for mercy and to intercede with the victors, both for you and for them, than to fight.'

We are told that when the first decree was presented to Alexander, in which the Athenians refused to hand over the men he had demanded, he flung it from him, turned his back on the envoys and left the room. But the second one, which was brought by Phocion, he accepted, since he had learned from the older Macedonians that Philip had always admired this man. Alexander not only consented to receive Phocion and hear his petition, but he actually listened to his advice, which was as follows. If it was peace that Alexander wanted above all, then he should make an end of the fighting, but if it was glory, then

1. *Odyssey* ix, 494. The reference is to Polyphemus.   2. 335 B.C.

he should transfer the theatre of the war and turn his arms away from Greece against the barbarians. Phocion spoke at length and his words were well chosen to fit Alexander's character and aspirations, with the result that he quite transformed the king's mood and allayed his resentment against the Athenians. In this frame of mind, Alexander told Phocion that the Athenians ought to watch the course of events with great care, since if anything happened to him, they were the people who should become the leaders of Greece. In private too he welcomed Phocion as his friend and guest and treated him with greater honour than even most of his closest associates enjoyed. At any rate the historian Douris tells us that after Alexander had become great and had conquered Darius, he left out the customary word of greeting, *chairein* in all his letters, except when he wrote to Phocion. For two men alone, Phocion and Antipater, he used the word: this detail is also recorded by Chares.

18. As regards the story of the money offered to Phocion, it is generally agreed that Alexander sent him a present of a hundred talents. When this arrived in Athens, Phocion asked those who brought it why, when there were so many Athenians to choose from, Alexander should have singled out him as the recipient of such a huge sum. They answered, 'Because Alexander considers that only you are a good and honourable man.' Phocion's reply was, 'In that case let him allow me to continue in that state and to enjoy that reputation always.' But when the messengers followed him to his house and saw his frugal way of life, how his wife kneaded the bread, while Phocion with his own hands drew water from the well and washed their feet, they were indignant, and pressed him even more insistently to accept the money: they exclaimed that it was monstrous that Phocion, who was an honoured friend of the king should live in such poverty. Phocion caught sight of a poor old man who was walking by dressed in a squalid cloak, and so he asked them which of the two they thought inferior, himself or the old man. They begged him not to make such a comparison, whereupon Phocion replied, 'Well, this man has less to live on than I have, and yet he finds it quite enough. In other words,' he went on, 'either I make no use of this enormous sum, or if I do, I shall destroy my good name with the Athenians and with the king as well.'

So the treasure went back from Athens to where it had come from, after it had served to prove to the Greeks that the man who did not need such a sum was richer than the man who had offered it. For his part Alexander was displeased, and wrote to Phocion that he did not consider those who refused to accept anything from him to be his friends. Even then Phocion would not take the money, but he did ask for the release of Echecratides the sophist, Athenodorus of Imbros and two Rhodians, Demaratus and Sparton, who had been arrested on various charges and imprisoned at Sardis. Alexander immediately set these men free, and years later, when he sent Craterus back to Macedonia,[1] he ordered him to make over to Phocion the revenue of whichever one of four cities he might choose. The cities were Cius, Gergittus, Mylasa and Elea, and he insisted even more vehemently than before that he would be angry if Phocion did not accept this gift. But Phocion again declined, and soon afterwards Alexander died. Phocion's house, which is in the quarter of Athens known as Melite, can be seen to this day. It is decorated with a number of plates of bronze, but in other respects it is simple and unpretentious.

19. As for Phocion's wives we have no record of the first, except for the fact that she was a sister of Cephisodotus the sculptor. But his second wife was as celebrated among the Athenians for her modesty and simplicity as was Phocion for his integrity. On one occasion when the Athenians were watching a performance of some new tragedies, the actor who was to play the part of the queen asked the *choregus*, the sponsor of the festival, to provide him with a large number of women attendants, all of them dressed in expensive costumes. When the sponsor declined to provide these, the actor became indignant and kept the audience waiting by refusing to make his entrance. At this the sponsor, whose name was Melanthius, pushed him on to the stage, shouting out at the same time, 'Don't you see Phocion's wife, who always goes out with only one maidservant to wait on her? Why should you give yourself these airs and turn all our wives' heads with your extravagance?' His words could be heard by the whole audience, and were greeted with loud applause. It was Phocion's wife too who remarked, when an Ionian woman who was staying with her showed off her gold ornaments and her collars and necklaces glittering with

1. 324 B.C. Craterus had been ordered to bring back some of Alexander's veterans to Macedonia.

jewels, 'My ornament is Phocion, who is just now serving his twentieth year as a general of Athens.'

20. When Phocion's son Phocus was anxious to take part in the Panathenaic games as an equestrian acrobat, Phocion gave him permission. This was not because he cared whether or not his son won a prize, but rather because he hoped that the young man would benefit from the exercise and physical training that were needed for the race, for in general Phocus had led a disorderly life and was fond of drinking. He won the race and received many invitations from friends who wished to celebrate his victory in their houses, but Phocion allowed only one host to have this honour, and declined all the other invitations. When Phocion came to the house and saw the magnificence of the preparations, he was particularly struck by the basins of spiced wine which were provided to wash the feet of the guests as they arrived, and he called his son and said, 'Phocus, won't you prevent your friend from spoiling your victory?' Later he decided to remove his son altogether from the Athenian style of living, and so he took him to Sparta and placed him among the young men who were undergoing the traditional course of Spartan discipline. This annoyed the Athenians, since it implied that Phocion had a poor opinion of their own customs and institutions, and on one occcasion Demades said to him, 'Phocion, why don't we try to persuade the Athenians to adopt the Spartan constitution? If you give me the word, I am quite ready to introduce the necessary legislation.' 'Yes, why not?', replied Phocion, 'With all these exotic perfumes and lotions you put on you would be just the man to sing the praises of Lycurgus and sell the Athenians the idea of plain food and state-controlled dining halls.'

21. When Alexander wrote requesting the Athenians to send him warships and the other orators opposed the idea, the Council invited Phocion to give his opinion. 'My advice,' he said, 'is that you should either possess superior strength yourselves, or be on good terms with those who do possess it.' When Pytheas, who at that time was just beginning to speak in public, reeled off a long harangue with complete self-confidence, Phocion remarked, 'You had better hold your tongue and remember that you are a servant of the people, and a newly bought one at that.' Again when Harpalus,[1] Alexander's treas-

1. Harpalus deserted Alexander's administration in Asia, absconded with large sums of money and sought refuge in Attica. See also *Demosthenes*, ch. 25.

urer, landed in Attica, and those of the demagogues who were in the habit of trading their political influence rushed to him and vied eagerly for his favours, he scattered a few trifles among them from his hoard to whet their appetite. But he immediately sent a message to Phocion, offered him seven hundred talents and placed himself and the whole of his property at his disposal in return for his protection. Phocion answered sharply that Harpalus would regret it if he did not give up his attempts to corrupt the city, and for the moment the man was abashed, and ceased his efforts. But soon afterwards, when the Athenians met to consider his case, he discovered that those who had accepted money from him were now changing sides and denouncing him to prevent themselves from being found out, while Phocion who had refused to accept anything, was showing some regard for his safety, if this could be reconciled with the public interest. This encouraged Harpalus to try to ingratiate himself with Phocion a second time, but he found him completely impervious to bribes and as unassailable on every side as a fortress. However he succeeded in making a friend and associate of Phocion's son-in-law, Charicles: Harpalus trusted him and employed him in all his affairs, with the result that he ruined Charicles' reputation.

22. For example Harpalus had been passionately in love with the courtesan Pythonice, who had borne him a daughter. When Pythonice died, Harpalus resolved to build a magnificent monument to her memory, and entrusted the supervision of the work to Charicles. This was a disreputable enough assignment in itself, but it was made even more so by the appearance of the tomb when it was completed. The monument can still be seen at Hermus on the way from Athens to Eleusis, but there is nothing in its character to justify the sum of thirty talents, which Charicles is said to have charged Harpalus for its construction. And yet after Harpalus' death Charicles and Phocion took his daughter under their protection and educated her with every care. On the other hand when Charicles was prosecuted for his dealings with Harpalus and appealed to Phocion to appear with him in court and speak on his behalf, Phocion refused and said, 'When I made you my son-in-law, it was only for honourable purposes.'

It was Asclepiades, the son of Hipparchus, who first brought the news of Alexander's death to Athens. When it was made public, Demades urged the people not to believe it: if Alexander were really dead, he declared, the stench of the corpse would have filled the whole world long before. But Phocion, who immediately saw that the people were bent on revolt against the Macedonians, tried his utmost to quieten and restrain them. And when many of them rushed to the public platform and shouted that the report which Asclepiades had brought was true, Phocion merely said, 'Very well then, if he is dead today, he will be dead tomorrow and the day after. We shall have all the more quiet to debate the matter, and all the more safety to decide what we should do.'

23. When Leosthenes had involved the Athenians in the Lamian War,[1] and saw that Phocion strongly disapproved of his action, he scornfully asked him what good *he* had done the city in all the years he had served her as general. 'Do you think it is nothing, then,' retorted Phocion, 'that our citizens are all buried at home in their own tombs?' On another occasion when Leosthenes was making a boastful and arrogant speech in the assembly, Phocion said, 'Your speeches, young man, remind me of cypress trees. They are towering and stately, but they bear no fruit.' And when Hypereides once rose and demanded of Phocion, 'Will the time ever come when you will advise Athens to go to war?' Phocion retorted, 'Yes, she can go to war when I see the young men willing to observe discipline, the rich to make contributions, and the demagogues to refrain from embezzling public funds.' Many people admired the force which Leosthenes had mobilized,[2] and they asked Phocion what he thought of the city's preparations. 'They are good enough for a sprint,' he said. 'But if it is to be a long race, then I fear for Athens, since we have no reserves, either of money, or of ships, or of men.' And events proved him right. At first Leosthenes achieved some brilliant successes, defeating the Boeotians in a pitched battle, and driving Antipater into Lamia. At this point the Athenians were buoyed up with high hopes, and were constantly holding festivals and offering sacrifices to the gods to celebrate the good news. Some of the citizens thought they could prove

1. 323–322 B.C. It was known as the Lamian War because the allied Greek forces besieged Antipater for some time in the town of Lamia in south-eastern Thessaly.

2. Apart from the Athenian contingent, Leosthenes mobilized 8,000 mercenaries who had returned from Asia to the Peloponnese. Antipater at this time was seriously short of men.

to Phocion that he had been wrong, and asked him whether he would not have been glad to have achieved these successes. 'Certainly I would,' he said, 'but I am still glad to have given the advice I did.' And again when one dispatch after another arrived, either in writing or by messenger from the camp, he remarked, 'I wonder when we shall stop winning victories.'

24. But the time came when Leosthenes was killed.[1] Then those who were afraid that if Phocion were elected general he would put an end to the war, arranged with an obscure person that he should rise to speak in the assembly. He was to make out that he was a friend and intimate associate of Phocion's and urge the people to spare him and keep him safe since they had no one else like him in Athens. They should therefore not send him into the field, but appoint Antiphilus to command the army. The Athenians approved his proposal, whereupon Phocion came forward and declared that he had never been associated with the man, and, so far from his being a close friend, he had not the slightest knowledge of him. 'But from this day,' he went on, 'I shall regard you as my friend and companion, for you have given advice which suits me very well.'

Later on, when the Athenians were eager to invade Boeotia, Phocion began by opposing the plan, and some of his friends warned him that he would be put to death if he continually came into conflict with his fellow countrymen. 'That will be an injustice' he said, 'so long as I am acting in their interests: it will be just if I lead them astray.' Later, when he saw that the people would not give up the project but continued to clamour for it, he ordered the herald to make a proclamation that all Athenian citizens under the age of sixty should take rations for five days and follow him immediately out of the assembly. At this there was an instant uproar, as the older citizens leaped to their feet and shouted their disagreement. 'There is nothing extraordinary about this,' Phocion told them 'after all, I who am to lead you am in my eightieth year.' For the moment, then, he quietened them down, and persuaded them to give up their intention.

25. Not long after[2] the northern sea coast of Attica was being ravaged by Micion, who had landed at Rhamnus with a large force of Macedonians and mercenaries and was overrunning the countryside near-

by. Phocion led out the Athenian army against him, and as they marched, men kept running up to him from all sides and telling him what to do. One advised him to occupy a hill on this side, another to send his cavalry round that way, a third to launch an attack on the enemy. 'Hercules!' Phocion exclaimed, 'how many generals I see around me, and how few soldiers!' Again, when he had drawn up his infantry in battle, one of his soldiers ran a long way out in front of the ranks, was overcome with fear when an opponent ran out to meet him, and raced back again to his position. 'Young man,' said Phocion sternly, 'you ought to be ashamed at deserting your post twice in one day, first the position which I gave you, and then the one you gave yourself.' He then immediately attacked the enemy and utterly routed them, killing Micion their commander along with many others. At the same time the Greek army in Thessaly also defeated Antipater, although he had been reinforced by Leonnatus and his Macedonian troops from Asia. The Greek infantry were commanded by Antiphilus, and the cavalry by Menon, the Thessalian: in this battle Leonnatus was killed.

26. A few months later Craterus crossed over from Asia with a large army, and another pitched battle was fought at Crannon, in which the Greeks were beaten. This was not a crushing defeat, nor were many men killed. But the Greek commanders were young men, and were too lenient to maintain a strict discipline, while at the same time Antipater made tempting offers to a number of the Greek cities from which the confederate army had been drawn: the result was that the troops melted away and disgracefully betrayed the cause of Greek freedom. Antipater at once marched upon Athens, and Demosthenes and Hypereides fled from the city. As for Demades, he had found it impossible to pay any part of the fines which had been imposed on him by the city: he had been convicted of putting forward illegal proposals on seven occasions, had been deprived of his civic rights, and was therefore disqualified from speaking in the assembly. But he discovered that at a moment of crisis these disabilities were ignored, and so he brought forward a proposal that delegates should be sent to Antipater with full powers to sue for peace. However the people distrusted him, and called upon Phocion, declaring that he was the only man in whom they felt confidence. 'If you had trusted me in the first place,' he reminded them, 'we should not now be debating this

question at all.' At any rate the motion was carried, and Phocion was sent to Antipater, who was encamped in the Cadmeia,[1] and was preparing to invade Attica at once. Phocion's first request was that Antipater should stay where he was and arrange terms. Craterus protested that it was unfair of Phocion to try to persuade the Macedonians to remain in the territory of a friend and ally, thereby inflicting all the damage which is caused by an occupying army, when they were quite free to plunder the territory of their enemy, but Antipater took his colleague by the hand and said, 'We must grant Phocion this favour.' However as for the remainder of the terms of peace, Antipater told the Athenians that these must be dictated by the victors: this was exactly what he in his turn had been told by Leosthenes at Lamia.[2]

27. Accordingly when Phocion returned to Athens and reported these demands, the people accepted them, since they had no choice. Phocion then visited Thebes again with the rest of the Athenian delegation, which had now been reinforced by the philosopher Xenocrates.[3] In the eyes of the Athenians, at least, Xenocrates' reputation for virtue, together with his fame and prestige, could not fail to command consideration: no man's heart, they imagined, could be so full of pride, or anger, or cruelty, that it would not at the mere sight of the man be moved to a feeling of reverence and a desire to do him honour. But in this case the opposite happened, for they had reckoned without a certain ruthlessness in Antipater's disposition and a positive antagonism to virtue. In the first place he refused to salute Xenocrates at all, although he greeted the other ambassadors, at which Xenocrates is said to have remarked, 'Antipater does well to feel ashamed before me alone, if he intends to show no mercy to our city.' Then when Xenocrates began to speak, Antipater would not listen to him, brutally interrupted him and reduced him to silence. Finally after Phocion had spoken, Antipater replied that the Athenians could be admitted to friendship and alliance with him on the following conditions. First they must deliver up Demosthenes and Hypereides; secondly they must revert to their earlier constitution, whereby the

1. The citadel of Thebes.
2. When Leosthenes had the advantage, see ch. 23.
3. He was then head of the Academy where he had succeeded Plato and Speusippus.

franchise was limited to those who possessed a property qualification;[1] thirdly they must admit a garrison into Munychia, and fourthly they must pay the whole expense of the war, as well as a fine.

The other delegates considered these terms tolerable, and even humane, but Xenocrates remarked that Antipater was treating the Athenians leniently if he regarded them as slaves, harshly if as free men. Phocion begged Antipater not to install a garrison in Athens, to which Antipater, so we are told, replied, 'Phocion, we are ready to do you any favour which will not bring ruin on you and on ourselves.' However some writers give a different account. They say that Antipater asked whether, if he made a concession to the Athenians in the matter of the garrison, Phocion could give him a guarantee that the city would abide by the terms of the peace and not stir up trouble. They also report that when Phocion was silent and hesitated as to how to answer, a certain Callimedon, nicknamed 'The Stag-beetle', who was an arrogant man and a hater of democracy, leaped to his feet and shouted out, 'But even if this fellow goes on talking nonsense, Antipater, and gives you his promise, will you believe him, and not carry out what you have already decided?'

28. In this way the Athenians were obliged to admit a Macedonian garrison: it was commanded by Menyllus, who was a fair-minded man and a friend of Phocion's. But the posting of a garrison in the city was regarded as a demonstration of power which was deliberately carried out to humiliate the Athenians, and not as the occupation of a strong-point which was dictated by necessity. Moreover the moment that was chosen for this action was even more galling for the Athenians, for the garrison was installed on the twentieth day of the month Boedromion, while the Mysteries were being celebrated. It is on that day that the god Iacchus is conducted from the town of Eleusis, and this disturbance of the ceremony caused the people to compare the present celebration of the rites with those of years gone by. In those earlier days mystic apparitions had been seen and voices heard which had coincided with the city's most glorious successes, and had struck terror and dismay into the hearts of their enemies.[2] But now,

1. As in her dealings with other Greek states it was Macedonian policy to establish and support a friendly oligarchy. This reduced the voters from 22,000 to 9,000 citizens.

2. As for example before the victory over the Persians at Salamis. (See *The Rise and Fall of Athens*, Themistocles, ch. 15.)

even in the midst of these same observances, the gods apparently looked down unmoved, while the most crushing misfortunes fell upon Greece. So the desecration of this season which hitherto had been the most hallowed and beloved in the eyes of the Athenians henceforth made them associate its name with their greatest disasters. And in fact a few years before this the priestess of Dodona had sent an oracle to Athens warning the people to 'guard the heights of Artemis'[1] and make sure that no strangers should seize them. Again, on this occasion, when they dyed the fillets which are twined around the sacred chests that are carried in the procession, instead of taking on their usual purple colour, they turned a pale and deathly hue; and, more ominous still, all the articles belonging to private individuals which were dyed with them at the same time retained their natural colour. Besides this one of the initiates, who was washing a pig in the harbour of Cantharus,[2] was seized by a shark, which devoured all the lower parts of his body as far as the belly: by this omen the gods were believed to be making a clear prophecy that the Athenians would lose the lower parts of the city which bordered on the sea, but would keep the upper city.

Now the garrison at Munychia did not harm the citizens in any way, thanks to the influence of Menyllus. But the Athenians who were now deprived of the vote because they were too poor to possess the property qualification, numbered more than twelve thousand. Those of them who remained in Athens were considered to have received harsh and humiliating treatment: on the other hand those who because of this measure left the capital and migrated to the town and the territory which Antipater provided for them in Thrace, regarded themselves as no better than the exiles of a captured city.

29. The death of Demosthenes at Calauria and of Hypereides at Cleonae, which I have described elsewhere, caused the Athenians to look back on the times of Philip and Alexander with regret and almost to long for their return. At a later period after Antigonus had been killed in battle, and those who had taken his life had begun to oppress and tyrannize over their subjects, a peasant in Phrygia who was digging on his farm was asked by a passer-by what he was doing, and re-

1. Artemis was the patron goddess of Munychia.
2. One of the harbours of Piraeus.

plied, 'I am searching for Antigonus.' So now the same sentiments occurred to the Athenians, when they recalled the greatness and generosity of those kings, and how these qualities made their anger easy to appease. By contrast Antipater, although he tried to conceal his power by counterfeiting the appearance of a private citizen who dressed meanly and followed a simple mode of life, was really a harsher and more tyrannical master to those who had to endure his rule. However by pleading with Antipater Phocion managed to save many Athenians from banishment, while for those who were obliged to go into exile he obtained the concession of living in the Peloponnese, instead of being sentenced to live beyond the Keraunian mountains or Cape Taenarus, as was the fate of many of those who were expelled from other Greek cities. One of these men was Hagnonides, the informer.[1] Phocion also succeeded in regulating the city's internal affairs so that government was carried on without disturbances and in a law-abiding fashion. He found means to keep the men of education and culture continuously in office, while the agitators and busybodies by the very fact of their being constantly excluded from power gradually faded into insignificance and ceased to trouble the state: instead, he encouraged such men to find satisfaction in staying at home and cultivating the soil. He noticed that Xenocrates paid tax as a resident alien and offered to enrol him as a citizen, but the philosopher declined, saying that he could not acknowledge a regime, the establishment of which he had been publicly delegated to oppose.

30. When Menyllus offered him a gift of money, Phocion replied that Menyllus was no better a man than Alexander, and that there was no stronger reason for him to accept it now than on the previous occasion when he had refused the present from Alexander. Menyllus pressed him to accept the money, if only for the benefit of his son Phocus, whereupon Phocion said, 'If Phocus becomes converted to a modest style of living, then his inheritance will be enough for him, but as he is now, nothing will satisfy him.' However when Antipater wished him to perform some service which he considered dishonourable, Phocion answered him sharply and said, 'Antipater cannot have me as a friend and a flatterer at once.' Antipater himself declared, so we are told, that he had two friends at Athens, Phocion and Demades:

1. This man showed his gratitude at the end of Phocion's life; see ch. 34.

he could never influence the one, whatever he offered him, or satisfy the other, whatever he gave him. Indeed Phocion could point to his poverty as the most conspicuous evidence of his virtue: he had served Athens times without number as a general, he had enjoyed the friendship of kings, and now he had reached old age and was still a poor man, whereas Demades prided himself on his wealth and on his contempt for the laws which had enabled him to acquire it. For example there was a law in force in Athens at this time which forbade the sponsor of a choric festival to include a foreigner in his chorus on pain of a fine of a thousand drachmae. So Demades presented a chorus of a hundred, every one of whom were foreigners, and at the same time brought into the theatre the fine of a thousand drachmae for each of them. Again on the occasion of the marriage of his son Demeas, he said to him, 'My boy, when I married your mother, not even our next-door neighbours knew about it, but at your wedding you will have presents from kings and princes.'

The presence of the garrison at Munychia was a standing grievance to the Athenians, and the people plagued Phocion with requests that he should appeal to Antipater to remove it. Whether it was that he had no hope of persuading Antipater to agree, or because he saw that the fear which it inspired obliged the Athenians to conduct their affairs in a more reasonable and law-abiding fashion, at any rate he continually contrived to put off the task. However he succeeded in persuading Antipater not to insist on immediate payment of the fine that had been inflicted on the city, but to allow a moratorium. So the people turned to Demades and appealed to him on the subject of the garrison; he willingly accepted the mission and set off for Macedonia, taking his son with him. He arrived, as if by some divine dispensation, at the precise moment when Antipater had fallen sick, and when his son Cassander who had taken charge of affairs, had just discovered a letter written by Demades to Antigonus in Asia. In this he had urged Antigonus to appear suddenly in Greece and Macedonia, for these territories were hanging by an old and rotten thread, as he scornfully referred to Antipater. So as soon as Cassander saw Demades after his arrival in Macedonia, he placed him under arrest. First of all he had Demades' son slaughtered in his presence: the two were standing so close that the young man's blood poured into the folds of his father's tunic and filled them: then he reviled and abused Demades for his ingratitude and treachery, and dispatched him in the same fashion.

31. Shortly before he died,[1] Antipater appointed Polyperchon commander-in-chief and Cassander second in command. Cassander, however, soon overturned this arrangement and hastened to seize power for himself. He sent out Nicanor with all speed to relieve Menyllus of the command of the garrison in Athens, and ordered him to seize Munychia before Antipater's death had become publicly known. These orders were carried out, and when the Athenians learned a few days later that Antipater was dead, they indignantly blamed Phocion, alleging that he had received information in advance, but had kept quiet as a favour to Nicanor. Phocion ignored these accusations: he made it his business to arrange meetings with Nicanor, pleaded the cause of the Athenians and secured lenient and considerate treatment for them: in particular he persuaded Nicanor to sponsor various costly athletic festivals in his capacity as president of the games.

32. Meanwhile Polyperchon the regent, who had the king[2] in his personal charge and who was opposing Cassander's schemes, sent a letter to Athens. In this he announced that the king had restored to the Athenians their democratic form of government and called upon the citizens to exercise their political rights according to their original constitution. This was a plot designed to destroy Phocion. Polyperchon's plan, as his actions revealed later, was to win over the city to his side. He had little hope of achieving his design unless he could secure Phocion's banishment, but he calculated that this might well come about if the mass of disfranchised citizens overwhelmed the government and the assembly was once more dominated by demagogues and public informers.

Nicanor soon saw that the Athenians were intensely excited by this communication from Macedon, and he was anxious to address them. A meeting of the Council was summoned at Piraeus and he appeared before it, his personal safety having been previously guaranteed by Phocion. Dercyllus, the Athenian general who was in charge of the district, tried to arrest him, but Nicanor, who had been warned in time, eluded the attempt and soon made it clear that he intended to

1. 319 B.C. Antipater, one of Philip of Macedon's senior generals, was then seventy-nine.
2. The imbecile Philip Arrhidaeus, Alexander's half-brother. Polyperchon was another senior general and contemporary of Antipater.

take reprisals against the city. When Phocion was blamed for failing to detain Nicanor and allowing him to escape, he replied that he had confidence in the Macedonian and had no reason to suspect him of any harmful intention, but that in any case he preferred suffering wrong to inflicting it. Now such a sentiment may seem honourable and high-minded enough if a man is speaking for his own interests alone. But if he endangers his country's safety, especially when he is the commander and chief magistrate, it seems to me that he violates an even more important and more sacred obligation, that is his duty towards his fellow citizens. It is not a good enough defence that Phocion refrained from arresting Nicanor because he was afraid of plunging the city into war, and that he justified his unwillingness to act by his professions of good faith and fair dealing in the hope that Nicanor would respect these obligations and do no harm to the Athenians. The truth seems to have been that Phocion was firmly convinced Nicanor was trustworthy: he believed this so strongly that even when many people warned him against the Macedonian and alleged that he was plotting to seize Piraeus, that he had sent mercenary troops over to Salamis and had corrupted a number of the inhabitants of Piraeus, Phocion would not believe the report or even pay any attention to it. Indeed even after Philomelus of Lamptrae had introduced a decree that all Athenians should take up arms and await orders from Phocion as their general, he still took no action until Nicanor marched his troops out of Munychia and began to surround Piraeus with a trench.

33. When matters had reached this pass, Phocion was willing to lead out the Athenians, but by now he was shouted down and treated with contempt. Then Alexander, the son of Polyperchon, arrived with his army. He had come ostensibly to bring help to the citizens in their struggle against Nicanor, but his real purpose was to seize the city if he could, now that it was fatally divided. The exiled Athenians, who accompanied him when he invaded Attica, quickly made their way into the city. A horde of foreigners and disfranchised citizens hurried in to join them, and a motley and disorderly assembly of the people was held, at which Phocion was removed from his command and other generals were elected. And but for the fact that Alexander and Nicanor were seen to be meeting alone near the walls, and that these conferences were so frequent that they roused the Athenians' suspic-

ions, the city would not have escaped the danger in which it stood. The orator Hagnonides[1] then attacked Phocion and denounced him as a traitor, and this so much alarmed Callimedon and Charicles[2] that they fled from the city, while Phocion and those of his friends who remained loyal to him set out to visit Polyperchon. They were accompanied out of regard for Phocion by Solon of Plataea and Deinarchus[3] of Corinth, both of whom were believed to be close friends of Polyperchon. However Deinarchus fell sick and his party was detained for many days at Elateia, and during this time the people of Athens passed a decree proposed by Archestratus and supported by Hagnonides, as a result of which they dispatched a delegation to denounce Phocion. The two parties reached Polyperchon simultaneously, as he was on the march with the king and had arrived at a village named Pharygae in Phocis: this lies at the foot of Mount Acrurium, which is now known as Galata.

Here Polyperchon set up the throne with the golden canopy and had the king and his friends seated beneath it. Before anything else was done, he ordered Deinarchus to be seized, tortured and put to death, and then he gave audience to the delegation from Athens. However they quickly reduced the interview to chaos by shouting, accusing and contradicting one another in the council, until at last Hagnonides came forward and said, 'Best pack us all into one cage and send us back to Athens to be tried.' At this the king burst out laughing, but the Macedonians and foreigners who happened to be in attendance at the council and had nothing else to do, were curious to listen, and nodding to the delegates, they encouraged both sides to state their case. But in fact the hearing was very far from impartial. When Phocion tried to speak, he was continually interrupted by Polyperchon, until at last he struck the ground with his staff, turned away, and did not utter another word. Again when Hegemon[4] claimed that Polyperchon could testify to his goodwill towards the people, Polyperchon exclaimed angrily, 'Be so good as not to slander

1. See ch. 29.
2. Supporters of Antipater and therefore suspect to Polyperchon.
3. Both men had been supporters of Antipater: Deinarchus had been his principal agent in the Peloponnese. This meant that they owed some allegiance to his son Cassander, and hence that they were now regarded by Polyperchon as enemies.
4. One of Phocion's friends who was likewise accused of supporting Cassander rather than Polyperchon.

me to the king', while the king himself jumped to his feet and made
as if to run Hegemon through with a spear. But Polyperchon quickly
threw his arms around the king and the council immediately broke
up.

34. Phocion and his companions were placed under guard, and at the
sight of this his friends who were standing some way apart covered
their faces and made their escape. Cleitus then took the prisoners back
to Athens: it was given out that they were to be tried, but in reality
they had already been condemned to death. The manner in which
this was done created a particularly distressing scene, for they were
transported in carts through the Cerameicus to the theatre, where
Cleitus kept them in custody until the archons had summoned the
assembly. This gathering included slaves, foreigners, and those who
had recently been disfranchised: all alike, both men and women were
allowed free access to the theatre and the rostrum. First a letter from
the king of Macedon was read aloud, in which he declared that he
personally was convinced that the men were traitors, but that he left
it to their fellow countrymen to pass judgement upon them, since
they were free individuals governed by their own laws, and then
Cleitus led the men in. At the sight of Phocion the best of the citizens
covered their faces, lowered their heads and wept. But one of them
rose to his feet and had the courage to say that since the king had entrusted so important a trial to the citizens of Athens, it would be well
for all foreigners and slaves to leave the assembly. The mob would not
allow this, but shouted out, 'Down with the oligarchs and the enemies of the people.' Nobody came forward to speak on Phocion's
behalf, but at last he succeeded with great difficulty in making himself heard and asked, 'Do you wish to put us to death justly or un-
justly?', and when some voices answered 'Justly!' he rejoined, 'And
how will you do that without hearing me?' The people showed no
sign of being any more ready to hear him, and so coming closer he
said 'I admit my own guilt, and I propose the penalty of death for my
political actions,[1] but why, men of Athens, should you put to death
these others, who have done no wrong?' 'Because they are your

1. According to Athenian law, in cases where the penalty was not legally
fixed, the accuser proposed a penalty and the accused had the right to propose a
counter-penalty: the court then chose between them. This was the procedure
which was followed at the trial of Socrates.

friends', a chorus of voices answered him, and at this Phocion turned
away and said no more. Hagnonides then read the motion he had
prepared, according to which the people were to decide by a show of
hands whether they considered the accused guilty, and the men, if
found guilty, were to be put to death.

35. When the decree was read, there were some who demanded an
additional clause sentencing Phocion to be tortured before he was put
to death, and they urged that the rack should be brought and the
executioners summoned. However Hagnonides saw that even Cleitus
was disgusted at this proposal and considered it detestable, and he
said, 'Whenever we catch that villain Callimedon, men of Athens,
let us put him to the torture, but I will not propose anything of the
kind for Phocion.' At this one of the more scrupulous citizens shouted
out, 'And quite right too, for if we are to torture Phocion, what
should we do to you?' So it was that the decree was confirmed, and
when the show of hands was taken, nobody remained seated, but the
entire assembly rose to their feet, many of them wearing garlands of
flowers, and condemned the men to death. These, besides Phocion
were Nicocles, Thudippus, Hegemon and Pythocles, while Demetrius of Phaleron, Charicles and various others were condemned to
death in their absence.

36. After the assembly had broken up and the condemned men were
being led to the prison, the others walked along lamenting and shedding tears, while their friends and relatives clung about them. As for
Phocion his expression looked exactly the same as it had in the days
when he served as general and had often been escorted back from the
assembly, and as men gazed at him, they marvelled at his grandeur of
spirit and composure. But some of his enemies ran along by his side
shouting abuse at him, and one even came up and spat in his face. At
this, we are told, Phocion turned towards the archons and said, 'Will
nobody make this fellow behave himself?' Later when they were in
the prison Thudippus, as he watched the executioner crushing the
hemlock, grew angry and cried out aloud against his hard fate, protesting that he did not deserve to lose his life with Phocion. 'What
then?', the old man asked, 'Is it nothing to you to die in Phocion's
company?' And when one of his friends asked if he had any message
for his son Phocus, Phocion said, 'Yes, certainly, my message is that

he should not hold my death as a grievance against the Athenian people.' When Nicocles, the most loyal of all his friends, begged from him the privilege of drinking the poison first, he replied, 'My friend, that is a hard thing you ask, and it is painful to me to grant it, but since I have never refused you anything in my life, I agree to this too.' But when all the rest had drunk it, the poison ran short, and the executioner refused to crush another portion unless he were paid twelve drachmae, which was the price of the weight that was needed. After some delay, Phocion sent for one of his friends. He remarked that it was hard if a man could not even die at Athens without paying for it, and told him to give the executioner the fee.

37. The day of Phocion's death was the nineteenth of the month Munychion,[1] and the knights who took part in the sacred procession in honour of Zeus, had to ride past the prison. Some of them took off their garlands and others wept as they looked towards the door of the prison. All those who were still capable of humanity and whose better feelings had not been swept away by rage or jealousy felt that it was sacrilege not to postpone the execution for a single day and thus preserve the city from the pollution incurred by carrying out a public execution while a festival was being celebrated. However Phocion's enemies, as if they were still not satisfied with their triumph, had a resolution passed that Phocion's body should be taken beyond the frontiers of Attica, and that no Athenian should provide fire for his funeral. The result was that no friend dared to touch the body, but a man named Conopion, who was accustomed to provide such services for payment, carried the body beyond Eleusis, had fire brought from Megarian territory, and burned it. Phocion's wife, who was present at the ceremony with her maid-servants, raised a mound on the spot and poured the customary libations on it. Then she took Phocion's bones to her bosom and brought them back to her house by night. There she buried them by the hearth with these words: 'To thee, my beloved hearth, I entrust these remains of a good man. Do thou restore them to the tomb of his fathers when the Athenians recover their senses.'

38. And indeed only a short time elapsed before the course of events taught the Athenians how great a protector and champion of modera-

1. May 318 B.C.

tion and justice they had lost. Then they set up a statue of him and gave his bones a public burial. As for his accusers, they themselves condemned Hagnonides and put him to death, while Epicurus and Demophilus, who had fled from the city, were tracked down by Phocion's son, who took his revenge on them. This son of Phocion's, we are told, turned out to be a man of little worth in most respects. On one occasion he had fallen in love with a girl who earned her living in a brothel. He happened to have heard a discussion in the Lyceum in which Theodorus the atheist put forward the argument that if there is no disgrace in ransoming a man with whom you are in love, the same should be true of a woman: if the principle applies to a comrade, it applies equally to a mistress. At any rate he determined to use the argument to justify his passion, and so bought the girl's freedom.

But Phocion's fate reminded the Greeks once more of that of Socrates: they felt that in each case the wrong which the city of Athens had done and the misfortune she had suffered were almost identical.

7

ALEXANDER[1]

[356–23 B.C.]

* *

*

My subject in this book is the life of Alexander, the king, and of Julius Caesar, the conqueror of Pompey.[2] The careers of these men embrace such a multitude of events that my preamble shall consist of nothing more than this one plea: if I do not record all their most celebrated achievements or describe any of them exhaustively, but merely summarize for the most part what they accomplished, I ask my readers not to regard this as a fault. For I am writing biography, not history, and the truth is that the most brilliant exploits often tell us nothing of the virtues or vices of the men who performed them, while on the other hand a chance remark or a joke may reveal far more of a man's character than the mere feat of winning battles in which thousands fall, or of marshalling great armies, or laying siege to cities. When a portrait painter sets out to create a likeness, he relies above all upon the face and the expression of the eyes and pays less attention to the other parts of the body: in the same way it is my task to dwell upon those actions which illuminate the workings of the soul, and by this means to create a portrait of each man's life. I leave the story of his greatest struggles and achievements to be told by others.

2. On his father's side Alexander was descended from Hercules through Caranus,[3] and on his mother's from Aeacus[4] through Neoptolemus:

1. For places mentioned in this *Life*, see Maps 1, 2 and 4, pp. 433–4, 437.

2. See Introduction, pp. 9–10.

3. Reputedly the founder in the ninth century B.C. of the dynasty to which Alexander belonged. Even in Alexander's day Macedonia still kept some of the characteristics of a Homeric kingdom.

4. The legendary king of Aegina and grandfather of Achilles.

so much is accepted by all authorities without question. It is said that his father Philip fell in love with Olympias, Alexander's mother, at the time when they were both initiated into the mysteries at Samothrace.[1] He was then a young man and she an orphan, and after obtaining the consent of her brother Arybbas, Philip betrothed himself to her. On the night before the marriage was consummated, the bride dreamed that there was a crash of thunder, that her womb was struck by a thunderbolt, and that there followed a blinding flash from which a great sheet of flame blazed up and spread far and wide before it finally died away. Then, some time after their marriage, Philip saw himself in a dream in the act of sealing up his wife's womb, and upon the seal he had used there was engraved, so it seemed to him, the figure of a lion. The soothsayers treated this dream with suspicion, since it seemed to suggest that Philip needed to keep a closer watch on his wife. The only exception was Aristander of Telmessus,[2] who declared that the woman must be pregnant, since men do not seal up what is empty, and that she would bring forth a son whose nature would be bold and lion-like. At another time a serpent was seen stretched out at Olympias' side as she slept, and it was this more than anything else, we are told, which weakened Philip's passion and cooled his affection for her, so that from that time on he seldom came to sleep with her. The reason for this may either have been that he was afraid she would cast some evil spell or charm upon him or else that he recoiled from her embrace because he believed that she was the consort of some higher being.

However there is another version of this story. It appears that from very ancient times all the women of this region have been initiates of the Orphic religion and of the orgiastic rites of Dionysus. For this reason they were known as Klodones and Mimallones[3] and they followed many of the observances of the Edonian and Thracian women who live around Mount Haemus, from whom the word *threskeuein*[4]

1. Between 365 and 361 B.C. when Philip was between seventeen and twenty-one. The mysteries at Samothrace concerned the Cabeiri, earth-gods who promoted fertility and also protected sailors. Although so young, Philip had already been married twice, but still had no son. His first wife died in childbirth in 357, his second a few months later, and he married Olympias in the autumn of the same year.

2. He later accompanied Alexander to Asia as a diviner: see chs. 31 & 33.

3. Macedonian names for Bacchantes.

4. Plutarch derives this word from *Thressai* (Thracian women).

has come to denote the celebration of extravagant and superstitious ceremonies. It was Olympias' habit to enter into these states of possession and surrender herself to the inspiration of the god with even wilder abandon than the others, and she would introduce into the festal procession numbers of large snakes, hand-tamed, which terrified the male spectators as they raised their heads from the wreaths of ivy and the sacred winnowing-baskets, or twined themselves around the wands and garlands of the women.

3. At any rate after Philip had seen this apparition, he dispatched Chaeron of Megalopolis to Delphi to consult the oracle of Apollo. In reply the god commanded him to sacrifice to Zeus Ammon and to revere him above all other deities; but he also warned Philip that he was fated to lose the eye with which he had peered through the chink of the half-open door on the night when he saw the god in the form of a serpent sharing his wife's bed. According to Eratosthenes, Olympias, when she sent Alexander on his way to lead his great expedition to the East, confided to him and to him alone the secret of his conception and urged him to show himself worthy of his divine parentage. But other authors maintain that she repudiated this story and used to say, 'Will Alexander never stop making Hera jealous of me?'

However this may be, Alexander was born on the sixth day of the month Hecatombaeon, which the Macedonians call Loüs, the same day on which the temple of Artemis at Ephesus was burned down.[1] It was this coincidence which inspired Hegesias of Magnesia to utter a joke which was flat enough to have put the fire out: he said it was no wonder the temple of Artemis was destroyed, since the goddess was busy attending to the birth of Alexander.[2] But those of the Magi who were then at Ephesus interpreted the destruction of the temple as the portent of a far greater disaster, and they ran through the city beating their faces and crying out that that day had brought forth a great scourge and calamity for Asia.

1. The year was 356 B.C. and the date about 20 July. The exact date is controversial and it seems likely that it was manipulated by historians for the sake of a striking coincidence

2. The temple of Artemis at Ephesus was one of the wonders of the ancient world, 425 feet in length and supported by columns 60 feet high. Artemis was the goddess not only of hunting but also of childbirth.

At that moment Philip had just captured the city of Potidaea, and he received three messages on the same day. The first was that his general Parmenio had overcome the Illyrians in a great battle, the second that his race-horse had won a victory in the Olympic games, and the third that Alexander had been born. Naturally he was over-joyed at the news, and the soothsayers raised his spirits still higher by assuring him that the son whose birth coincided with three victories would himself prove invincible.

4. The best likeness of Alexander which has been preserved for us is to be found in the statues sculpted by Lysippus, the only artist whom Alexander considered worthy to represent him. Alexander possessed a number of individual features which many of Lysippus' followers later tried to reproduce, for example the poise of the neck which was tilted slightly to the left, or a certain melting look in his eyes, and the artist has exactly caught these peculiarities. On the other hand when Apelles painted Alexander wielding a thunderbolt, he did not repro-duce his colouring at all accurately. He made Alexander's complexion appear too dark-skinned and swarthy, whereas we are told that he was fair-skinned, with a ruddy tinge that showed itself especially upon his face and chest. Aristoxenus also tells us in his memoirs that Alex-ander's skin was fresh and sweet-smelling, and that his breath and the whole of his body gave off a peculiar fragrance[1] which permeated the clothes he wore.

The cause of this may have been the blend of hot and dry elements which were combined in his constitution, for fragrance, if we are to believe Theophrastus,[2] is generated by the action of heat upon moist humours. This is why the hottest and driest regions of the earth pro-duce the finest and most numerous spices, for the sun draws up the moisture which abounds in vegetable bodies and causes them to decay. In Alexander's case it was this same warmth of temperament which made him fond of drinking, and also prone to outbursts of choleric rage.

Even while he was still a boy, he gave plenty of evidence of his powers of self-control. In spite of his vehement and impulsive nature, he showed little interest in the pleasures of the senses and indulged

1. This fragrance was also regarded as a sign of his superhuman nature.
2. A pupil of Aristotle and the author of two treatises on botany: best known or his *Characters* (sketches of contemporary social types).

in them only with great moderation, but his passionate desire for fame implanted in him a pride and a grandeur of vision which went far beyond his years. And yet it was by no means every kind of glory that he sought, and, unlike his father, he did not seek it in every form of action. Philip, for example, was as proud of his powers of eloquence as any sophist, and took care to have the victories won by his chariots at Olympia stamped upon his coins. But Alexander's attitude is made clear by his reply to some of his friends, when they asked him whether he would be willing to compete at Olympia, since he was a fine runner. 'Yes,' he answered, 'if I have kings to run against me.' He seems in fact to have disapproved of the whole race of trained athletes. At any rate although he founded a great many contests of other kinds, including not only the tragic drama and performances on the flute and the lyre, but also the reciting of poetry, fighting with the quarter-staff and various forms of hunting, yet he never offered prizes either for boxing or for the *pancration*.[1]

5. On one occasion some ambassadors from the king of Persia arrived in Macedon, and since Philip was absent, Alexander received them in his place. He talked freely with them and quite won them over, not only by the friendliness of his manner, but also because he did not trouble them with any childish or trivial inquiries, but questioned them about the distances they had travelled by road, the nature of the journey into the interior of Persia, the character of the king, his experience in war, and the military strength and prowess of the Persians. The ambassadors were filled with admiration. They came away convinced that Philip's celebrated astuteness was as nothing compared to the adventurous spirit and lofty ambitions of his son. At any rate, whenever he heard that Philip had captured some famous city or won an overwhelming victory, Alexander would show no pleasure at the news, but would declare to his friends, 'Boys, my father will forestall me in everything. There will be nothing great or spectacular for you and me to show the world.' He cared nothing for pleasure or wealth but only for deeds of valour and glory, and this was why he believed that the more he received from his father, the less would be left for him to conquer. And so every success that was gained by Macedonia inspired in Alexander the dread that another opportunity for action had been squandered on his father.

1. A contest which combined wrestling and boxing.

He had no desire to inherit a kingdom which offered him riches, luxuries and the pleasures of the senses: his choice was a life of struggle, of wars, and of unrelenting ambition.

It was natural, of course, that a great number of nurses, pedagogues[1] and teachers were appointed to take part in his upbringing, but the man who supervised them all was Leonidas, a severe disciplinarian, who was also a relative of Olympias. Although his duties were both important and honourable, he did not disdain the title of pedagogue, but because of his natural dignity and of his connection with the queen's family, other people referred to him as Alexander's foster-father and mentor. The person who took on both the title and the role of pedagogue was an Acarnanian named Lysimachus. He was neither an educated nor a cultivated man, but he managed to ingratiate himself by calling Philip Peleus, Alexander Achilles, and himself Phoenix,[2] and he held the second place in the prince's household.

6. There came a day[3] when Philoneicus the Thessalian brought Philip a horse named Bucephalas,[4] which he offered to sell for thirteen talents. The king and his friends went down to the plain to watch the horse's trials, and came to the conclusion that he was wild and quite unmanageable, for he would allow no one to mount him, nor would he endure the shouts of Philip's grooms, but reared up against anyone who approached him. The king became angry at being offered such a vicious animal unbroken, and ordered it to be led away. But Alexander, who was standing close by, remarked, 'What a horse they are losing, and all because they don't know how to handle him, or dare not try!' Philip kept quiet at first, but when he heard Alexander repeat these words several times and saw that he was upset, he asked him, 'Are you finding fault with your elders because you think you know more than they do, or can manage a horse better?' 'At least I could manage this one better', retorted Alexander. 'And if you cannot,' said his father, 'what penalty will you pay for being

1. The Greek word *paidagogus* signifies a slave whose task it was to accompany a child to and from school and keep him out of mischief. It was not his job to teach.

2. Achilles' tutor.

3. The date is uncertain. Alexander may have been about fourteen. Thessaly was the finest breeding-ground for horses in Greece.

4. The name of a famous breed of Thessalian horses which were branded on the shoulder with the sign of an ox's head.

so impertinent?' 'I will pay the price of the horse',[1] answered the boy. At this the whole company burst out laughing, and then as soon as the father and son had settled the terms of the bet, Alexander went quickly up to Bucephalas, took hold of his bridle, and turned him towards the sun, for he had noticed that the horse was shying at the sight of his own shadow, as it fell in front of him and constantly moved whenever he did. He ran alongside the animal for a little way, calming him down by stroking him, and then, when he saw he was full of spirit and courage, he quietly threw aside his cloak and with a light spring vaulted safely on to his back. For a little while he kept feeling the bit with the reins, without jarring or tearing his mouth, and got him collected. Finally, when he saw that the horse was free of his fears and impatient to show his speed, he gave him his head and urged him forward, using a commanding voice and a touch of the foot.

At first Philip and his friends held their breath and looked on in an agony of suspense, until they saw Alexander reach the end of his gallop, turn in full control, and ride back triumphant and exulting in his success. Thereupon the rest of the company broke into loud applause, while his father, we are told, actually wept for joy, and when Alexander had dismounted he kissed him and said, 'My boy, you must find a kingdom big enough for your ambitions. Macedonia is too small for you.'

7. Philip had noticed that his son was self-willed, and that while it was very difficult to influence him by force, he could easily be guided towards his duty by an appeal to reason, and he therefore made a point of trying to persuade the boy rather than giving him orders. Besides this he considered that the task of training and educating his son was too important to be entrusted to the ordinary run of teachers of poetry, music and general education: it required, as Sophocles puts it

> The rudder's guidance and the curb's restraint,

and so he sent for Aristotle,[2] the most famous and learned of the philosophers of his time, and rewarded him with the generosity that

---

1. The speed of change of money values makes it futile to try to convert the asking price of thirteen talents into modern figures. It is enough to say that by the Greek standards of the time this was a very high price.
2. When Alexander was thirteen.

his reputation deserved. Aristotle was a native of the city of Stageira, which Philip had himself destroyed. He now repopulated it and brought back all the citizens who had been enslaved or driven into exile.

He gave Aristotle and his pupil the temple of the Nymphs near Mieza as a place where they could study and converse, and to this day they show you the stone seats and shady walks which Aristotle used. It seems clear too that Alexander was instructed by his teacher not only in the principles of ethics and politics, but also in those secret and more esoteric studies which philosophers do not impart to the general run of students, but only by word of mouth to a select circle of the initiated. Some years later, after Alexander had crossed into Asia, he learned that Aristotle had published some treatises dealing with these esoteric matters, and he wrote to him in blunt language and took him to task for the sake of the prestige of philosophy. This was the text of his letter:

Alexander to Aristotle, greetings. You have not done well to write down and publish those doctrines you taught me by word of mouth. What advantage shall I have over other men if these theories in which I have been trained are to be made common property? I would rather excel the rest of mankind in my knowledge of what is best than in the extent of my power. Farewell.

Aristotle wished to encourage this ambition of his pupil's and so when he replied to justify his action, he pointed out that these so-called oral doctrines were in a sense both published and not published. For example it is true that his treatise on metaphysics is written in a style which makes it useless for those who wish to study or teach the subject from the beginning: the book serves simply as a memorandum for those who have already been taught its general principles.

8. It was Aristotle, I believe, who did more than anyone to implant in Alexander his interest in the art of healing as well as that of philosophy. He was not merely attracted to the theory of medicine, but was in the habit of tending his friends when they were sick and prescribing for them various courses of treatment or diet, as we learn from his letters. He was also devoted by nature to all kinds of learning and was a lover of books. He regarded the *Iliad* as a handbook of the art of war and took with him on his campaigns a text annotated by

Aristotle, which became known as 'the casket copy',[1] and which he always kept under his pillow together with his dagger. When his campaigns had taken him far into the interior of Asia and he could find no other books, he ordered his treasurer Harpalus to send him some. Harpalus sent him the histories of Philistus,[2] many of the tragedies of Aeschylus, Sophocles and Euripides, and the dithyrambic poems of Telestes and Philoxenus.

At first Alexander greatly admired Aristotle and became more attached to him than to his father, for the one, he used to say, had given him the gift of life, but the other had taught him how to live well. But in later years he came to regard Aristotle with suspicion. He never actually did him any harm, but his friendship for the philosopher lost its original warmth and affection, and this was a clear proof of the estrangement which developed between them.[3] At the same time Alexander never lost the devotion to philosophy which had been innate in him from the first, and which matured as he grew older: he proved this on many occasions, for example by the honours which he paid to Anaxarchus,[4] the fifty talents which he presented to Xenocrates,[5] and the encouragement which he lavished upon Dandamis and Calanus.[6]

9. While Philip was making an expedition against Byzantium,[7] Alexander, although he was only sixteen years old, was left behind as regent of Macedonia and keeper of the royal seal. During this period he defeated the Maedi[8] who had risen in revolt, captured their city, drove out its barbarous inhabitants, established a colony of Greeks assembled from various regions, and named it Alexandroupolis. He also took part in the battle against the combined armies of Greece at Chaeronea,[9] and is said to have been the first to break the line of the

1. See ch. 26.
2. Author of a history of Sicily. See *Life of Dion*, ch. 11.
3. Partly because of Aristotle's connection with Callisthenes. See chs. 53–6.
4. See ch. 28.
5. He became head of the Academy at Athens in 339 B.C. but declined to accompany Alexander to Asia.
6. See chs. 65, 69.
7. In 340 B.C.
8. A tribe in north-eastern Macedonia.
9. In 338 B.C., one of the decisive battles of Greek history, which resulted in the subjection of the city-states to the Macedonian monarchy.

Theban Sacred Band. Even in my own time an oak tree used to be pointed out near the river Cephisus which was known as Alexander's oak, because his tent had been pitched beside it at that time, and not far away is the mass-grave of the Macedonians who fell in the battle. Because of these achievements Philip, as was natural, became extravagantly fond of his son, so much so that he took pleasure in hearing the Macedonians speak of Alexander as their king and Philip as their general.

But before long the domestic strife that resulted from Philip's various marriages and love-affairs caused the quarrels which took place in the women's apartments to infect the whole kingdom, and led to bitter clashes and accusations between father and son. This breach was widened by Olympias, a woman of a jealous and vindictive temper, who incited Alexander to oppose his father. Their quarrel was brought to a head on the occasion of the wedding of Cleopatra, a girl with whom Philip had fallen in love and whom he had decided to marry, although she was far too young for him. Cleopatra's uncle Attalus, who had drunk too much at the banquet, called upon the Macedonians to pray to the gods that the union of Philip and Cleopatra might bring forth a legitimate[1] heir to the throne. Alexander flew into a rage at these words, shouted at him, 'Villain, do you take me for a bastard, then?' and hurled a drinking-cup at his head. At this Philip lurched to his feet, and drew his sword against his son, but fortunately for them both he was so overcome with drink and with rage that he tripped and fell headlong. Alexander jeered at him and cried out, 'Here is the man who was making ready to cross from Europe to Asia, and who cannot even cross from one table to another without losing his balance.' After this drunken brawl Alexander took Olympias away and settled her in Epirus, while he himself went to live in Illyria.

Meanwhile Demaratus the Corinthian came to visit Philip. He was an old friend of the Macedonian royal family and so was privileged to speak freely. After the formal greetings and courtesies had been exchanged, Philip asked him whether the various city states of Greece

1. This may mean one of pure Macedonian blood, as distinct from the off-spring of the semi-barbarous Olympias, who came from Epirus. A marriage with the nobly born Cleopatra threatened Alexander's prospects of succession. The wedding took place in 337. Philip had not divorced Olympias: Macedonian tradition did not require the king to be monogamous.

were at harmony with one another. Demaratus retorted, 'It is all very well for you to show so much concern for the affairs of Greece, Philip. How about the disharmony you have brought about in your own household?' This reply sobered Philip to such an extent that he sent for Alexander, and with Demaratus' help persuaded him to return.[1]

10. In the following year Pixodarus, the satrap of Caria, tried to form a family union with Philip, hoping by this means to insinuate himself into a military alliance. His plan was to offer the hand of his eldest daughter to Philip's son Arrhidaeus,[2] and he sent Aristocritus to Macedonia to try to negotiate the match. Alexander's mother and his friends sent him a distorted account of this manoeuvre, making out that Philip was planning to settle the kingdom upon Arrhidaeus by arranging a brilliant marriage and treating him as a person of great consequence. Alexander was disturbed by these stories and sent Thessalus, the tragic actor, to Caria to tell Pixodarus that he should pay no attention to Arrhidaeus, who was not only an illegitimate son of Philip's but was weak-minded as well: instead, he should offer his daughter's hand to Alexander.

Pixodarus was far more pleased with this suggestion than with his original proposal. When Philip discovered this, he went to Alexander's room, taking with him Philotas the son of Parmenio, one of the prince's companions. There he scolded his son and angrily reproached him for behaving so ignobly and so unworthily of his position as to wish to marry the daughter of a mere Carian, who was no more than the slave of a barbarian king.[3] As for Thessalus, he wrote to the Corinthians ordering them to send him to Macedonia in chains, and at the same time he banished four of Alexander's friends, Harpalus, Nearchus, Erygius and Ptolemy. Later Alexander recalled all of these men and raised them to the highest honours.

Not long afterwards a Macedonian named Pausanias assassinated

1. Late in 337 B.C.

2. An illegitimate son of Philip's by Philinna of Larissa. He later succeeded Alexander, see ch. 77 and Appendix. The fact that Alexander could believe the story suggests how precarious he thought his position had become. Cleopatra had already given birth to a girl early in 336 and was again pregnant by the summer.

3. It also seems probable that such a match would have been embarrassing to Philip in view of his plans to invade Persia.

the king: he did this because he had been humiliated by Attalus and Cleopatra and could get no redress from Philip.[1] It was Olympias who was chiefly blamed for the assassination, because she was believed to have encouraged the young man and incited him to take his revenge. It was said that when Pausanias met the young prince and complained to him of the injustice he had suffered, Alexander quoted the verse from Euripides' *Medea*, in which Medea is said to threaten

> The father, bride and bridegroom all at once[2]

However this may be, he took care to track down and punish those who were involved in the plot, and he showed his anger against Olympias for the horrible revenge which she took upon Cleopatra during his absence.[3]

11. Alexander was only twenty years old when he inherited his kingdom, which at that moment was beset by formidable jealousies and feuds, and external dangers on every side. The neighbouring barbarian tribes were eager to throw off the Macedonian yoke and longed for the rule of their native kings: as for the Greek states, although Philip had defeated them in battle, he had not had time to subdue them or accustom them to his authority. He had swept away the existing governments, and then, having prepared their peoples for drastic changes, had left them in turmoil and confusion, because he had created a situation which was completely unfamiliar to them. Alexander's Macedonian advisers feared that a crisis was at hand and urged the young king to leave the Greek states to their own devices and refrain from using any force against them. As for the barbarian tribes, they considered that he should try to win them back to their allegiance by using milder methods, and forestall the first signs of revolt by offering them concessions. Alexander, however, chose precisely the opposite course, and decided that the only way to make

1. Pausanias had been outraged by Attalus some eight years before.
2. The allusion is to Medea's wish to murder Creon , Creusa and Jason, who in the context are identified with Attalus, Cleopatra and Philip. The murder took place on the day of the wedding of Philip's daughter Cleopatra to Alexander of Epirus in June, 336.
3. According to Pausanias viii, 7, Olympias had Cleopatra (that is, Philip's widow) and her infant son roasted over a brazier. Attalus was executed by Alexander for allegedly treasonable correspondence with Athens. Other accounts suggest that the assassination was organized by Persian initiative.

his kingdom safe was to act with audacity and a lofty spirit, for he was certain that if he were seen to yield even a fraction of his authority, all his enemies would attack him at once. He swiftly crushed the uprisings among the barbarians by advancing with his army as far as the Danube, where he overcame Syrmus, the king of the Triballi, in a great battle. Then when the news reached him that the Thebans had revolted and were being supported by the Athenians, he immediately marched south through the pass of Thermopylae. 'Demosthenes', he said, 'called me a boy while I was in Illyria and among the Triballi, and a youth when I was marching through Thessaly; I will show him I am a man by the time I reach the walls of Athens.'

When he arrived before Thebes,[1] he wished to give the citizens the opportunity to repent of their actions, and so he merely demanded the surrender of their leaders Phoenix and Prothytes, and offered an amnesty to all the rest if they would come over to his side. The Thebans countered by demanding the surrender of Philotas and Antipater and appealing to all who wished to liberate Greece to range themselves on their side, and at this Alexander ordered his troops to prepare for battle. The Thebans, although greatly outnumbered, fought with a superhuman courage and spirit, but when the Macedonian garrison which had been posted in the citadel of the Cadmeia made a sortie and fell upon them from the rear, the greater part of their army was encircled, they were slaughtered where they stood, and the city was stormed, plundered and razed to the ground. Alexander's principal object in permitting the sack of Thebes was to frighten the rest of the Greeks into submission by making a terrible example. But he also put forward the excuse that he was redressing the wrongs done to his allies, for the Plataeans and Phocians had both complained of the actions of the Thebans against them. As for the population of Thebes, he singled out the priests, a few citizens who had friendly connections with Macedonia, the descendants of the poet Pindar, and those who had opposed the revolt to be spared: all the rest were publicly sold into slavery to the number of twenty thousand. Those who were killed in the battle numbered more than six thousand.

12. Among the many outrages and acts of violence which accompanied the sacking of the city, some Thracian troops broke into the

1. September 335 B.C.

house of Timocleia, a woman of noble birth and character. While the soldiers were plundering her property, their leader raped her and then demanded whether she had any gold or silver hidden. She told him that she had, and led him alone into the garden. There she pointed out to him a well, and explained that while the city was being stormed she had thrown into it all her most valuable possessions. Then as the Thracian leaned over and peered down the shaft, she moved behind him, pushed him in, and hurled stone after stone down on him until he was dead. The Thracians seized her, tied her hands, and led her to Alexander, who immediately saw from her expression and from her calm and fearless bearing as she followed her captors that she was a woman of dignity and spirit. When the king asked her who she was, she replied, 'I am the sister of Theagenes who commanded our army against your father, Philip, and fell at Chaeronea fighting for the liberty of Greece.' Alexander was filled with admiration not only at her words but at what she had done, and gave orders that she and her children should be freed and allowed to depart.

13. After this Alexander came to terms with the Athenians, in spite of their open sympathy with the sufferings of the Thebans. They had been on the point of celebrating the Mysteries of Demeter, but abandoned the festival as an act of mourning, and they treated all the fugitives who reached Athens with the greatest kindness. It may be that Alexander's fury had been sated with blood, like a lion's, or perhaps that he wished to efface his cruel and savage treatment of the Thebans by performing an act of clemency. At any rate he not only agreed to overlook the causes of complaint which he had against the Athenians, but advised them to pay the most careful attention to their affairs, since if anything should happen to him, they might once again become the leaders of Greece. In later years Alexander often felt distressed, we are told, at the harsh fate of the Thebans, and the recollection of it made him milder in his treatment of many other peoples. Certainly he believed that the murder of Cleitus, which he committed when he was drunk, and the cowardly refusal of the Macedonians to cross the Ganges and attack the Indians, which cut short his campaign and robbed him of its crowning achievement, were both caused by the anger of the god Dionysus, who wished to avenge the destruction of his favourite city. And of those Thebans who survived, it was remarked that all who came to him with a

request were granted whatever they asked. So much for Alexander's
dealings with Thebes.

14. In the previous year a congress of the Greek states had been held
at the Isthmus of Corinth: here a vote had been passed that the states
should join forces with Alexander in invading Persia and that he should
be commander-in-chief of the expedition. Many of the Greek statesmen and philosophers visited him to offer their congratulations, and
he hoped that Diogenes of Sinope, who was at that time living in
Corinth, would do the same. However since he paid no attention
whatever to Alexander, but continued to live at leisure in the suburb
of Corinth which was known as Craneion, Alexander went in person
to see him and found him basking at full length in the sun. When he
saw so many people approaching him, Diogenes raised himself a
little on his elbow and fixed his gaze upon Alexander. The king
greeted him and inquired whether he could do anything for him.
'Yes,' replied the philosopher, 'you can stand a little to one side out of
my sun.' Alexander is said to have been greatly impressed by this
answer and full of admiration for the hauteur and independence of
mind of a man who could look down on him with such condescen-
sion. So much so that he remarked to his followers, who were
laughing and mocking the philosopher as they went away, 'You
may say what you like, but if I were not Alexander, I would be
Diogenes.'

Next he visited Delphi, because he wished to consult the oracle of
Apollo about the expedition against the Persians. It so happened that
he arrived on one of those days which are called inauspicious, when it
is forbidden for the oracle to deliver a reply. In spite of this he sent
for the prophetess, and when she refused to officiate and explained
that the law forbade her to do so, he went up himself and tried to
drag her by force to the shrine. At last, as if overcome by his persist-
ence, she exclaimed, 'You are invincible, my son!' and when
Alexander heard this, he declared that he wanted no other prophecy,
but had obtained from her the oracle he was seeking. When the time
came for him to set out,[1] many other prodigies attended the departure
of the army: among these was the phenomenon of the statue of
Orpheus which was made of cypress wood and was observed to be
covered with sweat. Everyone who saw it was alarmed at this omen,

1. The early spring of 334 B.C.

but Aristander urged the king to take courage, for this portent signified that Alexander was destined to perform deeds which would live in song and story and would cause poets and musicians much toil and sweat to celebrate them.

15. As for the size of his army, the lowest estimate puts its strength at 30,000 infantry and 4,000 cavalry and the highest 43,000 infantry and 4,000 cavalry.[1] According to Aristobulus the money available for the army's supplies amounted to no more than seventy talents, Douris says that there were supplies for only thirty days, and Onesicritus that Alexander was already two hundred talents in debt. Yet although he set out with such slender resources, he would not go aboard his ship until he had discovered the circumstances of all his companions and had assigned an estate to one, a village to another, or the revenues of some port or community to a third. When he had shared out or signed away almost all the property of the crown, Perdiccas asked him, 'But your majesty, what are you leaving for yourself?' 'My hopes!' replied Alexander. 'Very well, then,' answered Perdiccas, 'those who serve with you will share those too.' With this, he declined to accept the prize which had been allotted to him, and several of Alexander's other friends did the same. However those who accepted or requested rewards were lavishly provided for, so that in the end Alexander distributed among them most of what he possessed in Macedonia. These were his preparations and this was the adventurous spirit in which he crossed the Hellespont.

Once arrived in Asia, he went up to Troy, sacrificed to Athena and poured libations to the heroes of the Greek army. He anointed with oil the column which marks the grave of Achilles, ran a race by it naked with his companions, as the custom is, and then crowned it with a wreath: he also remarked that Achilles was happy in having found a faithful friend while he lived and a great poet to sing of his deeds after his death. While he was walking about the city and looking at its ancient remains, somebody asked him whether he wished

1. Modern estimates give totals of about 43,000 infantry and 6,000 cavalry: about one quarter of these were the advance guard, which had already crossed to Asia. The cavalry included as many Thessalians as Macedonians, while the other Greek city-states contributed about 7,000 infantry and 600 cavalry. Besides the operational troops, the expedition included reconnaissance staff and many other specialists – geographers, historians, astronomers, zoologists, etc.

to see the lyre which had once belonged to Paris.[1] 'I think nothing of
that lyre,' he said, 'but I wish I could see Achilles' lyre, which he
played when he sang of the glorious deeds of brave men.'

16. Meanwhile Darius' generals had gathered a large army and
posted it at the crossing of the river Granicus, so that Alexander was
obliged to fight at the very gates of Asia, if he was to enter and
conquer it. Most of the Macedonian officers were alarmed at the
depth of the river and of the rough and uneven slopes of the banks
on the opposite side, up which they would have to scramble in the
face of the enemy. There were others too who thought that Alexander
ought to observe the Macedonian tradition concerning the time of
year, according to which the kings of Macedonia never made war
during the month of Daesius.[2] Alexander swept aside these scruples
by giving orders that the month should be called a second Artemisius.
And when Parmenio advised him against risking the crossing at such
a late hour of the day, Alexander declared that the Hellespont would
blush for shame if, once he had crossed it, he should shrink back from
the Granicus; then he immediately plunged into the stream with
thirteen squadrons of cavalry.[3] It seemed the act of a desperate madman rather than of a prudent commander to charge into a swiftly
flowing river, which swept men off their feet and surged about them,
and then to advance through a hail of missiles towards a steep bank
which was strongly defended by infantry and cavalry. But in spite
of this he pressed forward and with a tremendous effort gained the
opposite bank, which was a wet treacherous slope covered with mud.
There he was immediately forced to engage the enemy in a confused
hand to hand struggle, before the troops who were crossing behind
him could be organized into any formation. The moment his men
set foot on land, the enemy attacked them with loud shouts, matching
horse against horse, thrusting with their lances and fighting with the
sword when their lances broke. Many of them charged against
Alexander himself, for he was easily recognizable by his shield and

1. There is a pun here: Paris was also known as Alexander.
2. May–June: this was the time for the gathering of the harvest.
3. Diodorus gives an account which is more plausible in military terms.
According to this Alexander marched downstream under cover of darkness,
found a suitable ford, crossed at dawn, and had most of his infantry over before
the Persians discovered his new position.

by the tall white plume which was fixed upon either side of his helmet. The joint of his breast-plate was pierced by a javelin, but the blade did not penetrate the flesh. Rhoesaces and Spithridates, two of the Persian commanders then rode at him; he evaded the charge of the one and struck Rhoesaces, who wore a breast-plate, with his spear, but the shaft of the weapon snapped, whereupon he fought with his sword. While he was engaged with Rhoesaces, Spithridates rode up on the other side, and rising in his stirrups brought down a barbarian battle-axe with all his strength upon Alexander's head. The stroke split the crest of his helmet, sheared away one of his plumes, and all but cleft the head-piece, in fact the edge of the axe penetrated it and grazed the hair on the top of Alexander's head. But just as Spithridates raised his arm for another blow, 'Black' Cleitus,[1] as he was called, struck first and ran him through with a spear, and at the same moment Rhoesaces was cut down by Alexander's sword.

While Alexander's cavalry was engaged in this furious and dangerous action, the Macedonian phalanx crossed the river and the infantry of both sides joined battle. The Persians offered little resistance, but quickly broke and fled, and it was only the Greek mercenaries who held their ground. They rallied together, made a stand on the crest of a hill and sent a message to Alexander asking for quarter. In this instance he allowed himself to be guided by passion rather than by reason, led a charge against them and lost his horse (not Bucephalas on this occasion), which was pierced through the ribs by a sword-thrust. It was in this part of the field that the Macedonians suffered greater losses in killed and wounded than in all the rest of the battle, since they were fighting at close quarters with men who were expert soldiers and had been rendered desperate.

The Persians are said to have lost twenty thousand infantry and two thousand five hundred cavalry, whereas on Alexander's side, according to Aristobulus, only thirty four soldiers[2] in all were killed, nine of them belonging to the infantry. Alexander gave orders that each of these men should have his statue set up in bronze and the work was carried out by Lysippus. At the same time he was anxious to give

1. Commander of the Royal Squadron of Companion Cavalry: called 'Black' to distinguish him from Cleitus the White, an infantry commander.
2. According to Arrian, *Anabasis*, I, 16, 4, twenty-five of Alexander's picked cavalry, the Companions, fell in the first charge: it was these men whose statues were carved by Lysippus.

the other Greek states a share in the victory. He therefore sent the Athenians in particular three hundred of the shields captured from the enemy, and over the rest of the spoils he had this proud inscription engraved:

Alexander, the son of Philip, and all the Greeks, with the exception of the Spartans, won these spoils of war from the barbarians who dwell in Asia.

As for the drinking vessels, purple hangings and other such plunder, he sent it all with the exception of a few items to his mother.

17. This battle brought about a great and immediate change in Alexander's situation. Even the city of Sardis, which was the principal seat of Persian power on the Asiatic seaboard, at once surrendered to him and the rest of the region likewise made its submission.[1] Only Halicarnassus[2] and Miletus held out, and these cities were stormed and the surrounding territory subdued. At this point Alexander hesitated as to what his next step should be. Time and again he was impelled to seek out Darius and risk everything upon the issue of a single battle, and then as often he would decide that he must build up his strength by securing the coastal region and its resources and training his army, and only then strike inland against the king. It is said that there was a spring near the city of Xanthus in the province of Lycia, which at this moment overflowed and cast up from its depths a bronze tablet: this was inscribed with ancient characters which foretold that the empire of the Persians would be destroyed by the Greeks. Alexander was encouraged by this prophecy and pressed on to clear the coast of Asia Minor as far as Cilicia and Phoenicia. His advance through Pamphylia inspired various historians to compose a highly wrought and extravagant description of his progress. They imply that through some extraordinary stroke of providence the tide receded to make way for him, although at other times it came flooding in strongly from the open sea, so that the beach of small rocks which lies directly under the steep and broken face of the cliffs was hardly ever left uncovered. Menander alludes to this prodigy in one of his comedies, where he says:

1. At this stage of his campaign Alexander made it his policy to support democratic regimes in the Greek cities of Asia Minor.

2. The principal Persian naval base in the southern Aegean. It was defended by Memnon the Rhodian, a mercenary in Darius' service, and was captured in the autumn of 334.

> Like Alexander, if I want to meet
> A man, he's there before me in the street,
> And if I am obliged to cross the sea,
> The waves at once will make a path for me.

Alexander makes no mention in his letters of any such miracle, but says that he started from Phaselis in Lycia, and marched through Pamphylia by the pass known as *Klimax*, or The Ladder. It was for this reason that he spent several days in Phaselis, where he noticed in the market-place a statue which had been erected in honour of Theodectas,[1] a former citizen of the place. One evening after dinner when he had drunk well, he had the impulse to pay a convivial tribute to his association with Aristotle and with philosophy, and so he led a band of revellers to the statue and crowned it with a garland.

18. Next he marched into Pisidia where he subdued any resistance which he encountered, and then made himself master of Phrygia. When he captured Gordium,[2] which is reputed to have been the home of the ancient king Midas, he saw the celebrated chariot which was fastened to its yoke by the bark of the cornel-tree, and heard the legend which was believed by all the barbarians, that the fates had decreed that the man who untied the knot was destined to become the ruler of the whole world. According to most writers the fastenings were so elaborately intertwined and coiled upon one another that their ends were hidden: in consequence Alexander did not know what to do, and in the end loosened the knot by cutting through it with his sword, whereupon the many ends sprang into view. But according to Aristobulus he unfastened it quite easily by removing the pin which secured the yoke to the pole of the chariot, and then pulling out the yoke itself.

After this Alexander marched northward and won over the peoples of Cappadocia and Paphlagonia. He also learned of the death of Memnon,[3] the general to whom Darius had entrusted the defence of

1. The author of some fifty tragedies: he had been a pupil of Aristotle, hence Alexander's interest.

2. In March 333 B.C.

3. A Greek mercenary officer from Rhodes. After escaping from Halicarnassus when Alexander captured it, he had been appointed commander of the Persian fleet. In 333 B.C. he captured Chios, overran most of Lesbos and laid siege to Mitylene where he died. The Persians had hoped that he would threaten Alexander's rear by stirring up revolts in the islands and even in mainland Greece.

the coast of Asia Minor, and who, if he had lived, was likely to have
offered the most stubborn resistance to Alexander's advance and caused
him the greatest trouble. This news confirmed his resolve to invade
the interior. By this time Darius was also marching upon the coast
from Susa. He was full of confidence in the strength of his forces, for
he was leading an army of six hundred thousand men, and he had
been encouraged by a dream which the Magi had interpreted in
such a way as to please him rather than to discover the most likely
meaning. He had dreamed that he saw the Macedonian phalanx
encircled with flames and Alexander waiting upon him as a servant
and wearing a cloak which resembled one that Darius himself had
once worn when he had been a royal courier, and that after this
Alexander had entered the temple of Belos and had disappeared.
But what the gods really intended to prophesy through this dream,
it would appear, was that the Macedonians would accomplish brilliant and glorious exploits, that Alexander would become the ruler
of Asia – just as Darius had become its ruler when he rose to be a
king from having been a mere courier – and that he would soon die
and leave his glory behind him.

19. Darius was also encouraged by the many months of apparent
inactivity which Alexander had spent in Cilicia, for he imagined
that this was due to cowardice. In fact the delay had been caused by
sickness, which some said had been brought on by exhaustion, and
others by bathing in the icy waters of the river Cydnus. At any rate
none of his other physicians dared to treat him, for they all believed
that his condition was so dangerous that medicine was powerless to
help him, and dreaded the accusations that would be brought against
them by the Macedonians in the event of their failure. The only exception was Philip, an Acarnanian, who saw that the king was desperately
ill, but trusted to their mutual friendship. He thought it shameful not
to share his friend's danger by exhausting all the resources of his art
even at the risk of his own life, and so he prepared a medicine and
persuaded him to drink it without fear, since he was so eager to regain
his strength for the campaign. Meanwhile Parmenio had sent Alexander a letter from the camp warning him to beware of Philip, since
Darius, he said, had promised him large sums of money and even
the hand of his daughter if he would kill Alexander. Alexander read
the letter and put it under his pillow without showing it to any of his

friends. Then at the appointed hour, when Philip entered the room with the king's companions carrying the medicine in a cup, Alexander handed him the letter and took the draught from him cheerfully and without the least sign of misgiving. It was an astonishing scene, and one well worthy of the stage – the one man reading the letter and the other drinking the physic, and then each gazing into the face of the other, although not with the same expression. The king's serene and open smile clearly displayed his friendly feelings towards Philip and his trust in him, while Philip was filled with surprise and alarm at the accusation, at one moment lifting his hands to heaven and protesting his innocence before the gods, and the next falling upon his knees by the bed and imploring Alexander to take courage and follow his advice. At first the drug completely overpowered him and, as it were, drove all his vital forces out of sight: he became speechless, fell into a swoon, and displayed scarcely any sign of sense or of life. However Philip quickly restored him to consciousness, and when he had regained his strength he showed himself to the Macedonians, who would not be consoled until they had seen their king.

20. There was at this time[1] in Darius' army, a man named Amyntas a refugee from Macedonia, who was acquainted with Alexander's character. When he learned that Darius was eager to advance and attack Alexander as he marched through the mountain passes, he begged the Persian king to remain where he was in the flat open plains, where his immense numbers would have the advantage in fighting the small Macedonian army. Darius said that he was afraid the enemy might run away before he could come to grips with them, and that Alexander might thus escape him, to which Amyntas retorted: 'Your majesty need have no fears on that score. Alexander will march against you, in fact he is probably on his way now.' Darius refused to listen to Amyntas' advice, but broke camp and advanced into Cilicia, while at the same time Alexander marched against him into Syria. During the night they missed one another and both turned back. Alexander, delighted at his good fortune, hastened to catch his enemy in the narrow defile which leads into Cilicia, while Darius was no less eager to extricate his forces from the

1. September 333 B.C. In the late summer and before his illness Alexander had accomplished the difficult march south from Gordium across Anatolia and through the key pass of the Cilician Gates.

mountain passes and regain his former camping-ground in the plains. He already saw the mistake he had made by advancing into country which was hemmed in by the sea on one side and the mountains on the other, and divided by the river Pinarus which ran between them. Here the ground prevented him from using his cavalry, forced him to split up his army into small groups, and favoured his opponent's inferior numbers. Fortune certainly presented Alexander with the ideal terrain for the battle, but it was his own generalship which did most to win the victory. For although he was so heavily outnumbered, he not only gave the enemy no opportunity to encircle him, but leading his own right wing in person, he managed to extend it round the enemy's left, outflanked it, and fighting in the foremost ranks, put the barbarians to flight. In this action he received a sword wound in the thigh: according to Chares this was given him by Darius, with whom he engaged in hand to hand combat. Alexander sent a letter to Antipater describing the battle, but made no mention in it of who had given him the wound: he said no more than that he had been stabbed in the thigh with a dagger and that the wound was not a dangerous one.

The result of this battle[1] was a brilliant victory for Alexander. His men killed one hundred and ten thousand of the enemy, but he could not catch Darius, who had got a start of half a mile or more, although he captured the king's chariot and his bow before he returned from the pursuit. He found the Macedonians busy carrying off the spoils from the enemy's camp, for this contained an immense wealth of possessions, despite the fact that the Persians had marched into battle lightly equipped and had left most of their baggage in Damascus. Darius' tent which was full of many treasures, luxurious furniture, and lavishly dressed servants had been set aside for Alexander himself. As soon as he arrived, he unbuckled his armour and went to the bath, saying 'Let us wash off the sweat of battle in Darius's bath.' 'No, in Alexander's bath, now,' remarked one of his companions. 'The conqueror takes over the possessions of the conquered and they should be called his.' When Alexander entered the bath-room he saw that the basins, the pitchers, the baths themselves and the caskets containing unguents were all made of gold and elaborately carved, and noticed that the whole room was marvellously fragrant with spices and perfumes, and then passing from this into a spacious and

1. The battle of Issus: November 333 B.C.

lofty tent, he observed the magnificence of the dining-couches, the tables and the banquet which had been set out for him. He turned to his companions and remarked. 'So this, it seems, is what it is to be a king.'[1]

21. As he was about to sit down to supper, word was brought to him that the mother, the wife and the two unmarried daughters of Darius were among the prisoners, and that at the sight of the Persian king's bow and chariot they had beaten their breasts and cried out, since they supposed that he must be dead. When he heard this Alexander was silent for some time, for he was evidently more affected by the women's grief than by his own triumph. Then he sent Leonnatus[2] to tell them that Darius was not dead and that they need have no fear of Alexander: he was fighting Darius for the empire of Asia, but they should be provided with everything they had been accustomed to regard as their due when Darius was king. This kindly and reassuring message for Darius' womenfolk was followed by still more generous actions. Alexander gave them leave to bury as many of the Persians as they wished, and to take from the plunder any clothes and ornaments they thought fit and use them for this purpose. He also allowed them to keep the same attendants and privileges that they had previously enjoyed and even increased their revenues. But the most honourable and truly regal service which he rendered to these chaste and noble women was to ensure that they should never hear, suspect nor have cause to fear anything which could disgrace them: they lived out of sight and earshot of the soldiers, as though they were guarded in some inviolable retreat set aside for virgin priestesses rather than in an enemy's camp. This was the more remarkable because the wife of Darius was said to have been the most beautiful princess of her time, just as Darius himself was the tallest and handsomest man in Asia, and their daughters resembled their parents.

At any rate Alexander, so it seems, thought it more worthy of a king to subdue his own passions than to conquer his enemies, and

1. A remark intended to express not admiration but pity for Darius, for thinking that royalty consisted of mere wealth and luxury.

2. A friend who had grown up with Alexander: he helped to save his life in the battle against the Malli (ch. 63), and was himself killed at Crannon (322 B.C.).

so he never came near these women, nor did he associate with any other before his marriage, with the exception only of Barsine. This woman, the widow of Memnon, the Greek mercenary commander, was captured at Damascus. She had received a Greek education, was of a gentle disposition, and could claim royal descent, since her father was Artabazus who had married one of the Persian king's daughters. These qualities made Alexander the more willing – he was encouraged by Parmenio, so Aristobulus tells us – to form an attachment to a woman of such beauty and noble lineage. As for the other prisoners, when Alexander saw their handsome and stately appearance, he took no more notice of them than to say jokingly, 'These Persian women are a torment for our eyes.'[1] He was determined to make such a show of his chastity and self-control as to eclipse the beauty of their appearance, and so he passed them by as if they had been so many lifeless images cut out of stone.

22. When Philoxenus, the commander of his forces on the sea coast, wrote to say that he had with him a slave merchant from Tarentum named Theodorus who was offering exceptionally handsome boys for sale and asked whether Alexander wished to buy them, the king was furious and angrily demanded of his friends what signs of degeneracy Philoxenus had ever noticed in him that he should waste his time procuring such debased creatures. He wrote a letter to Philoxenus telling him what he thought of him and ordering him to send Theodorus and his merchandise to the devil. He also sharply rebuked Hagnon, who had written that he wanted to buy as a present for him a young man named Crobylus, whose good looks were famous in Corinth. And when he discovered that Damon and Timotheus, two Macedonian soldiers who were serving under Parmenio, had seduced the wives of some of the Greek mercenaries, he sent orders to Parmenio that if the two men were found guilty, they should be put to death as wild beasts which are born to prey upon mankind. In the same letter he wrote of himself: 'In my own case it will be found not only that I have never seen nor wished to see Darius' wife, but that I have not even allowed her beauty to be mentioned in my presence.' He also used to say that it was sleep and sexual intercourse which more than anything else, reminded him

1. i.e. because they incite the body to rebel against the discipline of the will.

that he was mortal; by this he meant that both exhaustion and pleasure proceed from the same weakness of human nature.

He was exceptionally temperate in what he ate, as he showed in
many different ways, but above all in the answer he gave to Queen
Ada,[1] whom he honoured with the official title of Mother and made
Queen of Caria. To show her affection for him she had formed the
habit of sending him delicacies and sweetmeats every day, and finally
offered him bakers and cooks who were supposed to be the most skilful
in the country. Alexander's reply was that he did not need them,
because his tutor Leonidas had provided him with better cooks than
these, that is a night march to prepare him for breakfast, and a light
breakfast to give him an appetite for supper. 'This same Leonidas,'
he went on, 'would often come and open my chests of bedding and
clothes, to see whether my mother had not hidden some luxury
inside.'

23. Alexander was also more moderate in his drinking than was
generally supposed. The impression that he was a heavy drinker arose
because when he had nothing else to do, he liked to linger over each
cup, but in fact he was usually talking rather than drinking: he
enjoyed holding long conversations, but only when he had plenty
of leisure. Whenever there was urgent business to attend to, neither
wine, nor sleep, nor sport, nor sex, nor spectacle, could ever distract
his attention, as they did for other generals. The proof of this is his
life-span, which although so short, was filled to overflowing with
the most prodigious achievements. When he was at leisure, his first
act after rising was to sacrifice to the gods, after which he took his
breakfast sitting down.[2] The rest of the day would be spent in hunting,
administering justice, planning military affairs or reading. If he were
on a march which required no great haste, he would practise archery
as he rode, or mounting and dismounting from a moving chariot,
and he often hunted foxes or birds, as he mentions in his journals.
When he had chosen his quarters for the night and while he was being
refreshed with a bath or rubbed down, he would ask his cooks and
bakers whether the arrangements for supper had been suitably made.

His custom was not to begin supper until late, as it was growing
dark. He took it reclining on a couch, and he was wonderfully

1. The sister of Pixodarus of Caria.
2. That is, not reclining, as for the evening meal.

attentive and observant in ensuring that his table was well provided, his guests equally served, and none of them neglected. He sat long over his wine, as I have remarked, because of his fondness for conversation. And although at other times his society was delightful and his manner full of charm beyond that of any prince of his age, yet when he was drinking he would sometimes become offensively arrogant and descend to the level of a common soldier, and on these occasions he would allow himself not only to give way to boasting but also to be led on by his flatterers. These men were a great trial to the finer spirits among his companions, who had no desire to compete with them in their sycophancy, but were unwilling to be outdone in praising Alexander. The one course they thought shameful, but the other was dangerous. When the drinking was over it was his custom to take a bath and sleep, often until midday, and sometimes for the whole of the following day.[1]

As for delicacies, Alexander was so restrained in his appetite that often when the rarest fruits or fish were brought him from the sea coast, he would distribute them so generously among his companions that there would be nothing left for himself. His evening meal, however, was always a magnificent affair, and as his successes multiplied, so did his expenditure on hospitality until it reached the sum of ten thousand drachmae. At this point he fixed a limit and those who entertained Alexander were told that they must not exceed this sum.

24. After the battle of Issus[2] he sent a force to Damascus and there captured the whole of the Persian army's treasure and baggage, together with their wives and children. On this occasion it was the Thessalian cavalry[3] who obtained the richest share of the plunder. They had particularly distinguished themselves at Issus, and Alexander had deliberately sent them on this expedition to reward them for their courage, but the booty proved so inexhaustible that there was enough to make the whole army rich. It was here that the Macedonians received their first taste of gold and silver and women and of the

1. Plutarch does his best here to pay tribute to Alexander's self-discipline, but the evidence of this sentence is significant. Nobody in fighting trim who has gone to bed sober would be likely to sleep till midday, or sometimes all day.
2. November 333 B.C. (see ch. 20).
3. These were heavy cavalry customarily placed under Parmenio on the left wing, where they fought a holding action, while Alexander attacked on the right.

luxury of the barbarian way of life, and henceforth, like hounds which have picked up a scent, they pressed on to track down the wealth of the Persians.

However this did not divert Alexander from his strategy of securing the whole of the Asiatic seaboard before striking inland. The kings of Cyprus promptly visited him to hand over the island, and the whole of Phoenicia surrendered to him except for the city of Tyre. He besieged Tyre for seven months,[1] constructing moles and siege artillery on the landward side, and blockading it with two hundred triremes by sea. During the siege he had a dream in which he saw Hercules stretching out his hand to him from the wall and beckoning him to enter. Many of the Tyrians also dreamed that Apollo appeared to them and announced that he was going away to Alexander because he was displeased at what had been done in the city. At this the citizens treated him as if he were a deserter caught in the act of going over to the enemy. They fastened cords to his statue, nailed it to its base and reviled him as a supporter of Alexander. On another occasion Alexander dreamed that he saw a satyr who mocked at him from a distance and evaded his grasp when he tried to seize him, but who at last after much coaxing and pursuing, allowed himself to be caught. The soothsayers gave a plausible interpretation of this dream by dividing the word *sa-tyros* into two, to which they gave the meaning 'Tyre will be thine'. To this day the inhabitants show a well, near which they say Alexander dreamed that he saw the satyr.

In the midst of this siege Alexander led a force against the Arabian tribes who inhabit the mountains of the Anti-Lebanon. During this expedition he risked his life to rescue his tutor Lysimachus, who had insisted on accompanying him, since he claimed that he was neither older nor weaker than Achilles' tutor Phoenix. When the force drew near the mountains, they were obliged to leave their horses and climb the slopes on foot, and the main body pressed far ahead of the rearguard. Lysimachus could not keep up the pace and grew more and more exhausted, but Alexander refused to leave him, since by then it was growing dark and the enemy were close at hand: instead he tried to encourage him and urge him along. But before he knew it, he found himself separated from the main body with only a handful of men and forced to spend a night of bitter cold in country which

1. January–August 332 B.C.

offered him no shelter. At last he saw in the distance a number of scattered watch-fires which belonged to the enemy. It was always his habit in a crisis to encourage the Macedonians by sharing in their dangers, and so, trusting to his speed and agility, he dashed to the nearest camp fire, dispatched with his dagger the two barbarians who were sitting by it, and snatching up a firebrand ran back to his own party. His companions quickly built up a huge fire which frightened some of the enemy into flight, while those who ventured to attack were quickly routed and the Macedonians spent the rest of the night in safety. This is the account of the incident which we have from Chares.

25. The siege finally ended as follows. Alexander was resting the greater part of his army, which was exhausted after the hard fighting it had undergone, but in order to give the enemy no respite he led a small party against the walls. At the same time his diviner Aristander offered up a sacrifice, and after inspecting the omens, confidently announced to all those present that the city would be captured in the course of that month: this pronouncement was greeted with laughter and even some derision because by then it was the last day of the month. The king saw that Aristander was at a loss to explain the omens, and as he was always anxious to uphold the credibility of his prophecies, gave orders that that day should be counted not as the thirtieth of the month but as the twenty-eighth. The trumpet then sounded the advance and he launched a fiercer attack against the walls than he had originally intended. The fighting grew hotter, until the troops who had been left in camp could not bear to stay inactive, but came running up to join the attackers, and thereupon the Tyrians gave up the struggle. So it came about that Alexander captured the city on that day.

In the autumn of the same year he laid siege to Gaza,[1] the most important city in Syria. While he was engaged in these operations, a bird flying overhead let fall a clod of earth which struck him on the shoulder. The bird then perched upon one of the siege engines and immediately became entangled in the network of sinews which were used to tighten the ropes. On this occasion too the portent was fulfilled as Aristander had prophesied: the city was taken, and Alexander was wounded in the shoulder. He sent a great part of the spoils

1. September and October, 332 B.C.

captured at Gaza to Olympias, to his sister Cleopatra and to his friends. He also remembered his tutor Leonidas and presented him with five hundred talents' weight of frankincense and one hundred of myrrh: this was in remembrance of the hopes with which his teacher had inspired him in his boyhood. It seems that one day when Alexander was sacrificing and was throwing incense on to the altar by the handful, Leonidas remarked to him, 'Alexander, when you have conquered the countries that produce these spices, you can make as extravagant sacrifices as you like: till then, don't waste it!' On this occasion Alexander wrote to him, 'I have sent you plenty of myrrh and frankincense, so that you need not be stingy towards the gods any longer.'[1]

26. One day a casket was brought to him which was regarded by those who were in charge of Darius' baggage and treasure as the most valuable item of all, and so Alexander asked his friends what he should keep in it as his own most precious possession. Many different suggestions were put forward, and finally Alexander said that he intended to keep his copy of the *Iliad* there. This anecdote is supported by many reliable historians, and if the tradition which has been handed down by the Alexandrians on the authority of Heracleides is true, then certainly the poems of Homer were by no means an irrelevant or an unprofitable possession to accompany him on his campaigns. According to this story, after Alexander had conquered Egypt, he was anxious to found a great and populous Greek city there,[2] to be called after him. He had chosen a certain site on the advice of his architects, and was on the point of measuring and marking it out. Then as he lay asleep he dreamed that a grey-haired man of venerable appearance stood by his side and recited these lines from the *Odyssey*:

> Out of the tossing sea where it breaks on the beaches of Egypt
> Rises an isle from the waters: the name that men give it is Pharos[3]

Alexander rose the next morning and immediately visited Pharos: at that time it was still an island near the Canopic mouth of the

1. About thirteen and a half tons of frankincense and two and a half tons of myrrh. Alexander never forgot a slight.
2. In particular a maritime capital which should eclipse Piraeus, Carthage, Syracuse and any other rival.
3. *Odyssey* iv, 354–5.

Nile,[1] but since then it has been joined to the mainland by a causeway. When he saw what wonderful natural advantages the place possessed – for it was a strip of land resembling a broad isthmus, which stretched between the sea and a great lagoon, with a spacious harbour at the end of it – he declared that Homer, besides his other admirable qualities, was also a very far-seeing architect, and he ordered the plan of the city to be designed so that it would conform to this site. There was no chalk to mark the ground plan, so they took barley meal, sprinkled it on the dark earth and marked out a semi-circle, which was divided into equal segments by lines radiating from the inner arc to the circumference: the shape was similar to that of the *chlamys* or military cloak, so that the lines proceeded, as it were, from the skirt, and narrowed the breadth of the area uniformly. While the king was enjoying the symmetry of the design, suddenly huge flocks of birds appeared from the river and the lagoon, descended upon the site and devoured every grain of the barley. Alexander was greatly disturbed by this omen, but the diviners urged him to take heart and interpreted the occurrence as a sign that the city would not only have abundant resources of its own but would be the nurse of men of innumerable nations, and so he ordered those in charge of the work to proceed while he himself set out to visit the temple of Ammon.[2]

This was a long and arduous journey, which was beset by two especial dangers. The first was the lack of water, of which there was none to be found along the route for many days' march. The second arises if a strong south wind should overtake the traveller as he is crossing the vast expanse of deep, soft sand, as is said to have happened to the army of Cambyses long ago: the wind raised great billows of sand and blew them across the plain so that fifty thousand men were swallowed up and perished. These dangers were present in the minds of almost all of Alexander's companions, but it was difficult to dissuade him from any course once he had set his heart on it. Fortune, by giving way to his insistence on every occasion had made his resolve unshakeable, and the proud spirit which he carried into all his undertakings had created in him a passion for surmounting obstacles, so that in the end he was able to overcome not only his enemies but even places and seasons of the year.

1. Later the site of the famous octagonal lighthouse.
2. In the winter of 332 B.C.

27. At any rate during this journey the assistance he received from the gods in his difficulties was more readily believed than the oracles that followed, or rather it was because of this assistance that the oracles were believed. First of all the abundant rain and continual showers which fell from heaven relieved the expedition from any fear of thirst, saturated the dry sand so that it became moist and firm to the tread, and rendered the air pure and refreshing to breathe. Besides this whenever the travellers became separated, lost the track, or wandered about because the landmarks used by their guides had become obliterated, a number of ravens appeared and proceeded to guide their march, flying swiftly ahead of them when they followed, and waiting for them when they marched slowly or lagged behind. And what was most miraculous of all, according to Callisthenes, was that if any of the company went astray in the night, the birds would croak and caw over them, until they had found their way back to the track.

When Alexander had crossed the desert and arrived at the shrine, the high priest of Ammon welcomed him on the god's behalf as a father greeting his son.[1] Alexander's first question was to ask whether any of his father's murderers had escaped punishment. At this the high priest commanded him to speak more guardedly, since his father was not a mortal. Alexander therefore changed the form of his question and asked whether the murderers of Philip had all been punished, and he added another inquiry concerning his own empire, and asked whether he was destined to rule over all mankind. This, the god replied, would be granted to him, and he also assured him that Philip's death had been completely avenged, whereupon Alexander dedicated some magnificent offerings to the god and presented large sums of money to his priests.

This is the account which most writers have given of the oracles pronounced by the god, but Alexander himself in a letter to his mother says that he received certain secret prophecies which he would confide to her, and her alone, after his return. Others say that the priest, who wished as a mark of courtesy to address him with the Greek phrase 'O, paidion' (O, my son) spoke the words because of his

[1]. The shrine of Zeus Ammon had been regarded for centuries, together with Dodona and Delphi, as one of the three great oracles of the Greek world. The priests of Ammon had contact with those of Zeus in Greece, and since Egypt had become a vassal of Persia, prophecies had begun to look to the kingdoms of the north, Macedonia and Epirus, for the rise of a deliverer and universal ruler.

barbarian origin as 'O, *pai Dios*' (O, son of Zeus), and that Alexander was delighted at this slip of pronunciation, and hence the legend grew up that the god had addressed him as 'O, son of Zeus'. We are also told that while he was in Egypt he listened to the lectures of Psammon the philosopher, and especially approved his saying to the effect that all men are ruled by God, because in every case that element which imposes itself and achieves the mastery is divine. Even more philosophical was Alexander's own opinion and pronouncement on this subject, namely that while God is the father of all mankind, it is the noblest and best whom he makes especially his own.

28. In general Alexander adopted a haughty and majestic bearing towards the barbarians, as a man who was fully convinced of his divine birth and parentage, but towards the Greeks he was more restrained, and it was only on rare occasions that he assumed the manner of divinity. He made an exception when he wrote to the Athenians on the subject of Samos and said, 'I would never have given you that free and glorious city: it was from your master at that time that you received it and now hold it – my so-called father.'[1] By this he was referring to Philip. But some years later, when he had been wounded by an arrow and was in great pain, he remarked, 'What you see flowing, my friends, is blood, and not that

Ichor which flows in the veins of the blessed immortals in heaven.'[2]

On another occasion too, when there was a loud crash of thunder, and all those in his company were frightened by it, Anaxarchus the sophist asked him, 'Since you are the son of Zeus, could you make a noise like that?' Alexander laughed and replied, 'I have no wish to terrify my friends as you would have me do. It is you who apparently despise my table, because, so you say, what you see on it is merely fish, and not a row of satraps' heads!' For there is a story that this remark had been made by Anaxarchus when he saw a present of small fish that the king had sent to Hephaestion: he seemed to be disparaging and belittling those who undertake immense enterprises and run great risks in pursuit of their ambitions, which in the end leave them no happier or better able to enjoy themselves than other men. At any rate it is evident from what I have said that Alexander did not allow

1. i.e. he was disowning Philip as his father.   2. *Iliad* v, 340.

himself to become vain or foolishly conceited because of his belief in his divinity, but rather used it to assert his authority over others.

29. On his return from Egypt to Phoenicia[1] he honoured the gods with sacrifices and solemn processions and arranged contests of dithyrambic choruses and tragedies: these were remarkable not only for the splendour of their presentation but also for the rivalry between those who organized them. Just as at Athens those who present these spectacles are the *choregi*, rich citizens chosen by lot from the tribes, so on this occasion the sponsors were the kings of Cyprus, each of whom vied to outdo his competitors in the most spectacular fashion. The keenest contest of all took place between Nicocreon of Salamis and Pasicrates of Soli, who had been given by lot the services of two of the most celebrated actors of the day: Athenodorus was assigned to Pasicrates and Thessalus, in whom Alexander was particularly interested, to Nicocreon. Alexander did not reveal his preference until Athenodorus had been proclaimed the victor by a majority of the judges' votes. Then, as he was leaving the theatre, it seems, he remarked that he approved of the verdict of the judges, but would gladly have sacrificed a part of his kingdom rather than see Thessalus defeated. However when Athenodorus, who had been fined by the Athenians for breaking his undertaking to appear at their Dionysiac festival, appealed to the king to write a letter on his behalf, Alexander, although he refused to do this, settled the fine at his own expense. Again when Lycon of Scarpheia, who was giving a successful performance before Alexander, introduced into the comedy he was playing a line asking for a present of ten talents, Alexander laughed and gave him the money.

Darius wrote Alexander a letter[2] and sent it by the hand of some of his friends. He appealed to Alexander to accept ten thousand talents as a ransom for his Persian prisoners: he further offered him all the territory west of the Euphrates and the hand of one of his daughters in marriage, and on these terms proposed that they should become friends and allies. Alexander told his companions of this offer, whereupon Parmenio said, 'I would accept those terms if I were Alexander.'

1. Early in 331 B.C.
2. According to Arrian (*Anabasis*, II, 25, 1) this episode had taken place earlier, at the time of the siege of Tyre, and Alexander's reply was the conclusion of a more arrogantly phrased letter.

A.A. — 14

'So would I, by Zeus,' retorted Alexander, 'if I were Parmenio!' In reply he wrote that if Darius would come and give himself up, he would receive every courtesy: if not, Alexander would immediately march against him.

30. However not long after, when Darius' wife died in childbirth, Alexander felt remorse for having written in these terms. It is clear that he was distressed at having lost the chance to show his magnanimity, and he spared no expense to give the queen a magnificent funeral. One of her attendants, a eunuch named Teireos who had been captured with her, escaped from the camp, made his way to Darius on horseback and brought the news of the queen's death. When Darius heard it, he beat his head, broke into lamentations and cried aloud: 'Alas for the evil genius of the Persians! Was it not enough that the king's consort and sister should have become a prisoner while she lived, but she must also be deprived of a royal funeral at her death?' 'As for her burial, sire,' the eunuch replied, 'and all the honours that were due to her state, you have no cause to accuse the evil genius of the Persians. To my knowledge neither your queen Stateira while she lived, nor your mother nor your children lacked any of their former blessings, except for the light of your countenance, which the Lord Oromazdes will surely cause to shine again in its former glory. Neither was she deprived of any funeral ornament when she died, but was even honoured with the tears of her enemies. Alexander is as gentle after victory as he is terrible in battle.'

When Darius heard this, his agitation and misery were so great that he was quite carried away and began to entertain the most extravagant suspicions. He took the eunuch aside into a more secluded part of his tent and said: 'If you have not deserted me like the good fortune of Persia and gone over to the Macedonians, and if I, Darius, am still your lord and master, tell me, I charge you as you revere the great light of Mithras and the right hand of the king, was not her death which I am now lamenting the least of Stateira's misfortunes? Did I not suffer an even crueller blow of fate while she was still alive? Would not my unhappy destiny at least have been more honourable if I had met a harsher and more inhuman enemy? For how can a young man's treatment of his enemy's wife be virtuous, if it expresses itself in such tributes?'

While the king was still speaking, Teireos threw himself at his feet and implored him to hold his peace. He should not do Alexander so much injustice, he told him, nor shame his dead queen and sister. Nor should he deprive himself of the greatest consolation left him in his adversity, the belief that he had been conquered by a man whose powers raised him above the mortal state: indeed he should admire Alexander for having shown a restraint towards Persian women which even surpassed the valour he had shown against their husbands. While the eunuch reassured the king, he swore the most solemn oaths to attest the truth of his words, and he described the magnanimity and self-restraint which Alexander had shown on other occasions. Then Darius went out to his companions and lifting up his hands to heaven uttered this prayer: 'You gods of my race and my kingdom, grant me above all that the fortunes of Persia may be restored to the prosperity in which I found them. I ask this so that I may be able to requite Alexander for the favours I received from him, when I lost everything that is dearest to me. But if the fated time is at hand when the rule of the Persians must cease, and if our downfall is a debt we must pay to the envy of the gods and the laws of change, grant that no other man but Alexander shall sit upon the throne of Cyrus.' Most historians agree with this account of what was said and done on that occasion.

31. Meanwhile[1] Alexander, after subduing the whole region which lay on his line of march between the Tigris and the Euphrates, resumed his advance against Darius, who was on his way to meet him with a million men.[2] On this march one of his companions mentioned to Alexander to amuse him that the camp followers had divided themselves for sport into two armies, and had appointed a general and commander for each, one of whom they had named Alexander and the other Darius. At first they had only pelted one another with clods of earth, then they had come to blows with their fists, and finally, inflamed with the heat of battle, they had fought in earnest with stones and clubs. More and more men had joined in, until at last it had become hard to separate them. When Alexander heard of this, he ordered the leaders to be matched so as to fight in single combat: he

1. The late summer of 331 B.C.
2. A propagandist figure. Modern estimates put the Persian strength at a maximum of 100,000 infantry and 34,000 cavalry. On this occasion Darius put his faith in his superiority in cavalry, in which he outnumbered the Greeks by five to one.

himself gave weapons and armour to his namesake, and Philotas gave them to the so-called Darius. The whole army watched this contest and saw in it something of an omen for their own campaign. After a strenuous fight, 'Alexander' finally prevailed, and received as a prize twelve villages and the right to wear the Persian dress. This at least is the story we have from Eratosthenes.

The great battle that was fought against Darius did not take place at Arbela, as the majority of writers say, but at Gaugamela. The word signifies 'the house of the camel': one of the ancient kings of this country escaped the pursuit of his enemies on a swift camel and gave the animal a home there, setting aside various revenues and the pro-duce of several villages to maintain it. It happened that in the month of Boedromion, about the same time as the beginning of the festival of the mysteries at Athens,[1] there was an eclipse of the moon. On the eleventh night after this, by which time the two armies were in sight of one another, Darius kept his troops under arms and held a review of them by torchlight. Alexander allowed his Macedonians to sleep, but himself spent the night in front of his tent in the company of his diviner Aristander, with whom he performed certain mysterious and sacred ceremonies and offered sacrifice to the god Fear. Meanwhile some of the older of his companions and Parmenio in particular looked out over the plain between the river Niphates and the Gordy-aean mountains and saw the entire plain agleam with the watch-fires of the barbarians, while from their camp there arose the confused and indistinguishable murmur of myriads of voices, like the distant roar of a vast ocean. They were filled with amazement at the sight and remarked to one another that it would be an overwhelmingly difficult task to defeat an enemy of such strength by engaging him by day. They therefore went to the king as soon as he had performed his sacrifice and tried to persuade him to attack by night, so as to conceal from his men the most terrifying element in the coming struggle, that is the odds against them. It was then that Alexander gave them his celebrated answer, 'I will not steal my victory.' Some of his com-panions thought this an immature and empty boast on the part of a young man who was merely joking in the presence of danger. But others interpreted it as meaning that he had confidence in his present situation and that he had correctly judged the future. In other words he was determined that if Darius were defeated, he should have no

1. 20 September 331 B.C.

cause to summon up courage for another attempt: he was not to be allowed to blame darkness and night for his failure on this occasion, as at Issus he had blamed the narrow mountain passes and the sea. Certainly Darius would never abandon the war for lack of arms or of troops, when he could draw upon such a vast territory and such immense reserves of man-power. He would only do so when he had lost courage and become convinced of his inferiority in consequence of an unmistakable defeat suffered in broad daylight.

32. When his friends had gone, Alexander lay down in his tent and is said to have passed the rest of the night in a deeper sleep than usual. At any rate when his officers came to him in the early morning, they were astonished to find him not yet awake, and on their own responsibility gave out orders for the soldiers to take breakfast before anything else was done. Then, as time was pressing, Parmenio entered Alexander's tent, stood by his couch and called him two or three times by name: when he had roused him, he asked how he could possibly sleep as if he were already victorious, instead of being about to fight the greatest battle of his life. Alexander smiled and said, 'Why not? Do you not see that we have already won the battle, now that we are delivered from roving around these endless devastated plains, and chasing this Darius, who will never stand and fight?' And indeed not only beforehand, but at the very height of the battle Alexander displayed the supremacy and steadfastness of a man who is confident of the soundness of his judgement.

As the action developed, the left wing under Parmenio was driven back and found itself hard pressed, first by a violent charge from the Bactrian cavalry, and later by an outflanking movement when Mazaeus sent a detachment of horsemen to ride round the line and attack the troops who were guarding the Macedonian baggage. Parmenio, who was disconcerted by both these manoeuvres, sent messengers to warn Alexander that his camp and his baggage train were lost, unless he could immediately move strong reinforcements from the front to protect his rear. It so happened that at that moment Alexander was about to give the signal to the right wing, which he commanded, to attack: when he received this message, he exclaimed that Parmenio must have lost his wits and forgotten in his agitation that the victors will always take possession of their enemy's baggage in any event, and that the losers must not concern themselves with their property or their slaves, but only with how to fight bravely and die with honour.

After he had sent this message to Parmenio, he put on his helmet. He was already wearing the rest of his armour when he left his tent, a tunic made in Sicily which was belted around his waist and over this a thickly quilted linen corslet, which had been among the spoils captured at Issus. His helmet, the work of Theophilus, was made of steel which gleamed like polished silver, and to this was fitted a steel gorget set with precious stones. His sword, which was a gift from the king of Citium, was a marvel of lightness and tempering, and he had trained himself to use this as his principal weapon in hand-to-hand fighting. He also wore a cloak which was more ornate than the rest of his armour. It had been made by Helicon, an artist of earlier times, and presented to Alexander as a mark of honour by the city of Rhodes, and this too he was in the habit of wearing in battle. While he was drawing up the phalanx in formation, reviewing the troops, or giving out orders, he rode another horse to spare Bucephalas, who was by now past his prime: but when he was about to go into action Bucephalas would be led up, and he would mount him and at once begin the attack.

33. On this occasion Alexander gave a long address to the Thessalians and the rest of the Greeks. They acclaimed by shouting for him to lead them against the barbarians, and at this he shifted his lance into his left hand, so Callisthenes tells us, and raising his right he called upon the gods and prayed that if he were really the son of Zeus they should protect and encourage the Greeks. Then Aristander the diviner, who was wearing a white robe and a crown of gold, rode along the ranks and pointed out to the men an eagle which hovered for a while over Alexander's head and then flew straight towards the enemy. The sight acted as an immediate inspiration to the watching troops, and with shouts of encouragement to one another the cavalry charged the enemy at full speed and the phalanx rolled forward like a flood. Before the leading ranks could engage, the barbarians began to fall back, hotly pursued by Alexander, who drove the retreating enemy towards the centre, where Darius was stationed.

Alexander had sighted his adversary through the ranks of the royal squadron of cavalry, as they waited drawn up in deep formation in front of him. Darius was a tall and handsome man and he towered conspicuously above this large and superbly equipped body of horse-men, who were closely massed to guard the lofty chariot in which he stood. But the horseguards were seized with panic at the terrible sight of Alexander bearing down upon them and driving the fugitives before him against those who still held their ground, and the greater number of them broke and scattered. The bravest and most highly born, however, stood fast and were slaughtered in front of their king: they fell upon one another in heaps, and in their dying struggles they clung to the legs of horses and riders, entwining themselves about them so as to hinder the pursuit. As for Darius, all the horrors of the battle were now before his eyes. The forces which had been stationed in the centre for his protection had now been driven back upon him: it had become difficult to turn his chariot round and drive it away, since the wheels were encumbered and entangled with heaps of bodies, and the horses which were surrounded and almost covered by the dead began to rear and plunge so that the charioteer could not control them. In this extremity the king abandoned his chariot and his armour, mounted a mare which, so the story goes, had recently foaled, and rode away. It is believed that he would not have escaped at that moment, had not Parmenio sent another party of horsemen begging Alexander to come to his rescue, because he was engaged with a strong enemy force which still held together and would not give way. In this battle Parmenio is generally accused of having been sluggish and lacking in spirit, either because old age had dulled his courage, or because he had become envious of the authority and pomp, to use Callisthenes' words, which Alexander now displayed. Alexander was vexed by this appeal for help, but at the time he did not reveal to his men the fact that it had been made. Instead he ordered the recall to be sounded on the ground that it was growing dark and that he wished to bring the slaughter to an end. Then as he rode back to the part of the field where Parmenio's troops were supposedly threatened, he learned on his way that the enemy had been utterly defeated and put to flight.

34. After the battle had ended in this way, the authority of the Persian empire was regarded as having been completely overthrown. Alexander was proclaimed king of Asia and after offering splendid sacrifices to the gods, he proceeded to reward his friends with riches, estates and governorships. As he wished to increase his prestige in the Greek world, he wrote to the states saying that all tyrannies were

now abolished and that henceforth they might live under their own laws: to the Plataeans in particular he wrote that he would rebuild their city because their ancestors had allowed the Greeks to make their territory the seat of war in the struggle for their common freedom.[1] He also sent a share of the spoils to the people of Croton in Italy in honour of the spirit and valour shown by their athlete Phaÿllus: this man, when the rest of the Greeks in Italy had refused to give any help to their compatriots in the Persian wars, had fitted out a ship at his own expense and sailed with it to Salamis to share in the common danger. Such was Alexander's desire to pay tribute to any manifestation of courage and to prove himself the friend and guardian of noble actions.

35. He then advanced through the province of Babylonia which immediately surrendered to him. On his march he was particularly impressed by the fissure in the earth from which fire continually poured forth as if it came from a well, and by the stream of naphtha which gushed forth so abundantly that it formed a lake not far from the chasm. This naphtha is in many ways like bitumen, but is so inflammable that a flame can set it alight by its very radiance without actually touching it, and it often kindles all the intermediate air. To demonstrate the nature of the liquid and the force of its action the barbarians sprinkled a small quantity along the street which led to Alexander's quarters. Then standing at the far end they applied their torches to the trail of moisture, as it was growing dark. The first drops instantly ignited, and in a fraction of a second with the speed of thought the flames darted to the other end and the whole street was ablaze.

Among the attendants who waited upon the king, whenever he bathed and anointed himself, was an Athenian named Athenophanes, who had the task of providing him with diversions and amusements. On one occasion a boy named Stephanus, who possessed an absurdly ugly face but an agreeable singing voice, was also in attendance in the bathroom, and Athenophanes asked the king, 'Would you care for us to try an experiment with the naphtha upon Stephanus? If it catches fire on him and is not immediately put out, then its strength must be extraordinary and irresistible.' Surprisingly, the boy agreed to try the experiment, and no sooner had he touched the liquid and anointed himself with it than the flames broke out and enveloped his body so

1. In the final phase of the Persian wars, 479 B.C.

completely that Alexander was appalled and began to fear for his life. If there had not happened to be many attendants close by holding pitchers of water for the bath, he would have been burned to death before any help could reach him. Even as it was they had great difficulty in putting out the flames, and his whole body was so severely burned that he was critically ill for a long time after.

It is natural therefore that some of those who wish to reconcile legend with fact should say that this was the drug used by Medea when in the tragedy she anoints the crown and the robe which she presents to Creon's daughter. The fire did not originate from these objects, they explain, nor did it break out of its own accord, but a flame must have been placed near them, with which the liquid was then drawn into contact so quickly that the process was invisible to the naked eye. The rays and emanations which proceed from a flame at a certain distance have no more effect on some substances than to give them light and warmth, but in the case of those which are dry and porous, or possess a sufficiently oily moisture, the heat is concentrated, then bursts into fierce flames and transforms the substance. There has been much dispute as to how naphtha is produced: whether, for example, the liquid combustible matter that feeds the flame flows out from a soil which is naturally oily and inflammable. Certainly the soil of Babylonia is very fiery, so much so that grains of barley are often thrown up out of the earth and bound away, as if the heat of the soil made the ground throb, and in the hottest part of the summer the inhabitants sleep on skins filled with water. When Harpalus, Alexander's treasurer, was left as governor of the province, he was anxious to adorn the royal gardens and walks with Greek plants and shrubs, and he succeeded with all except ivy: the soil would not nourish this, but always killed it. The plant could not endure the temper of the soil which was fiery, whereas ivy loves a cold soil. I hope the impatient reader will bear with digressions of this kind, so long as they are kept within reasonable limits.

36. After Alexander had made himself master of Susa, he found forty thousand talents of coined money in the palace, besides furniture and other treasures of incalculable value. Among these it was said were five thousand talents weight of cloth dyed with purple from Hermione,[1] which still kept a fresh and vivid colour even after it had been

1. A port on the Gulf of Spetsae in the eastern Peloponnese.

stored there for one hundred and ninety years. The reason for this, we are told, is that honey was used in the purple dyes and white olive oil in the white dyes, and each of these substances, it is said, will preserve the lustre and brilliance of the colour and prevent any fading. Deinon also tells us that the kings of Persia had water transported from the Nile and the Danube, and stored among their treasures as a testimony to the extent of their dominions and a proof that they were masters of the world.

37. When Alexander advanced beyond Susa, he found the province of Persis difficult to penetrate: not only was the country mountainous, but it was defended by the bravest of the Persians since Darius had taken refuge there. In spite of these obstacles Alexander found a guide who showed him the way by making a short diversion.[1] This man had a Lycian father and a Persian mother and spoke both Greek and Persian, and it was to him, so the story goes, that the Pythian priestess had referred when she prophesied while Alexander was still a boy that a *lykos* (wolf) would guide him on his march against the Persians. During the advance across Persis the Greeks massacred great numbers of their prisoners, and Alexander has himself recorded that he gave orders for the Persians to be slaughtered because he thought that such an example would help his cause. It is said that in Persepolis, the capital of the province, he found as much gold as he had in Susa, and that it required two thousand pairs of mules and five hundred camels to carry away the furniture and other treasures that were found there.

It was in Persepolis that Alexander saw a gigantic statue of Xerxes. This had been toppled from its pedestal and heedlessly left on the ground by a crowd of soldiers, as they forced their way into the palace, and Alexander stopped and spoke to it as though it were alive. 'Shall I pass by and leave you lying there because of the expedition you led against Greece, or shall I set you up again because of your magnanimity and your virtues in other respects?' For a long while he gazed at the statue and reflected in silence, and then went on his way. It was by then winter, and he stayed in Persepolis for four months to allow his soldiers time to rest. It is said that when he first took his seat on the royal throne under the golden canopy, Demaratus the

1. This brief allusion refers to one of Alexander's most brilliant operations, the forcing of the pass known as the Persian Gates, which on this occasion was guarded by an army of over 40,000 men (in midwinter 331 B.C.).

Corinthian, who was much attached to Alexander, as he had been to his father, began to weep, as old men are apt to do, and exclaimed that any Greek who had died before that day had missed one of the greatest pleasures in life by not seeing Alexander seated on the throne of Darius.

38. In the spring[1] Alexander again took the field against Darius, but a short while before it so happened that he accepted an invitation to a drinking party held by some of his companions, and on this occasion a number of women came to meet their lovers and joined in the drinking. The most celebrated of these was Thais, an Athenian, at that time the mistress of the Ptolemy who later became the ruler of Egypt. As the drinking went on, Thais delivered a speech which was intended partly as a graceful compliment to Alexander and partly to amuse him. What she said was typical of the spirit of Athens, but hardly in keeping with her own situation. She declared that all the hardships she had endured in wandering about Asia had been amply repaid on that day, when she found herself revelling luxuriously in the splendid palace of the Persians, but that it would be an even sweeter pleasure to end the party by going out and setting fire to the palace of Xerxes, who had laid Athens in ashes. She wanted to put a torch to the building herself in full view of Alexander, so that posterity should know that the women who followed Alexander had taken a more terrible revenge for the wrongs of Greece than all the famous commanders of earlier times by land or sea. Her speech was greeted with wild applause and the king's companions excitedly urged him on until at last he allowed himself to be persuaded, leaped to his feet, and with a garland on his head and a torch in his hand led the way. The other revellers followed, shouting and dancing, and surrounded the palace, and those of the Macedonians who had heard what was afoot delightedly ran up bringing torches with them. They did this because they hoped that the act of burning and destroying the palace signified that Alexander's thoughts were turned towards home, and that he was not planning to settle among the barbarians. According to a number of historians it was in this way that the palace was burned down, that is on impulse, but there are others who maintain that it was an act of deliberate policy. However this may be, it is agreed that Alexander quickly repented and gave orders for the fire to be put out.

1. 330 B.C.

39. Alexander was by nature exceptionally generous and became even more so as his wealth increased. His gifts were always bestowed with grace and courtesy, and it is this alone, to tell the truth, which makes the giver's generosity welcome. I may mention a few instances of this. When Ariston the commander of the Paeonians[1] had killed one of his enemies, he brought the man's head, showed it to Alexander and remarked, 'In my country, sire, a present such as this is always rewarded with a gold cup.' Alexander laughed and replied, 'Yes, but with an empty one. I will drink your health with a cup full of neat wine, and give it you as well.' On another occasion one of the Macedonian soldiers was driving a mule laden with the king's gold, and when the animal became too exhausted to carry it, he took off the load and put it on his own shoulders. When Alexander saw him struggling along in distress and learned what had happened, he called out as the soldier was about to put down his burden, 'Hold on, don't give up! Finish your journey and take what you are carrying to your own tent.' Indeed he was always more offended with those who refused his gifts than with those who asked for them. He wrote to Phocion telling him that in future he would not regard him as a friend if he declined all his favours, and in the case of Serapion, one of the youths who used to play ball with him, he never gave him anything because he never asked for anything. So one day whenever the ball came to Serapion, he made a point of throwing it to the others, until the king said, 'Aren't you going to throw it to me?' 'No,' retorted Serapion, 'You never ask for it!' whereupon the king burst out laughing and loaded him with presents.

Then there was Proteas, one of the king's drinking companions, who had a reputation as a jester, and who seemed on one occasion to have made the king angry. At this his friends pleaded for him and he himself begged for forgiveness with tears in his eyes, until Alexander said that he pardoned him. 'Then will you first give me something to prove it?' Proteas asked him, whereupon the king gave orders for him to be presented with five talents. His friends and bodyguards were apt to put on airs as a result of the riches he showered on them, and this is revealed in a letter Olympias once wrote him, in which she said, 'I wish you would find other ways of rewarding those you love and honour: as it is you are making them all the equals of kings and enabling *them* to make plenty of friends, but leaving yourself without

1. A regiment of light cavalry from the borders of Macedonia.

any.' Olympias often wrote to him in this strain, but Alexander kept her letters to himself with one exception. Hephaestion was in the habit of reading the king's letters with him, and on this occasion his eye fell on a letter which had been opened. The king did not prevent him from reading it, but took the ring from his own finger and pressed the seal to his lips, so much as to tell him to keep silence.

Mazaeus had been the most powerful of Darius' officials, and although his son was already the governor of a province, Alexander now proposed to add an even larger one to it. The young man declined it, however, and said to him, 'In the past, sire, there was only one Darius, but now you have made many Alexanders.' Besides this he presented Parmenio with the house of Bagoas at Susa, in which it is said clothes were found to the value of a thousand talents. Alexander also wrote to Antipater, warning him to keep bodyguards around him, since he was in danger of plots against his life.[1] He sent a great many presents to his mother, but he would not allow her to interfere in affairs of state or in the management of his campaigns, and when she complained about this, he bore her scoldings with great tolerance. But on one occasion when Antipater had written him a long letter finding fault with her, he exclaimed that Antipater did not understand that one tear shed by his mother would wipe out ten thousand letters such as this.

40. Alexander now noticed that his companions had acquired thoroughly luxurious habits and had become vulgar in the extravagance of their way of living. There was Hagnon of Teos, who wore silver nails in his boots; Leonnatus, who had the dust with which he sprinkled his body for wrestling brought by camel-train from Egypt; and Philotas who hunted with nets that could enclose a space of twelve miles. When his friends bathed, they often anointed themselves with myrrh, rather than with plain oil, and were attended by masseurs and body-servants. Alexander reasoned with them and gently reproved them for these excesses. He told them he was amazed to see that men who had fought and conquered in such great battles could have forgotten that those who labour sleep more sweetly than those who are laboured for. Could they not understand, when they compared their style of living with that of the Persians, that there is nothing more slavish than the love of pleasure and nothing more princely than the

1. Plots laid by Olympias, who was on bad terms with Antipater.

life of toil? How can a man attend to his horse, he asked them, or
keep his spear and his helmet clean and bright, if he has lost the habit
of using his hands to look after his own precious body? Did they not
know that the end and perfection of conquest is to avoid doing the
same things as the conquered have done? And so, to set an example,
he exerted himself more strenuously than ever in campaigns and
hunting expeditions, exposing himself to hardship and danger, so that
an envoy from Sparta, who was by his side when he speared a great
lion, remarked, 'Alexander, you fought nobly with this lion to decide
which of you should be king!' Craterus later had this hunting scene
represented in bronze and dedicated it at Delphi: it showed the figures
of the lion, the hounds, the king fighting with the lion, and Craterus
advancing to help him. Some of these sculptures were executed by
Lysippus, and some by Leochares.

41. Alexander made a point of risking his life in this way both to
exercise himself and to inspire others to acts of courage, but his
friends, because of the wealth and pomp with which they were surrounded, desired only to lead a life of luxury and idleness. They found
his expeditions and campaigns an intolerable burden, and little by
little went so far as to abuse and find fault with the king. Alexander
bore this treatment with great tolerance at first, and remarked that it
is the part of a king to do good to his subjects and be maligned for it.
And indeed even in the most trivial services which he rendered to his
friends, he revealed the affection and regard which he had for them. I
will give a few examples of this.

He wrote to Peucestas, who had been bitten by a bear, to complain
that he had described his injury to other friends but had said nothing
to Alexander. 'Now,' he went on, 'you must write to tell me how
you are, and whether you were let down by any of your fellow hunts-
men, so that I can punish them.' When Hephaestion was absent on
some business, Alexander wrote with the news that while they had
been amusing themselves hunting an ichneumon, Craterus had acci-
dentally been run through the thighs with Perdiccas' lance. After
Peucestas had recovered from some illness, Alexander wrote to his
friend's physician Alexippus congratulating him on the cure. When
Craterus was sick, Alexander had a dream in which he offered certain
sacrifices to the gods on his friend's behalf and told him to do the
same, and he wrote to Craterus' physician Pausanias, when the latter

wished to treat him with hellebore, expressing his anxiety and advising him how to use the drug. Ephialtes and Cissus were the first to bring the news that Harpalus[1] had deserted, and Alexander had them put in chains because he believed that they were making a false accusation against the man. Again, when he was sending home his invalid and superannuated soldiers, Eurylochus of Aegae contrived to have his name put on the list of the sick, and when it was discovered that there was nothing wrong with him, he confessed that he was in love with a girl named Telesippe, and had planned to travel with her on her journey to the coast. Alexander made inquiries about her parentage, and when he found that she was a free-born Greek courtesan, he said, 'I will help you with your love affair, Eurylochus, but since she is a free woman, you must see whether you can win her either by presents or by courtship, but not use other means.'

42. It is in fact astonishing that he could find time to write so many letters to his friends. For example he wrote one ordering a search to be made for a slave belonging to Seleucus who had run away to Cilicia, and another praising Peucestas because he had caught Nicon, a runaway slave of Craterus, and a third to Megabyzus about a slave who had taken refuge in a sanctuary. In this he told him to try, if possible, to lure the slave outside and then arrest him, but not to lay hands on him within the sacred precincts. We are also told that when he was trying a prisoner on a capital charge, he would place a hand over one of his ears while the prosecutor was speaking, so as to keep it free and impartial for listening to the defendant. But later so many accusations were laid before him that he grew harsh and was inclined to believe even the false charges, because so much that he was told was true. Above all, if anybody spoke ill of him, his judgement was apt to desert him and his mood would become cruel and merciless, since he valued his good name more than his life or his crown.

He now set out again in pursuit of Darius,[2] fully expecting that he would have to fight another battle. However when he learned that the

---

1. Harpalus, who had been guilty of maladministration during Alexander's campaigns, deserted in 325 B.C. He fled to Cilicia and after Alexander's return from India took refuge in Attica in 324. He was murdered in Crete by one of his fellow-adventurers. See *Life of Demosthenes*, chs. 25–6.

2. In the spring of 330 B.C. Darius had assembled a force of some 6,000 infantry and 3,000 cavalry at Ecbatana.

king had been arrested by Bessus, the satrap of Bactria, he sent his Thessalian cavalry back to Greece, after first giving them a gratuity of two thousand talents,[1] besides their regular pay. The pursuit of Darius turned out to be long and exhausting. Alexander covered more than four hundred miles in eleven days, and by this time most of his horsemen were on the verge of collapse for lack of water. At this point he met some Macedonians, who were carrying water from a river in skins on the backs of their mules, and when they saw Alexander almost fainting with thirst in the midday heat, they quickly filled a helmet and brought it to him. He asked them for whom they were carrying the water. 'For our own sons,' they told him, 'but so long as your life is safe, we can have other children, even if we lose these.' At this Alexander took the helmet in his hands. But then he looked up and saw the rest of his troop craning their heads and casting longing glances at the water, and he handed it back without drinking a drop. He thanked the men who had brought it, but said to them, 'If I am the only one to drink, the rest will lose heart.' However no sooner had his companions witnessed this act of self-control and magnanimity than they cried out and shouted for him to lead them on boldly. They spurred on their horses and declared that they could not feel tired or thirsty or even like mortal men, so long as they had such a king.

43. All his horsemen were fired with the same enthusiasm, but only sixty of his men, so the story goes, had kept up with Alexander when he burst into the enemy's camp. They rode over great heaps of gold and silver vessels which had been scattered on the ground, passed waggons full of women and children that were moving aimlessly about without their drivers, and at length caught up with the Persian vanguard, imagining that Darius must be among them. At last they found him lying in a waggon, riddled with javelins and at his last gasp. He asked for a drink, and when he had swallowed some cold water which a Macedonian named Polystratus brought him, he said, 'This is the final stroke of misfortune, that I should accept a service from you, and not be able to return it, but Alexander will reward you for your kindness, and the gods will repay him for his courtesy towards my mother and my wife and my children. And so through you, I give him my hand.' As he said this, he took Poly-

1. Each of the 2,000 cavalrymen received one talent.

stratus by the hand, and died. When Alexander came up, he showed his grief and distress at the king's death, and unfastening his own cloak, he threw it over the body and covered it. Later, after he had captured Bessus, who had murdered the king, he had him torn limb from limb. He had the tops of two straight trees bent down so that they met, and part of Bessus' body was tied to each. Then when each tree was let go and sprang back to its upright position, the part of the body attached to it was torn off by the recoil. As for Darius' body, he sent it to his mother to be laid out in royal state, and he enrolled his brother Exathres into the number of the Companions.

44. Meanwhile he himself with the flower of his army pressed on into Hyrcania. Here he came in sight of a bay of the open sea which appeared to be as large as the Black Sea, and was sweeter than the Mediterranean. He could not obtain any certain information about it, but guessed that it was probably a stagnant overflow from Lake Maeotis.[1] However various geographers had already discovered the truth and many years before Alexander's expedition they had recorded their conclusion that this was the most northerly of four gulfs which run inland from the outer Ocean[2] and was called the Hyrcanian or Caspian Sea. In this neighbourhood the barbarians surprised the grooms, who were leading Alexander's horse Bucephalas, and captured him. Alexander was enraged and sent a herald with the threat that unless they gave back his horse, he would exterminate the whole tribe, together with their women and children. However when they returned with the horse and surrendered their cities to him, he treated them all kindly, and even gave a reward to the men who had captured Bucephalas.

45. From this point he advanced into Parthia,[3] and it was here during a pause in the campaign that he first began to wear barbarian dress. He may have done this from a desire to adapt himself to local habits, because he understood that the sharing of race and of customs is a great step towards softening men's hearts. Alternatively, this may

1. The Sea of Azov.
2. According to the beliefs of Plutarch's time, the outer Ocean encircled the world and the Caspian flowed into it. Alexander planned an expedition to determine whether the Caspian was a lake or a gulf, but did not live to carry it out.
3. In the autumn of 330 B.C.

have been an experiment which was aimed at introducing the obeisance among the Macedonians, the first stage being to accustom them to accepting changes in his own dress and way of life. However he did not go so far as to adopt the Median costume, which was altogether barbaric and outlandish, and he wore neither trousers, nor a sleeved vest, nor a tiara.[1] Instead he adopted a style which was a compromise between Persian and Median costume, more modest than the first, and more stately than the second. At first he wore this only when he was in the company of barbarians or with his intimate friends indoors, but later he put it on when he was riding or giving audience in public. The sight greatly displeased the Macedonians, but they admired his other virtues so much that they considered they ought to make concessions to him in some matters which either gave him pleasure or increased his prestige. For besides all his other hardships, he had recently been wounded below the knee by an arrow which splintered the shin-bone so that the fragments had to be taken out, and on another occasion he had received such a violent blow on the neck from a stone that his vision became clouded and remained so for a long time afterwards. In spite of this, he continued to expose himself unsparingly to danger: for example he crossed the river Orexartes, which he believed to be the Tanais, routed the Scythians and pursued them for twelve miles or more, even though all this while he was suffering from an attack of dysentery.

46. It was here that he was visited by the queen of the Amazons, according to the report we have from many writers, among them Cleitarchus, Polycleitus, Onesicritus, Antigenes and Ister. On the other hand Aristobulus, Chares the royal usher, Ptolemy, Anticleides, Philo the Theban and Philip of Theangela, and besides these Hecataeus of Eretria, Philip the Chalcidian and Douris of Samos all maintain that this is a fiction, and this judgement seems to be confirmed by Alexander's own testimony. In a letter to Antipater in which he describes the details of the occasion, he mentions that the king of the Scythians offered him his daughter in marriage, but he makes no reference to an Amazon. There is also a story that many years afterwards, when Lysimachus had become king of Macedonia, Onesicritus was reading aloud the fourth book of his history, which contained the tale of the Amazon, at which Lysimachus smiled and asked

1. The conical Persian head-dress which was wound like a turban.

quietly, 'I wonder where I was then.' In any case our admiration for Alexander is not diminished if we reject this story, nor increased if we regard it as true.

47. Alexander was by now becoming anxious that the Macedonians might refuse to follow him any further in his campaigns. He therefore quartered the main body on the country and allowed them to rest, but pressed on with his best troops, consisting of twenty thousand infantry and three thousand cavalry, and marched into Hyrcania. He then addressed this picked force and told them that up to now the barbarians had watched them as if they were in a dream, but that if they merely threw the whole country into disorder and then retired, the Persians would fall upon them as if they were so many women. He went on to say that he would allow any of them who desired it to go back, but he called on them to witness that at the very moment when he was seeking to conquer the whole inhabited world for the Macedonians, he found himself deserted and left only with his friends and those who were willing to continue the expedition. These are almost the exact words which he used in his letter to Antipater, and he says that after he had spoken in this way, the whole of his audience shouted aloud and begged him to lead them to whatever part of the world he chose. Once he had tested the loyalty of these troops, he found no difficulty in winning over the main body, indeed they followed him with a will.

From this point he began to adapt his own style of living more closely to that of the country and tried to reconcile Asiatic and Macedonian customs: he believed that if the two traditions could be blended and assimilated in this way his authority would be more securely established when he was far away, since it would rest on goodwill rather than on force. For this reason he selected thirty thousand boys and gave orders that they should be taught to speak the Greek language and to use Macedonian weapons, and he appointed a large number of instructors to train them. His marriage to Roxane[1] was a love match, which began when he first saw her at the height of her youthful beauty taking part in a dance at a banquet, but it also played a great part in furthering his policy of reconciliation. The barbarians were encouraged by the feeling of partnership which their alliance created, and they were completely won over by Alexander's

1. This took place in August 327 B.C.

moderation and courtesy and by the fact that without the sanction of marriage he would not approach the only woman who had ever conquered his heart.

Alexander noticed that among his closest friends it was Hephaestion who approved of these plans and joined him in changing his habits, while Craterus[1] clung to Macedonian customs, and he therefore made use of the first in his dealings with the barbarians and of the second with the Greeks and Macedonians. In general he showed most affection for Hephaestion and most respect for Craterus, for he had formed the opinion and often said that Hephaestion was a friend of Alexander's, while Craterus was a friend of the king's. For this reason a feeling of hostility grew and festered between the two and they often came into open conflict. Once on the expedition to India they actually drew their swords and came to blows, and as their friends appeared and began to join in the quarrel, Alexander rode up and publicly reprimanded Hephaestion: he told him that he must be a fool and a madman if he did not understand that without Alexander's favour he was nothing. Then later in private he sharply rebuked Craterus. Finally he called both men together and made them be friends again. He swore by Zeus Ammon and the rest of the gods that these were the two men he loved best in the world, but that if he ever heard them quarrelling again, he would kill them both, or at least the one who began the quarrel. After this, it is said, neither of them ever did or said anything to offend the other even in jest.

48. Among the Macedonians at this time[2] few men enjoyed a more prominent position than Philotas, the son of Parmenio:[3] he had a high reputation for courage and for his ability to endure hardship and after Alexander he had no equal for generosity and devotion to his friends. At any rate we are told that when one of his intimate friends asked him for money and his steward replied that he had none

1. Probably the ablest of Alexander's younger officers. He became second in command after Parmenio's death in 330 B.C. He led part of the army back from India and in 324 brought the veterans back to Macedonia. He was killed in battle against Eumenes in 321.

2. The narrative now moves back to the period immediately following the murder of Darius, the autumn of 330 B.C.

3. Philotas was older than Alexander: he commanded the Companion cavalry, eight squadrons strong.

to give, he asked the man, 'What do you mean – have I no plate or furniture to sell?' However, Philotas also displayed an arrogance, an ostentation of wealth, and a degree of luxury in his personal habits and his way of living which could only cause offence in his position as a private subject. At this time in particular his efforts to imitate a lofty and majestic presence carried no conviction, appeared clumsy and uncouth, and succeeded only in provoking envy and mistrust to such a degree that even Parmenio once remarked to him, 'My son, do not make so much of yourself.' And indeed Philotas had fallen under suspicion a long while before this. When Darius had been defeated in Cilicia and his treasure captured at Damascus, one of the many prisoners who were brought into Alexander's camp was discovered to be a beautiful Greek girl who had been born in Pydna and was named Antigone. She was handed over to Philotas and he – like many a young man who, when he has drunk well, is apt to talk freely to his mistress in the boastful fashion of a soldier – often confided to her that all the greatest achievements in the campaign had been the work of his father and himself. Then he would speak of Alexander as a mere boy who owed his title of ruler to their efforts. Antigone repeated these remarks to one of her friends, and he naturally enough passed them on until they reached the ears of Craterus, who took the girl and brought her privately to Alexander. When the king heard her story, he ordered her to continue visiting Philotas, but to come and report everything that she learned from him.

49. Philotas had no suspicion of the trap that was being set for him and in his conversations with Antigone he uttered many indiscretions and often spoke slightingly of the king, sometimes through anger and sometimes through boastfulness. Even so Alexander, although he now had overwhelming evidence against Philotas, endured these insults in silence and restrained himself either because he had confidence in Parmenio's loyalty, or perhaps because he feared the power and prestige of father and son. But meanwhile a Macedonian from Chalaestra named Dimnos organized a conspiracy against Alexander, and invited a young man named Nicomachus whose lover he was to take part in the plot. Nicomachus refused to be involved, but told his brother Cebalinus of the attempt. Cebalinus then went to Philotas and demanded that he should take them both to Alexander,

as they had something of the greatest urgency to tell him. Philotas, however, for some unknown reason, did not arrange the interview, making out that the king was engaged on more important business, and he did this not once but twice. By this time the brothers had become suspicious of Philotas, and so they turned to somebody else who brought them into the king's presence. First of all they revealed Dimnos' plot and then they made a number of insinuations against Philotas, because he had twice disregarded their requests to see the king.

This news enraged Alexander, and when he learned that Dimnos had resisted arrest, and had been killed by the men who had been sent to fetch him, he became still more disturbed, as he concluded that he had lost the chance to uncover the plot. He felt bitter resentment against Philotas and became all the more ready to listen to those who had long hated his friend. These enemies now said openly that it was folly on the king's part to suppose that a man such as Dimnos who came from the obscure town of Chalaestra would ever have undertaken such a daring enterprise on his own account: it was obvious that he was a mere agent, a tool in the hands of somebody of much greater power, and that Alexander must look for the source of the conspiracy among those who had most interest in keeping it concealed. Once the king had begun to listen to these insinuations and suspicions, Philotas' enemies brought innumerable accusations against him. He was arrested, interrogated, and tortured in the presence of the king's Companions, while Alexander himself listened to the examination from behind a curtain. We are told that when he heard Philotas uttering broken and pitiful cries and pleas for mercy to Hephaestion he exclaimed, 'Ah, Philotas, if you are so weak and unmanly as this, how could you involve yourself in such a dangerous business?' Philotas was executed, and immediately afterwards Alexander sent messengers to Media and had Parmenio put to death as well. This was a man who had rendered many great services to Philip and who, of all Alexander's older friends, had urged him most strongly to undertake the invasion of Asia: of his three sons he had seen two die in battle and now he was put to death with the third.

These actions[1] made Alexander dreaded by his friends, above all by

1. Parmenio's son-in-law Alexander of Lyncestis was also put to death as a possible pretender to the throne: unlike Parmenio he was of royal blood.

Antipater,[1] and caused him at a later date to enter into secret negotiations with the Aetolians and make an alliance with them. These people were especially afraid of Alexander, because they had destroyed the city of the Oeniadae,[2] and because the king, when he heard of it, had declared that the sons of the Oeniadae would not need to seek their revenge, since he himself would punish the Aetolians.

50. Not long after[3] this came the killing of Cleitus, whose treatment on the bare facts of the case appears to have been even more shocking than that of Philotas. However, if we consider both the occasion and the cause, we may see that it was a misfortune rather than a deliberate act, and that it was Cleitus' evil genius[4] which took advantage of Alexander's anger and intoxication to destroy him. This was how it came about. Some men arrived from the coast bringing a present of Greek fruit for the king. Alexander admired its beauty and ripeness and sent for Cleitus to share it with him. It so happened that Cleitus was in the midst of sacrificing, but he at once left the ceremony, and three of the sheep on which libations had been poured followed him. When the king heard of this, he consulted Aristander his diviner and Cleomantis the Spartan. Since they interpreted this as an evil omen, he ordered them to offer up a sacrifice at once for Cleitus' safety. Alexander was all the more disturbed because two days before he had dreamed a strange dream in which he saw Cleitus sitting with the sons of Parmenio: they were dressed in black and all four of them were dead. However before the sacrifice offered on Cleitus' behalf was concluded, he came at once to dine with the king, who had already sacrificed on that day to the Dioscuri.

After the company had drunk a good deal somebody began to sing the verses of a man named Pranichus (or Pierio according to another account), which had been written to humiliate and make fun of some Macedonian commanders who had recently been defeated by the barbarians. The older members of the party took offence at this and showed their resentment of both the poet and the singer,

1. Antipater had been left as regent in Macedonia in Alexander's absence.
2. A town in Acarnania at the mouth of the Acheloos.
3. Two years after in the autumn of 328 B.C. at Marakanda (Samarkand).
4. It was widely believed that every man receives at birth a *daimon* which is associated with him for life. It may be good or evil. See the *Lives of Dion, Brutus* and *Julius Caesar*.

but Alexander and those sitting near him listened with obvious pleasure and told the man to continue. Thereupon Cleitus, who had already drunk too much and was rough and hot-tempered by nature, became angrier than ever and shouted that it was not right for Macedonians to be insulted in the presence of barbarians and enemies, even if they had met with misfortune, for they were better men than those who were laughing at them. Alexander retorted that if Cleitus was trying to disguise cowardice as misfortune, he must be pleading his own case. At this Cleitus sprang to his feet and shouted back, 'Yes, it was my cowardice that saved your life, you who call yourself the son of the gods, when you were turning your back to Spithridates' sword.[1] And it is the blood of these Macedonians and their wounds which have made you so great that you disown your father Philip and claim to be the son of Ammon!'

51. These words made Alexander furious. 'You scum,' he cried out, 'do you think that you can keep on speaking of me like this, and stir up trouble among the Macedonians and not pay for it?' 'Oh, but we Macedonians do pay for it,' Cleitus retorted. 'Just think of the rewards we get for all our efforts. It's the dead ones who are happy, because they never lived to see Macedonians being beaten with Median rods, or begging the Persians for an audience with our own king.' Cleitus blurted out all this impulsively, whereupon Alexander's friends jumped up and began to abuse him, while the older men tried to calm down both sides. Then Alexander turned to Xenodochus of Cardia and Artemius of Colophon and asked them, 'When you see the Greeks walking about among the Macedonians, do they not look to you like demi-gods among so many wild beasts?' But Cleitus refused to take back anything and he challenged Alexander to speak out whatever he wished to say in front of the company, or else not invite to his table free-born men who spoke their minds: it would be better for him to spend his time among barbarians and slaves, who would prostrate themselves before his white tunic and his Persian girdle. At this Alexander could no longer control his rage: he hurled one of the apples that lay on the table at Cleitus, hit him, and then looked around for his dagger. One of his bodyguards, Aristophanes, had already moved it out of harm's way,[2] and the others crowded

1. See ch. 16.
2. This may have made Alexander suspect treachery.

around him and begged him to be quiet. But Alexander leaped to his feet and shouted out in the Macedonian tongue for his bodyguard to turn out, a signal that this was an extreme emergency; then he ordered his trumpeter to sound the alarm, and because the man was unwilling to obey, he struck him with his fist. Afterwards the trumpeter was highly praised for his conduct, because it was chiefly thanks to him that the whole camp was not thrown into a turmoil. Meanwhile as Cleitus still refused to give way, his friends with great difficulty pushed him out of the banqueting room. But soon afterwards he came in by another door, and, as he did so, recited in a loud and contemptuous voice this line from Euripides' *Andromache*

Alas, what evil customs reign in Greece.[1]

At this Alexander seized a spear from one of his guards, faced Cleitus as he was drawing aside the curtain of the doorway, and ran him through. With a roar of pain and a groan, Cleitus fell, and immediately the king's anger left him. When he came to himself and saw his friends standing around him speechless, he snatched the weapon out of the dead body and would have plunged it into his own throat if the guards had not forestalled him by seizing his hands and carrying him by force into his chamber.

52. There he spent the rest of the night and the whole of the following day sobbing in an agony of remorse.[2] At last he lay exhausted by his grief, uttering deep groans but unable to speak a word, until his friends, alarmed at his silence, forced their way into his room. He paid no attention to what any of them said, except that when Aristander the diviner reminded him of the dream he had had concerning Cleitus and its significance, and told him that these events had long ago been ordained by fate, he seemed to accept this assurance. For this reason they brought to him two philosophers, Callisthenes, who was the great-nephew of Aristotle, and Anaxarchus of Abdera. Callisthenes used a gentle and comforting manner towards the king to relieve his suffering, skirting round the subject and never referring to it directly in order to spare his feelings. Anaxarchus, on the other hand, had always pursued an independent approach to philosophy

1. Line 683.
2. Cleitus was some twenty years older than Alexander, whom he had often tended in his childhood: his sister had been the young prince's wet-nurse.

and had acquired a reputation for slighting and looking down on his associates. As soon as he entered the room, he exclaimed, 'Here is this Alexander whom the whole world now looks to for an example, and he is lying on the floor weeping like a slave, terrified of the law and of what men will say of him. And yet all the time it should be he who represents the law and sets up the criterion of justice. Why else did he conquer, unless it was to govern and command? It was certainly not to allow himself to submit like a slave to the foolish opinions of others. Do you not know that Zeus has Justice and Law seated by his side to prove that everything that is done by the ruler of the world is lawful and just?' By using arguments such as these Anaxarchus certainly succeeded in relieving Alexander's sufferings, but he made him in many ways more proud and autocratic than before. He also gained great favour for himself and managed to make Callisthenes' company, which had never been very welcome because of his austerity, even more disagreeable to the king.

The story goes that one day at table, when the conversation turned upon the climate and the temperature of the air, Callisthenes, who took the view of those who said it was colder in Persia than in Greece, was contradicted by Anaxarchus in his usual aggressive manner, whereupon he retorted, 'Surely you must admit that it is colder here, for in Greece you used to wear just one cloak all through the winter, while here you are sitting at table with three rugs wrapped round you.' This remark naturally made Anaxarchus dislike him more than ever.

53. Callisthenes also annoyed the other sophists and flatterers of Alexander's court because he attracted the young men by his eloquence and because he was equally admired by the older generation[1] on account of his orderly, dignified and self-sufficient way of life. His behaviour certainly confirmed the reports which were current as to why he had left Greece, namely that he had come to Alexander in the hope of persuading him to re-settle his native city of Olynthus.[2] His great reputation naturally exposed him to some envy, but his behaviour at times also made it easy for his detractors to malign him, since he often refused invitations, and when he did appear in company, he was apt to make it plain that he disliked or disapproved of what

1. The older men disliked Alexander's 'orientalism'.
2. Olynthus had been destroyed by Philip in 348 B.C.

was going on by sitting wrapped in a morose silence, so that even Alexander said of him that he could not abide

> A sage who is blind to his own interests.[1]

There is a story that on one occasion when a large company had been invited to dine with the king, Callisthenes was called upon, as the cup passed to him, to speak in praise of the Macedonians. This theme he handled so eloquently that the guests rose to applaud and threw their garlands at him. At this Alexander quoted Euripides' line from the *Bacchae*

> On noble subjects all men can speak well.[2]

'But now,' he went on, 'show us the power of your eloquence by criticizing the Macedonians so that they can recognize their short-comings and improve themselves.' Callisthenes then turned to the other side of the picture and delivered a long list of home truths about the Macedonians, pointing out that the rise of Philip's power had been brought about by the divisions among the rest of the Greeks, and quoting the verse

> Once civil strife has begun, even scoundrels may find themselves honoured.[3]

This speech earned him the implacable hatred of the Macedonians, and Alexander remarked that it was not his eloquence that Callisthenes had demonstrated, but his ill will towards them.

54. According to Hermippus, this is the account which Stroebus, the slave who read aloud for Callisthenes, gave to Aristotle of the quarrel between Callisthenes and Alexander. He also says that when Callisthenes understood that he had antagonized the king, he repeated two or three times, as he was taking his leave, this verse from the *Iliad*

> Braver by far than yourself was Patroclus, but death did not spare him.[4]

Aristotle seems to have come near the truth when he said that Callisthenes possessed great eloquence, but lacked common sense.

1. A line from an unknown play of Euripides.
2. Line 260.
3. A proverb in hexameters attributed to Callimachus.
4. Achilles to Hector, *Iliad* xxi, 107.

But at least in the matter of the obeisance[1] he behaved like a true philosopher, not only in his sturdy refusal to perform it, but also in being the only man to express in public the resentment which all the oldest and best of the Macedonians felt in private. By persuading the king not to insist on this tribute, he delivered the Greeks from a great disgrace and Alexander from an even greater one, but at the same time he destroyed himself, because he left the impression that he had gained his point by force rather than by persuasion.

Chares of Mitylene says that on one occasion at a banquet Alexander, after he had drunk, passed the cup to one of his friends, who took it and rose so as to face the shrine of the household; next he drank in his turn, then made obeisance to Alexander, kissed him and resumed his place on the couch. All the guests did the same in succession, until the cup came to Callisthenes. The king was talking to Hephaestion and paying no attention to Callisthenes, and the philosopher, after he had drunk, came forward to kiss him. At this Demetrius, whose surname was Pheido, called out, 'Sire, do not kiss him; he is the only one who has not made obeisance to you.' Alexander therefore refused to kiss him, and Callisthenes exclaimed in a loud voice, 'Very well then, I shall go away the poorer by a kiss.'

55. Once this rift between them had occurred, it was easy for Hephaestion to be believed when he said that the philosopher had promised him to make obeisance to Alexander and had then broken his word. Besides this, men such as Lysimachus and Hagnon persistently spread the story that the sophist went round giving himself great airs as though he were determined to abolish a tyranny, and that the young men flocked to him and followed him everywhere, as though he were the only free spirit among so many tens of thousands.

1. The obeisance was originally a gesture which consisted of blowing a kiss, latterly of prostration to the ground. In Persia it was a *social* gesture, performed by the inferior to the superior, and by all Persians to the king. But it was not a *religious* gesture, for the Persians did not worship their kings. The Greeks, on the other hand, prostrated themselves only before their gods. Hence the Persian custom seemed to them an ignoble demonstration of reverence, which degraded the free Greeks to the level of barbarians. Alexander wished to introduce a uniform procedure which would apply to Greeks and Persians equally. The difficulty was that to forbid prostration to the Persians might imply that he was not a real king: on the other hand the Macedonians resented being placed on the same footing as the Persians. For Alexander a possible solution seemed to be to have himself regarded officially, but only officially, as a god by his Greek subjects, and in particular by the Greek cities of Asia Minor.

These slanders spread by Callisthenes' enemies became all the more plausible when the plot that had been laid against Alexander by Hermolaus and his fellow conspirators was discovered. According to these accusers, when Hermolaus asked the philosopher how he might become the most famous of men, Callisthenes said, 'By killing the most famous of men,' and further that when he was encouraging Hermolaus to make the attempt, he told him not to be overawed by Alexander's golden couch, but to remember that he was dealing with a man who was subject to sickness and wounds like anybody else. Yet the fact remains that not one of Hermolaus' accomplices, even under the stress of torture, denounced Callisthenes. And even Alexander himself in the letters which he immediately wrote to Craterus, Attalus and Alectas says that the youths had confessed under torture that the conspiracy was entirely their own and that nobody else knew of it. However, in a letter which he wrote later to Antipater and in which he includes Callisthenes in the general accusation, he says: 'The youths were stoned to death by the Macedonians, but as for the sophist I shall punish him myself, and I shall not forget those who sent him to me, or the others who give shelter in their cities to those who plot against my life.' In these words, at least, he plainly reveals his hostility to Aristotle in whose house Callisthenes had been brought up, since he was a son of Hero, who was Aristotle's niece. As for Callisthenes' death, according to some accounts Alexander ordered him to be hanged, but others have it that he was thrown into chains and died of disease. Chares tells us that after his arrest he was kept in prison for seven months in order to be tried by the Council of the League of Corinth in the presence of Aristotle, but that about the time when Alexander was wounded in India he died of excessive corpulence and the disease of lice.

56. These events, however, belong to a later period. In the meanwhile Demaratus of Corinth,[1] although he was by now an old man, was eager to visit Alexander, and when the king had received him, Demaratus declared that those Greeks who had died before they could see Alexander seated on the throne of Darius had missed one of the greatest pleasures in the world. However he did not live

1. An old friend of Alexander. He had helped to reconcile Philip and Alexander (see ch. 9). This episode seems deliberately placed to contrast Alexander's treatment of a friend with that of an enemy.

long to enjoy the king's friendship, but fell sick and died soon after-wards. He was given a magnificent funeral. The army raised a mound of eighty cubits in height and of a great circumference as a memorial to him, and his ashes were carried down to the coast in a four-horse chariot which was richly adorned.

57. Alexander was now about to launch his invasion of India.[1] He had already taken note that his army was over-encumbered with booty and had lost its mobility, and so early one morning after the baggage waggons had been loaded, he began by burning those which belonged to himself and the Companions, and then gave orders to set fire to those of the Macedonians. In the event his decision proved to have been more difficult to envisage than it was to execute. Only a few of the soldiers resented it: the great majority cheered with delight and raised their battle-cry: they gladly shared out the neces-sities for the campaign with those who needed them and then they helped to burn and destroy any superfluous possessions with their own hands. Alexander was filled with enthusiasm at their spirit and his hopes rose to their highest pitch. By this time he was already feared by his men for his relentless severity in punishing any dereliction of duty. For example he put to death Menander, one of the Companions, because he had been placed in command of a garrison and had refused to remain there, and he shot down with his own hand one of the barbarians named Orsodates who had rebelled against him.[2]

About this time a ewe brought forth a lamb whose head was covered with a substance which in shape and colour resembled the tiara of the king of Persia, with testicles on either side of it. Alexander was revolted by this prodigy and had himself purified by the Baby-lonian priests, whom he had become accustomed to bring on his campaigns for such purposes. When he spoke of this portent to his friends, he explained that he was alarmed not for his own sake but for theirs, because he feared that in the event of his death the gods might allow his power to fall into the hands of some unworthy and feeble successor. However a more encouraging phenomenon fol-lowed, which dispelled his misgivings. The head of Alexander's

1. In the spring of 327 B.C.
2. Alexander had reorganized the army to include some Oriental troops especially among the cavalry. His force for the invasion of India may have numbered some 35,000 fighting men.

household servants, a man named Proxenus, was digging a place to pitch the royal tent by the bank of the river Oxus, when he uncovered a spring of a smooth and fatty liquid. When the top of this was strained off, there gushed forth a pure and clear oil which appeared to be exactly like olive oil both in odour and in taste, and was also identical in smoothness and brightness, and this too in a country where there were no olive trees. It is said that the water of the Oxus itself is extraordinarily soft and gives a glossy texture to the skin of all those who bathe in it. It is clear that Alexander was delighted with this portent, if we may judge from a letter he wrote to Antipater, in which he speaks of it as one of the greatest signs of favour ever granted to him by the gods. The diviners, however, interpreted the omen as forecasting a campaign which would be a glorious one but also arduous and painful, for oil, they pointed out, was given to men by the gods as a refreshment for their labours.

58. This was certainly how events turned out. Alexander encountered many dangers in the battles he fought and was severely wounded, but the greatest losses his army suffered were caused by lack of provisions and by the rigours of the climate. But for his part he was anxious to prove that boldness can triumph over fortune and courage over superior force: he was convinced that while there are no defences so impregnable that they will keep out the brave man, there are likewise none so strong that they will keep the coward safe. It is said that when he was besieging the fortress of a ruler named Sisimithres,[1] which was situated upon a steep and inaccessible rock, his soldiers despaired of capturing it. Alexander asked Oxyartes whether Sisimithres himself was a man of spirit and received the reply that he was the greatest coward in the world. 'Then what you are telling me,' Alexander went on, 'is that we can take the fortress, since there is no strength in its defender.' And in fact he did capture it by playing upon Sisimithres' fears. Later, when he was attacking another equally inaccessible stronghold, he was encouraging the younger Macedonians and spoke to one who also bore the name of Alexander. 'You at least,' he told him, 'will have to prove yourself a brave man to live up to your name.' After this the young man fought with the utmost gallantry, and was killed to the great sorrow of the king. On another

1. This operation took place in the winter of 328/7. In this chapter Plutarch describes various incidents at random to illustrate Alexander's character.

occasion when the Macedonians were hesitating to attack the fortress of Nysa, because there was a deep river in front of it, Alexander halted on the bank and cried out, 'What a wretch I am! Why did I never learn to swim?', and he made ready to ford it, carrying his shield on his arm. After he had ordered a halt in the fighting, ambassadors came from a number of the cities he was besieging to beg for terms, and they were amazed to find him still unkempt and clad in full armour. Then when a cushion was brought for him, he ordered the most senior of the ambassadors, whose name was Acouphis, to seat himself on it. Acouphis, who was much impressed with his magnanimity and courtesy, asked what he wanted the people to do to earn his friendship. Alexander told him, 'I should like your countrymen to appoint you as their ruler and send me a hundred of their best men.' At this Acouphis laughed and replied, 'I shall rule them better, sire, if I send you the worst men rather than the best.'

59. There was a prince named Taxiles[1] whose territory, we are told, was as large as Egypt and contained good pasturage as well as fertile arable land. He was a wise ruler, and after he had greeted Alexander, he asked him, 'Why should we fight battles with one another? You have not come here to rob us of water or of the necessities of life, and these are the only things for which sensible men are obliged to fight. As for other kinds of wealth and property so-called, if I possess more than you, I am ready to be generous towards you, and if I have less, I shall not refuse any benefits you may offer.' Alexander was delighted at this, took his hand and said, 'Perhaps you think that after your kind words and courtesy our meeting will pass off without a contest. No, you shall not get the better of me in this way: I shall fight with you to the last, but only in the services I offer you, for I will not have you outdo me in generosity.' Alexander received many gifts from him, but returned even more, and finally presented him with a thousand talents in coin. This behaviour greatly annoyed his friends, but it made many of the barbarians far better disposed towards him.

Now the best fighters among the Indians were mercenaries, whose custom it was to travel from one city to another as they were needed: they defended their clients vigorously and caused Alexander heavy losses. So he concluded a truce with them when they were in one city,

1. The ruler of the great city of Taxila about twenty miles north-west of the modern Rawalpindi.

allowed them to leave, and then attacked them on the march and annihilated them. This action remains a blot on his career as a soldier: on all other occasions he observed the normal usages of war and behaved like a king. As for the philosophers,[1] they gave him as much trouble as the mercenaries, because they denounced those of the local rulers who went over to him and at the same time encouraged the free peoples to revolt: for this reason he had many of them hanged.

60. The events of the campaign against Porus are described in Alexander's letters. He tells us that the river Hydaspes flowed between the two camps, and that Porus stationed his elephants on the opposite bank and kept the crossing continually watched. Alexander caused a great deal of noise and commotion to be made day after day in his camp and in this way accustomed the barbarians not to be alarmed by his movements.[2] Then at last on a stormy and moonless night he took a part of his infantry and the best of his cavalry, marched some distance along the river past the enemy's position, and then crossed over to a small island. Here he was overtaken by a violent storm of rain accompanied by tremendous bursts of thunder and lightning. Although he saw that a number of his men were struck dead by the lightning, he continued the advance and made for the opposite bank. After the storm the Hydaspes, which was roaring down in high flood, had scooped out a deep channel, so that much of the stream was diverted in this direction and the ground between the two currents had become broken and slippery and made it impossible for his men to gain a firm footing. It was on this occasion that Alexander is said to have exclaimed, 'O you Athenians, will you ever believe what risks I am running just to earn your praise?'

This is the version which Onesicritus gives of the battle.[3] But according to Alexander's own account, the Macedonians left their rafts and waded across the breach in full armour, up to their chests in water. After making the crossing, Alexander rode on for more than two miles ahead of the infantry; he calculated that if the enemy attacked with their cavalry he could overcome them easily, and that if

1. The Brahmans of Sind.
2. Alexander could not get his horses to cross in the face of the elephants: the object of his repeated feints was that Porus should cease to send out the elephants to meet every threat.
3. July 326 B.C.

they moved up their infantry, there would still be time for his own to join him. His judgement proved quite correct. He was attacked by a thousand of the enemy's cavalry and sixty of their chariots, and killed four hundred of their horsemen. Then Porus, understanding that Alexander had crossed, advanced against him with his whole army, but left behind a force sufficient to prevent the remainder of the Macedonians from crossing. Alexander, remembering the threat of the enemy's elephants and their superior numbers, attacked their left wing and ordered Coenus to charge against the right. Both flanks of the Indian army were routed, and the defeated troops fell back upon the elephants and crowded into the centre. Here they rallied and a stubborn hand-to-hand struggle ensued, so that it was not until the eighth hour that the enemy was overcome. This is the account we have from the conqueror himself in one of his letters.

Most historians agree that Porus was about six feet three inches tall, and that his size and huge physique made him appear as suitably mounted upon an elephant as an ordinary man looks on a horse. His elephant too was very large and showed an extraordinary intelligence and concern for the king's person. So long as Porus was fighting strongly, it would valiantly defend him and beat off his attackers, but as soon as it recognized that its master was growing weak from the thrusts and missiles that had wounded him, it knelt quietly on the ground for fear that he might fall off, and with its trunk took hold of each spear and drew it out of his body. When Porus was taken prisoner, Alexander asked him how he wished to be treated. 'As a king,' Porus answered, and when Alexander went on to ask whether he had anything more to say, the reply came, 'Those words, "as a king" include everything.' At any rate Alexander not only allowed him to govern his former kingdom, but he also added to it a province, which included the territory of the independent peoples he had subdued. These are said to have numbered fifteen nations, five thousand towns of considerable size, and innumerable villages. His other conquests embraced an area three times the size of this, and he appointed Philip, one of the Companions, to rule it as satrap.

61. After this battle with Porus Bucephalas also died, not immediately, but some while later. Most historians report that he died of wounds received in the battle for which he was being treated, but according to Onesicritus it was from old age, for by this time he was thirty

years old. Alexander was plunged into grief at his death, and felt that he had lost nothing less than a friend and a comrade. He founded a city in his memory on the banks of the Hydraspes and called it Bucephalia, and there is also a story that when he lost a dog named Peritas of which he was very fond and which he had brought up from a puppy, he again founded a city and called it after the dog. The historian Sotion tells us that he learned this from Potamon of Lesbos.

62. Another consequence of this battle with Porus was that it blunted the edge of the Macedonians' courage and made them determined not to advance any further into India. It was only with great diffi-culty that they had defeated an enemy who had put into the field no more than twenty thousand infantry and two thousand cavalry, and so, when Alexander insisted on crossing the Ganges,[1] they opposed him outright. The river, they were told, was four miles across and one hundred fathoms deep, and the opposite bank swarmed with a gigantic host of infantry, horsemen and elephants. It was said that the kings of the Gandaridae and the Praesii were waiting for Alexander's attack with an army of eighty thousand cavalry, two hundred thousand infantry, eight thousand chariots and six thousand fighting elephants, and this report was no exaggeration, for Sandrocottus,[2] the king of this territory who reigned there not long afterwards, presented five hundred elephants to Seleucus, and overran and conquered the whole of India with an army of six hundred thousand men.

At first Alexander was so overcome with disappointment and anger that he shut himself up and lay prostrate in his tent. He felt that unless he could cross the Ganges, he owed no thanks to his troops for what they had already achieved; instead he regarded their having turned back as an admission of defeat. However his friends set them-selves to reason with him and console him and the soldiers crowded round the entrance to his tent, and pleaded with him, uttering loud

1. The date was September 326 B.C. Alexander did not, of course, reach the Ganges. The river where the troops mutinied was the Hyphasis: the upper Ganges was some two hundred and fifty miles further east. There is much dis-pute as to his real intentions and whether he planned to advance as far as the 'eastern ocean'. (See Arrian, *Anabasis* 5, 26 for his speech at the Hyphasis.)

2. The Hellenized form of Chandragupta, whose accession took place about 326 B.C. He later wiped out the Macedonian garrisons in India.

cries and lamentations, until finally he relented and gave orders to break camp. But when he did so he devised a number of ruses and deceptions to impress the inhabitants of the region. For example he had arms, horses' mangers and bits prepared, all of which exceeded the normal size or height or weight, and these were left scattered about the country. He also set up altars for the gods of Greece[1] and even down to the present day the kings of the Praesii whenever they cross the river do honour to these and offer sacrifice on them in the Greek fashion. Sandrocottus, who was then no more than a boy, saw Alexander himself, and we are told that in later years he often remarked that Alexander was within a step of conquering the whole country, since the king who ruled it at that time was hated and despised because of his vicious character and his lowly birth.

63. Alexander was now eager to see the outer Ocean. He had a large number of oar-propelled ferries and rafts constructed, and was rowed down the rivers on these at a leisurely speed. But his voyage was by no means a peaceful and certainly not a passive affair. As he travelled downstream he would land, assault the cities near the banks, and subdue them all. However when he attacked the tribe known as the Malli, who are said to be the most warlike of all the Indian peoples, he nearly lost his life. After the defenders had been driven from the walls by volleys of missiles, he was the first[2] to scramble to the top of the wall by means of a scaling ladder. The ladder was smashed, so that no more Macedonians could join him, and the barbarians began to gather inside along the bottom of the wall and to shoot at him from below. Finding himself almost alone and exposed to their missiles, Alexander crouched down, leaped into their midst, and by good luck landed on his feet. Then, as he brandished his arms, it seemed to the barbarians as if a dazzling sheet of flame suddenly took shape in front of his body, and they scattered and fled. But when they saw that there were no more than two of his guards accompanying him, they rushed in to attack him. Some of them engaged him hand to hand, and rained blows upon his armour with sword and spear as he strove to defend himself, while another, standing a little way apart, shot at him with a bow. The shaft was so well aimed and struck him

1. Twelve altars for the twelve gods of Greece.
2. His object was evidently to shame his own troops into attacking with more *élan*.

with such force that it pierced his breastplate and lodged in his chest between the ribs. The impact was so violent that Alexander staggered back and sank to his knees; his attacker rushed up with his drawn scimitar in his hand, while Peucestas and Limnaeus threw themselves in front of him. Both men were wounded and Limnaeus was killed, but Peucestas stood firm, while Alexander killed the barbarian with his own hand. But he was wounded over and over again, and at last received a blow on the neck from a club which forced him to lean against the wall, although he still faced his assailants. At this moment the Macedonians swarmed round him, snatched him up as he lost consciousness, and carried him to his tent. Immediately the rumour ran through the camp that he had been killed. Meanwhile his attendants with great difficulty sawed off the wooden shaft of the arrow and thus succeeded in removing his breastplate; they then had to cut out the arrow-head, which was embedded between his ribs and measured, so we are told four fingers width in length and three in breadth. When it was extracted the king fainted away and came very near to death, but finally he recovered. Even when the danger was past he remained weak, and for a long time needed careful nursing and was obliged to remain on a diet. Then one day, as he heard a clamour outside his tent, he understood that the Macedonians were yearning to see him, and so he took his cloak and went out to them. After sacrificing to the gods, he once more boarded his vessel and proceeded down the river, subduing great cities and large tracts of territory as he went.

64. He captured ten of the Indian philosophers who had played the most active part in persuading Sabbas to revolt and had stirred up most trouble for the Macedonians. These philosophers enjoyed a great reputation for their ingenuity in devising short pithy answers to questions, and so Alexander confronted them with a series of conundrums. He had previously announced that he would put to death the first man who gave a wrong answer, and then the rest in order according to their performance, and he ordered one of them, the eldest, to act as judge in the contest. The examination then proceeded as follows.

FIRST PHILOSOPHER

  Question: Which are more numerous, the living or the dead?
  Answer: The living, since the dead no longer exist.

SECOND PHILOSOPHER

    Question: Which breeds the larger creatures, the land or the sea?

    Answer: The land, since the sea is only a part of it.

THIRD PHILOSOPHER

    Question: Which is the most cunning of animals?

    Answer: The animal which man has not yet discovered.

FOURTH PHILOSOPHER

    Question: Why did you incite Sabbas to revolt?

    Answer: Because I wished him either to live or to die with honour.

FIFTH PHILOSOPHER

    Question: Which was created first, the day or the night?

    Answer: The day, by one day.

When the philosopher saw that the king was astonished by this reply, he added, 'Abstruse questions will necessarily produce abstruse answers.'

SIXTH PHILOSOPHER

    Question: How can a man make himself most beloved?

    Answer: If he possesses supreme power, and yet does not inspire fear.

SEVENTH PHILOSOPHER

    Question: How can a man become a god?

    Answer: By doing something a man cannot do.

EIGHTH PHILOSOPHER

    Question: Which is the stronger: life or death?

    Answer: Life, since it endures so many evils.

NINTH PHILOSOPHER

    Question: How long is it good for a man to live?

    Answer: So long as he does not regard death as better than life.

Finally Alexander turned to the judge and told him to give his verdict: this was that each of them had answered worse than the one before. 'In that case,' Alexander replied, 'you shall be executed first yourself for having given such a verdict.' 'That is not right, your majesty', returned the judge, 'unless you did not mean what you said when you announced that you would put to death first the man who gave the worst answer.'

65. Alexander distributed presents to all ten and sent them away unharmed. He then sent Onesicritus to those philosophers who

enjoyed the highest reputation but lived a secluded and contemplative life, and invited them to visit him. Onesicritus himself belonged to the school of Diogenes the Cynic, and he tells us that one of the Indians, Calanus, treated him most arrogantly and insolently and told him to take off his clothes and listen to him naked if he wished to hear any of his doctrines, otherwise he would not carry on a conversation, even if the Greek came from Zeus himself. Onesicritus reports that another sage named Dandamis received him more courteously, and when he had spoken at length about Socrates, Pythagoras and Diogenes, Dandamis remarked that they seemed to him to have been men of good natural parts, but to have spent their lives with too submissive an attitude to the laws. According to other writers, however, the only remark which Dandamis made at this meeting was, 'Why did Alexander come all this way to India?' Nevertheless the prince Taxiles was able to persuade Calanus to visit Alexander. His real name was Sphines, but because he greeted everyone he met not with the Greek salutation, *chairete*, but with the Indian word *cale*, the Greeks called him Calanus. It was he, we are told, who first propounded to Alexander the celebrated parable about government, which ran as follows. Calanus threw on to the ground a dry and shrunken piece of hide and put his foot on the outer edge: the hide was thus pressed down at one point on the surface, but rose up at others. He walked round the circumference and showed that this was what happened whenever he trod on the edge: then finally he put his weight on to the middle, whereupon the whole of the hide lay flat and still. The demonstration was intended to show that Alexander should concentrate the weight of his authority at the centre of his empire and not go wandering around the borders of it.

66. Alexander's voyage to the mouth of the Indus occupied seven months. When he reached the open sea with his ships,[1] he sailed out to an island which he himself named Scillustis, while others called it Psiltukis. Here he landed and sacrificed to the gods, and made what observations he could on the nature of the sea and of the coast, as far as it was accessible. Then he offered up a prayer that no man after him might ever pass beyond the bounds of his expedition.

He appointed Nearchus to the supreme command of the fleet with Onesicritus as its chief pilot, and ordered them to follow the

1. In July 325 B.C.

line of the sea coast, keeping India on their right.[1] Meanwhile, he himself set out by land and marched through the territory of the Oreites. Here he endured terrible privations and lost great numbers of men, with the result that he did not bring back from India so much as a quarter of his fighting force. And yet his strength had once amounted to a hundred and twenty thousand infantry and fifteen thousand cavalry.[2] Some of his men died from disease, some of the wretched food, some of the scorching heat, but most from sheer hunger, for they had to march through an uncultivated region whose inhabitants only eked out a wretched existence. They possessed few sheep and even these were of a stunted breed, and the sea fish on which they subsisted made the animals' flesh rank and unsavoury. It was only with great difficulty that Alexander succeeded in crossing this region in sixty days, but once he reached Gedrosia, he was immediately in a land of plenty, and the satraps and local rulers provided him with all his needs.

67. After resting his force here he set out again and marched for seven days through the territory of Carmania, a march which soon developed into a kind of Bacchanalian procession. Alexander himself feasted continually, day and night, reclining with his Companions on a dais built upon a high and conspicuous rectangular platform, the whole structure being slowly drawn along by eight horses. Innumerable waggons followed the royal table, some of them covered with purple or embroidered canopies, others shaded by the boughs of trees, which were constantly kept fresh and green: these vehicles carried the rest of Alexander's officers, all of them crowned with flowers and drinking wine. Not a single helmet, shield or spear was to be seen, but along the whole line of the march the soldiers kept dipping their cups, drinking-horns or earthenware goblets into huge casks and mixing-bowls and toasting one another, some drinking as they marched, others sprawled by the wayside, while the whole

1. The plan was that the fleet should sail up the Persian Gulf and rejoin Alexander at the mouth of the Euphrates.

2. Alexander is said to have chosen this desert route both to support the fleet by digging wells and establishing depots and to restore his own reputation for superhuman achievement. For the strength of Alexander's operational force see note on ch. 57. Plutarch here seems to be referring to a total which includes all camp-followers. The non-combatants were the principal sufferers on this march.

landscape resounded with the music of pipes and flutes, with harping and singing and the cries of women rapt with the divine frenzy. Not only drinking but all the other forms of bacchanalian license attended this straggling and disorderly march, as though the god himself were present to lead the revels.[1] Then when Alexander arrived at the palace of Gedrosia, he again allowed the army time to rest and celebrated another festival. It is said that one day, after he had drunk well, he went to watch some contests in dancing and singing and that his favourite Bagoas won the prize; thereupon the young man came across the theatre, still in his performer's costume and wearing his crown as victor, and seated himself beside the king. At the sight the Macedonians applauded loudly and shouted to Alexander to kiss the winner, until at last the king put his arms around him and kissed him.

68. Here Nearchus and his officers joined him, and Alexander was so delighted with their reports[2] of their voyage that he suddenly had the impulse to sail down the Euphrates himself with a large fleet, and then to coast round Arabia and Africa and re-enter the Mediterranean by way of the Pillars of Hercules. He began to have vessels of many different kinds constructed at Thapsacus and to collect sailors and pilots from all parts of the world. But meanwhile the difficulties he had encountered during the whole eastern campaign, the wound he had received in the battle with the Malli, and the heavy losses which his army was reported to have suffered had raised doubts as to his safe return: this combination of events had encouraged the subject peoples to revolt and his various viceroys and satraps to act in an unjust, rapacious and arrogant manner. In short the whole empire was in turmoil and an atmosphere of instability prevailed everywhere. Even at home his mother Olympias and his sister Cleopatra had been intriguing against the regent, Antipater, and had divided the kingdom between them, Olympias taking Epirus and Cleopatra Macedonia. When Alexander heard of this, he remarked that his mother had made the wiser choice, since the Macedonians would never tolerate being governed by a woman. For these reasons he now sent Nearchus back

1. The authenticity of this account is very doubtful. It echoes Dionysius' triumphant return from the conquest of India and probably refers to the celebrations held when Nearchus rejoined the army in Carmania.

2. In December 325 Nearchus landed at Harmezeia and joined Alexander after five days' march inland.

to sea: his plan was to carry the war into the provinces which bordered the coast, while he himself would march down from Upper Asia and punish those of his officers who had abused their powers. He killed Oxyartes, one of the sons of Abuletes the satrap of Susiana with his own hands, running him through with a Macedonian pike, and when Abuletes brought him three thousand talents in coin instead of the provisions which he ought to have supplied, Alexander ordered the money to be thrown to the horses. Then, when they did not touch it, he asked Abuletes, 'What use are your provisions to us?' and ordered him to be imprisoned.

69. One of his first acts when he reached Persis was to distribute money to the women: in this he was following the custom of the Persian kings,[1] who whenever they arrived in this province presented each matron with a gold coin. For this reason, it is said, some of the kings seldom visited Persis, and Ochus never set foot there at all: he was mean enough to exile himself from his native land. Not long afterwards Alexander discovered that the tomb of Cyrus had been plundered and had the offender put to death, even though he was a prominent Macedonian from Pella named Polymachus. When he had read the inscription on the tomb, he ordered it to be repeated below in Greek characters. The text was as follows. 'O man, whoever you are and wherever you come from, for I know you will come, I am Cyrus who won the Persians their empire. Do not therefore grudge me this little earth that covers my body.' These words made a deep impression on Alexander, since they reminded him of the uncertainty and mutability of mortal life.

It was here too that Calanus, who had suffered for some while from a disease of the intestine, asked for a funeral pyre to be made ready for him. He rode up to it on horseback, said a prayer, poured a libation for himself, and cut off a lock of hair to throw on the fire. Then he climbed on to the pyre, greeted the Macedonians who were present, and urged them to make this a day of gaiety and celebration and to drink deep with the king, whom, he said, he would soon see in Babylon.[2] With these words he lay down and covered himself. He made no movement as the flames approached him, and continued to lie in exactly the same position as at first, and so immolated himself

1. A custom instituted by Cyrus.
2. A prophecy of Alexander's death.

in a manner acceptable to the gods, according to the ancestral custom of the wise men of his country. Many years afterwards an Indian who belonged to the retinue of Augustus Caesar performed the same action in Athens, and the so-called Indian's tomb can be seen there to this day.

70. After Alexander had left the funeral pyre, he invited a number of his friends and officers to dine with him and proposed a contest in drinking neat wine, the winner of which was to receive a crown. The victor was Promachus, who downed four pitchers, or about twelve quarts: the prize was a crown worth a talent, but he lived for only three days afterwards. Of the other competitors forty-one, according to Chares, died of the effects of the wine: they were seized by a violent chill after the drinking.

Alexander now celebrated the marriages of a number of his Companions at Susa.[1] He himself married Stateira, the daughter of Darius, and he matched the noblest of the Persian women with the bravest of his men. On this occasion[2] he gave a banquet to which he invited all the Macedonians who had already married Persian wives. We are told that nine thousand guests attended this feast and each of them was given a gold cup for the libations. The whole entertainment was carried out on the grand scale and Alexander went so far as to discharge all the debts owed by any of his guests: the outlay for the occasion amounted to nine thousand eight hundred and seventy talents. Antigenes, one of Alexander's officers who had only one eye, contrived to get himself fraudulently enrolled as a debtor. He produced a witness who pretended to have lent him a sum at the bank and repaid him the money. Later the fraud was discovered and Alexander deprived him of his command and banished him from the court. Antigenes had a brilliant military record. While he was still a young man he had served under Philip at the siege of Perinthus, and when he was hit in the eye by a bolt from a catapult, he had refused to leave the fighting or have the dart extracted until he had helped to drive back the enemy and shut them up in the city. He could not endure the humiliation of his disgrace, and it was clear that he intended to kill himself out of grief and despair. The king was afraid that he would

1. Ninety-two of the Companions married Persian women, but many repudiated them after Alexander's death.
2. 324 B.C.

really carry out his intention, and so he pardoned him and told him to keep the money.

71. The thirty thousand boys whom he had left behind to be given a Greek education and military training had now grown into active and handsome men and had developed a wonderful skill and agility in their military exercises. Alexander was delighted with their progress, but the Macedonians were disheartened and deeply disturbed for their own future, because they assumed that the king would henceforth have less regard for them. So when he arranged to send the sick and disabled among them to the sea-coast, they protested that he was not only doing them an injustice but deliberately humiliating them. He had first worn them out in every kind of service, and now he was turning them away in disgrace and throwing them upon the mercy of their parents and native cities, where they would be in worse case than when they had set out for Asia. Why not send them all home and write off the Macedonians as useless, now that he had this corps of young ballet-soldiers, with whom he could go on to conquer the world? These words stung Alexander and he angrily rebuked the Macedonians, dismissed his guards, handed over their security duties to Persians and recruited from these his royal escort and personal attendants. When the Macedonians saw him surrounded by these men, while they were barred from his presence and treated as being in disgrace, they were greatly humbled, and when they considered the matter, they understood that they had been almost beside themselves with jealousy and rage. Finally when they had come to their senses, they presented themselves at Alexander's tent unarmed and dressed only in their tunics, and there they cried out and lamented, threw themselves on his mercy and begged him to deal with them as their baseness and ingratitude deserved. Alexander refused to receive them, although he had already begun to relent, but the men would not go away and remained for two days and nights outside his tent weeping and calling him their master. At last on the third day he came out, and when he saw them reduced to such a forlorn and pitiful state, he himself wept for a while. He reproached them gently for their behaviour and finally spoke to them kindly: afterwards he dismissed those who were no longer fit for service and gave them generous gratuities. Besides this he sent instructions to Antipater that at all public contests and in the theatres these men should occupy

the best seats and wear garlands on their heads. He also gave orders that the orphaned children of those who had died in his service should continue to receive their fathers' pay.

72. In the spring[1] he left Susa for Ecbatana in Media and there, after he had dealt with the most pressing of his concerns, he once more turned his attention to plays and spectacles, since three thousand players had arrived from Greece.[2] At this time it happened that Hephaestion had caught a fever, and being a young man who was accustomed to a soldier's life, he could not bear to remain on a strict diet. No sooner had his physician Glaucus gone off to the theatre, than he sat down to breakfast, devoured a boiled fowl and washed it down with a great cooler-full of wine. His fever quickly mounted and soon afterwards he died. Alexander's grief was uncontrollable. As a sign of mourning he gave orders that the manes and tails of all horses should be shorn, demolished the battlements of all the neighbouring cities, crucified the unlucky physician and forebade the playing of flutes or any other kind of music for a long time until finally an oracle was announced from the temple of Ammon, commanding him to honour Hephaestion and sacrifice to him as a hero.[3] To lighten his sorrow he set off on a campaign, as if the tracking down and hunting of men might console him, and he subdued the tribe of the Cossaeans,[4] massacring the whole male population from the youths upwards: this was termed a sacrifice to the spirit of Hephaestion. He determined to spend ten thousand talents on the funeral and the tomb for his friend, and as he wished the ingenuity and originality of the design to surpass the expense he was especially anxious to employ Stasicrates, as this artist was famous for his innovations, which combined an exceptional degree of magnificence, audacity and ostentation.

It was Stasicrates who had remarked to Alexander at an earlier interview that of all mountains it was Mount Athos which could

1. 324 B.C.
2. These were the so-called 'Artists of Dionysus'. By the fourth century actors and other theatrical artists had become organized into a guild of this name and travelled all over the Greek world.
3. In this context the word means a semi-divine personage.
4. The metaphor is not inappropriate. The Cossaeans were a mountain tribe who had made brigandage their livelihood.

most easily be carved into the form and shape of a man and that if it pleased Alexander to command him, he would shape the mountain into the most superb and durable statue of him in the world: its left hand would enfold a city of ten thousand inhabitants, while out of its right would flow the abundant waters of a river which would pour, like a libation, into the sea. Alexander declined this proposal, but now he spent his time with his engineers and architects planning projects which were even more outlandish and extravagant.

73. Towards the end of the year Alexander travelled to Babylon. Before he arrived he was joined by Nearchus, who had sailed through the ocean and up the Euphrates: Nearchus told him that he had met some Chaldaeans who had advised the king to stay away from Babylon. Alexander paid no attention to this warning and continued his journey, but when he arrived before the walls of the city, he saw a large number of ravens flying about and pecking one another, and some of them fell dead in front of him.[1] Next he received a report that Apollodorus the governor of Babylon had offered up a sacrifice to try to discover what fate held in store for Alexander, and he then sent for Pythagoras, the diviner who had conducted the sacrifice. Pythagoras admitted that this was true, and Alexander then asked him in what condition he had found the victim. 'The liver,' Pythagoras told him, 'had no lobe.' 'Indeed,' replied Alexander, 'that is a threatening omen.' He did Pythagoras no harm and he began to regret that he had not taken Nearchus' advice, and so he spent most of his time outside the walls of Babylon, either in his tent or in boats on the Euphrates. Many more omens now occurred to trouble him. A tame ass attacked the finest lion in his menagerie and kicked it to death. On another occasion Alexander took off his clothes for exercise and played a game of ball. When it was time to dress again, the young men who had joined him in the game suddenly noticed that there was a man sitting silently on the throne and wearing Alexander's diadem and royal robes. When he was questioned, he could say nothing for a long while, but later he came to his senses and explained that he was a citizen of Messenia named Dionysius. He had been accused of some crime, brought to Babylon from the coast, and kept for a long time in chains. Then the god Serapis had appeared to him, cast off his chains and brought him to this place, where he had

1. The fighting of birds was customarily regarded as an ominous sign.

commanded him to put on the king's robe and diadem, take his seat
on the throne and hold his peace.

74. When he had heard the man's story, Alexander had him put to
death, as the diviners recommended. But his confidence now
deserted him, he began to believe that he had lost the favour of the
gods, and he became increasingly suspicious of his friends. It was
Antipater and his sons whom he feared most of all. One of them
named Iolas was his chief cup-bearer. The other, Cassander, had only
lately arrived in Babylon, and when he saw some of the barbarians
prostrate themselves before the king, he burst into loud and dis-
respectful laughter, for he had been brought up as a Greek and had
never seen such a spectacle in his life. Alexander was furious at this
insult, seized him by the hair with both hands and dashed his head
against the wall. On another occasion when Cassander wished to
reply to some men who were making accusations against his father
Antipater, Alexander interrupted him and said, 'What do you mean?
Are you really saying that these men have suffered no wrong, but
have travelled all this way just to bring a false accusation?' When
Cassander replied that the very fact of their having travelled so far
from those who could contradict them might point to the charges
being false, Alexander laughed and said, 'This reminds me of some
of Aristotle's sophisms, which can be used equally well on either side
of a question: but if any of you are proved to have done these men
even the smallest wrong, you will be sorry for it.' In general, we
are told, this fear was implanted so deeply and took such hold of
Cassander's mind that even many years later, when he had become
king of Macedonia and master of Greece, and was walking about
one day looking at the sculptures at Delphi, the mere sight of a
statue of Alexander struck him with horror, so that he shuddered
and trembled in every limb, his head swam and he could scarcely
regain control of himself.

75. Meanwhile Alexander had become so much obsessed by his fears
of the supernatural and so overwrought and apprehensive in his own
mind, that he interpreted every strange or unusual occurrence, no
matter how trivial, as a prodigy or a portent, with the result that the
palace was filled with soothsayers, sacrificers, purifiers and prog-
nosticators. Certainly it is dangerous to disbelieve or show contempt

for the power of the gods, but it is equally dangerous to harbour superstition, and in this case just as water constantly gravitates to a lower level, so unreasoning dread filled Alexander's mind with foolish misgivings, once he had become a slave to his fears. However, when the verdict of the oracle concerning Hephaestion was brought to him, he laid aside his grief and allowed himself to indulge in a number of sacrifices and drinking-bouts. He gave a splendid banquet in honour of Nearchus, after which he took a bath as his custom was, with the intention of going to bed soon afterwards. But when Medius invited him, he went to his house to join a party, and there after drinking all through the next day, he began to feel feverish. This did not happen 'as he was drinking from the cup of Hercules',[1] nor did he become conscious of a sudden pain in the back as if he had been pierced by a spear: these are details with which certain historians felt obliged to embellish the occasion, and thus invent a tragic and moving finale to a great action. Aristobulus tells us that he was seized with a raging fever, that when he became very thirsty he drank wine which made him delirious, and that he died on the thirtieth day of the month Daesius.[2]

76. According to his journals, the course of his sickness was as follows. On the eighteenth day of the month Daesius[3] he slept in the bathroom because he was feverish. On the next day, after taking a bath, he moved into the bedchamber and spent the day playing dice with Medius. He took a bath late in the evening, offered sacrifice to the gods, dined and remained feverish throughout the night. On the twentieth he again bathed and sacrificed as usual, and while he was lying down in the bathroom he was entertained by listening to Nearchus' account of his voyage, and his exploration of the great sea. On the twenty-first he passed the time in the same way, but the fever grew more intense: he had a bad night and all through the following day his fever was very high. He had his bed moved and lay in it by the side of the great plunge-bath, and there he discussed with his commanders the vacant posts in the army and how to fill them with experienced officers. On the twenty-fourth his fever was still worse

1. Plutarch is contradicting the account given by Diodorus Siculus xviii, 117 and Quintus Curtius x, 4. The so-called cup of Hercules was according to Athenaeus, a large vessel with two handles.

2. 10 June 323 B.C.   3. 2 June 323 B.C.

and he had to be carried outside to offer sacrifice. He gave orders to the senior commanders to remain on call in the courtyard of the palace and to the commanders of companies and regiments to spend the night outside. On the twenty-fifth day he was moved to the palace on the other side of the river, and there he slept a little, but his fever did not abate. When his commanders entered the room he was speechless and remained so on the twenty-sixth. The Macedonians now believed that he was dead: they thronged the doors of the palace and began to shout and threaten the Companions, who were at last obliged to let them in. When the doors had been thrown open they all filed slowly past his bedside one by one, wearing neither cloak nor armour. In the course of this day too Python and Seleucus were sent to the temple of Serapis to ask whether Alexander should be moved there, and the god replied that they should leave him where he was. On the twenty-eighth towards evening he died.

77. Most of this account follows the version that is given in the journals almost word for word. Nobody had any suspicion at the time that Alexander had been poisoned, but it is said that five years afterwards some information was given, on the strength of which Olympias put many men to death and had the ashes of Iolas, Antipater's son, scattered to the winds on the supposition that he had administered the poison.

According to some writers it was Aristotle who advised Antipater to arrange the murder and it was entirely through his efforts that the poison was provided. They cite a man named Hagnothemis as their authority: he claimed to have heard the details from Antigonus, and according to this story the poison consisted of ice-cold water drawn from a certain cliff near the town of Nonacris,[1] where it was gathered up like a thin dew and stored in an ass's hoof. No other vessel could hold the liquid, which was said to be so cold and pungent that it would eat through any other substance. But most authorities consider that this tale of poisoning is pure invention, and this view is strongly supported by the fact that during the quarrels between Alexander's commanders, which continued for many days, the body

1. A small town in northern Arcadia. The water came from the river Styx. It was not poisonous but intensely cold, as the river rises from the snow-fields of Mount Chelmus. It was because of its supposedly deadly nature that oaths were sworn by the waters of the Styx.

showed no sign of any such corruption but remained pure and fresh, even though it lay for all that time without receiving any special care.

At this time Roxane was expecting a child and she was therefore held in special honour by the Macedonians. But she was jealous of Alexander's second wife, Stateira, whom she tricked into visiting her by means of a forged letter, which purported to have come from Alexander. When she had thus got her into her power she had her murdered together with her sister, threw the bodies into a well, and filled it up with earth. In this crime her accomplice was Perdiccas, who after Alexander's death at once succeeded in concentrating the greatest power in his hands, using Arrhidaeus as a figure-head for the authority of the royal house. This Arrhidaeus was a son of Philip's by an obscure and humbly born woman named Philinna, and was backward as a result of some disease. This was neither hereditary nor was it produced by natural causes. On the contrary, it is said that as a boy he had shown an attractive disposition and displayed much promise, but Olympias was believed to have given him drugs which impaired the functions of his body and irreparably injured his brain.

8

DEMETRIUS[1]

[337–283 B.C.]

* *
*

WHOEVER first conceived the idea that there is a parallel between
the arts and our bodily senses seems to me to have grasped one fact
very clearly, namely that both possess a power to make distinctions
which enables us to perceive opposites, alike on the physical and on
the aesthetic plane. The arts and the senses have this faculty in
common, but the ways in which they apply it are quite different.
Thus our senses are no better equipped to distinguish black objects,
for example, than white, or sweet things than bitter, or soft and
yielding substances than hard and resistant ones: their function is to
register impressions from all objects alike as they occur, and to
communicate the sensation as it has been experienced to the brain.
The arts, on the other hand, function with the help of reason in such
a way as to select and apprehend what is conformable to their nature
and to avoid and reject what is alien to it: accordingly they contem-
plate the one category of objects deliberately and by preference, but
while they also incidentally take note of the other, they do so in
order to avoid it. Thus to promote health the art of medicine has
incidentally investigated the nature of disease, and to create harmony
the art of music has studied that of discord, each in order to produce
its opposite.

Finally the most consummate arts of all – those of self-control,
justice and wisdom – have the task of distinguishing not only what
is good, useful and just, but also what is harmful, disgraceful and
unjust; and these arts, we find, by no means prize that kind of
innocence which boasts of its inexperience of evil. On the contrary
they regard it as folly, and as ignorance of all the things that a man

1. For places mentioned in this *Life*, see Maps 1, 2 and 4, pp. 433–5, 437.

who intends to lead an upright life is most concerned to know. It was for a similar reason that the ancient Spartans had the custom of compelling the Helots at their festivals to drink large quantities of neat wine: then they would bring them into the public dining-halls as an object lesson to their young men of what it was like to be drunk. For my part I think it is wrong both in human and in political terms to try to raise the standards of one section of society by demoralizing another. But on the same principle it may serve as a useful example in my *Parallel Lives* if I include one or two pairs of men who have been careless of their reputations, and who because they exercised supreme power or were engaged in great enterprises made themselves conspicuous by their misconduct. My purpose in doing so is not merely to divert or entertain my readers by giving variety to my writings. I am rather following the example of Ismenias the Theban, who when he taught the flute used to show his pupils both good and bad performers, and tell them 'You should play like this one', or 'You should not play like that one'. Antigenidas went further and believed that young men would appreciate good fluteplayers better if they were given experience of bad ones. In the same way it seems to me that we shall be all the more ready to study and imitate the lives of good men if we know something of those of the wicked and infamous.

This book, then, will contain the lives of Demetrius, nicknamed the Besieger of Cities, and Antony the Imperator,[1] men whose lives conspicuously illustrate the truth of Plato's saying that great natures produce great vices as well as great virtues. Both men were redoubtable womanizers, drinkers and fighters, both were open-handed, extravagant and arrogant, and these resemblances were reflected in the similarity of their fortunes. During their careers they met with prodigious triumphs and disasters, conquered great empires and as easily lost them, rose to the heights of success as unexpectedly as they plumbed the depths of failure, and ended their lives the one as a prisoner of his enemies, and the other narrowly escaping the same fate.

2. According to most historians, Antigonus had two sons from Stratonice the daughter of Corrhagus. One of them he named Demetrius after his brother, the other Philip after his father. But some writers tell us that Demetrius was Antigonus' nephew, not his

1. See Introduction, p. 9.

son: they say that his father died when he was quite young, and that his mother married Antigonus, who thus came to be regarded as Demetrius' father. Philip, who was a few years the younger, died at an early age. Demetrius grew up to be a tall man, although not so tall as his father, and both in form and in feature he was so strikingly handsome that no painter or sculptor ever succeeded in fashioning a likeness of him. His features combined charm and seriousness, beauty and a capacity to inspire fear, but hardest of all to represent was the blend in his appearance of the eagerness and fire of youth with a heroic aspect and an air of kingly dignity. In his disposition he was equally capable of making himself loved and feared. He could be the most delightful of companions, more voluptuous than any other ruler of his age in his addiction to drinking and other luxurious habits of life, and yet when action was required, he could show the utmost energy, perseverance and practical ability. It was for this reason that he took Dionysus as his model, since this god was most terrible when waging war, but also most skilful at exploiting the ensuing peace for the pursuit of pleasure and enjoyment.

3. Demetrius was also deeply attached to his father, and to judge by the devotion he showed to his mother, it was evident that his feeling for Antigonus sprang from genuine affection, not from mere regard for his power. On one occasion when Antigonus was giving audience to some foreign envoys, Demetrius happened to come home from hunting. He walked straight up to his father, and then sat down beside him in his hunting clothes and with his javelins still in his hand. When the envoys had received their answer and were about to leave his presence, Antigonus called out to them in a loud voice and said, 'Gentlemen, when you return home, you may also report that this is how my son and I live,' for he felt that this demonstration of the harmony and confidence which prevailed between him and his son was the best proof of the power and stability of his kingdom. How difficult it is to share absolute power, and how much ill will and suspicion it breeds around itself we may judge from this episode – from the fact that the oldest and greatest of the successors of Alexander could make it his boast that he was not afraid of his son, but allowed him to sit close by his side with a spear in his hand. And indeed it is a fact that Antigonus' was the only royal house whose history remained unsullied by crimes of this kind for many generations; or,

to put the matter more precisely, the only one of the descendants of Antigonus who put a son to death was Philip.[1] The chronicles of almost all the other dynasties are full of examples of men who murdered their sons, their mothers or their wives, while the murder of brothers had come to be regarded almost as axiomatic, as a recognized precaution to be taken by all rulers to ensure their safety.

4. The following story is worth quoting, because it shows that Demetrius in his early years was by nature humane and well disposed towards his friends. Mithridates, the son of Ariobarzanes, was of the same age as Demetrius and a close friend and companion. He was one of Antigonus' courtiers, but although he enjoyed a well-earned position of trust, he incurred the king's suspicion on account of a dream. Antigonus had dreamed that he was crossing a large and beautiful field and was sowing it with gold dust. At first a crop of gold immediately sprang up, but when after a little while he returned to the field, he could see nothing but stubble. Then in his disappointment and vexation he seemed to hear a number of voices saying that Mithridates had gathered the golden harvest for himself and escaped to the coast of the Black Sea. The vision preyed on Antigonus, and finally he sent for his son, and after making him take an oath of silence, he described to him what he had seen and added that he had decided to rid himself of Mithridates. Demetrius was greatly distressed at this, but when the young man arrived, as was his habit, to spend the day with the prince, Demetrius did not dare to refer to the subject or to warn him of his danger, on account of the oath he had sworn. Instead he drew him aside, away from his friends, and when they were alone together he wrote on the ground with the butt of his spear as the others watched him, the words, 'Fly, Mithridates!' Mithridates understood and made his escape by night to Cappadocia. But not long afterwards fate caused Antigonus' vision to come to pass. Mithridates made himself master of a large and prosperous territory, and founded the dynasty of kings of Pontus, which was overthrown eight generations later by the Romans.[2] At any rate the story may serve to illustrate Demetrius' natural tendency to behave in a just and humane fashion.

1. Philip V of Macedonia.
2. In 63 B.C. when Pompey defeated Mithridates VI.

5. Empedocles tells us that the principles of love and hatred produce perpetual strife among the elements of the universe, especially among those elements which are adjacent to or in contact with one another. In the same way wars continually broke out among the successors of Alexander, and these were particularly violent or bitter when the rival interests or disputed territories happened to lie close to one another. This was the situation in which Antigonus and Ptolemy found themselves. Antigonus was at that moment[1] in Phrygia, and as soon as he received the news that Ptolemy had crossed over from Cyprus, was ravaging Syria and was compelling or subverting the cities there to transfer their allegiance, he sent his son Demetrius to oppose him. Demetrius was then only twenty-two years of age, and now found himself for the first time on trial as the supreme commander of an expedition in which great interests were at stake. In the event his youth and inexperience proved no match for an opponent who had been trained in the school of Alexander, and who had since fought many great campaigns on his own account. Demetrius was crushingly defeated near the city of Gaza, five thousand of his men were killed, eight thousand taken prisoner, and he lost his tent, his money and all his personal possessions. Ptolemy returned all these to him, together with his friends and added the courteous and humane message that they were not engaged in a struggle for life or death, but only for honour and power. Demetrius accepted this generous gesture: at the same time he uttered a prayer to the gods that he should not remain long in Ptolemy's debt, but should soon repay him in like fashion. He did not allow the disaster to cast him down, as if he were a boy who had received a check at the beginning of his first campaign, but behaved like an experienced general who has known all the vicissitudes of fortune. He promptly occupied himself with enrolling new troops, preparing fresh supplies of arms, keeping the cities firmly in hand, and training his recruits.

6. When the news of the battle reached Antigonus, he remarked that Ptolemy had so far conquered beardless youths,[2] but would now have to fight with grown men: but he was anxious not to crush or humble the spirit of his son and so he granted the young man's request to be

1. In the spring of 312 B.C.
2. The competitors at Greek athletic contests were divided into three classes, boys, beardless youths and men.

allowed to fight again on his own account. Soon after this Cilles, one of Ptolemy's generals, arrived in Syria. He brought with him a splendidly equipped army, he regarded Demetrius with contempt because of his earlier defeat, and his intention was to drive him out of the province altogether. But Demetrius launched a sudden attack and achieved complete surprise. He routed Cilles' troops, and seized his camp, generals and all, capturing seven thousand prisoners and a vast quantity of treasure. Demetrius was delighted at this success, not so much for what he had acquired as for what he could give back, and he prized the victory less for the glory and the spoils he had won than for the power it gave him to repay Ptolemy's generosity and return the favours he had received. However he did not take this action on his own responsibility, but wrote first to his father. When Antigonus granted him permission to dispose of the spoils as he pleased, he loaded Cilles and his companions with gifts and sent them back to Ptolemy. This reverse drove Ptolemy out of Syria and brought Antigonus down from Celaenae. He was overjoyed at the victory and eager to see the son who had won it.

7. After this Demetrius' next mission was to subdue the Arab tribe known as the Nabataeans,[1] and in this campaign he ran great dangers by marching through completely waterless country, but by his cool and resolute leadership he so overawed the barbarians that he captured from them seven hundred camels and great quantities of booty and returned in safety.

Some years before this Seleucus[2] had been driven out his capital of Babylon by Antigonus, but he had later won back the province and re-established his authority there. He now made an expedition to the east with the intention of annexing the tribes living on the borders of India and the provinces in the neighbourhood of Mount Caucasus. So Demetrius, calculating that he would find Mesopotamia undefended, suddenly crossed the Euphrates and made a surprise attack on Babylon. He captured one of the two citadels of the capital, drove out

1. The Nabataeans occupied a region in Arabia Petraea south of Petra and east of the Gulf of Aqaba.

2. Seleucus (c. 356–281 B.C.), the founder of the Seleucid dynasty, had accompanied Alexander to Asia and distinguished himself in the expedition to India. He became governor of the province of Babylonia in 321 and was driven out of it in 316. He then took refuge with Ptolemy, returning to Babylon in 312.

the garrison left by Seleucus and replaced it with a force of seven thousand of his own troops. Then he gave orders to his soldiers to seize and plunder everything that they could carry or drive out of the country and marched back to the coast. But in the event his action only left Seleucus more firmly established in possession of his kingdom than before, for by ravaging the country he appeared to admit that it no longer belonged to him and his father. Then as Demetrius was returning through Syria, he learned that Ptolemy had laid siege to Halicarnassus, whereupon he swiftly marched to the city and relieved it.

8. This feat won great renown for Demetrius and Antigonus and fired them with the inspiring ambition to restore freedom to the whole of Greece, which had been deprived of its liberty by the rule of Cassander and Ptolemy. None of the kings who succeeded Alexander ever waged a nobler or a juster war than this, for Demetrius now took the huge quantities of treasure which they had amassed from their victories over the barbarians and devoted it for their own honour and good name to the cause of delivering the Greeks. They decided to begin their campaign by sailing against Athens, whereupon one of Antigonus' friends remarked that if they captured the city they must keep possession of it, since it was the gangway that led to all the rest of Greece. But Antigonus would not hear of this. He declared that he needed no better or steadier gangway than a people's goodwill, that Athens was the watch-tower of the whole world, and that through her reputation she would swiftly beacon forth his deeds to all mankind.

So Demetrius sailed to Athens with a fleet of two hundred and fifty ships and five thousand talents. The city was at this time governed by Demetrius of Phaleron as Cassander's deputy, and a force of Macedonians was garrisoned in Munychia. Demetrius arrived on the twenty-fifth day of the month Thargelion,[1] and through a combination of good fortune and good management his approach took his opponents completely by surprise. When his ships were first sighted off the coast, everybody took them for Ptolemy's fleet and prepared to receive them. Then at last the generals discovered their mistake and hurried down to the shore, where all was tumult and confusion, as is natural when men suddenly find themselves obliged to repel a sur-

1. May–June 307 B.C.

prise landing. For Demetrius, as he found the entrances to the harbours undefended, sailed straight in, and was soon in full view of the Athenians on the deck of his ship: he then signalled to the citizens to be quiet and allow him a hearing. When silence had been restored, he ordered a herald standing by his side to announce that he had been sent by his father on what he prayed would prove a happy mission for the Athenians, for his orders were to set the city free, to expel the garrison and to restore to the people the use of their laws and their ancestral constitution.

9. When they heard this proclamation, most of the Athenians immediately threw down their shields at their feet and burst into applause. Then with loud cheers they called upon Demetrius to land, acclaiming him as their benefactor and saviour. The supporters of Demetrius of Phalerum decided that they must at all events receive the conqueror, even if he did not fulfil any of his promises, but they also sent a delegation to beg for his protection. Demetrius received the envoys courteously and sent back with them one of his father's friends, Aristodemus of Miletus. Demetrius of Phalerum was an Athenian, and the political changes which he expected would follow made him more frightened of his fellow countrymen than of the invader. Demetrius the Macedonian took note of this, and because he admired his opponent's courage and reputation, he granted his request to be sent under safe conduct to Thebes. As for himself, he declared that although he was eager to see the city, he would not do so until he had completed its deliverance by expelling the garrison. He then surrounded the fortress of Munychia with a trench and a palisade, thus cutting off its communications with the rest of the city, and sailed against Megara, where Cassander had also stationed a garrison.

Soon after this he heard news of Cratesipolis, a famous beauty who had been the wife of Polyperchon's son Alexander. It seemed that she was living at Patrae and would be glad to pay him a visit, and so he left his army in the territory of Megara and set off across country, taking only a few lightly armed attendants with him. When he reached the meeting place, he had his tent pitched apart from his guard, so that Cratesipolis could visit him unobserved. Some of the enemy discovered this and made a sudden attack on his camp. In his alarm he only had time to snatch up a shabby cloak and run for his life. In this disguise he made his escape, but through his inability to control his passion he narrowly avoided being ignominiously captured, and the enemy seized his tent and possessions and carried them off.

When Megara was captured and Demetrius' troops were about to plunder the city, the Megarians were only saved from this fate because the people of Athens pleaded strongly on their behalf. Demetrius then expelled the Macedonian garrison and gave the city its freedom. While he was engaged in these operations, he remembered Stilpo the philosopher, a man who had become famous because he had chosen a life of tranquillity and study. Demetrius sent for him and asked whether any man had robbed him of anything. 'No,' replied Stilpo, 'I have seen nobody carrying away any knowledge.' However the soldiers had carried off almost all the slaves in Megara and so when Demetrius once more paid his respects to Stilpo and remarked, as he was about to take his departure, 'I leave this a city of free men, Stilpo!', the philosopher retorted, 'You may say that indeed, for you have not left a single one of our slaves.'

10. Demetrius then returned to Munychia, encamped before it, drove out the garrison and demolished the fortress. Then at last, having fulfilled his promise, he accepted the pressing invitation of the Athenians and made his entry into the city. Here he called the people together and formally restored to them their ancestral constitution. He also promised that his father would supply one hundred and fifty thousand bushels of wheat and enough timber to build a fleet of a hundred triremes. It was by then fourteen years since the Athenians had been deprived of their democratic constitution, and in the intervening period since the Lamian war and the battle of Crannon[1] they had in theory been governed by an oligarchy but in practice by a single man, because of the continuously growing power of Demetrius of Phalerum.

The benefactions which Demetrius[2] had lavished on the Athenians had made his name great and glorious, but the people themselves now began to make it obnoxious by the extravagance of the honours which they voted him. For example they were the first people in the world to confer upon Antigonus and Demetrius the title of king. Both men had hitherto made it a matter of piety to decline this appellation, for they regarded it as the one royal honour which was still reserved for the lineal descendants of Philip and Alexander and

1. 322 B.C. See *Life of Phocion*, chs. 23 & 26.   2. The Macedonian.

which it would be wrong for others to assume or share. The Athenians were also the only people who described them as saviour-gods, and they even abolished the ancient office of the archon, from whom the year received its name, and elected in his place a priest to officiate at the altar of the saviour-gods. They also decreed that the figures of Demetrius and Antigonus should be woven into the sacred robe of Athene, together with those of the other gods.[1] They consecrated the spot where Demetrius had first alighted from his chariot and built an altar there, which was known as the altar of the Descending Demetrius. Besides this they created two new tribes and named them Demetrias and Antigonis, and in consequence raised the number of senators from five hundred to six hundred, since each tribe supplies fifty.

11. It was a man named Stratocles who had been the initiator of these extravagant and sophisticated forms of flattery, but the most preposterous of his ideas was the proposal that any envoys sent to Antigonus or Demetrius by public decree or at the public expense should be referred to not as ambassadors but as sacred deputies, in the same way as the envoys who conveyed the traditional sacrifices on behalf of the various cities to the great Hellenic festivals at Olympia and at Delphi. In other respects too this Stratocles was a man of extraordinary effrontery. He lived a shamelessly debauched life and through his buffoonery and scurrilous behaviour he had come to be regarded as a deliberate imitator of the kind of familiarity with which Cleon had treated the people.[2] He kept a mistress named Phylacion, and one day when she had bought some brains and neck-bones in the market-place for their dinner, he said to her, 'Ah, I see you have bought me the very things that we politicians play ball with!' On another occasion when the Athenians had suffered a defeat in a naval battle off Amorgos,[3] Stratocles hurried to the city before the news of the disaster had arrived. He then put on a garland and drove through the Cerameicus and after announcing that a victory had been won, he proposed a sacrifice to the gods and had meat distributed at the public

1. Every fifth year at the Panathenaic festival a sacred robe was carried in procession and deposited in the Parthenon. It was embroidered with the exploits of Athena and her fellow Olympians.
2. See *The Rise and Fall of Athens, Life of Nicias*, chs. 7–8.
3. 322 B.C. The Athenians were beaten by a Macedonian fleet.

expense to all the tribes. A little later when the sailors returned bringing back the wrecks from the battle and the people angrily called him to account for his deception, he faced their clamour with his usual impudence and asked them, 'What harm have I done if for two days you have been happy?' Such was the audacity of Stratocles.

12. However there are some things even hotter than fire, as Aristophanes puts it,[1] and there was another Athenian whose servility eclipsed even that of Stratocles. This man proposed that whenever Demetrius visited Athens he should be received with the same divine honours that were paid to Demeter and Dionysus, and that whichever citizen surpassed the rest in the magnificence and lavishness of his arrangements for the festival should be granted a sum of money from the public treasury to enable him to dedicate an offering. Finally the Athenians changed the name of the month Munychion to Demetrion, gave the name of Demetrion to the odd day which falls between the end of the old month and the beginning of the new, and re-named the festival of the Dionysia the Demetria. Most of these innovations were greeted with signs of displeasure from the gods. The sacred robe, in which it had been decreed that the figures of Antigonus and Demetrius should be woven beside those of Zeus and Athena, was struck by a violent gust of wind[2] as it was being carried in procession through the midst of Cerameicus, and was torn in pieces: great quantities of hemlock suddenly sprang up around the altars of the so-called saviour gods, although there are many parts of the country in which this poisonous herb does not grow at all: on the day of the celebration of the Dionysia the sacred procession had to be cancelled because of a sudden spell of cold weather which arrived out of season, and this was followed by a heavy frost, which not only blasted all the vines and fig-trees but destroyed most of the corn in the blade. It was for this reason that Philippides, who was an enemy of Stratocles, attacked him in a comedy with these verses

> It was through him that frost attacked the vines,
> Through his impiety the robe was rent,
> Because he would bestow on mortal men
> The honours that belong to gods alone:
> Such acts destroy a people, not its comedy.

1. *Knights*, 382.
2. The robe was spread like a sail on the mast of the processional ship at the Panathenaic festival.

This Philippides was a friend of Lysimachus and on his account the Athenians received many favours from the king. He even believed that it was a good omen if he were to meet or catch sight of Philippides at the start of any expedition or enterprise. Besides this Philippides enjoyed a good reputation, since he was no busybody and had none of the self-important habits of a courtier. One day Lysimachus wished to do him a kindness and asked him, 'Philippides, which of my possessions shall I give you?' 'Whichever you please, sire,' he replied, 'but not one of your secrets.' I have purposely made a comparison of this man with Stratocles, in order to contrast the man of the theatre with the man of the hustings.

13. But the strangest and most exaggerated of all the honours devised for Demetrius was the one proposed by Dromoclides of Sphettus. This man, when the question arose concerning the consecration of certain shields at Delphi, put down a motion that the people should obtain an oracular response from Demetrius. I reproduce the actual words of the motion, which read as follows.

May it be propitious.[1] It has been decreed by the people that they shall elect one man from the Athenians, who shall go to the saviour-god, and after he has sacrificed and obtained good omens, shall inquire of the saviour-god what is the most reverent, decorous and expeditious manner in which the people may ensure the restitution of the intended offerings to their proper places. And whatsoever answer he shall please to give them, the people shall comply with it.

By such absurd flattery, they completely turned Demetrius' head, which even before was not as sound as it should have been.

14. During the months which he spent in Athens at this time, he married a widow named Eurydice. She was descended from the famous Miltiades, the hero of Marathon, had married Ophelas, the king of Cyrene, and after his death had returned to Athens. The Athenians chose to regard this marriage as a special mark of favour and as an honour to their city. But in general Demetrius was very free in his attitude towards marriage, and had many wives at the same time. Among these the one who enjoyed most respect and honour was Phila: she owed her privileged position to the fact that she was the daughter of Antipater and had been married to Craterus, the man

1. A pious formula, prefixed to official documents.

who of all the successors of Alexander had been remembered with the greatest affection by the Macedonians. Antigonus had persuaded Demetrius to marry her when he was quite young, in spite of her being considerably older, and it is said that when Demetrius expressed his reluctance, his father whispered in his ear Euripides' words

> Where it is profitable, a man should marry
> Even against his nature.[1]

He substituted the word 'marry' for 'serve', as the verse was originally phrased. But such regard as Demetrius showed for Phila or the rest of his wives did not prevent him from keeping many mistresses, not only courtesans, but women of free birth, and in this respect he had the worst reputation of all the rulers of his time.

15. Soon after this[2] his father sent for him to take command of the operations against Ptolemy with the object of capturing Cyprus. Demetrius had no choice but to obey the order, but he was most unwilling to abandon the campaign he had undertaken for the liberation of Greece, which he regarded as a nobler and more glorious enterprise. He therefore offered a sum of money to Cleonides, Ptolemy's general who commanded the troops garrisoning Sicyon and Corinth, to evacuate the cities and set them free. But Cleonides refused the bribe and so Demetrius hurriedly put to sea and, gathering reinforcements on his way, brought his fleet to Cyprus. There he attacked Menelaus, Ptolemy's brother, and immediately defeated him. Soon afterwards Ptolemy himself appeared on the scene with a large fleet and army, and the two commanders exchanged haughty and threatening messages. Ptolemy called upon Demetrius to sail away before he concentrated all his forces and crushed him, while Demetrius offered to allow Ptolemy to withdraw from Cyprus, on condition that he surrendered Corinth and Sicyon. The battle which then followed was of the greatest moment, not only to the combatants themselves but to all the other rulers of the eastern Mediterranean, for apart from the uncertainty of the outcome, they believed that the prize was not merely the possession of Cyprus and Syria, but an absolute supremacy over all their rivals.

16. Ptolemy advanced to the attack with a fleet of a hundred and fifty sail and ordered Menelaus to move out of Salamis with a detachment

1. *Phoenissae*, 396.   2. 306 B.C.

of sixty vessels at the moment when the battle was at its height, so as to fall upon Demetrius' fleet from the rear and throw it into disorder. Demetrius detached no more than ten ships to oppose Menelaus' sixty, since these were enough to block the narrow channel which led out of the harbour. He then deployed his land forces in extended order along various headlands which jutted out into the water, and put to sea with a hundred and eighty ships. He bore down upon the opposing fleet with great speed and dash and utterly routed Ptolemy, who after his defeat fled with a squadron of eight ships. This was all that remained of his fleet: of the rest, some had been sunk in the battle and seventy had been captured, crews and all. At the same time the whole of Ptolemy's enormous train of attendants, friends and women who had been embarked in transports near his fleet, all fell into Demetrius' hands: so too did all his arms, money and engines of war. Demetrius rounded up the entire expedition and escorted it to his camp. Among these prizes of war was the celebrated Lamia, who had first won fame for her skill as a flute-player and had later become renowned as a courtesan. By this time her beauty was on the wane and Demetrius was many years her junior: in spite of this her charm took possession of him to such an extent that although many other women had a passion for him, he had no passion save for her.

After the battle Menelaus offered no further resistance, but surrendered Salamis to Demetrius together with his land forces of twelve thousand infantry and twelve hundred horse.

17. Demetrius added more lustre to his brilliant victory by the generosity and humanity which he showed to his opponents: he not only buried the enemy's dead with full honours but he also set his prisoners free. He then chose twelve hundred complete suits of armour from the spoils and presented them to the Athenians.

He sent Aristodemus of Miletus as his personal messenger to carry the news of the victory to his father. Of all those in Demetrius' entourage this man was the arch-flatterer and on this occasion he set out, it seems, to crown his achievement and surpass any of his previous efforts. After he had made the crossing from Cyprus, he would not allow the ship to approach the land. Instead he ordered the crew to cast anchor and to remain quietly on board, while he had himself rowed ashore in a small boat and landed alone. Then he continued his journey to Antigonus, who was awaiting the news of the battle in a state of suspense and with all the anxiety which is natural to a man who is contending for such high stakes. When he heard that Aristodemus was on his way his agitation reached such a pitch that he could scarcely keep himself indoors, but sent servants and friends one after the other to discover from Aristodemus what had happened. Aristodemus refused to utter a word to anybody, but walked on in complete silence, keeping a measured pace and wearing a grave expression on his face. By this time Antigonus was thoroughly alarmed and could bear the suspense no longer; he came to the door to meet Aristodemus, and found him accompanied by a large crowd which was hastening to the palace. At last when Aristodemus was near enough, he stretched out his hand and cried in a loud voice, 'Hail, King Antigonus, we have defeated Ptolemy in a sea battle. We are the masters of Cyprus and we have taken sixteen thousand, eight hundred prisoners.' Antigonus replied, 'Hail to you likewise, by Zeus. But I shall punish you for torturing us for so long. You can wait a while for the reward for your good news.'

18. After this success the people for the first time acclaimed Antigonus and Demetrius as kings. Antigonus was immediately crowned, and Demetrius received a diadem from his father with a letter addressing him as king. At the same time when the news reached Ptolemy's followers in Egypt, they also conferred the title of king on him, so as not to appear unduly cast down by their defeat, and this spirit of rivalry proved infectious among the other successors of Alexander. Lysimachus began to wear a diadem, and Seleucus who had already assumed royal prerogatives when he gave audience to the barbarians, now adopted the same practice in his interviews with Greeks. Cassander, however, although others addressed him as king both in letters and in speech continued to sign letters with his own name, as he had always done.

The assumption of these dignities meant something more than the mere addition of a name or a change in appearance. It stirred the spirits of these men, raised their ideas to a different plane and introduced an element of pride and self-importance into their daily lives and their dealings with others, in the same way as tragic actors, when they put on royal robes, alter their gait, their voice, their deportment and their mode of address. As a result they also became harsher in their administration of justice, and they cast off the various disguises whereby they had previously concealed their power and which had made them treat their subjects more gently and tolerantly. Such was the effect of a single word from a flatterer, which in this way brought about a revolution throughout the world.

19. Antigonus, elated by his son's achievements in Cyprus, immediately launched another expedition against Ptolemy.[1] He himself took command of the land forces, while Demetrius in charge of the fleet supported his operations from the sea. The outcome of the campaign was foretold to Medius, a friend of Antigonus, in his sleep. He dreamed that Antigonus together with the whole army was running in a race in the stadium. Over the first part of the course he ran strongly and swiftly, but then little by little his strength failed him: then after he had rounded the half-way mark, he became weak, began to pant heavily and could barely finish the race. As events turned out, Antigonus encountered many difficulties on land while Demetrius ran into a violent storm and heavy seas, and was driven on to a rocky shore which offered no shelter. In the end he lost many of his ships and returned home without having accomplished anything.

Antigonus was almost eighty years old and by this time it was his corpulence and weight even more than his age which incapacitated him for playing an active part in military operations. He therefore made more and more use of his son, for Demetrius with the help of experience combined with good luck was now conducting the greatest enterprises with success, and neither his luxury nor his extravagance nor his drinking habits troubled his father. The fact was that in peace time Demetrius threw himself headlong into these excesses and devoted his time exclusively to the pursuit of pleasure in the most abandoned and wanton fashion, yet in time of war he was as sober as those to whom abstinence was the natural way of life. There is a story that when Demetrius was completely under the spell of Lamia, a fact which had become common knowledge, he returned home from abroad and greeted his father with a kiss: Antigonus laughed and said, 'Anybody would think, my boy, that you were kissing Lamia.' On another occasion when Demetrius had been drinking for several days continuously, he excused his absence by saying that he had been laid up with a severe cold. 'So I heard,' remarked

1. In the same year, 306 B.C.: the intention was to invade Egypt.

Antigonus, 'but did your cold come from Chios or from Thasos?'[1] Another time after hearing that his son was sick, Antigonus went to visit him and met one of his beautiful mistresses coming away from his room. Antigonus went inside, sat down by his side, and felt his pulse. 'The fever has left me now,' Demetrius told him, 'Yes, so I see,' his father replied, 'I met it just now as it was going away.' Antigonus was willing to indulge these faults in his son because of his achievements in other respects. The Scythians have a custom of twanging their bow-strings in the midst of their drinking and carousing, as though they were summoning back their courage at the moment when it melts away in pleasure. Demetrius on the other hand was in the habit of surrendering his whole being, now to pleasure and now to action: he succeeded in keeping the two spheres completely separate and never allowed his diversions to interfere with his preparations for war.

20. As a general he had the reputation of being more effective in preparing an army than in handling it. He insisted on being abundantly supplied for every eventuality, he had an insatiable ambition to embark upon larger and larger projects, whether in shipbuilding or the construction of siege engines, and he took an intense pleasure in watching the working of these creations. He had a good natural intelligence and a speculative mind and he did not apply his talents to mere pastimes or useless diversions, like some other kings, who played the flute or painted or worked in metal. Aeropus the king of Macedonia, for example, used to devote his leisure to making little tables or lampstands. Attalus Philometer made a hobby of cultivating poisonous herbs, not only henbane or hellebore but also hemlock, aconite, or dorycnium. He used to sow and plant these in the royal gardens, and he made it his business to know their various juices and fruits and to gather them at the proper season. The kings of Parthia in the same way used to pride themselves on notching and sharpening with their own hands the points of their spears and arrows. But when Demetrius played the workman he did it in regal fashion. He approached his projects on a grand scale and his creations were not only skilfully and inventively conceived, but they bore the marks of a lofty mind and purpose, so that men thought them worthy not only of the genius and wealth of a king but also of his handiwork. Their sheer size alarmed

1. Two islands famous for their wine.

even his friends, while their beauty delighted even his enemies, and this description is true and not merely elegantly phrased. His enemies would stand on the shore and gape in wonder at his galleys of fifteen or sixteen banks of oars as they sailed past, while his 'city-takers', as events actually testify, were a spectacle to the inhabitants of the towns he besieged. For example Lysimachus, who was the bitterest of Demetrius' enemies among the kings of his time, came to try to raise the town of Soli in Cilicia which Demetrius was besieging, and sent a message asking to be allowed to see his siege engines and his ships under sail: after Demetrius had displayed these to him he expressed his admiration and went away. Likewise the people of Rhodes, after they had resisted a long siege and had come to terms with Demetrius, asked him for some of his machines which they wished to keep as a memorial of his power and of their own courage.

21. Demetrius went to war with the people of Rhodes[1] because they were allies of Ptolemy and he moved up against their walls the great-est of his so-called 'city-takers'.[2] This was a siege tower with a square base, each side of which measured seventy-two feet at the bottom. It was ninety-nine feet high with the upper part tapering off to narrower dimensions. Inside it was divided into many separate storeys and com-partments, the side which faced the enemy being pierced with aper-tures on each storey through which missiles could be discharged, and it was manned with troops who were equipped with every kind of weapon. The machine never tottered or leaned in any direction, but rolled forwards firm and upright on its base, advancing with an even motion and with a noise and an impetus that inspired mingled feelings of alarm and delight in all who beheld it.

For this campaign Demetrius was sent two iron coats of mail from Cyprus,[3] each of which weighed only forty pounds. In order to demonstrate the armour's strength and power of resistance, Zoilus, the maker, had a bolt from a catapult shot at one of them at a range of twenty paces. The armour remained unbroken at the point of impact

1. 305–304 B.C.
2. Diodorus Siculus, xx, 92, records that the machine had nine storeys, rolled on four wheels each of them sixteen feet high, and was worked by 3,400 men.
3. According to Pliny Cyprus was famous for making supposedly impreg-nable coats of mail. Agamemnon had been sent such a cuirass by Cinyras, king of Cyprus (*Iliad* xi, 20).

and its surface showed nothing more than a small scratch such as might have been made by an engraver. Demetrius wore this suit himself and gave the other to Alcimus the Epirot, the man who combined the greatest physical strength and the most warlike spirit in his army, and the only one whose armour weighed nearly a hundred and twenty pounds, the others carrying only half this weight. Alcimus was later killed at Rhodes in the fighting near the theatre.

22. The Rhodians defended their city with great courage and Demetrius achieved no success worth mentioning against them. However he kept the siege going out of sheer vexation, because when his wife Phila despatched a ship carrying letters, bedding and clothing for him, the Rhodians captured the vessel and sent it with all its cargo to Ptolemy. In this matter they did not follow the civilized example set by the Athenians who, when Philip was at war with them, captured one of his messengers and read all the letters he was carrying except for one written by Olympias: this they did not open but returned to Philip with the seal unbroken. However although Demetrius was furious at the Rhodians' action, he did not stoop to retaliating against them when, a little later, he had the opportunity to do so. It happened that they had commissioned Protogenes of Caunus to paint a portrait of Ialysus and that this picture, which was almost finished, had been captured by Demetrius in one of the suburbs of the city. The Rhodians sent a herald and begged him to spare the painting and not destroy it, to which he replied that he would rather burn the statues of his father than a masterpiece which had cost so much labour, for Protogenes was reputed to have worked for seven years on the painting. Apelles tells us that when he first set eyes on it, he was so filled with admiration that he could not utter a word, and that when speech returned to him he exclaimed, 'A tremendous labour and a wonderful achievement,' but he added that it lacked something of the grace which raised his own paintings to the heavens. This picture later shared the fate of many other Greek works of art: it was taken to Rome, crowded into a general collection with many other Greek masterpieces, and destroyed by fire.[1]

The Rhodians continued to hold out vigorously and at last Demet-

---

1. Ialysus was one of the legendary heroes of Rhodes. The painting was brought to Rome by Cassius, the murderer of Julius Caesar, and placed in the Temple of Peace.

rius, who was anxious to find a pretext for abandoning the siege, was persuaded to make terms through the mediation of the Athenians: the treaty which they concluded stipulated that the Rhodians should act as the allies of Demetrius in his wars, but should not take up arms against Ptolemy.

23. Soon afterwards the Athenians appealed to Demetrius because their city was being besieged by Cassander, and Demetrius sailed to their rescue with a fleet of three hundred and thirty ships and a large land force. He not only drove Cassander out of Attica but pursued him as far as Thermopylae. There he routed Cassander's army, occupied Heracleia whose citizens came over to him, and was joined by six thousand Macedonians who had deserted from Cassander's army. On his return he freed the Greeks living south of Thermopylae from Macedonian rule, concluded an alliance with the Boeotians and captured Cenchreae. He also took possession of the strongholds of Phyle and Panactum, fortresses in Attica which had been garrisoned by Cassander and restored them to the Athenians. It might have been thought that the people of Athens had exhausted all the honours which could possibly be bestowed upon Demetrius during his earlier stay, but they went on to show that they could still invent new forms of flattery. They gave him the rear part of the temple of the Parthenon for his quarters, and there he lodged throughout his visit. He was entertained, so the arrangement implied, by his hostess Athena, but it could not be said that he was a well-behaved guest or that he conducted himself under her roof with the decorum that is due to a virgin-goddess. There is a story that on an earlier occasion when Antigonus had learned that Demetrius' brother Philip was billeted in a house which was occupied by three girls, he had said nothing to Philip but sent for the officer responsible for requisitioning houses and told him, 'I suggest that you find less crowded quarters for my son.'

24. Demetrius affected to call Athena his elder sister,[1] and for this reason, if for no other, he ought at least to have shown her respect. But in fact he filled her temple with so many outrages committed against the persons of free-born youths and Athenian women that the place was considered to be unusually pure when he was content to live there with well-known courtesans such as Chrysis, Lamia, Demo

    1. Because the Athenians had given him the title of Saviour-god.

and Anticrya. For the sake of the city's good name I shall not enter into the details of Demetrius' other debaucheries, but it would be wrong to pass over the virtue and modesty of a boy named Democles. He was young and was known as Democles the Beautiful: indeed the epithet betrayed him, since reports of his good looks soon reached the ears of Demetrius. Democles refused the advances of many who tried to win him by persuasion or gifts or threats, and finally stopped appearing at the public wrestling schools or gymnasia and used only a private bath. Demetrius watched his opportunity and one day surprised him there alone. When the boy saw that there was no one to help him and that he had no choice but to yield, he snatched the lid off the cauldron, leaped into the boiling water and killed himself. In this way he suffered a fate which was certainly undeserved but he showed a spirit which was worthy both of his personal beauty and of his country. His behaviour may be contrasted with that of Cleaenetus the son of Cleomedon. This man's father had been sentenced to pay the sum of fifty talents, and in the attempt to obtain a letter from Demetrius remitting the fine he not only disgraced himself, but caused great trouble to the city. The people excused Cleomedon from this penalty, but they also passed a resolution that no citizen should ever again bring a letter from Demetrius before the assembly. Demetrius was furious when he heard the news, whereupon the people took fright and not only rescinded the motion but actually put to death some of those who had introduced and supported it and banished others. They even went so far as to pass a further decree to the effect that whatever thing Demetrius might command in future should be regarded as holy in the sight of the gods and just towards all men. One of the better class of citizens remarked on this occasion that Stratocles was mad to propose such a motion, to which Demochares of Leuconoe replied that he would certainly be mad if he did not show this kind of madness, for Stratocles was amply rewarded for his flattery. Demochares, on the other hand, was publicly charged for this utterance and sent into exile. Such was the fate of the Athenians, who fondly imagined that because they had got rid of the occupying garrison they had become a free people.

25. Demetrius next marched into the Peloponnese,[1] where not one of his enemies opposed him, but all abandoned their cities and fled. He

1. In 303 B.C.

accepted the allegiance of the eastern part of the coast, which is known as Aete, and of the region of Arcadia with the exception of Mantinea and liberated the cities of Argos, Sicyon and Corinth by paying to their garrisons a hundred talents to evacuate them. It happened that at Argos the festival of Hera was being held and Demetrius presided over the games, joined in the celebration of the festival with the Greeks who had gathered there, and married Deidamia, who was the daughter of Aeacides the king of the Molossians and the sister of Pyrrhus of Epirus. He told the inhabitants of Sicyon that their city was sited in the wrong place and persuaded them to move to the ground which it now occupies, and he also had its name changed and styled Demetrias instead of Sicyon.

A little later a general assembly of the city-states was held at the Isthmus of Corinth, which was attended by a huge concourse of delegates. Here Demetrius was proclaimed commander-in-chief of the Greeks, as Philip and Alexander had been before him, and in the elation of success and of the power which he enjoyed at that moment he could even consider himself their superior. In one respect at least he outdid Alexander, for the latter never deprived other kings of their royal title, nor did he proclaim himself King of Kings, although many other rulers received their style and position from him. Demetrius on the other hand mocked and ridiculed those who gave the title of king to anybody other than his father and himself, and at his drinking parties it flattered his vanity to hear the guests propose toasts to himself as king, but to Seleucus as master of the elephants, Ptolemy as admiral, Lysimachus as treasurer, and Agathocles the Sicilian as lord of the islands. The other kings when they heard of these affectations merely laughed at Demetrius, but Lysimachus was enraged at the idea that Demetrius regarded him as a eunuch, because it was the general custom to appoint eunuchs to the post of treasurer. In fact it was Lysimachus who of all these rulers felt the bitterest hatred for Demetrius, and on one occasion when he was sneering at his rival's passion for Lamia, he remarked that this was the first time he had ever seen a whore take part in a tragedy, to which Demetrius retorted that his mistress was a more modest woman than Lysimachus' consort Penelope.

26. When Demetrius was preparing to return to Athens from the Peloponnese, he wrote to inform the people that he wished to be

initiated into the Mysteries as soon as he arrived, and to be admitted to every one of the various grades in the ceremony, from the lowest to the highest, which were known as the *Epoptica*. This request was both unprecedented and unlawful, since the lesser rites were enacted in the month of Anthesterion and the greater in Boedromion. But when Demetrius' letter was read out, the only man who dared to refuse his request was Pythodorus the torch-bearer, and his opposition achieved nothing. Instead a motion was proposed by Stratocles that the current month which happened to be Munychion should be declared to be Anthisterion, and during this period the lesser rites were performed for Demetrius at Agrae. Next the month of Munychion was again changed and this time became Boedromion, during which Demetrius passed through the remaining rites of initiation, and was admitted to the highest grade of *Epoptos*. It was for this reason that Philippides poured scorn on Stratocles as the man who

> Crowded the whole year into a single month

and referred to the quartering in the Parthenon of Demetrius

> Who treated the Acropolis as his inn
> And used the temple of the virgin-goddess
> As lodgings for his mistresses.

27. Of all the many outrages and abuses which Demetrius committed at this time, the one that most angered the Athenians was his action in commanding them to levy immediately the sum of two hundred and fifty talents for his services. The money was then extorted from the people in the harshest and most peremptory fashion, and when he saw the amount that had been raised, he ordered it to be given to Lamia and his other mistresses to buy soap and cosmetics. What the Athenians resented was not so much the loss of the money as the humiliation of this imposition and the words which accompanied it, although according to some accounts it was not they but the people of Thessaly who were treated in this fashion. Apart from this episode, Lamia also extorted money from many of the citizens when she was preparing to entertain Demetrius, and indeed the extravagance of this banquet became so legendary that it was described in full by Lynceus of Samos; it was for this reason that one of the comic poets wittily described Lamia as a 'city-taker' in herself, and Demochares of Soli

called Demetrius *Mythos* or *Fable*, because he too, like the fable, had his Lamia.[1]

Demetrius' passion for Lamia and the favours which he lavished on her roused the enmity and animosity not only of his other wives but of his friends. For example he once sent some ambassadors to Lysimachus, and one day when they were at leisure the king showed them a number of deep scars on his thighs and shoulders which had been made by a lion's claws, and told them of the battle he had fought with the beast when Alexander had shut him up in a cage with it. The ambassadors laughed and declared that their own king also carried on his neck the marks of a terrible wild beast, a Lamia. The wonder was that Demetrius, who in the beginning had found fault with Phila because she was older than himself, should now be captivated by Lamia and love her so long when she was well past her prime. At any rate one evening when Lamia had been playing the flute at a banquet, Demetrius asked the courtesan Demo, who was surnamed Mania, what she thought of her. 'Your majesty,' she replied, 'I think she is an old woman.' Another time when some sweetmeats had been placed on the table, Demetrius remarked to Mania, 'You see how many presents Lamia sends me?' 'My mother,' answered Mania, 'will send you many more if you will sleep with her.'

Another story has come down to us of what Lamia had to say about the celebrated judgement of Bocchoris. An Egyptian fell in love with Thonis the courtesan, who asked him for a large sum of money in return for her favours. Afterwards he dreamed that he had enjoyed her, and his passion for her then died away. At this Thonis brought an action against him for the payment which she claimed was her due. When he had heard the case, Bocchoris ordered the defendant to bring into court in its coffer the exact amount of money which had been demanded from him, and to move it backwards and forwards with his hand: meanwhile the courtesan was to clutch at its shadow, since the thing which is imagined is the shadow of the reality. Lamia thought this judgement unjust, because although the young man's dream had delivered him from his passion, the shadow of the money did not deliver the courtesan from her desire for it. So much then for Lamia.

1. A legendary queen of Libya who, in revenge for the loss of her own children, was reputed to have had those of other women brought for her to devour. The name has been conjectured to be derived from the Phoenician word *lahama*, to devour.

28. And now our story, as it traces the fortunes and achievements of my subject, moves from the comic to the tragic stage. All the other kings at this point[1] formed an alliance against Antigonus and combined their forces. Demetrius sailed away from Greece to join him, and was greatly heartened to find his father full of resolution for the war, and buoyed up by a spirit that belied his years. And yet it seems probable that if only Antigonus could have made some small concessions and curbed his passion for extending his rule, he could have retained his supremacy among the successors of Alexander and bequeathed it to his son. But he was by nature imperious and disdainful of others and as overbearing in his words as in his actions, and he therefore exasperated many young and powerful men and provoked them to act against him: he boasted that he would scatter the alliance they had formed with a single stone and a single shout, as easily as one scares away a flock of birds from a field.

Antigonus took the field with more than seventy thousand infantry, ten thousand cavalry and seventy-five elephants, while his opponents had sixty-four thousand infantry, five hundred more cavalry, four hundred elephants and a hundred and twenty war chariots. But once Antigonus had drawn near the enemy, a change in his demeanour became noticeable, not in his resolution, but rather in his presentiments. In the past it had been his custom to show a lofty and aggressive spirit before he went into action; he would speak in a loud voice and use arrogant language, and often by uttering some casual joke or piece of mockery when the enemy was close at hand, he would reveal his own assurance and the contempt he felt for his opponent. But this time he was observed to be thoughtful and silent for the most part. He presented his son to the army and formally pronounced him to be his successor, but what astonished everybody most of all was that he now held a long conference alone in his tent with Demetrius, whereas it had never been his practice in the past to enter into secret consultations even with his son. Instead he had always relied upon his own judgement, formed his own plans, and issued his orders openly. At any rate there is a story that when Demetrius was still only a boy he had asked his father at what hour he intended to break camp, to which Antigonus retorted roughly, 'Why, are you afraid that you will be the only man who does not hear the trumpet?'

1. 302 B.C.

29. On this occasion they were also disheartened by threatening omens. Demetrius dreamed that Alexander appeared before him in shining armour and asked him what would be their watchword for the battle. Demetrius told him, 'Zeus and victory', whereupon Alexander replied, 'In that case I shall go and join your adversaries: they will certainly receive me,' for he was offended to find that Antigonus had not chosen 'Alexander and victory' for his watchword. Then while the phalanx was already forming in order of battle, Antigonus, as he stepped out of his tent, stumbled, fell on his face and hurt himself severely. When he rose to his feet, he stretched out his hands towards heaven and prayed that the gods should either grant him victory or else a painless death before his army was routed.

When the battle began,[1] Demetrius led his strongest and best squadrons of cavalry in a charge against Antiochus, Seleucus' son. He fought brilliantly and put the enemy to flight, but by pressing the pursuit too far and too impulsively he threw away the victory. The enemy placed their elephants in his way to block his return and he was prevented from rejoining the infantry: meanwhile Seleucus, seeing that his opponent's phalanx had been left unprotected by cavalry, altered his tactics accordingly. He did not actually launch a mounted attack, but by riding round Antigonus' infantry and continually threatening to charge, he kept them in a state of alarm and at the same time gave them the opportunity of changing sides. And this indeed was what finally happened, for a large group of them who had become separated from the main body came over to him of their own accord, and the rest were routed. Then as great numbers of the enemy bore down Antigonus, one of his attendants cried out, 'They are making for you, sire,' to which the king replied, 'Yes, what other object could they have? But Demetrius will come to our rescue.' In this hope he persisted to the last and kept looking for his son's approach on every side, until the enemy overwhelmed him with a cloud of javelins and he fell. The rest of his friends and attendants abandoned him, and only Thorax of Larissa remained by his body.

30. After the battle had been decided in this way, the victorious kings proceeded to carve up the realm which Antigonus and Demetrius had ruled like the carcass of some great slaughtered beast, each of them taking a limb and adding new provinces to those they already

1. Near the village of Ipsus in Phrygia, 301 B.C.

possessed. Demetrius got away with five thousand infantry and four thousand cavalry and marched straight to Ephesus. Here everybody supposed that as he needed money he would inevitably plunder the treasures of the temple of Artemis, but as he was afraid that the troops would do precisely this, he immediately left the city and sailed for Greece. He placed his remaining hopes principally in Athens, for he had left his wife there, together with his ships and his treasure, and he believed that his safest refuge in his misfortune lay in the goodwill of the Athenian people. But as he approached the Cyclades, he met a delegation from the city who requested him to keep away, since the people had passed a resolution not to admit any of the kings within their walls: at the same time they informed him that his wife Deidameia had been escorted to Megara with appropriate honours and ceremony. At this Demetrius, who had borne his other trials serenely and who despite the complete reversal in his fortunes had never behaved in a mean or ignoble fashion, was transported with rage and quite lost control of himself. He was cut to the heart at being unexpectedly disappointed and betrayed by the Athenians in this fashion, and at discovering that their apparent goodwill proved to be empty and false as soon as it was put to the test. And indeed it would seem that the bestowing of extravagant honours is really the least substantial proof of the goodwill of a people towards a ruler, for the true value of such tributes lies in the intentions of those who bestow them. They are worthless if they are prompted by fear, for an identical decree may equally well be passed out of motives of fear or of affection. Accordingly men of sense will consider first of all the substance of their actions and achievements, and only afterwards the statues, paintings or deifications which have been offered to them: they can then judge whether these can be trusted as genuine acts of homage or distrusted as obligatory ones, since it often happens that people in the very act of conferring honours will hate those who accept them arrogantly and without modesty or respect for the free will of the givers.

31. However this may be, Demetrius felt that he had been shamefully treated by the Athenians, but as he was powerless to avenge the affront, he sent them a message in which he courteously protested at their decision and requested that his ships should be returned to him, among them the vessel which had thirteen banks of oars. These were

duly handed over to him and he then sailed for the Isthmus of Corinth, where he found that his affairs had greatly deteriorated. Everywhere his garrisons were being expelled from the towns in which he had stationed them and the whole region was going over to his enemies. He therefore left Pyrrhus of Epirus to act as his lieutenant in Greece, while he himself put to sea and sailed for the Thracian Chersonese. There he plundered the territory of Lysimachus and out of the spoils he collected was able to maintain and hold together his army, which was now beginning to recover its spirits, and to build up a force of formidable strength. In the meanwhile the other kings made no attempt to help Lysimachus: they considered that he was by no means more reasonable than Demetrius, and that because he possessed more power, he was more to be feared.

Not long after this Seleucus approached Demetrius to ask for the hand of Stratonice, who was his daughter by Phila. He already had one son Antiochus by his Persian wife, Apame, but he considered that his empire had room in it for more than one heir, and he was anxious to form an alliance with Demetrius because he saw that Lysimachus had already married one of Ptolemy's daughters himself and had taken the other for his son Agathocles. For his part Demetrius regarded a marriage alliance with Seleucus as an unexpected stroke of good fortune, and so he took his daughter on board ship and sailed with his whole fleet to Syria. In the course of his voyage he was forced to touch at a number of places, and in particular he landed on the coast of Cilicia, a province ruled by Pleistarchus the brother of Cassander, who had been given it by the kings after their victory over Antigonus. Pleistarchus regarded Demetrius' arrival in his territory as a violation of his sovereignty: besides this he wished to protest to Seleucus against his having made an alliance with their common enemy without consulting the other kings, and so he went up to see him.

32. When Demetrius learned of this he marched inland to the city of Quinda. There he found twelve hundred talents of the public treasury still intact, a sum which had belonged to his father, and so he collected this, embarked without any hindrance, and quickly put to sea. His wife Phila had by then joined him and at Rhosus he met Seleucus. No sooner had the two men come together than they received one another in princely style without the least deception or

suspicion. First Seleucus gave a banquet for Demetrius in his camp, and then Demetrius in his turn received Seleucus on board his galley with the thirteen banks of oars. There were entertainments and the two rulers conversed at leisure and spent whole days in one another's company without either guards or arms, until at length Seleucus took Stratonice and escorted her in great state to Antioch. Demetrius then made himself master of Cilicia and sent his wife Phila to Cassander, who was also her brother, to answer the accusations which had been made against him by Pleistarchus. In the meanwhile his wife Deidameia, whom he had married at Argos, arrived by sea, but they had only been together for a short while before she fell sick and died. Then through Seleucus' good offices Demetrius was reconciled with Ptolemy, and it was arranged that he should marry the king's daughter, Ptolemais.

So far Seleucus had behaved with the utmost courtesy, but soon afterwards he requested Demetrius to cede Cilicia to him in return for a sum of money, and when Demetrius refused, he angrily insisted that Tyre and Sidon should be handed over to him. This seemed a violent and quite unjustifiable demand. Seleucus had become the ruler of the whole region from India to the coast of Syria. Why should he be so needy or so mean in spirit as to quarrel with a man who had just become related to him by marriage and who had suffered a great reversal in his fortunes, all for the sake of two cities? In short Seleucus was a conspicuous example of the wisdom that Plato showed when he argued that the man who wishes to be really rich should seek not to increase his possessions but to decrease his desires. He who can never restrain his avarice will never be free from the sense of poverty and want.

33. Demetrius on this occasion showed no lack of courage. He declared that even if he should lose ten thousand battles as great as that of Ipsus, he would never consent to pay for the privilege of having Seleucus as his son-in-law. In the meanwhile he strengthened the garrisons of Tyre and Sidon. About this time[1] he had news that Lachares had taken advantage of the civil dissensions which had occurred in Athens and made himself tyrant there, and Demetrius calculated that if he suddenly appeared on the scene he could take the

city with ease. He crossed the Aegean safely with a large fleet, but as he was sailing along the coast of Attica, he ran into a storm in which most of his ships were destroyed and a great number of his men were drowned. He himself escaped and opened a petty campaign against the Athenians, but when he found he was getting no results, he dispatched officers to assemble another fleet for him: meanwhile he marched into the Peloponnese and laid siege to the town of Messene. Here during an assault on the walls he was nearly killed, for he was struck in the face by a bolt from a catapult which pierced his jaw and entered his mouth. But he recovered from the wound, and after receiving the submission of a number of cities that had revolted from him, he again invaded Attica, captured Eleusis and Rhamnus and devastated the countryside. He also seized a ship loaded with grain that was bound for Athens, and hanged the pilot and the owner of the cargo. This action so frightened other vessels that they turned away from the city, which was reduced to a state of famine and a great shortage of other commodities. The price of a bushel of salt rose to forty drachmas and a peck of wheat to three hundred. The Athenians gained a short respite from their sufferings when a fleet of a hundred and fifty ships sent to help them by Ptolemy was sighted off the coast of Aegina. But then Demetrius was reinforced by a strong naval contingent from the Peloponnese and by another from Cyprus, so that he was able to concentrate a fleet of three hundred vessels. In consequence Ptolemy's ships hoisted sail, abandoned the city and made their escape.

34. Earlier the Athenians had passed a resolution decreeing the death penalty for anyone who even mentioned the possibility of negotiating a peace or an agreement with Demetrius, but now they opened the nearest gates and sent a delegation to his camp. They had been forced into this action by sheer destitution, and so did not expect any favours. Among many examples of the extremities to which they had been reduced, it happened that a father and son were sitting in a room and had abandoned all hope that they could survive. Suddenly a dead mouse fell from the ceiling and as soon as the two saw it, they sprang up and began to fight for the prize. It was at this time too, we are told, that the philosopher Epicurus kept his disciples alive with beans, counting out and distributing a ration for them each day.

Such was the condition of the city when Demetrius entered it,[1] and his first action was to order the whole population to assemble in the theatre. He surrounded the rear and sides with troops and lined the stage with his bodyguards, while he himself just like a tragic actor made his appearance down one of the stairways which led through the auditorium. This frightened the Athenians more than ever, but with the very first words that he uttered Demetrius dispelled their fears. He avoided any hint of bitterness either in his tone or his words, but he reproached them in a gentle and friendly fashion for their behaviour towards him and finally declared that he had forgiven them. He presented them with a hundred thousand bushels of wheat and appointed as magistrates the leaders who were most acceptable to the people. At this Democlides the orator, when he saw that the populace could hardly find words to express their joy and wished to eclipse the panegyrics which the demagogues were accustomed to lavish on Demetrius, put down a motion that Piraeus and Munychia should be handed over to king Demetrius. This resolution was passed, but Demetrius went further still by posting another garrison in the Mouseion: he did this to prevent the Athenians from shaking off his yoke yet again and distracting his attention from his other enterprises.

35. Now that he had made himself master of Athens, he at once laid plans against Sparta. He engaged Archidamus, the king of Sparta near Mantinea, defeated him, routed his army and then invaded Laconia. Next he fought a second pitched battle before the walls of Sparta itself in which he killed two hundred men and took five hundred prisoner and seemed to have the city within his grasp, although up to that moment no enemy had ever captured it. But for Demetrius, as for no other king, Fortune always held the greatest and most sudden vicissitudes in store; there was no man whose destiny was so often transformed by her caprice, from obscurity to renown, from triumph to humiliation and from abasement to the heights of power. It was for this reason, so we are told, that when he was in the depths of adversity, Demetrius would call upon Fortune in the words of Aeschylus,

> You fan my flame one moment: in the next
> Extinguish it.[2]

1. 294 B.C.   2. Nauck, *Tragoedia Graeca Fragmenta* p. 107.

And so just when the whole course of events seemed to be moving in conjunction to increase his power and sovereignty, the news reached him that Lysimachus had seized the cities in Asia which had belonged to him, and that Ptolemy had captured the whole of Cyprus except for the city of Salamis, where Demetrius' mother and children were now besieged. But like the woman in Archilochus' poem, who treacherously offered water in one hand while she bore fire in the other, so Fortune drew him away from Sparta with this dire and threatening news and at the same instant kindled his hopes of fresh achievements on the grandest scale. This was how it happened.

36. After the death of Cassander, his eldest son Philip ruled the Macedonians for a short while, and then died, whereupon Philip's two surviving brothers contested the succession. One of these, Antipater, murdered his mother Thessalonice, while the other, Alexander, appealed to Pyrrhus to come to his help from Epirus and Demetrius from the Peloponnese. Pyrrhus arrived first, and as he promptly annexed a large slice of Macedonia as the reward for his help, he at once became a neighbour whom Alexander dreaded. Demetrius, as soon as he had received Alexander's letter, set out for Macedonia with his army and frightened the young man even more because of his power and reputation. The result was that Alexander met Demetrius at the town of Dium, received him as an honoured guest, and then told him that the situation no longer required his presence. This was enough to arouse suspicions on both sides: moreover when Demetrius was on his way to a banquet to which the young prince had invited him, he was warned that there was a plot to kill him in the midst of the drinking. Demetrius was not at all disconcerted and merely delayed his arrival a little, gave orders to his officers to keep their men under arms, and arranged that his personal attendants and pages, who far outnumbered Alexander's retinue, should accompany him into the banqueting room and remain there until he rose from the table. Alexander and his followers were alarmed by these precautions and did not dare to attempt any violence, while Demetrius for his part excused himself on the ground that his health forbade him to drink wine, and took his leave early in the evening. The next day he began making preparations to depart, explaining that fresh emergencies had arisen which called him away. He asked Alexander to excuse him for leaving so soon

and assured him that he would make a longer stay when he was more at leisure. Alexander was delighted at this, since he imagined that Demetrius was leaving of his own free will and without any hostile intentions, and escorted him on his way to Thessaly. When they reached Larissa they once more exchanged invitations to a banquet and plotted to kill one another. It was this fact more than any other which delivered Alexander into Demetrius' power, as he hesitated to take precautions for fear of provoking a similar action on Demetrius' part: but in the event he was the first to suffer the fate he had intended for his enemy, because he delayed taking steps to prevent the other from escaping. He accepted Demetrius' invitation to a banquet, in the middle of which his host suddenly rose from the table. Alexander was filled with alarm, started to his feet, and following close behind made for the door. Demetrius' bodyguards were standing beside it, and as he reached them he merely said, 'Kill the man who follows me.' He passed through by himself, but Alexander was cut down by the guards, together with those of his friends who rushed up to help him. One of these is said to have cried out as he was killed that Demetrius had been too quick for them by just one day.

37. The night following was one of disorder and alarm, as might be expected. The next day found the Macedonians in a state of confusion and fearful of Demetrius' army, but when instead of an attack there came a message from Demetrius proposing that he should meet them and explain what had been done, they took heart and decided to receive him in a friendly spirit. When he appeared, there was no need for him to make a long speech. The Macedonians hated Antipater for having murdered his mother, and as they were at a loss to find a better ruler, they hailed Demetrius as king and at once escorted him back to Macedonia. At home too the people were ready to welcome the change, for they still remembered and detested the crimes which Cassander had committed against the family of Alexander the Great.[1] If there remained any regard for the moderation and justice with which the elder Antipater had ruled, it was Demetrius who profited from it, since he had married Antipater's daughter Phila, and their son, Antigonus Gonatas, who was almost

1. Cassander had put to death Alexander the Great's mother Olympias in 316 and the young king Alexander IV and his mother Roxane in 310.

grown up and was serving with his father in this campaign, could be regarded as the heir to the throne.

38. In the midst of this spectacular revival of his fortunes, Demetrius received the news that his mother and his children had been set free by Ptolemy and that he had pressed gifts and honours upon them: at the same time he also learned that his daughter Stratonice, who had been married to Seleucus, had now become the wife of Seleucus' son Antiochus and bore the title of Queen of Upper Asia. It appeared that Antiochus had fallen in love with Stratonice, who was still a young girl, although she had already borne a child to Seleucus. Antiochus was distressed and for a time he struggled to conceal his passion. But at last he decided that his malady was incurable, his desires sinful and his reason too weak to resist them: he therefore determined to make his escape from life and to destroy himself gradually by neglecting his body and refusing all nourishment, under the pretext that he was suffering from some disease. Erasistratus, his physician, found no difficulty in diagnosing his condition, namely that he was in love, but it was less easy to discover with whom. He made a habit of spending day after day in the young prince's room, and when any particularly good-looking girl or young man entered, he would study his patient's face minutely and watch those parts and movements of the body which nature has formed so as to reflect and share the emotions of the soul. Sure enough, when anybody else came in, Antiochus remained unmoved, but whenever Stratonice visited him, as she often did either alone or with Seleucus, all the symptoms which Sappho describes immediately showed themselves: his voice faltered, his face began to flush, his eye became languid, a sudden sweat broke out on his skin, his heart began to beat violently and irregularly, and finally as if his soul were overpowered by his passions, he would sink into a state of helplessness, prostration and pallor.

Besides all this, Erasistratus reflected, it was most unlikely that the king's son, if he had fallen in love with any other woman, would have persisted to the point of death in saying nothing about it. He saw the difficulty of revealing a secret of this nature to Seleucus, but still, trusting in the king's affection for his son, he ventured to tell him one day that love was the disorder from which Antiochus was suffering, a love that could neither be satisfied nor cured. 'How is it incurable?', the king asked him in astonishment. 'Because,' Erasistratus replied, 'he is in love with my wife.' 'Well then, Erasistratus,' said the king,' since you are my son's friend, could you not give up your wife and let him marry her, especially when you see that he is my only son, the only anchor of our troubled dynasty, and this is the only means of saving him?' 'You are his father,' the physician answered, 'would you do such a thing if Antiochus were in love with Stratonice?' 'My friend,' replied Seleucus,'I only wish that someone, whether a god or a man, could turn this passion of his towards her. I should be happy to give up my kingdom if only I could save Antiochus.'

Seleucus uttered these words with deep emotion, and wept as he spoke, and thereupon the physician clasped him by the hand and said, 'Then you have no need of Erasistratus: you, sire, are a father, a husband and a king, and you are also the best physician for your own household.' After this Seleucus summoned the people to meet in full assembly and announced that it was his will and pleasure that Antiochus should marry Stratonice, and that they should be proclaimed King and Queen of all Upper Asia. He believed, he said, that his son, who had always been accustomed to obey his father, would not oppose his desire, and that if his wife should be unwilling to take this extraordinary step, he would appeal to his friends to persuade her to accept as just and honourable whatever seemed right to the king and advantageous to the kingdom. This is how Antiochus came to be married to Stratonice, so we are told.

39. Having secured the crown of Macedonia, Demetrius proceeded to make himself master of Thessaly. Next, as he already controlled the greater part of the Peloponnese and, east of the Isthmus, the territories of Megara and Athens, he marched against Boeotia. At first the Boeotians made a pact of friendship with him on reasonable terms. But a little later Cleonymus the Spartan entered Thebes with an army, and at the same time Pisis of Thespiae, at that time the most prominent and influential man in the city, urged the Thebans to recover their independence, and these events so much heartened the Boeotians that they rose in revolt. But when Demetrius brought up his famous siege train[1] and surrounded the city, Cleonymus took fright and stole away, and the Boeotians were likewise overawed and

1. In 293 B.C.

surrendered. Demetrius stationed garrisons in the Boeotian cities, levied large sums of money from the people and installed the historian Hieronymus as governor and commander: by these measures and most of all by his treatment of Pisis he earned a reputation for clemency. When this man was brought before him as a prisoner Demetrius did him no harm, but even greeted him, treated him courteously and appointed him polemarch in Thespiae. But not long after Lysimachus was taken prisoner by Dromichaetes and Demetrius marched with all speed to Thrace hoping to find it undefended. The Boeotians took this opportunity to rise yet again and at the same time the news was brought that Lysimachus had been released. Enraged at these events Demetrius retraced his steps southwards, and finding that the Boeotians had been defeated by his son Antigonus, he again laid siege to Thebes.

40. However at this moment Pyrrhus overran Thessaly and advanced as far as Thermopylae, whereupon Demetrius left his son Antigonus to carry on the siege and himself marched against Pyrrhus. Pyrrhus quickly withdrew, and Demetrius, leaving a force of ten thousand infantry and a thousand cavalry in Thessaly, returned to press the siege of Thebes. He brought up his famous 'city-taker' for the assault, but because of its huge size and weight, the machine was so slowly and laboriously propelled that in the space of two months it hardly advanced two furlongs. The Boeotians defended their city bravely and Demetrius often forced his soldiers to risk their lives in assaulting the city, though he did this out of sheer exasperation rather than any real necessity for fighting. Antigonus, when he saw them losing so many men, was distressed and asked him, 'Why, father, do we allow these lives to be thrown away so unnecessarily?' Demetrius was angry and retorted 'Why do you trouble yourself about that? Do you have to find rations for the dead?' However Demetrius was anxious to prove that he was not careless only of other men's lives and careful of his own, but that he was ready to share the dangers of battle, and exposing himself in the siege he was pierced through the neck by a bolt from a catapult. He suffered great pain from this wound, but he refused to relax his efforts and finally captured Thebes a second time. When he entered the city, the Thebans were filled with fear and expected that he would carry out the most terrible reprisals, but Demetrius only put to death thirteen of the rebels,

banished a few more and pardoned the remainder. Thus it was the fate of Thebes to be captured twice within ten years, after it had been rebuilt.

The time was now approaching when the Pythian games[1] were due to be held and Demetrius took it upon himself to introduce an extraordinary innovation. Since the Aetolians held the passes which led to Delphi, he himself presided over the celebration of the games and other festivities at Athens and proclaimed that it was especially appropriate for Apollo to be honoured there because he was a patron deity of the Athenians and was reputed to be a founder of their race.

41. From Athens he returned to Macedonia. His temperament made it impossible for him to lead a quiet life, and since he had discovered that his Macedonian subjects were easy for him to control when they were on a campaign, but restless and troublesome whenever they stayed at home, he led out an expedition against the Aetolians. After ravaging the country, he left a large part of his army under Pantauchus while he himself marched against Pyrrhus. Pyrrhus at the same time advanced to meet him, but the two armies missed each other with the result that Demetrius went on to plunder Epirus, while Pyrrhus fell upon Pantauchus. A pitched battle followed in the course of which the two commanders fought hand to hand and wounded one another, but Pyrrhus routed his adversary, killed many of his soldiers, and took five thousand prisoners. This battle played a great part in weakening Demetrius' cause: the Macedonians did not feel hostile to Pyrrhus for the harm he had done them, but rather admired him because his victories owed so much to his personal prowess. The action earned him a great and glorious reputation amongst them, and many declared that Pyrrhus was the only king in whom they could see an image of the great Alexander's courage: the others, and especially Demetrius, only imitated Alexander in the pomp and outward show of majesty, like actors on a stage. And indeed it is true that there was something intensely theatrical about Demetrius. He possessed an elaborate wardrobe of hats and cloaks, broad-brimmed hats with double mitres and robes of purple interwoven with gold, while his feet were clad in shoes of the richest purple felt embroidered with gold. One of his robes had taken many months to weave on the looms: it

1. The Pythian games, contests in music and athletics, were held every four years at Delphi in honour of Apollo as the slayer of the serpent Python.

was a superb piece of work in which the world and the heavenly
bodies were represented. It was still only half finished at the time of
Demetrius' downfall, and none of the later kings of Macedon ever
presumed to wear it, although several of them had a taste for pomp
and ceremony.

42. Demetrius' ostentatious tastes offended the Macedonians, who
were not accustomed to see their kings dressed in this fashion, and so
did the luxury and extravagance of his way of living, but what
annoyed them most of all was the difficulty of speaking to him or
even coming into his presence. Sometimes he would refuse to see
anybody at all, and on other occasions he would behave harshly and
discourteously even to those who had been granted an audience. For
example he kept an Athenian embassy waiting for two years, even
though he favoured Athens more than any other Greek city, and
another time he considered himself insulted and lost his temper when
a deputation arrived from Sparta which consisted of only one envoy.
When Demetrius demanded, 'What do you mean, have the Spartans
sent no more than one?' he received the neat and laconic reply, 'Yes,
sire, one ambassador to one king.'

One day when Demetrius was riding abroad and appeared to be in
a more obliging mood than usual, and more willing to converse with
his subjects, a large crowd gathered to present him with written
petitions, all of which he accepted and placed in the fold of his cloak.
The people were delighted and followed him on his way, but when
he came to the bridge over the Axios river, he shook out the fold
and emptied all the petitions into the water. This infuriated the
Macedonians, who felt that Demetrius was insulting them, not
governing them, and they recalled or listened to those who were old
enough to remember how accessible Philip had been and how considerate in such matters. On another occasion an old woman accosted
Demetrius and kept asking him to give her an audience. Demetrius
replied that he could not spare the time, whereupon the old woman
screamed at him, 'Then don't be king!' This rebuke stung Demetrius
to the quick. He went back to his house, put off all other business and
for several days gave audience to everybody who asked for it,
beginning with the old woman.

And indeed there is nothing that becomes a king so much as the
task of dispensing justice. Ares, the god of war, is a tyrant, as Timo-

theus tells us, but Law, in Pindar's words, is the monarch of all things. Homer tells us that Zeus entrusts kings not with 'city-takers' or bronze-beaked ships, but with the decrees of Justice, which are to be protected and kept inviolate, and it is not the most warlike or unjust or murderous of kings but the most righteous to whom he gives the title of Zeus' confidant and disciple. Demetrius on the other hand took pleasure in being given a nickname which is the opposite of the one bestowed on the king of the gods, for Zeus is known as the protector or defender of cities but Demetrius as the besieger. It is through such an attitude that naked power, if it lacks wisdom, allows evil actions to usurp the place of good, and glorious achievements to be associated with injustice, and so it happened with Demetrius.

43. Not long after this, while Demetrius was lying dangerously ill at Pella, he almost lost his kingdom, for Pyrrhus invaded Macedonia and rapidly advanced as far as Edessa. But as soon as Demetrius had recovered, he easily drove Pyrrhus out of his territory and came to terms with him, for he was anxious not to be distracted by continual petty entanglements and border warfare from his main objective, which was nothing less than to recover the whole of the empire which had been ruled by his father. Besides this he had the keels laid for a fleet of five hundred ships, some of which were being constructed at Piraeus, some at Corinth, some at Chalkis and some at Pella. He visited each of these places in person, giving instructions to the artificers and even taking part in the work, and there was general wonder not only at the number but at the size of the vessels that were being constructed. Until then nobody had even seen a ship of fifteen or sixteen banks of oars, although it is true that at a later date Ptolemy Philopator built a vessel of forty banks of oars, which was four hundred and twenty feet long and seventy-two feet high to the top of her stern. She was manned by four hundred sailors who did not row and four thousand at the oars, and apart from these she could carry on her decks and gangways nearly three thousand soldiers. But this vessel was only intended for show: she differed little from a stationary building on land, and since she was designed for exhibition rather than for use, she could only be moved with great difficulty and danger. But in the case of Demetrius' ships, their beauty did not at all detract from their fighting qualities, nor did the magnificence of their equipment make them any less operational: on the contrary

their speed and their performance were even more remarkable than their size.

44. Nothing comparable to this great expedition against Asia had been assembled by any man since the days of Alexander, but as it was preparing to sail, the three kings, Seleucus, Ptolemy and Lysimachus formed an alliance against Demetrius. Next they sent a combined delegation to Pyrrhus urging him to attack Macedonia. He should consider himself at liberty to disregard his treaty with Demetrius, in which the latter had given no guarantee of leaving him unmolested, but had claimed for himself the right to make war upon the enemy of his choice. Pyrrhus responded to their appeal and Demetrius thus found himself drawn into a war on several fronts before his preparations were complete. While Ptolemy sailed to Greece with a powerful fleet and incited various cities to revolt,[1] Lysimachus invaded Macedonia from Thrace and Pyrrhus from Epirus, each of them plundering the country as he advanced. Demetrius left his son in command in Greece, while he hurried back to relieve Macedonia and marched against Lysimachus. On his way news reached him that Pyrrhus had captured Verroia. The report quickly spread to the Macedonians and Demetrius could no longer control his army. The whole camp resounded with tears and lamentations mingled with shouts of anger and execration against their commander. The men refused to stay with Demetrius and insisted on dispersing, ostensibly to return to their homes, but in reality to desert to Lysimachus. In this situation Demetrius determined to remove himself as far from Lysimachus as he could and to march against Pyrrhus. He reckoned that Lysimachus might be popular with the Macedonians because he was a fellow-countryman and on account of his association with Alexander, while Pyrrhus was a newcomer and a foreigner whom they would be unlikely to prefer to himself. But these calculations proved quite unfounded. When he approached his adversary's camp and pitched his own close by, the admiration which his men had felt in the past for Pyrrhus' brilliant feats of arms quickly revived, and besides this their traditions had accustomed them to believe that the man who proved himself the best fighter was also the best ruler. Besides, the soldiers also learned that Pyrrhus dealt leniently with his prisoners and since they were now anxious to transfer their allegiance either to Pyrrhus or to another master, but in

1. The spring of 288 B.C.

any event to rid themselves of Demetrius, they began to desert him. At first they came over stealthily and in small groups, but presently the climate of disorder and sedition spread through the whole camp. At last some of the soldiers plucked up courage to go to Demetrius and told him to clear out and save himself, for the Macedonians were tired of fighting wars to pay for his extravagances. Demetrius thought this very reasonable advice compared to the hostility shown him by the others, and so he went to his tent, and just as if he were an actor rather than a real king, he put on a dark cloak in place of his royal robe and slipped away unnoticed. Most of his men at once fell to tearing down his tent, and while they were looting it and fighting over the spoils, Pyrrhus came up and finding that he met no resistance immediately took possession of the camp. After this the whole kingdom of Macedonia, which Demetrius had ruled securely for seven years, was divided between Lysimachus and Pyrrhus.[1]

45. When Demetrius had thus completely lost his power, he took refuge in the city of Cassandreia.[2] His wife Phila was quite overwhelmed by his misfortunes and could not bear to see her husband, the most unlucky of kings, reduced once more to the condition of a private citizen and an exile. Henceforth she gave up all hope, and in her bitter resentment of a destiny which seemed to be far more consistent in adversity than in prosperity, she took poison and died. But Demetrius was still determined to save what he could from the wreck of his fortunes, and so he went to Greece and tried to rally those of his generals and supporters who were still there. In one of Sophocles' plays Menelaus uses this image to describe the vicissitudes of his destiny,

> But my fate on the turning wheel of heaven
> For ever whirls, for ever changes shape,
> Even as the face of the inconstant moon
> That never keeps her form two nights the same;
> Out of the dark she rises, young and new,
> Her countenance grows fairer, fills with light,
> Until, the moment of her glory past,
> She turns away and shrinks to nothingness.[3]

1. In 288 B.C.
2. This city, situated on the westernmost of the three peninsulas of Chalcidice, had earlier been known as Potidaea.
3. Nauck, *Tragoedia Graeca Fragmenta*, p. 315.

This figure of speech seems even more apt to describe the fortunes of Demetrius, as they first waxed and then waned, appeared at one moment at the full and at the next in eclipse. Even so at this point, just as his power seemed to be completely spent and extinguished, it suddenly burst forth and through various accessions of strength, it began to fill up once more the measure of his hopes. At first he visited the various states as a private citizen and dressed without any of the insignia of royalty, and somebody who saw him in Thebes in this condition very aptly quoted those verses of Euripides which describe the arrival of Dionysius in Thebes

> Changing his godhead into mortal guise
> He comes to Ismene's waters and Dirce's stream.[1]

46. No sooner had he stepped back on to the path of hope, as it were upon a royal highway, and had gathered around him something of the form and substance of sovereignty, than he restored to the Thebans their ancestral constitution. The Athenians, on the other hand, revolted from him. They had the name of Diphilus erased from the public registers. It was he who as the priest of the saviour-gods had been granted the privilege of giving his name to the current year: it was now decreed instead that archons should be elected for this purpose according to the traditional Athenian custom. But when the Athenians saw that Demetrius was becoming more powerful than they had expected, they sent for Pyrrhus to come down from Macedonia and protect them. This action angered Demetrius and he marched against Athens and laid the city under close siege. However the people sent Crates the philosopher, a man of high reputation and authority to plead with him, and finally Demetrius raised the siege, partly because he was persuaded by the ambassador's appeal, and partly because Crates was able to suggest to him courses that were to his own advantage. He therefore assembled all the ships he possessed,[2] embarked eleven thousand soldiers and all his cavalry, and sailed for Asia with the object of winning over the provinces of Caria and Lydia from Lysimachus.

At Miletus he was met by Eurydice, a sister of Phila's, who brought with her Ptolemais, one of her daughters by Ptolemy. The girl had been betrothed to Demetrius several years before[3] through the

---

1. *Bacchae*, 4.   2. See ch. 43.   3. In 301 B.C., see ch. 32.

mediation of Seleucus. Demetrius now married her and Eurydice gave the bride away. Immediately after the wedding Demetrius set himself to win over the cities of Ionia. Many joined him of their own accord, while others were compelled to submit. He also captured Sardis and several of Lysimachus' officers deserted to him, bringing with them both money and troops. When Lysimachus' son Agathocles took the field against him with a strong force, Demetrius withdrew into Phrygia. His plan was to make his way to Armenia, stir up a revolt in Media, and from there gain control of the provinces of the interior, where a commander who was on the run could always find places of refuge and lines of retreat. Agathocles pursued him and although Demetrius came off the better in their skirmishes, his troops were reduced to desperate straits because he was cut off from his supplies of provisions and forage, and worse still, his soldiers began to suspect his intention of leading them into Armenia and Media. Famine now began to press upon the army, and when they attempted to cross the river Lycus, they mistook the ford so that many of his men were swept away by the current and drowned. In spite of this the men did not cease to joke, and one of them wrote up in front of Demetrius' tent the opening lines of Sophocles' *Oedipus Coloneus*, which he altered a little so that they read

> Child of the blind old man Antigonus,
> What is this region where we find ourselves?[1]

47. But at last the army began to be attacked by disease as well as by hunger, as so often happens when men are forced to subsist on whatever food they can find, and after Demetrius had lost no fewer than eight thousand men, he turned back with the remainder and descended from the interior to Tarsus. Here he would gladly have refrained from living on the country, which belonged to Seleucus, and so avoided giving the king any excuse to attack him, but this was impossible since his troops had by then been reduced to great privations and Agathocles had fortified the passes of the Taurus mountains against him. So he wrote a long letter to Seleucus in which he gave a pathetic account of his misfortunes and implored him as a kinsman by marriage to take pity on one who had suffered enough to deserve compassion even from his enemies.

[1] In the play the question is put to Antigone, the daughter of the blind Oedipus. The one-eyed Antigonus was Demetrius' father.

A.A. — 18

Seleucus seems to have been touched by this appeal and wrote to his generals in that province that they should supply Demetrius on the scale that was due to a king and make generous provision for his army. But then Patrocles, a man whose judgement was greatly valued and who was a trusted friend of Seleucus, came to him and pointed out that although the expense of maintaining Demetrius and his troops was small enough, it would be a great mistake to allow him to remain in the country. Demetrius, he reminded Seleucus, had always been the most violent of the kings and the one most addicted to ambitious and daring enterprises, and his fortunes had now sunk to a point at which even the most moderate of men might be tempted to embark on some desperate and unlawful attempt. Seleucus was put on his guard by this advice and marched into Cilicia at the head of a large army, while Demetrius, surprised and alarmed at the sudden change in the king's attitude, retreated into the fastnesses of the Taurus range. He then sent messengers to Seleucus and asked to be allowed as a final boon to conquer a petty realm for himself among the independent barbarian tribes, where he could live out the rest of his days without further wanderings and peregrinations: if this could not be allowed him, he begged the king to supply his troops with food for the winter and not to drive him out of the country in such an exposed and helpless condition that he would be completely at the mercy of his enemies.

48. Seleucus treated all these proposals with suspicion. He told Demetrius that he would be allowed, if he wished, to spend two months of the winter in Cataonia, on condition that his principal officers should be handed over as hostages: at the same time he fortified the passes leading into Syria against him. Then Demetrius feeling himself trapped like a wild beast and surrounded on all sides, was driven to use force. He overran the country, and on several occasions when Seleucus attacked him, he gained the upper hand. Once in particular, when Seleucus' scythe-carrying chariots bore down on him, he avoided the charge and put the enemy to flight, and he also succeeded in dislodging the garrison from one of the passes and gaining control of the road into Syria. These successes greatly raised his spirits and when he saw that his soldiers had recovered their courage, he prepared to engage Seleucus and put the issue to the supreme test. For his part Seleucus was at a loss as to what to do. He had refused an

offer of help from Lysimachus, because he both distrusted and feared him: on the other hand he shrank from engaging Demetrius, partly because his opponent now seemed to be buoyed up by the courage of despair, and partly because he dreaded those sudden vicissitudes of fortune which in the past had so often swung Demetrius from the depths of failure to the heights of success.

But at this moment Demetrius fell victim to a dangerous sickness which not only undermined his physical strength but completely ruined his cause, for its consequence was that some of his soldiers immediately deserted to the enemy, while others scattered. After forty days he recovered his strength with difficulty, and rallying the remnant of his army, he set out for Cilicia, so far as his enemies could discover his intention. But as soon as it was dark Demetrius promptly marched, without using his trumpets, in the opposite direction, crossed the pass of Amanus and ravaged the plains below as far as Cyrrhestica.

49. When Seleucus followed and encamped close by, Demetrius got his men on the march at night and advanced against him. For a long while Seleucus had no warning of his approach and his troops were asleep. But then some deserters arrived and warned him of the danger, and at this he started up in alarm and ordered his trumpets to be sounded, while at the same time he pulled on his boots and shouted to his companions that a terrible wild beast was about to attack them. Demetrius at once understood from the noise in the enemy's camp that they had been forewarned of his attack and pulled back his troops as quickly as he could. When daylight came he found that Seleucus was pressing him hard, and so he sent one of his officers to the other wing, while he drove back the one that faced him. But then Seleucus dismounted, took off his helmet and carrying only a light shield went up to hail Demetrius' mercenaries: he showed them who he was and appealed to them to come over to him, since they must have known for a long while that it was for their sake, not for their general's that he had refrained from attacking them. At this they all greeted him, acclaimed him as their king and went over to his side.

Demetrius who had experienced so many shifts of good and bad fortune in his career, understood that this reverse was final. He turned his back on the field and fled to the passes of Amanus, where he took refuge with a small company of friends and attendants and waited for nightfall. His plan was to reach the road to Caunus if possible and from there make his way to the sea, where he hoped to find his fleet. But when he discovered that his party did not have enough food even for the next day, he cast around for other plans. At that point one of his comrades named Sosigenes came up, who had four hundred gold pieces in his belt. With this money they hoped to get through to the sea and as soon as it was dark they started in the direction of the passes. But when they found the enemy's watch-fires blazing all along the heights, they despaired of breaking through that way, and returned to their hiding-place in the forest. By then they were fewer in number, for some had already deserted, and much of the spirit had gone out of them. One of them then ventured to suggest that Demetrius should surrender himself to Seleucus. At this Demetrius unsheathed his sword and would have killed himself, but his friends surrounded him, did their best to comfort him, and finally persuaded him to do as the man had proposed. So he sent a messenger to Seleucus and put himself into his hands.

50. When Seleucus heard of this he declared that it was his own good fortune, and not his opponent's, which had saved Demetrius' life and had added to her other favours this opportunity to show humanity and kindness. He sent for the officers of his household and ordered them to pitch a royal tent and to make all other arrangements to receive and entertain Demetrius in magnificent style. There was also at Seleucus' court a man named Apollonides, who had been a close friend of Demetrius, and Seleucus at once sent him to help put Demetrius at his ease and reassure him that he was coming into the presence of a man who was a friend and a relative. When Seleucus' intentions became clear, first of all a few of Demetrius' followers and then the great majority hurried to rejoin him, vying with one another in their efforts to reach him first, for they now expected that he would become a man of great influence at Seleucus' court.

But these actions soon transformed Seleucus' compassion into jealousy and gave the more skilful of the courtiers and those who were ill disposed to Demetrius the opportunity to thwart and defeat the king's generosity. They alarmed him by suggesting that the first moment Demetrius was seen in Seleucus' camp, all the troops would go over to him. By this time Apollonides had already arrived in high spirits and others of Demetrius' followers were joining him with wonderful tales of Seleucus' kindness. Even Demetrius himself after all his reverses and misfortunes, if he had at first regarded his surrender as a disgrace, had begun to change his mind as a result of recovering his spirits and beginning to feel some hope for the future. But then suddenly Pausanias appeared at the head of a detachment of a thousand soldiers and horsemen. He immediately surrounded Demetrius, sent away all his followers, and escorted him not into the presence of Seleucus, but away to the Syrian Chersonese.[1] Here for the rest of his life Demetrius was placed under a strong guard, but was granted attendance suitable to his rank: generous funds and provisions were supplied from day to day, and he was allowed to walk or ride in the royal estates and hunt game in the parks. He was free to enjoy the company of any of his comrades in exile who wished to join him, and a number of people contrived to visit him from Seleucus' court: they brought encouraging messages, urged him to keep up his spirits, and hinted that as soon as Antiochus arrived with Demetrius' daughter Stratonice, he would be set free.

51. But Demetrius, once he found himself in this situation, sent word to his son and his commanders in Athens and Corinth that henceforth they should pay no attention to any letters written in his name or under his seal, but should regard him as a dead man and hold in trust his cities and the rest of his possessions for his heir Antigonus. When Antigonus learned of his father's capture, he was deeply grieved and put on mourning. He wrote to the other kings and in particular to Seleucus entreating him, offering to give up all that was left of his own and Demetrius' possessions, and above all proposing himself as a hostage for his father. Many cities and their rulers supported this appeal. But Lysimachus stood aloof and even approached Seleucus with the offer of a large sum of money if he would put Demetrius to death. Seleucus had always felt a sense of revulsion against Lysimachus, and after this proposal he regarded him both as a villain and a barbarian. He therefore continued to keep Demetrius under guard until the arrival of Antiochus and Stratonice, as if to suggest that the favour of his release might come from their intercession.

1. This is believed to have been situated in a bend of the Orontes river in the neighbourhood of Antioch.

52. Demetrius at first manfully endured the misfortune that had befallen him, and then gradually became accustomed to it and learned to accept the situation with a better grace. At first he exercised his body as well as he could and made use of his privileges of riding or hunting, but then little by little he became indifferent and at last positively averse to such pastimes. Instead he took to drinking and playing dice and spent most of his leisure in this way. This may have been because he wished to escape from any thought of his condition, the consciousness of which so haunted him when he was sober that he tried to drown such reflections in liquor. Or perhaps he had come to the conclusion that this was the kind of life he had really desired all along, but had missed through folly and the pursuit of empty ambition. In this way he had brought many troubles both on himself and on others, by using weapons and fleets and armies to chase after the happiness he had now unexpectedly discovered in idleness, leisure and relaxation. And in fact for all these wretched kings, after all the risks they run and the wars they fight, what other goal is there than this? Truly these men are both wicked and stupid, not merely because they strive after luxury and pleasure rather than virtue and honour, but because they do not even know how to enjoy the real thing in either case.

However that may be, Demetrius after he had lived for three years in confinement in the Syrian Chersonese fell sick through inactivity and over-indulgence in food and wine and died in his fifty-fifth year. Seleucus was generally blamed and bitterly reproached himself for having harboured such suspicions against Demetrius and for having fallen so far below the standards even of Dromichaetes, a barbarous Thracian, who, when Lysimachus was his prisoner, had treated him in a manner that was far more humane and worthy of a king.

53. There was something dramatic and theatrical even in the funeral ceremonies which were arranged in Demetrius' honour. When Antigonus learned that his father's remains were being brought to him, he put to sea with his whole fleet and met Seleucus' ships near the Cyclades. The relics were presented to him in a golden urn, and he placed them in the largest of his admiral's galleys. Then at the various cities where the fleet touched during its passage, some brought garlands to adorn the urn, others sent representatives dressed in mourning to escort it home and bury it. When the fleet put in at

Corinth, the urn was placed in full view on the poop of the flagship covered with royal purple, crowned with a king's diadem and surrounded by an armed bodyguard of young men. Close to it was seated Xenophantus, the most celebrated flute-player of the time, who played a sacred hymn: the rowers kept time with the music and the rhythmical splashing of their oars matched the cadences of the flute and sounded like a mourner's beating of the breast. But it was the sight of Antigonus, his head bowed with grief and his eyes filled with tears, which excited most pity among the crowds who flocked to the sea-shore. After the remains had been crowned with garlands and other honours had been paid at Corinth, Antigonus brought them to Demetrias[1] to be buried. This was the town named after his father, who had settled in it the inhabitants from a number of villages round Iolcus.

Demetrius left the following descendants. Antigonus and Stratonice were his children by Phila. There were two sons named Demetrius, one surnamed the Thin, by a woman of Illyria, the other, who became the ruler of Cyrene, by Ptolemais. Alexander, who lived and died in Egypt was his son by Deidameia. He is also said to have had a son named Corrhagus by Eurydice. His descendants continued to rule over Macedonia in a direct line of kings of whom Perseus was the last: it was in his reign that the Romans subdued Macedonia. So now that the Macedonian drama has been performed, it is time to bring the Roman[2] on to the stage.

1. In Thessaly on the eastern shore of the Gulf of Pagasae.
2. Mark Antony, the parallel *Life* to Demetrius.

9

PYRRHUS[1]

[319–272 B.C.]

* *
*

ACCORDING to the historians the first king of the Thesprotians and
Molossians after the great flood was Phaethon: he was one of those
who came to Epirus with Pelasgus. But there is also a tradition that
Deucalion and Pyrrha[2] founded the sanctuary at Dodona[3] and lived
there among the Molossians. In later times Neoptolemus, the son of
Achilles, brought a whole people with him to Epirus, conquered the
country, and founded a dynasty. These were named 'the sons of
Pyrrhus' after him because he bore the name of Pyrrhus in his boyhood, and he afterwards also gave it to one of his legitimate children
by Lanassa, who was the daughter of Cleodaeus and grand-daughter
of Hyllus. This was how it came about that Achilles was granted
divine honours in Epirus and was known as Aspetus in the nomen-
clature of that region. However, the later kings of this line sank into
barbarism, and as a result of the decline of their power and the
insignificance of their lives, the dynasty lapsed into obscurity. It was
Tharrhypas, so the historians say, who was the first of their successors
to make himself famous by introducing Greek customs and letters and
who imposed order on the life of his cities by promulgating humane
laws. Tharrhypas was the father of Alcetas and his son Arybas married
Troas, who bore him Aeacides. This king married Phthia, the daughter of Menon of Thessaly, who had earned a high reputation in the
Lamian war:[4] after Leosthenes it was he who had distinguished himself most in the confederation which the Greek states formed against

1. For places mentioned in this *Life*, see Maps 1, 2 and 3, pp. 433–6.
2. The two survivors of the great flood, according to Greek legend.
3. The famous shrine and oracle of Zeus, near the modern Yannina.
4. 323–322 B.C. See *Life of Demosthenes*, ch. 27.

Macedonia. Phthia bore Aeacides two daughters, Deidamia and Troas, and a son, Pyrrhus.

2. After a time civil strife broke out among the Molossians, Aeacides was driven out and the descendants of Neoptolemus were restored to power. The supporters of Aeacides were captured and put to death; his enemies also made a search for Pyrrhus, who was still an infant, but Androclides and Angelus contrived to escape and carried off the young prince with them. They were obliged to take a few servants and women to nurse the child, with the result that they could only travel slowly and laboriously and soon found themselves being overtaken. They therefore entrusted Pyrrhus to three strong and reliable young men, Androcleion, Hippias and Neander, whom they ordered to press ahead as quickly as they could and make for Megara, a town in Macedonia: meanwhile they themselves, partly by entreaty and partly by force contrived to hold up the pursuers until late in the evening. They succeeded at last in driving off their enemies, and then hurried on to join the men who were carrying Pyrrhus. The sun had already set and the party had begun to hope that they were within reach of safety, when they suddenly found themselves cut off by the river which flowed between them and the town. The stream looked wild and dangerous, and when they attempted to cross they found this was impossible, for the rains had swollen the waters to a rushing torrent and the gathering darkness increased the terror of the scene. They decided that they would never be able to cross by their own efforts, since they had to carry both the child and the women who were looking after it, but when they saw several of the people of the locality standing on the opposite shore, they called out for help to cross and made gestures of entreaty, pointing at the infant Pyrrhus. Those on the far side could not hear what they were saying because of the dashing and the roar of the water, and much time was lost with one group shouting and the other unable to understand them, until one of the fugitives hit on a solution. He tore off a strip of bark from a tree and wrote on it with the pin of a brooch a few words explaining their predicament and who the child was. Then he wrapped the piece of bark round a stone to give weight to his throw and flung it over the torrent; according to another version of the story he wrapped the bark around a javelin and hurled this across the stream. At any rate when the people on the other side read the message and understood

that there was no time to be lost, they cut down some trees, lashed them together to form a raft and thus made the crossing. As chance would have it, the man who first came ashore and took Pyrrhus in his arms was named Achilles, and his companions ferried over the rest of the party.

3. Having thus escaped the pursuit and reached safety, the fugitives proceeded to Glaucias, the king of the Illyrians. They found him sitting at home with his wife, and laid the baby on the ground between them. The king was obliged to weigh the matter carefully. He was afraid of Cassander, the ruler of Macedon, who was an enemy of Aeacides, and for a long while he said nothing as he turned the problem over in his mind. Meanwhile Pyrrhus of his own accord crawled along the floor, took hold of the king's robe and pulled himself up at Glaucias' knees: the king at first burst out laughing, and then was moved to pity, as he saw the child standing there like a suppliant, clasping his knees and sobbing. According to one account Pyrrhus did not throw himself before Glaucias, but seized hold of an altar, and clasping his hands round it raised himself to his feet, and this the king regarded as a sign from heaven. For this reason he at once placed Pyrrhus in the arms of his wife and gave orders that he should be brought up with their own children. Then a little later, when Pyrrhus' enemies demanded that he should be handed over to them and Cassander offered two hundred talents for him, Glaucias refused to give him up. Indeed, after Pyrrhus had reached the age of twelve, Glaucias actually invaded Epirus with an army and set him on the throne there.

Pyrrhus' features were more likely to inspire fear in the beholder than to impress him with a sense of majesty. He did not have a regular set of teeth, but his upper jaw was formed of one continuous bone with small depressions in it, which resembled the intervals between a row of teeth. He was believed to have the power to cure diseases of the spleen. He would sacrifice a white cock, and then, while the patient lay flat on his back, he would gently press upon the region of the spleen with his right foot. There was nobody so poor or obscure that Pyrrhus would refuse him this healing touch, if he were asked for it. He would accept the cock as a reward after he had sacrificed it, and was always very pleased with this gift. The great toe of his right foot was also said to possess a divine power, so that when the rest of his body was burned after his death, this was found unharmed and untouched by the fire. These details, however, belong to a later period.

4. When he had reached the age of seventeen[1] and appeared to be firmly established on the throne, he left Epirus to attend the wedding of one of Glaucias' sons, with whom he had been brought up. Thereupon the Molossians again took the opportunity to rise in revolt; they drove out Pyrrhus' supporters, plundered his property and made another of Neoptolemus' descendants[2] their king. In this way Pyrrhus lost his kingdom, and since he was now completely destitute, he attached himself to Demetrius, the son of Antigonus, who had married his sister Deidameia. While she was still a young girl, she had nominally been married to Alexander, the son of Alexander the Great and Roxane, but fate had soon deprived her of her husband, and when she came of age Demetrius married her.[3] Pyrrhus served under Demetrius at the great battle of Ipsus,[4] in which all the kings who had succeeded Alexander the Great took part. He was only eighteen at the time, but he routed the contingent that was opposed to him and distinguished himself brilliantly in the fighting. He did not desert Demetrius after his defeat, but kept guard over the cities in Greece which were entrusted to his command,[5] and when Demetrius made a treaty with Ptolemy, Pyrrhus sailed to Egypt as a hostage. In Egypt he gave Ptolemy ample proof of his prowess and endurance both in hunting and in military exercises. He noticed that among Ptolemy's wives it was Berenice who enjoyed the highest esteem for her virtue and her intelligence and also who exercised the greatest influence, and so he went out of his way to court her favour. He was particularly skilful at winning over his superiors to his own interest, just as, on the other hand, he looked down on his inferiors, and since he was temperate and decorous in his private life, he was singled out from among many other young princes as a suitable husband for Antigone, who was the daughter of Berenice by her first husband Philip.[6]

1. In 302 B.C.
2. The grandson of the Neoptolemus mentioned in ch. 2.
3. See *Demetrius* ch. 25. 4. In 301 B.C.
5. See *Demetrius* ch. 31.
6. An obscure Macedonian, no connection with the father of Alexander the Great.

5. After this marriage Pyrrhus' reputation rose still higher, and since Antigone proved an excellent wife to him, he contrived to procure money and troops and to get himself sent to Epirus to recover his kingdom. Many of the Epirots welcomed his arrival, for they had come to hate Neoptolemus, who had proved himself a harsh and repressive ruler. Pyrrhus was afraid, however, that if he drove out his rival, Neoptolemus might turn for help to one of the other successors of Alexander, and so he made a pact with him, whereby they agreed to share the royal power. But as time went on some of their partisans secretly provoked friction between them and fomented their suspicions of one another. But the event which did most to arouse Pyrrhus to action is said to have originated as follows.

It was the custom for the kings of Epirus to offer sacrifice to Zeus Areius at Passaron, a place in Molossian territory, and there to exchange solemn oaths with their subjects: the kings swore to govern according to the laws and the people to support the kingdom as it had been established by the laws. This ceremony was duly performed, both the kings were present and conversed with one another together with their adherents, and many gifts were exchanged. On this occasion Gelon, a faithful supporter of Neoptolemus, greeted Pyrrhus warmly and presented him with two yoke of oxen for ploughing. Myrtilus, Pyrrhus' cup-bearer, asked him for these, and was deeply offended when the king refused him and gave them to somebody else. Gelon noticed this and invited Myrtilus to dine with him, and, according to some accounts, as Myrtilus was a good-looking young man, made love to him as they drank: then he began to talk seriously to him, and urged him to throw in his lot with Neoptolemus and dispatch Pyrrhus by poison. Myrtilus listened to the suggestion, pretended to approve and agree to it, but privately informed Pyrrhus. Then on the king's instructions, he introduced Alexicrates, Pyrrhus' chief cup-bearer to Gelon, making out that he was willing to take part in the plot, for Pyrrhus was anxious to have several witnesses to testify to the intended crime. In this way Gelon was completely deceived, and he in turn deceived Neoptolemus, who imagined that the plot was developing smoothly and could not restrain his delight, but kept talking about it to his friends. On one particular occasion, after a drinking-party at the house of his sister Cadmeia, he let his tongue run away with him: he imagined that he could not be heard, since there seemed to be nobody near them, except for Phaenarete, the wife of a man named Samon, Neoptolemus' chief herdsman, and she was lying on a couch, apparently asleep with her face to the wall. But in fact, while she took care not to arouse their suspicions, she had heard everything that was said, and next day she went to Pyrrhus' wife Antigone and reported the whole conversation. When Pyrrhus heard this, he took no action for the moment, but on a day when a sacrifice was due to be offered, he invited Neoptolemus to supper and killed him. He knew that the leading men in Epirus were on his side and were eager to see him rid himself of Neoptolemus. He was also aware of their desire that he should not content himself with a petty share in the government, but should follow his natural bent and engage in far more ambitious designs: moreover, now that his suspicion of Neoptolemus' treachery provided yet another motive for the deed, they were content for him to forestall Neoptolemus by putting him out of the way first.

6. Pyrrhus then honoured Ptolemy and Berenice by giving the name of Ptolemy to the infant son whom Antigone bore him, and Berenice to the city which he had built on the peninsula of Epirus.[1] Next he began to ponder a number of ambitious schemes, in particular designs directed against the territories of his neighbours, and he found an opportunity to intervene in the affairs of Macedon upon the following pretext.

After Cassander's death[2] Antipater, the elder of his sons, had his mother Thessalonice put to death and drove his brother Alexander into exile. Alexander appealed for help to Demetrius and also addressed himself to Pyrrhus. Demetrius' attention was taken up with other matters and he was slow to respond, but Pyrrhus came to Macedonia and demanded as the price of his alliance the districts known as Stymphaea and Paravaea within Macedonia itself, and of the territories conquered by the Macedonians, Ambracia, Acarnania and Amphilochia.[3] The young man agreed to the terms, and Pyrrhus at once occupied these regions and secured them for himself by posting garrisons there: then he proceeded to wrest the remaining parts of the kingdom from Antipater and handed them over to Alexander. Meanwhile Lysimachus, who was anxious to send help to Antipater, found himself too much occupied with other matters

1. Near the modern Preveza.   2. In 297 B.C.
3. These territories border the Ambracian Gulf to the south of Epirus.

to come to Macedonia in person. As he knew that Pyrrhus would never disoblige Ptolemy or refuse him anything, he sent him a forged letter which purported to come from Ptolemy and which ordered him to abandon his expedition on receipt of three hundred talents from Antipater. However, as soon as Pyrrhus opened the letter, he discovered Lysimachus' trick, because it did not begin with Ptolemy's usual greeting to him, which ran, 'The father to the son, greetings', but with the words 'King Ptolemy to King Pyrrhus, greetings'. Pyrrhus reproached Lysimachus for the deception, but he nevertheless made peace, and the three rulers met to confirm the agreement and swear a solemn oath at a sacrifice. A bull, a boar and a ram were led up for the ceremony, and the ram of its own accord suddenly fell down dead. The rest of the spectators burst out laughing, but Theodotus the diviner prevented Pyrrhus from taking the oath: he declared that through this portent the gods were foretelling the death of one of the three kings. For this reason, then, Pyrrhus withdrew from the pact.

7. Alexander's affairs had in fact already been settled with Pyrrhus' help, but this did not deter Demetrius from coming to Macedonia. However as soon as he arrived, it became clear that not only was his presence unnecessary, but that it alarmed the young king, and the two had only been together for a few days before their mutual distrust led them to plot against one another. Demetrius seized the opportunity to strike first against his youthful opponent, and had Alexander murdered, and himself proclaimed king of Macedonia.[1] He had clashed with Pyrrhus before this when the latter invaded and overran Thessaly. Now greed, the congenital disease of dynasties, made the two men distrustful and suspicious neighbours, and their fears of one another were intensified by the death of Deidameia, who was Demetrius' wife and Pyrrhus' sister.

Since they had both annexed different parts of Macedonia, their interests frequently collided and the occasions for quarrelling were multiplied still further. Demetrius made an expedition against the Aetolians and subdued them; then, leaving his general Pantauchus there with a strong force, he set out at once to attack Pyrrhus,[2] while Pyrrhus, as soon as he learned the news, marched against him. Somehow they mistook their way and their armies passed one another

1. 294 B.C.   2. 291 B.C.

without meeting. Demetrius went on to invade Epirus and plunder the country, while Pyrrhus came upon Pantauchus and promptly engaged him. A fierce battle ensued and the fighting was especially violent around the two commanders. Pantauchus was by general consent the best fighting-man of all Demetrius' generals. He combined courage, strength and skill in arms with a lofty and resolute spirit, and he challenged Pyrrhus to a hand-to-hand combat. Pyrrhus, for his part, yielded to none of the kings in valour and daring: he was determined to earn the fame of Achilles not merely through his ancestry but through his prowess in the field, and he advanced beyond the front rank of his troops to face Pantauchus. First they hurled their javelins at one another, and then coming to close quarters, they drew their swords and fought with all their strength and skill. Pyrrhus received one wound, but inflicted two on Pantauchus, one in the thigh and one along the neck. Finally he drove his opponent back and forced him to the ground, but could not kill him outright, as his friends came to the rescue and dragged him away. This victory of their king's uplifted the Epirots' spirits and inspired by his courage they succeeded in penetrating and breaking up the Macedonian phalanx: then they pursued their enemies as they fled, killed great numbers of them and took five thousand prisoners.

8. This battle, so far from filling the Macedonians with anger or hatred against Pyrrhus for having defeated them, caused all those who had fought in it and witnessed his exploits to talk about him endlessly and marvel at his courage. They compared his appearance and the speed and vigour of his movements to those of Alexander the Great,[1] and felt that they saw in him an image and a reflection of that hero's fire and impetuosity in the field. The other kings, they said, could only imitate Alexander in superficial details,[2] with their scarlet cloaks, their bodyguards, the angle at which they held their heads, or the lofty tone of their speech: it was Pyrrhus alone who could remind them of him in arms and in action.

As for Pyrrhus' knowledge and mastery of military tactics and the art of generalship, the best proof is to be found in the writings he left on those subjects. It is said that when Antigonus was asked who was the best general, he replied, 'Pyrrhus, if he lives to be old enough' – he was speaking, I should add, of the generals of his own time. Han-

1. See *Life of Demetrius*, ch. 41.   2. See *Life of Alexander* ch. 4.

nibal's verdict was that the greatest of all generals in experience and ability was Pyrrhus, that next to him came Scipio, and after that himself, as I have written in my *Life of Scipio*.[1] In a word, Pyrrhus seems to have continually studied and reflected upon this one subject, which he considered the most kingly of all branches of learning: the others he regarded as mere accomplishments and set little store by them. We are told that on one occasion he was asked at a drinking-party whether he preferred Python to Cephisias as a flute-player: his reply was that Polyperchon was a good general – so much as to say that this was the only subject on which a king needed to inform himself and pass judgement.

Towards his close friends he was considerate and not easily moved to anger: he was also appreciative of any favours that were done him and eager to repay them. Certainly when Aeropus died, he was deeply distressed: he remarked that Aeropus had only suffered what was the common lot of humanity, but he reproached himself, because he had been dilatory and had put off what he had intended doing and so had not repaid his friend's kindness. Debts of money can be repaid to the creditor's heirs, but a just and upright man will be tormented by his conscience if he does not repay debts of kindness to his friends at a time when they can feel his gratitude. In Ambracia there was a man who constantly abused and spoke ill of Pyrrhus, and many people considered that he should be banished. 'No,' declared Pyrrhus, 'he had better stay here, where he can only speak ill of me to a few people, rather than spread his slanders all round the world.' Again when some young men had insulted him in their cups and were later brought before him, Pyrrhus asked them whether they had uttered the abuse of which they were accused. 'We did, sire,' replied one of the youths, 'but we should have said worse things still if we had had more wine.' At this Pyrrhus burst out laughing and sent them away.

9. After Antigone's death, he married several wives so as to increase his power and further his political interests. One of these was the daughter of Autoleon, king of the Paeonians,[2] another was Bircenna, the daughter of Bardyllis, king of the Illyrians, and a third was Lanassa, daughter of Agathocles, the ruler of Syracuse, who brought him as her dowry the city of Corcyra which Agathocles had captured.

1. This *Life*, the parallel to the *Life of Epaminondas*, has been lost.
2. The northern neighbours of Macedonia.

By Antigone he had a son, Ptolemy, by Lanassa Alexander, and by Bircenna his youngest son, Helenus. He brought up all three to be fine soldiers, young men of fiery temperament who were well trained in arms, and he whetted their appetite for fighting from their earliest childhood. The story goes that one of them, while he was still a boy, asked him to whom he intended to leave his kingdom, to which Pyrrhus replied, 'To whichever of you keeps his sword the sharpest.' In fact, however, this saying differs very little from the tragic curse which Oedipus pronounced on his sons, to the effect that the brothers 'would divide their inheritance by whetted steel, not by lot'. So pitiless and ferocious a trait, we should remember, is greed.

10. After this battle with the Macedonians Pyrrhus returned home exulting in the glory and prestige he had won. When the Epirots gave him the title 'The Eagle' he told them, 'It is through you that I am an eagle: how should I not be, when I am borne up by your arms as if they were wings?' A little later, when he heard that Demetrius had fallen dangerously ill, he suddenly led an army into Macedonia. He had not intended to do more than make a swift raid and plunder a few districts, but he came near to subduing the whole country and gaining possession of the kingdom without striking a blow, for he advanced as far as Edessa without meeting any resistance, and many of the Macedonians flocked to his army and joined his expedition. At last the danger aroused Demetrius to leave his bed and disregard his sickness, while his friends quickly gathered a strong force and set out to offer a determined resistance to Pyrrhus. As the latter's plan had only been to plunder the country, he did not stand his ground but hastily withdrew and suffered considerable losses as the Macedonians harried his retreat.

However, although Demetrius had so easily and quickly driven Pyrrhus out of the country, he did not leave him out of his calculations. He had determined to embark on a great enterprise, nothing less than to win back his father Antigonus' dominions, for which he had collected a force of a hundred thousand soldiers and five hundred ships: in consequence he had no wish to embroil himself with Pyrrhus, nor to leave behind a restless and hostile neighbour on the frontier of Macedonia. As he had no time to fight a campaign against Pyrrhus, he was anxious to come to terms with him and make peace, and thus free himself to turn his arms against the other kings. Once he had reached an agreement with Pyrrhus, the size of his preparations revealed the true nature of his plans, and at this the kings became alarmed and sent messengers and letters to Pyrrhus. They were amazed, they said, that Pyrrhus should let slip the moment when it was most favourable for him to make war, but allow Demetrius to choose his own time. Just now Pyrrhus was well placed to drive Demetrius out of Macedonia, while his opponent was fully occupied and extended elsewhere. Did he intend to do nothing and wait for the time when Demetrius had grown strong again, and could then at his leisure make Pyrrhus fight for the temples and the tombs of his native Molossia, and would he allow all this to be done by a man who had lately taken Corcyra from him, not to mention his wife? I should explain that Lanassa, Pyrrhus' Sicilian wife, had quarrelled with him because he paid more attention to his barbarian wives than to her, and had gone to Corcyra. There she had invited Demetrius, since she was ambitious to make a royal match and had learned that he was the most ready of all the kings to entertain offers of marriage. So Demetrius sailed there, married Lanassa, and left a garrison in the city.

11. At the same time that they were writing to Pyrrhus in this strain, the kings did their utmost to distract Demetrius while he was completing his preparations for the campaign. Ptolemy sailed to Greece with a great fleet and set to work to persuade the cities there to revolt, while Lysimachus invaded the north of Macedonia from Thrace and pillaged the country, Pyrrhus chose the same moment to take the field and marched upon the city of Verroia: he calculated, rightly as it turned out, that Demetrius would march to meet Lysimachus and would thus leave southern Macedonia undefended. That night Pyrrhus dreamed that Alexander the Great sent for him, and that when he answered the summons, he found the king lying on a couch. Alexander welcomed him in a friendly fashion and promised his help, whereupon Pyrrhus ventured to ask him, 'How, sire, can you help me, when you are sick yourself?' 'With my name!', replied Alexander, and mounting a horse from Nisaea, he seemed to show Pyrrhus the way.

This vision gave Pyrrhus great confidence. He led his army by forced marches over the intervening country and occupied the city of Verroia. There he stationed the main body of his troops and sent out his commanders to subdue the remainder of the region. When Demetrius heard this news and became aware that a terrible commotion was taking place among the Macedonians in his camp, he halted his advance, because he was afraid that if his troops came any closer to a Macedonian king of such renown as Lysimachus, they would immediately go over to him. He therefore turned back and marched against Pyrrhus, calculating that he would be hated by the Macedonians because he was a foreigner. But no sooner had he pitched his camp in Pyrrhus' neighbourhood than many of the citizens of Verroia came out to visit him. They were loud in their praises of Pyrrhus, described him as an invincible soldier and a man of inspiring courage, and added that he treated his prisoners with kindness and consideration. Some of these visitors were Pyrrhus' agents: they were disguised as Macedonians and spread the word that now was the time to get rid of Demetrius and his overbearing rule by going over to Pyrrhus, a man who possessed the common touch and was devoted to his soldiers. In this way the majority of Demetrius' troops were roused to a high pitch of excitement and began to look everywhere for Pyrrhus. It so happened that he had taken off his helmet. Then he remembered that the soldiers did not know him, and so he put it on again and was instantly recognized by its high crest and the goat's horns which he wore at the sides. Some of the Macedonians ran up and asked him for the password of his army, and others, when they saw that his guards wore crowns of oak-leaves, garlanded their heads in the same way. Meanwhile some of Demetrius' followers had already summoned up courage to tell him that his best course would be to give up his ambitious plans and slip quietly away. Demetrius saw that this advice reflected only too clearly the mutinous state of his troops, and he took fright, put on a broad-brimmed hat and a private soldier's cloak, and stole off unnoticed. Pyrrhus came up, made himself master of the camp without a blow, and was proclaimed king of Macedonia.

12. When Lysimachus appeared upon the scene soon afterwards, he claimed that he had done as much as Pyrrhus to overthrow Demetrius, and demanded that the kingdom should be partitioned between them. Pyrrhus was by no means certain of the loyalty of the Macedonians, and so he accepted Lysimachus' terms, and they divided the cities and the territory. This compromise served its purpose for the

moment and prevented them from fighting one another, but it was not long before they recognized that the settlement, so far from allaying their mutual hostility, was a source of endless quarrels and disputes. For if two rulers are so greedy to acquire new territory that neither the sea nor the mountains nor the uninhabitable desert can limit their appetite, nor the boundaries which divide Europe and Asia serve as a barrier to their ambitions, it can hardly be expected when their frontiers actually run side by side that they will stay contented with what they have and do one another no wrong. On the contrary, they are continually at war, because to envy and to plot against one another becomes second nature, and they make use of the words war and peace just like current coin, to serve their purpose as the needs of the moment may demand, but quite regardless of justice. Indeed they are really better men when they openly admit that they are at war with one another than when they disguise under the names of justice and friendship those periods of leisure or inactivity which punctuate their acts of wrongdoing. Pyrrhus demonstrated this very clearly when he took up the cause of the Greeks and went to Athens expressly to check the growing power of Demetrius, and prevent its recovering, as it were, from a serious illness. There he climbed the Acropolis and offered sacrifice to Athena, and on the same day came down again and addressed the people. He expressed his pleasure at the confidence and goodwill they had shown him, but warned them for the future that if they knew what was best for them, they would never open their gates to any of the kings nor admit them into the city. Later he actually made peace with Demetrius, but then again, after Demetrius had set out for Asia, he attempted at Lysimachus' instigation to stir up a revolt in Thessaly, and he attacked the garrisons which Demetrius had left in various Greek cities. This was partly because he had discovered that the Macedonians were easier to manage when they were at war than when they were idle, and partly because his own nature could not endure inaction.

Later, however, after Demetrius had suffered a crushing defeat in Syria,[1] Lysimachus, who by then felt himself secure and had no other distractions, lost no time in marching against Pyrrhus. He found his opponent encamped at Edessa: there he attacked him, captured his supply columns, and caused his troops to suffer great hardship. Next, by writing letters to the leading Macedonians and spreading rumours,

1. At Ipsus in 301 B.C. See *Life of Demetrius*, ch. 29.

he contrived to subvert Pyrrhus' principal supporters. He reproached them for having chosen as their master a man who was a foreigner and whose ancestors had always been vassals of the Macedonians, and for having driven from their country the men who had been the friends and comrades of Alexander. When Pyrrhus discovered that many of the Macedonians were being won over, he took fright and withdrew, taking with him his Epirot troops and his allies, and in this way he lost Macedonia in exactly the same way that he had seized it. It follows that kings have no reason to blame the mass of humanity if it changes sides to suit its own interests, for the people are only imitating the kings themselves, who set them an example of bad faith and treachery, and who believe that the man who shows least regard for justice will always reap the greatest advantage.

13. At this time, then, when Pyrrhus had been forced to give up Macedonia and retire to Epirus, Fortune gave him the opportunity to enjoy his possessions without interference, and to live at peace ruling over his own subjects. But for Pyrrhus life became tedious to the point of nausea, unless he could stir up trouble for others, or have it stirred up for him. Like Achilles he could not endure inaction

> ... but heart-sick he brooded
> Pining at home for the war-cry, the noise of the battle.[1]

Yearning as he did for new adventures, he found his opportunity in the following circumstances.

The Romans were at this time[2] at war with the people of Tarentum, who were neither strong enough to carry on the struggle, nor, because of the reckless and unprincipled nature of their demagogues, inclined to put an end to it. They therefore conceived the idea of making Pyrrhus their leader and inviting him to take part in the war, since they believed that he was the most formidable general of all the Greek rulers and also that he was more free to act than the others. Among the older and more prudent citizens some, who were directly opposed to the plan, were silenced by the clamour and vehemence of the war-mongers, while others, seeing the way that matters were going, stayed away from the assembly. However there was a man named Meton, who was well known as a moderate. When the day

1. *Iliad* i, 491–2.   2. 281 B.C.

arrived on which the decree inviting Pyrrhus was to be confirmed, and while the people were taking their seats in the assembly, he snatched up a withered garland and a torch, as drunken revellers do, and came prancing and reeling into the assembly, accompanied by a flute-girl, who led the way for him. At this, as might be expected in a popular assembly which possessed little idea of decorum, some of the audience applauded and others laughed, but nobody made any move to stop him: instead they shouted to the girl to go on playing the flute and to Meton to come forward and give them a song, whereupon he made as if to obey them. But when silence had been restored, he made them a short speech as follows: 'Men of Tarentum, you are right not to hinder those who wish to make merry and enjoy themselves while they can. And if you are wise, you will make the most of your present freedom, for you may be sure that you will have other things to think of, and your way of life will be very different once Pyrrhus arrives in the city.' These words made an impression on the majority and a murmur of applause ran through the assembly. But those who were afraid that if peace were concluded they would be handed over to the Romans rebuked the people for tamely allowing a drunken reveller to insult them by such a disgraceful exhibition; then they banded together and drove Meton out of the assembly.

In this way the decree was ratified and the Tarentines sent a delegation to Pyrrhus, which included representatives of other Greek cities in Italy. They took with them gifts for the king, and explained to him that they needed an experienced commander, who had already earned a reputation. They also told him that they could provide large forces drawn from Lucania, Messapia, Samnium and Tarentum, which would total twenty thousand cavalry and three hundred and fifty thousand infantry. These promises not only stirred Pyrrhus' enthusiasm, but made the Epirots eager to take part in the expedition.

14. There was a man named Cineas, a Thessalian in Pyrrhus' entourage, whose judgement was greatly respected. He had been a pupil of Demosthenes and was considered to be the only public speaker of his time who could revive in his audience's minds, as a statue might do, the memory of the Athenian's power and eloquence. He was in Pyrrhus' service and was often sent as his representative to various cities, where he proved the truth of Euripides' saying

... words can achieve
All that an enemy's sword can hope to win.[1]

At any rate Pyrrhus used to say that Cineas had conquered more cities by his oratory than he himself by force of arms, and he continued to pay him exceptional honours and to make use of his services. This man noticed that Pyrrhus was eagerly preparing for his expedition to Italy, and finding him at leisure for the moment, he started the following conversation. 'Pyrrhus,' he said, 'everyone tells me that the Romans are good soldiers and that they rule over many warlike nations. Now if the gods allow us to defeat them, how shall we use our victory?' 'The answer is obvious,' Pyrrhus told him, 'If we can conquer the Romans, there is no other Greek or barbarian city which is a match for us. We shall straightaway become the masters of the whole of Italy, and nobody knows the size and the strength and the resources of the country better than yourself.' There was a moment's pause before Cineas went on. 'Then, sire, after we have conquered Italy, what shall we do next?' Pyrrhus did not yet see where the argument was leading. 'After Italy, Sicily, of course,' he said. 'The place positively beckons to us. It is rich, well-populated and easy to capture. Now that Agathocles is dead, the whole island is torn by factions, there is no stable government in the cities, and the demagogues have it all their own way.' 'No doubt what you say is true,' Cineas answered, 'but is our campaign to end with the capture of Sicily?' 'If the gods grant us victory and success in this campaign,' Pyrrhus told him, 'we can make it the spring-board for much greater enterprises. How could we resist making an attempt upon Libya and Carthage, once we came within reach of them? Even Agathocles very nearly succeeded in capturing them when he slipped out of Syracuse with only a handful of ships. And when we have conquered these countries, none of our enemies who are so insolent to us now, will be able to stand up to us. I do not have to emphasize that.' 'Certainly not,' replied Cineas. 'There is no doubt that when we have achieved that position of strength, we shall be able to recover Macedonia and have the rest of Greece at our feet. But after all these countries are in our power, what shall we do then?' Pyrrhus smiled benevolently and replied. 'Why, then we shall relax. We shall drink, my dear fellow, every day, and talk and amuse one another to our

1. *Phoenissae*, 517–8.

hearts' content.' Now that he had brought Pyrrhus to this point, Cineas had only to ask him, 'Then what prevents us from relaxing and drinking and entertaining each other *now*? We have the means to do that all around us. So the very prizes which we propose to win with all this bloodshed and toil and danger and all the suffering inflicted on other people and ourselves, we could enjoy without taking another step!'

These arguments disturbed Pyrrhus but did not convert him. He could see clearly enough the happiness he was leaving behind, but he could not give up the hopes he had set his heart on.

15. First, then, he sent Cineas ahead to Tarentum with three thousand soldiers. Next he assembled from Tarentum a large fleet of cavalry transports, decked ships and many other kinds of vessel, and on them he embarked twenty elephants, three thousand cavalry, twenty thousand infantry, two thousand archers and five hundred slingers. When all these were ready he set sail, but when he was half way across the Ionian sea the fleet was struck by a north wind which sprang up without warning and out of season. Although his ship was hard pressed, Pyrrhus himself, thanks to the courage and resolution of his sailors and helmsmen, was able to recover his course and after great labour and peril to make his landfall, but the rest were thrown into confusion and scattered. Some were driven away from the Italian coast altogether and on into Sicilian and Libyan waters; other vessels, which failed to round the Iapygian cape[1] before dark, were hurled by heavy and boisterous seas on to the rocky and harbourless coast, with the result that all were destroyed except the royal galley. This ship was so large and solidly constructed that she could hold out against the pounding of the water from the seaward side, but when the wind veered round and began to blow from the shore, she was in danger of going to pieces if she met the waves bows on, while to let her wallow in the rough open sea, battered by squalls which came from all directions, seemed the most dangerous course of all. At last Pyrrhus leaped to his feet and dived into the sea, and his friends and bodyguard vied with one another to follow him. But the darkness and the roar of the waves and the undertow made it difficult to help him, and it was not until daybreak, by which time the wind had begun to die down, that he was able to struggle ashore. By then his

1. The modern Cape Rizzuto in south-eastern Calabria.

strength was almost gone, but his courage and determination sustained him, even in this extremity. The Messapians, on whose coast he had been wrecked, quickly gathered and eagerly offered him all the help they could muster, and meanwhile some of his ships that had escaped the storm put in. These brought with them only a few cavalrymen, less than two thousand infantry, and two elephants.

16. With this force Pyrrhus set out for Tarentum, and Cineas, as soon as he learned of the king's arrival, led out his contingent to meet him. When Pyrrhus entered the city, he did nothing without the consent of the Tarentines, nor did he try to coerce them into any action, but waited until his fleet had safely reassembled and the greater part of his army had been regrouped. By then he had discovered that the people were quite incapable of helping him or themselves, unless circumstances compelled them. Their inclination was to allow him to do their fighting for them, while they stayed at home enjoying their baths and social entertainments. Accordingly Pyrrhus closed the gymnasia and public walks, where the citizens were in the habit of strolling about and fighting battles against the Romans with words. He also banned drinking-parties, banquets and festivals as unseasonable, conscripted the male population, and showed himself strict and inflexible in mobilizing all those required for military service. When they discovered this, many of the Tarentines left the city: they were so unaccustomed to discipline that they regarded it as slavery not to be allowed to live as they pleased.

The news now reached Pyrrhus that Laevinus, the Roman consul, was advancing on the city with a large army, plundering Lucania as he came. Pyrrhus' allies had not yet arrived, but he thought it disgraceful to remain inactive and allow the enemy to advance any nearer, and so he marched out with his troops. He had first dispatched a herald to the Romans to ask whether they would agree to receive satisfaction from the Italian Greeks before resorting to arms, and he offered his services as arbitrator and mediator. Laevinus' reply was that the Romans neither accepted Pyrrhus as a mediator nor feared him as an enemy, whereupon Pyrrhus advanced and pitched his camp in the plain between the cities of Pandosia and Heracleia.

When he discovered that the Romans were close by and had encamped on the other side of the river Siris, he rode up to reconnoitre the position. Their discipline, the arrangement of their watches, their orderly movements and the planning of their camp all impressed and astonished him, and he remarked to the friend nearest him, 'These may be barbarians, but there is nothing barbarous about their discipline: however we shall see in action what it is worth.' He had already begun to feel some uncertainty as to the outcome, and he now determined to wait for his allies to arrive. At the same time he posted a guard on the bank of the river to oppose the Romans if they tried to cross it. The Romans, however, were anxious to forestall the arrival of the forces for which Pyrrhus had decided to wait and immediately attempted the crossing. Their infantry made the passage at a ford, while the cavalry galloped through the water at many different points, and thereupon the Greeks who were on guard retreated from the bank, for fear that they might be encircled.

Pyrrhus was disturbed by this, so he ordered his infantry officers to take up their battle formation at once and wait under arms, while he himself advanced with his force of three thousand cavalry: he hoped to catch the Romans while they were still engaged in crossing the river and before they could regain their formation. But when he saw the glittering line of shields of the Roman infantry stretching along the bank, while their cavalry advanced against him in good order, he closed up his own ranks and led them in a charge. He stood out at once among his men for the beauty and brilliance of his elaborately ornamented armour, and he proved by his exploits that his reputation for valour was well deserved. Above all, although he exposed himself in personal combat and drove back all who encountered him, he kept throughout a complete grasp of the progress of the battle and never lost his presence of mind. He directed the action as though he were watching it from a distance, yet he was everywhere himself, and always managed to be at hand to support his troops wherever the pressure was greatest.

During the fighting Leonnatus the Macedonian noticed that one of the Italians had singled out Pyrrhus and was riding towards him, following his every movement. At length he said to the king, 'Do you see, sire, that barbarian who is riding the black horse with white feet? He looks like a man who is planning some desperate action. He never takes his eyes off you, he pays no attention to anybody else, and it looks as though he is reserving all his strength to attack you. You must be on your guard against him.' Pyrrhus replied, 'Leonnatus, no man can avoid his fate. But neither he nor any other Italian will find it an easy task once they get to close quarters with me.' Even as they were speaking, the Italian wheeled his horse, levelled his lance and charged at Pyrrhus. Then in the same instant that the Italian's lance struck the king's horse, his own was transfixed by Leonnatus. Both horses fell, but Pyrrhus was snatched up and saved by his friends, while the Italian, fighting desperately, was killed. His name was Hoplax: he was captain of a troop of horse and a Frentanian by race.

17. This episode taught Pyrrhus to be more cautious in future. He saw that his cavalry were now giving ground and he gave orders for the phalanx to take up formation. Then he gave his cloak and armour to one of his companions, Megacles, concealed himself after a fashion among his men, and charged the Romans with his infantry. The Romans resisted their onslaught bravely and for a long while the issue hung in the balance. It is said that the mastery of the field changed hands no less than seven times, as each side gave ground in turn or advanced. The king's change of armour, although well-timed for his personal safety, came near to losing him the battle. Many of the enemy attacked Megacles, and the man who first struck him, Decius, seized his cloak and helmet and rode up with them to Laevinus: as he did so he brandished them aloft and shouted out that he had killed Pyrrhus. The Romans, when they saw these trophies exultantly displayed and carried along their ranks, shouted aloud in triumph: the Greeks, on the other hand, were disheartened and dejected until Pyrrhus, discovering what had happened, rode along his line with bared head stretching out his hand to his allies and making himself known to them by his voice. At last, as the Romans began to be driven back by the elephants and their horses, before they could get near the great beasts, started to panic and bolt, Pyrrhus seized his opportunity: as the Romans faltered, he launched a charge with his Thessalian cavalry and routed the enemy with great slaughter.

According to Dionysius the Romans lost nearly fifteen thousand men and Pyrrhus thirteen thousand, while Hieronymus reduces these figures to seven thousand on the Roman side and four thousand on the Greek. But these were some of Pyrrhus' best troops, and in addition he lost many of the friends and commanders whom he trusted and employed the most. However he captured the Roman camp, which they abandoned, and he persuaded some of their allies to come over to his side. He also ravaged a large area, and advanced to a point less than forty miles distant from Rome. After the battle many of the Lucanians and Samnites flocked to join him. He reproached these peoples for coming so late, but it was clear that he was delighted and took especial pride in the fact that he had defeated such a great army of the Romans without any help but that of his own troops and the Tarentines.

18. The Romans did not remove Laevinus from his office as consul, but Gaius Fabricius is reported to have said that it was not the Epirots who had defeated the Romans, but Pyrrhus who had defeated Laevinus. Fabricius took the view that the Romans had been beaten through the fault of their general, not of the army. Meanwhile the fact that the Romans immediately brought the depleted legions back to full strength, raised others and spoke of the war only in a spirit of undaunted confidence made a deep impression on Pyrrhus. He decided to make an approach to them and discover whether they would come to terms, for he saw that to storm the city and subdue the whole Roman people would be an immense task and quite beyond the strength of his present force, whereas a pact of friendship and a settlement negotiated after his victory would greatly enhance his prestige. So Cineas was dispatched to Rome, where he conferred with the leading officials and brought gifts for their wives and children in Pyrrhus' name. Nobody was willing to accept his gifts, but they all declared, women and children alike, that if a peace were concluded by the will of the people, they for their part would show their regard and goodwill for the king. Again, when Cineas laid a number of tempting proposals before the Senate, not one of them was taken up with the least pleasure or enthusiasm: this in spite of the fact that Pyrrhus offered to release without any ransom all the prisoners he had taken in the battle, and undertook to help the Romans to subdue the rest of Italy. All he asked in return was that he should be treated as a friend and the Tarentines left unmolested.

On the other hand it was clear that the majority of the senators were inclined towards peace, for they recognized that they had been defeated in a great battle and must expect to have to fight another against an even stronger army, now that the Italian Greeks had joined Pyrrhus. It was at this point that Appius Claudius, a man of great distinction but one who had long been prevented by old age and blindness from playing an active part in politics, learned that the king's terms had been presented to the Senate, and that they were about to vote on the proposed cessation of hostilities. He could no longer bear to remain at home, but ordered his attendants to take him up, and had himself carried through the Forum to the Senate-house on a litter. When he arrived at the doors, his sons and sons-in-law supported him and guided him to his seat, while the senators honoured him by preserving a respectful silence.

19. Speaking from where he stood, Appius then addressed them as follows. 'Until now, my countrymen, I had felt the loss of my sight as a heavy affliction. But now it grieves me that I have not lost my hearing as well, when I learn of the shameful motions and decrees with which you propose to dishonour the great name of Rome. What has become of that boast which you have made famous throughout the world, that if the great Alexander had invaded Italy and encountered us when we were young men, or our fathers in their prime, he would not now be celebrated as invincible, but would either have fled or perhaps have fallen, and thus left Rome more glorious than ever before? Now, it seems to me, you are proving that this was mere bravado and empty boasting, since you shrink from these Chaonians and Molossians who have always been the prey and the spoil of the Macedonians, and you tremble before this Pyrrhus, who has spent most of his life dancing attendance on one or other of Alexander's bodyguards.[1] Now he comes wandering around Italy not so much to help the Greeks here as to escape from his own enemies at home, and he has the insolence to offer to help us subdue the country with this army which was not good enough to hold even a fraction of Macedonia for him. Do not imagine that you will get rid of this fellow by making him your friend. You will only bring other invaders after him, and they will despise you as a people whom anybody can subdue. This is what you can expect if you allow Pyrrhus to leave Italy not merely unpunished for the outrages he has committed against you, but actually rewarded for having made Rome a laughing-stock to the Tarentines and the Samnites.'

By the time Appius had finished, his audience were filled with the desire to continue the war, and Cineas was dismissed with the reply that Pyrrhus must first leave Italy, and only then, if he still wished it,

1. A sarcastic allusion to Pyrrhus' dealings with Ptolemy, Demetrius and Lysimachus.

would the Romans discuss the question of an alliance and a pact of friendship. So long as he remained on their soil in arms, they would fight him to the death, even though he defeated ten thousand Laevini in battle. It is reported that in the course of his mission Cineas took especial care to study the life and customs of the Romans, and to acquaint himself with the peculiar virtues of their form of government, and he also conversed with their most prominent men. On his return he had much to report to Pyrrhus. Among other things he told him that the Senate impressed him as an assembly of many kings, and as for the people, he feared that to fight against them would be like fighting the Lernaean Hydra. The consul had already raised an army twice the strength of the one which had faced Pyrrhus, and there were still many times this number of Romans who were able to bear arms.

20. After this a Roman delegation visited Pyrrhus to discuss the subject of the prisoners of war. It was headed by Gaius Fabricius, who, as Cineas advised the king, enjoyed the highest reputation among the Romans both as a fine soldier and as a man of honour, but who was also extremely poor. Pyrrhus entertained him privately and tried to persuade him to accept a present of money. He did not offer this for any dishonourable reason, he explained, but simply as a token of friendship and hospitality. Fabricius refused the gift, and for the moment Pyrrhus said nothing more. The next day, as he wished to startle a man who had never before seen an elephant, he ordered the largest he had to be placed behind a curtain, while they conversed on the other side. This was done and then at a given signal the curtain was drawn aside, the animal suddenly raised its trunk, held it over Fabricius' head and trumpeted with a loud and terrifying noise. Fabricius turned, smiled serenely at Pyrrhus and said, 'Your gold made no impression on me yesterday, and neither does your elephant today.'

Later when they dined together, they discussed many different topics, and in particular the subject of Greece and Greek philosophers. Cineas happened to mention Epicurus and expounded the theories of the Epicurean school concerning the gods, the conduct of politics, and the question of what is the highest good. He explained that the Epicureans considered pleasure to be the greatest good, but refrained from taking any active part in politics on the ground that it was injurious to and confused the pursuit of happiness; also that the

Epicureans believed the deity to be completely remote from feelings of benevolence, anger or concern for humanity, and conceived of the gods as leading a life which was devoid of cares and filled with comfort and enjoyment. Before Cineas could finish, Fabricius interrupted him, 'Hercules,' he exclaimed, 'pray grant that Pyrrhus and the Samnites continue to take these doctrines seriously so long as they are at war with us!'

After these encounters, Pyrrhus was filled with admiration for Fabricius' spirit and character, and he desired more than ever to make the Romans his friends instead of his enemies. He even went so far as to invite Fabricius, if he could bring about a settlement between the two peoples, to throw in his lot with the Greeks and live with him as the chief of his companions and generals. But Fabricius, so the story goes, quietly said to him, 'This arrangement, sire, would not be to your advantage. The same men who now admire and honour you, if they came to know me, would rather have me to rule them than yourself.' Such a man was Fabricius. For his part Pyrrhus did not take offence at this speech nor behave like a tyrant: he even told his friends of Fabricius' magnanimity, and entrusted the Roman prisoners of war to his charge alone. He did this on condition that if the Senate voted against making peace, the prisoners should be returned to Pyrrhus, though they were allowed first to greet their friends and spend the festival of Saturn with them. This was how matters turned out. The prisoners were sent back after the festival, and the Senate passed a decree that any who remained behind should be put to death.

21. Not long after, when Fabricius had become consul, a man arrived in the Roman camp with a letter for him. The writer was Pyrrhus' physician, who offered to poison the king, provided that the Romans would pay him a sufficient reward for putting an end to the war without any further danger to them. Fabricius was disgusted at the man's treachery and persuaded his colleague to take the same view: he immediately sent a letter to Pyrrhus, warning him to be on his guard against this plot. The letter ran as follows:

'Gaius Fabricius and Quintus Aemilius, the consuls of Rome, greet king Pyrrhus. It seems that you are a poor judge both of your friends and of your enemies. You will see when you read the letter I have sent you that you choose to make war against just and virtuous men and put your faith in rogues and traitors. We do not send you this information because of any love we bear you, but because we do not wish your downfall to bring any reproach upon us, nor to have men say of us that we brought this war to an end by treachery because we could not do so by our own valour.'

When Pyrrhus had read the letter and made further inquiries into the plot, he punished the physician and, by way of return to the Romans, delivered up his prisoners to them without ransom; he also once more sent Cineas to try to negotiate a peace for him. However, the Romans refused to take back the prisoners without payment; they were unwilling to accept a favour from an enemy or to be rewarded for having refrained from using treachery against him. As for Cineas' overtures concerning a treaty of peace and friendship, they declined to enter into any further discussion until Pyrrhus had removed his arms and his troops from Italy and returned to Epirus in the ships which had brought him.

Pyrrhus' affairs thus compelled him to fight another battle, and after he had rested his troops, he marched to the city of Asculum and attacked the Romans. Here he was obliged to manoeuvre on rough ground where his cavalry could not operate, and along the wooded banks of a swiftly flowing river where his elephants could not charge the enemy's infantry. There was fierce fighting in which both sides suffered heavy losses before night put an end to the engagement. The next day Pyrrhus regrouped his forces so as to fight on even terrain, where his elephants could be used against the enemy's line. At first light he detached troops to occupy the difficult ground, posted strong contingents of archers and slingers in the spaces between the elephants, and then launched his main body into the attack in close order and with an irresistible impetus. The Romans could not employ the feinting and skirmishing tactics they had used on the previous day and were compelled to receive Pyrrhus' charge on level ground and head on. They were anxious to repulse Pyrrhus' heavy infantry before the elephants came up, and so they hacked desperately with their swords against the Greek pikes, exposing themselves recklessly, thinking only of killing and wounding the enemy and caring nothing for their own losses. After a long struggle, so it is said, the Roman line began to give way at the point where Pyrrhus himself was pressing his opponents hardest, but the factor which did most to enable the Greeks to prevail was the weight and fury of the elephants' charge. Against this even the Romans' courage was of little avail: they felt as they might have done before the rush of a tidal wave or the shock of an earthquake, that it was better to give way than to stand their ground to no purpose, and suffer a terrible fate without gaining the least advantage.

The Romans had only a short distance to retreat before they reached their camp. They lost six thousand men killed, according to Hieronymus, who also records that Pyrrhus' casualties, according to the king's own commentaries, were three thousand five hundred and five. In Dionysius' account, on the other hand, there is no mention of two battles having been fought at Asculum nor that the Romans acknowledged any defeat: he says that the two armies fought on one occasion only and that this battle lasted until sunset, when they at last broke off the action with difficulty: he tells us that Pyrrhus was wounded in the arm by a javelin, that his baggage was plundered by the Daunians,[1] and that the losses of Pyrrhus and the Romans combined amounted to fifteen thousand men.

The two armies disengaged and the story goes that when one of Pyrrhus' friends congratulated him on his victory, he replied, 'One more victory like that over the Romans will destroy us completely!' He had lost a great part of the force he had brought with him, with a few exceptions almost all his friends and commanders had been killed, and there were no reinforcements which he could summon from home. At the same time he noticed that his allies were losing their enthusiasm, while the Roman army, by contrast, seemed to be fed, like a spring gushing forth indoors, by a constant stream of recruits, from which they could quickly and easily replace their losses. Defeat never seemed to undermine their self-confidence: instead their anger only gave them fresh strength and determination to pursue the war.

22. Even while he laboured under these difficulties, new prospects and fresh hopes presented themselves to divert him from his original purpose. News now reached him from two different quarters simultaneously. From Sicily there arrived a delegation which offered to put him in control of the cities of Agrigentum, Syracuse and Leontini, and begged him to help them expel the Carthaginians and free the island from its tyrants. And from Greece messengers

1. Roman auxiliaries from Apulia.

reported that Ptolemy, surnamed the Thunderbolt,[1] had been killed in a battle with the Gauls and his army annihilated, and that this was the moment for him to return to Macedonia, where the people needed a king. Pyrrhus railed against Fortune for presenting him with two opportunities of such importance at the same moment, and for a long while he hesitated in his choice, since he assumed that to take up the one would compel him to abandon the other. In the end it seemed to him that Sicily offered the more promising prospects, especially since Libya was so close at hand, and he immediately dispatched Cineas, as was his habit, to open preliminary negotiations with the cities, while he placed a garrison in Tarentum. The Tarentines were angry at this, and demanded that he should either devote his efforts to the task for which he had been invited, that is to help them fight the Romans, or else go away and leave their country as he had found it. He answered them roughly by telling them to keep quiet until he had time to attend to their affairs, and then sailed away.

When he arrived in Sicily[2] he found his hopes had already been effectively realized. The cities came over to him with enthusiasm, and even in those cases where it was necessary to use force, no place at first held out against him for long. He advanced with a combined expedition of thirty thousand infantry, two thousand five hundred cavalry and two hundred ships, and with these forces he routed the Carthaginians and overran the part of Sicily which had been under their rule. Next he decided to assault the citadel of Eryx,[3] which was the strongest of their fortresses and was held by a large garrison. When his army was ready for the attack, he donned his armour, appeared before his troops, and made a vow to Hercules that he would hold public games and offer sacrifice in his honour if the god would allow him on that day to prove himself before the Sicilian Greeks as a champion who was worthy to be descended from Achilles and fit to command an allied army of this size. Then he ordered the trumpet to sound the attack, drove the barbarians back from the battlements with a hail of missiles, had the scaling ladders brought forward, and was the first to climb the wall. There he engaged great numbers of the enemy. Some he forced off the wall and hurled to the ground on

1. The son of Ptolemy I of Egypt. In 280 B.C. he had assassinated Seleucus and made himself king of Macedonia.

2. Early in 278 B.C.

3. In the extreme west of Sicily, near the modern Trapani.

either side, but most of them he attacked with his sword, so that he was soon standing amid a heap of dead bodies. He himself was unscathed, but his appearance filled the enemy with terror, thus proving that Homer was right and was speaking from experience when he says that it is courage alone of all the virtues which often manifests itself in states of divine possession and frenzy.[1] After the city had been captured he offered up sacrifices to the god on a magnificent scale, and organized spectacles of many different kinds of contests.

23. The barbarians who lived in the neighbourhood of Messina had been the cause of many troubles to the Greeks and had compelled some of them to pay tribute. They formed a large and warlike population and had been given the name of Mamertines, which in the Latin language means the children of Mars. Pyrrhus first arrested their collectors of tribute and put them to death, and then he defeated the Mamertines in battle and destroyed many of their strongholds. Meanwhile the Carthaginians showed themselves ready to come to terms with him, and they offered to pay a sum of money and provide him with ships if a treaty were concluded between them. But Pyrrhus, who cherished much larger ambitions than these, replied that he could not consider the idea of a settlement or a pact of friendship between them except on one condition, namely that they should evacuate the whole of western Sicily and make the Libyan sea the frontier between themselves and the Greeks. Pyrrhus by now felt so elated by his success and the strength of his resources that he determined to pursue the ambitions with which he had originally sailed from Epirus, and make Libya his prime objective. Accordingly since many of the ships of his fleet were undermanned, he began to conscript rowers. However, he set about this in a thoroughly autocratic fashion: he made no attempt to treat the Greek cities with tact or consideration, but angrily resorted to force and punishments. He had not acted in this fashion at first, indeed he had gone out of his way to win friends by the courtesy of his manner, by his readiness to trust everybody and by his anxiety to do no harm. Now, however, he ceased to behave as a popular leader and became a tyrant, and besides the reputation for severity which he already possessed, he acquired another for ingratitude and bad faith.

1. See *Iliad* v, 185; vi, 101; ix, 238.

The Sicilians murmured against these impositions, but nevertheless put up with them as necessary evils: it was his treatment of Thoenon and Sosistratus which proved the turning-point in his dealings with the islanders. These two men were prominent citizens of Syracuse: they had been among the first to invite Pyrrhus to come to Sicily, and as soon as he had arrived they had placed the city in his hands and given him the greatest help in all he had achieved in Sicilian affairs. In spite of this, however, Pyrrhus would neither take them with him on his campaigns nor leave them behind, but treated them with suspicion. At length Sosistratus became alarmed at this behaviour and escaped, but Thonon was accused by Pyrrhus of plotting with Sosistratus against him, and was put to death. From this moment the attitude of the Sicilians towards him was transformed, and not only in Syracuse. All the cities now regarded him with feelings of mortal hatred, and some of them joined the Carthaginians, while others appealed to the Mamertines to help them. But at this moment, when Pyrrhus was faced on all sides with disaffection, insurrections against his authority, and a strongly united opposition, he received letters from the Tarentines and the Samnites, who begged for his help since they had been driven from their outlying territories, were confined to the boundaries of their cities, and could scarcely carry on the war even from within their own walls. This gave him a plausible excuse to sail away, so that his departure should not appear to be a flight or the result of his having despaired of his prospects on the island. But the truth was that he had failed to master Sicily, which was like a storm-tossed ship, and it was because he was anxious to escape that he once more threw himself into Italy. The story goes that as he was leaving, he looked back at the island and remarked to his companions, 'My friends, what a wrestling ground we are leaving behind us for the Romans and the Carthaginians.' And certainly it was not long before this prophecy of his was fulfilled.[1]

24. The barbarians combined to attack him while he was crossing to Italy. He fought a sea battle with the Carthaginians in the Straits of Messina and lost many of his ships, but escaped with the rest to Italy. Meanwhile a Mamertine army ten thousand strong had already crossed ahead of him. The Mamertines were afraid to face him in a pitched battle, but they harassed his march and caused great confusion

1. Pyrrhus left Sicily in 275 B.C. The First Punic War began eight years later.

to his army by attacking him at difficult points on his route. Two of his elephants were killed in these actions, and his rearguard suffered heavy losses. Pyrrhus had been at the head of his column, but he at once rode to the rear, helped to drive off the enemy, and exposed himself fearlessly in fighting against men who were not only courageous but well trained in battle. The enemy became all the more elated when Pyrrhus was struck on the head with a sword, and retired a little way from the fighting. One of the Mamertines, a man of giant stature clad in shining armour ran out in front of their ranks and challenged Pyrrhus in a loud voice to come forward if he were still alive. This infuriated Pyrrhus, and in spite of the efforts of his guards to protect him, he wheeled round and forced his way through them. His face was smeared with blood and his features contorted into a terrible expression of rage. Then before the barbarian could strike, he dealt him a tremendous blow on the head with his sword. So great was the strength of his arm and the keenness of the blade that it cleft the man from head to foot, and in an instant the two halves of his body fell apart. The barbarians immediately halted and came on no further, for they were amazed and bewildered at Pyrrhus and believed him to be superhuman. He was able to continue his march unopposed and arrived at Tarentum with a force of twenty thousand infantry and three thousand cavalry. He reinforced his army with the best of the Tarentine troops and immediately led them out against the Romans, who were encamped in the territory of the Samnites.

25. But in the meanwhile the many defeats which the Romans had inflicted on the Samnites had broken their power and subdued their spirit. They also harboured a grudge against Pyrrhus for having left them and sailed away to Sicily, and in consequence few of them joined him. Pyrrhus then divided his army into two parts. He sent one into Lucania to engage the other consul and prevent him from joining forces with his colleague: he himself led the main body of his forces against Manius Curius, who was encamped in a strong position near the city of Beneventum. Here the consul placed himself on the defensive: this was partly because he was waiting for the troops in Lucania, and partly because the soothsayers had advised against action on account of unfavourable omens from the sacrifices. Pyrrhus however was eager to attack this force before their comrades could arrive, and so he took his best troops and his most warlike elephants

and set out on a night march to the camp. But as he had chosen a long roundabout route, which led through wooded country, his torches went out, and the soldiers lost their way in the darkness and were thrown into confusion. Much time was lost in this way, the night passed, and daylight revealed his position to the Romans, as he bore down upon them from the heights.

The sight of the enemy created a great stir and commotion in the Roman camp, but the sacrifices now turned out to be favourable, and since action was forced upon him, Manius led out his troops and attacked the enemy's advance guard. He routed these and also succeeded in putting the main body to flight: many of them were killed and several of the elephants were left behind and captured. This success encouraged Manius to come down into the plain and engage the enemy there. In this action on open ground he drove back one wing of his opponent's army, but in another sector his own men were overwhelmed by the elephants and forced back to their camp. Manius now threw into the battle the troops who had been left to guard the camp and who were standing in great numbers along the ramparts, all under arms and fresh for the battle. They came down at the run from their strong position, flung their javelins at the elephants and forced them to wheel about, thus causing great confusion and dismay as they trampled on their own troops in their flight. This manoeuvre gave the victory to the Romans and finally established their superiority in the struggle with Pyrrhus. These battles not only steeled their courage and their fighting qualities, but also earned them the reputation of being invincible: the result was that they at once brought the rest of Italy under their sway, and soon after Sicily as well.

26. In this way Pyrrhus' hopes of the conquest of Italy and Sicily were finally demolished. He had squandered six years in his campaigns in these regions, but although he had been worsted in all his attempts, his spirit remained undaunted in the midst of defeat. The general opinion of him was that for warlike experience, daring and personal valour, he had no equal among the kings of his time; but what he won through his feats of arms he lost by indulging in vain hopes, and through his obsessive desire to seize what lay beyond his grasp, he constantly failed to secure what lay within it. For this reason Antigonus compared him to a player at dice, who makes many good throws,

but does not understand how to exploit them when they are made.

Pyrrhus brought back to Epirus[1] an army of eight thousand infantry and five hundred cavalry, and since he had no money, he looked about for a campaign to enable him to support this force. A number of Gauls joined him, and he made a raid on Macedonia,[2] originally intending only to strip and plunder the country, which was now ruled by Antigonus, the son of Demetrius. However after he had captured a number of cities and a force of two thousand Macedonians had come over to his side, his hopes began once more to rise. He marched against Antigonus, and making a surprise attack on him at the entrance to a narrow defile, threw his whole army into confusion. A strong contingent of Gauls who formed the rearguard of Antigonus' force stood their ground bravely, but after fierce fighting most of them were cut down, while the division of the army which contained the elephants was hemmed in and the drivers surrendered themselves and their animals. With this addition to his strength Pyrrhus decided to trust to his luck rather than his judgement, and disregarding the superior numbers against him, advanced to attack the Macedonian phalanx, which was already disorganized and demoralized because of the defeat of the rear-guard. They made no attempt to engage or resist their adversaries, and when Pyrrhus stretched out his right hand and called upon the commanders and captains by name, the whole of Antigonus' infantry went over to him. Antigonus escaped with a small detachment of cavalry and managed to secure some of the coastal cities, while Pyrrhus, who considered that of all his successes the victory over the Gauls was the one which added the most to his reputation, dedicated the finest and richest of the spoils to the temple of Athena Itonis. This was the inscription in elegiac verses which he had placed over them:

Pyrrhus the king dedicates these shields to Athena Itonis
    Trophies he earned from his victory over the valiant Gauls
When he defeated the host of Antigonus: that was no wonder
    Now, as of old, none can rival the Aeacidae[3] with the spear.

After the battle he immediately moved to occupy the cities of Macedonia. He captured Aegae, where he treated the inhabitants harshly and left a contingent of Gauls who were campaigning with

1. In 275 B.C.   2. In the spring of 274 B.C.

3. The sons of Aeacus, the ancestor of Achilles from whom Pyrrhus claimed descent.

him to garrison the city. As a race the Gauls possess an insatiable appetite for money, and they now dug up the tombs of the rulers of Macedon who are buried there, plundering the treasure and insolently scattering the bones. This outrage Pyrrhus treated with indifference; he either postponed action because he had too many urgent matters on his hands, or decided not to take any because he was afraid of punishing the barbarians. In any event the episode did much harm to his reputation with the Macedonians. Then while his affairs were still unsettled and before his position in Macedonia had been established, Pyrrhus' hopes suddenly veered in a new direction. He abused Antigonus and called him shameless because he continued to wear his royal robe of purple and had not yet exchanged it for a commoner's dress, and when Cleonymus the Spartan arrived and appealed to him to come to Lacedaemon, he sprang at the offer with enthusiasm.

Cleonymus, who was by now an elderly man, was of royal descent but was considered to possess a violent and autocratic disposition: he had failed to win the confidence or the goodwill of his people and the country was ruled by Areus. This was the cause of a long-standing grudge which Cleonymus bore against his fellow-citizens. In his later years he had married Chilonis the daughter of Leotychidas, a beautiful woman who also belonged to the Spartan royal family, but who had fallen passionately in love with Acrotatus, the son of Areus. Acrotatus was in the flower of his manhood, and so their relationship not only tormented Cleonymus, who loved his wife, but also dishonoured him, since every Spartan knew that she despised her husband. In this way Cleonymus' private troubles and his political grievances exacerbated one another, and it was these feelings of anger which had led him to bring Pyrrhus to Sparta.[1] Pyrrhus had with him twenty-five thousand infantry, two thousand cavalry and twenty-four elephants, and it was clear from the scale of his preparations that his aim was not to conquer Sparta for Cleonymus but the Peloponnese for himself. Of course he expressly denied any such intention, above all when the Spartan ambassadors met him at Megalopolis. He declared to them that he had come to liberate the cities which Antigonus was holding in subjection, and added that he planned to send his own sons to Sparta, if nothing prevented this, to be brought up according to the Lacedaemonian traditions, which

1. In the spring of 272 B.C.

would make them superior to all the other rulers of their time. These diplomatic inventions were fed to all those who came to meet him on his march, but no sooner had he reached Lacedaemonian territory than he began to ravage and plunder it. When the Spartan envoys complained that he was attacking their country without having declared war, he retorted, 'But neither do you Spartans, as we know very well, give any warning to others of what you are going to do.' At this one of the envoys named Madrocleidas remarked in the broad Spartan dialect, 'If you are a god, you will do us no harm, for we have done none to you. But if you are a man, you may meet one who is stronger than you are.'

27. After this Pyrrhus marched southward against the city of Sparta. Cleonymus strongly urged him to attack the city on the very first evening that he arrived. But Pyrrhus was afraid, it is said, that his troops would sack the city if they attacked it by night, and so he held them back, telling Cleonymus that they could achieve the same result by day. The town was only thinly defended and the speed of Pyrrhus' advance had taken the Spartans unawares, for King Areus was in Crete on an expedition to help the people of Gortyne. As events turned out, it was precisely the fact that Pyrrhus despised the city's apparent weakness and lack of defenders which proved to be its salvation. Pyrrhus assumed that there would be no resistance and pitched camp for the night, while Cleonymus' friends and helots prepared his house and decorated it, expecting that Pyrrhus would dine there with him.

When it was dark, the Lacedaemonians at first debated the possibility of sending their women-folk to Crete, but the women opposed this, and Archidamia walked into the Senate with a sword in her hand and reproached the senators on their behalf for proposing that their wives and daughters should survive while Sparta itself perished. Next it was resolved to dig a trench parallel with the enemy's camp and to place at each end waggons buried up to their axles, so that once embedded in this way, they could resist the charge of the elephants. As soon as this work began the women arrived on the scene, some of them in their robes with their tunics knotted round the waist, others dressed only in their tunics, and all joined in to help the older men. The younger males who had been assigned to the defence were ordered to rest, and the women dug a third of the trench with their hands. According to Phylarchus the trench was eight hundred feet long, nine feet wide and six feet deep, although Hieronymus says that its dimensions were rather smaller. When day dawned and the enemy began to move, the women brought the young men their arms, handed over the trench to them, and urged them to guard and keep it safe. They reminded them that it would be sweet to conquer in sight of the whole country and glorious to die in the arms of their wives and mothers, laying down their lives in a manner that was worthy of Sparta. As for Chilonis, she retired to her house and had a halter ready round her neck, so that she would not fall into Cleonymus' hands if the city were captured.

28. Pyrrhus now led a frontal attack at the head of his infantry. He strove to force a way through the wall of shields presented by the Spartans who were drawn up in deep formation, and to cross the trench, but this proved difficult because the freshly turned earth gave his soldiers no firm footing. Then his son Ptolemy led a picked force of Chaonians and two thousand Gauls round the end of the trench and tried to break through the barricade of waggons. These had been dug in so deeply and so close together that they not only obstructed his advance but made it difficult for the Lacedaemonians to reach the point he was attacking. The Gauls succeeded in pulling the wheels up, but as they began to haul the waggons down to the river, the young Acrotatus saw the danger, and running through the city with three hundred men, managed to get behind Ptolemy's soldiers, from whom he was concealed by some depressions in the ground; from here he attacked the rear of Ptolemy's detachment and forced them to turn and defend themselves. In this way the barbarians were crowded against one another, so that they fell into the trench and among the waggons, and at last they were driven back with great slaughter. The veterans and the crowd of women all witnessed Acrotatus' gallant exploit, and as he returned through the city to his appointed post, covered with blood, but triumphant and exulting in his victory, it seemed to the Spartan women that he had grown even taller and handsomer than before and they envied Chilonis her lover: some of the old men even followed him and shouted, 'Go, Acrotatus, and make love to Chilonis, but be sure that you beget brave sons for Sparta!' Meanwhile a fierce battle was also raging around Pyrrhus, and many of the Spartans fought magnificently, especially a man

named Phyllius who surpassed all his comrades in the stubbornness of his resistance and the numbers of the attackers whom he laid low. When he found that his strength was ebbing away on account of all the wounds he had received, he made way for one of his comrades to take his place and fell dead inside the line of shields, so as to be sure that his body should not fall into enemy hands.

29. As darkness fell, the fighting died down, and that night while Pyrrhus slept, he saw the following vision. He dreamed that Sparta was stricken with thunderbolts hurled from his own hand, that the whole countryside was ablaze, and that he was filled with rejoicing. This feeling of delight woke him and he gave orders to his commanders for the army to prepare for action: meanwhile he described his dream to his friends, for he was convinced that they would capture the city by storm. Most of them agreed with this interpretation and were full of admiration, except only for one named Lysimachus, who found the dream disturbing: he explained he was afraid that as places which have been struck by thunderbolts are held to be sacred, and may not be trodden by the foot of man, so the gods might be warning Pyrrhus that the city was not for him to enter. But Pyrrhus declared that this was idle chatter invented for those who knew no better, and he called upon his listeners to take up their weapons and act on the belief that

One is the best of all omens, to fight for the sake of King Pyrrhus![1]

Then he rose and at daybreak led out his army to the attack.

Once again the Spartans defended themselves with a resolution and courage out of all proportion to their numbers. The women too were in the thick of the action, handing the men arrows and javelins, bringing food and drink wherever they were needed, and carrying away the wounded. The Macedonians tried to fill up the trench, bringing up great quantities of material and throwing it over the weapons and the corpses which lay at the bottom, and when the Lacedaemonians tried to prevent these tactics, Pyrrhus appeared on horse-back, fighting his way past the trench and the waggons and into the city. Those who were defending this part of the Spartan

1. The line is adapted from *Iliad* xii, 243, Pyrrhus being substituted for *patris* (one's country).

line raised a shout, and the women began to shriek and run wildly about, but just as Pyrrhus had cleared a path through the waggons and was attacking the men in front of him, his horse was wounded in the belly by a Cretan javelin, and rearing up in its death agony threw the king on to the steep and slippery slope. This accident caused dismay and confusion among his companions, and the Spartans seized the moment to charge, and making good use of their missiles drove the enemy back. After this Pyrrhus gave the order to halt the fighting elsewhere on the battlefield; he believed that the Spartans were on the point of surrendering, since many of them had been killed and almost all were wounded. But at that moment the city's good fortune came to her rescue. It may be that she was satisfied that the courage of her citizens had been proved, or perhaps wished to show her own power to save the day when all seemed lost. At any rate, Ameinias the Phocian, one of Antigonus' generals, suddenly appeared from Corinth with a contingent of mercenaries, and no sooner had he been admitted into the city than Areus arrived from Crete with his army of two thousand soldiers. Thereupon the women returned to their homes, since they no longer thought it necessary to take part in the defence, and the soldiers relieved the veterans, who had been obliged in the emergency to arm themselves, and took their places in the order of battle.

30. For his part Pyrrhus was spurred on to make an even fiercer effort to capture the city now that it had been reinforced. But as his renewed attacks met with no success and his losses mounted, he abandoned the assault, took to plundering the countryside, and planned to spend the winter there. However, no man can escape his destiny. It happened that civil war had broken out at Argos between Aristeas and Aristippus, and since Aristippus was believed to be supported by Antigonus, Aristeas promptly invited Pyrrhus to Argos. Now Pyrrhus, as we have seen, kept his hopes in perpetual motion, and since he thought that every success could serve as the starting-point for a new enterprise, and every failure could be retrieved by a fresh start, he allowed neither defeat nor victory to limit his capacity to make trouble for himself or for others. So no sooner had he received this offer than he broke camp and set off for Argos. Areus, however, posted a number of ambushes, and by occupying the most difficult points on Pyrrhus' line of march, he succeeded

several times in cutting off the Gauls and the Molossians who formed Pyrrhus' rearguard.

Pyrrhus had been warned by one of his diviners that the liver of the victim of one of his sacrifices was without a lobe and that this portended the death of one of his kindred. But unluckily because of the commotion and disorder created by the ambush he forgot this warning, and ordered his son Ptolemy to go with his companions to relieve the rear-guard, while he himself hastened the advance of the main body and led them out of the defile. When Ptolemy arrived a fierce battle developed, and while a picked company of Spartans commanded by Evalcus engaged the troops who were fighting immediately in front of Ptolemy, a Cretan named Oryssus from Aptera, a man who combined exceptional strength of arm and speed of foot, sprinted round the flank, approached the young prince where he was fighting bravely, flung a javelin and struck him down. When Ptolemy fell, the rest of his troops gave ground, and the Spartans followed in headlong pursuit, until before they knew where they were they had broken out into the plain and were cut off by Pyrrhus' infantry. Pyrrhus himself had just learned of his son's death, and in an agony of grief ordered his Molossian cavalry to charge the Spartans. He himself rode at their head and strove to drown his sorrow in Spartan blood. He had always shown himself to be an irresistible and terrifying fighter, but this time his daring and his fury surpassed anything that had been seen before. When he rode at Evalcus, the Spartan side-stepped his charge and aimed a blow with his sword that just missed Pyrrhus' bridle-hand and sheared through the reins. Pyrrhus ran him through with his lance, but in the same moment fell from his horse: he went on fighting on foot, and cut to pieces the picked company of Spartans who were fighting round the body of Evalcus. This was a great loss to Sparta: the campaign against Pyrrhus was effectively over and the deaths of these men were really due to the desire of their commanders to distinguish themselves.

31. In this way Pyrrhus had offered up a sacrifice, so to speak, to the ghost of his son, and had made his death the occasion for a glorious victory. He had also found relief for much of his grief in the fury with which he had attacked the enemy and he proceeded to lead on his army towards Argos. He learned that Antigonus had already occupied the heights which commanded the plain, and so he pitched

his own camp close to Nauplia. On the next day he sent a herald to
Antigonus denouncing him as a robber and challenging him to come
down into the plain and fight for the realm of Argos. Antigonus
replied that when he was conducting a campaign, he chose his own
moment to fight, and that if Pyrrhus was weary of life, he could find
many ways to die. Meanwhile the two kings were visited by deputa-
tions from Argos, who begged them to go away and allow the city
to remain neutral but on friendly terms with them both. Antigonus
agreed to this and handed over his son to the Argives as a hostage.
Pyrrhus likewise agreed to go, but as he gave no pledge, he was
regarded with even greater suspicion than before. Pyrrhus was then
himself the witness of a remarkable portent. The heads of the cattle
which he had sacrificed were seen, as they lay apart from the bodies,
to put out their tongues and lap up their own blood, and besides this
the priestess of the temple of Lycian Apollo in the city of Argos ran
out of the shrine in a frenzy, crying that she saw the city full of
carnage and dead bodies, and that there was an eagle which visited
the battlefield and then disappeared.

32. At dead of night Pyrrhus marched his troops up to the walls,
found that the gate known as Diemperes had been opened for him by
Aristeas, and so his Gauls were able to enter the city and seize the
market-place before the alarm was raised. But the gate was too small
to let his elephants through, and the howdahs which they carried on
their backs had to be unfastened and then put on again when the
animals were inside. All these manoeuvres had to be carried out in
the darkness and so caused confusion and delay, and at length the
alarm was given and the Argives roused. They hurried to the place
known as The Shield and to other strong-points in the city, and sent
messengers to Antigonus calling on him to help. Antigonus marched
up close to the walls, halted there and sent his generals and his son
inside with a strong relieving force, while at the same time Areus
came up with a detachment consisting of a thousand Cretans and
light-armed Spartans. These troops joined forces, attacked the
Gauls and threw them into great confusion. Meanwhile Pyrrhus had
come up from the gymnasium outside the walls which is known as
Cytharabis, and his troops entered the city with warlike shouts. But
he noticed that the answering shouts from the Gauls in the market-
place sounded weak and undecided, and he at once guessed that they

were hard pressed. He therefore tried to quicken his pace and urged on the horsemen ahead of him: they were picking their way with great difficulty among the water-conduits with which the whole city is intersected and which endangered their advance. All the while in this night action there was great confusion as to what orders were being given and how they were being carried out. Men wandered about and lost their direction in the narrow alley-ways, and amid the darkness, the confused noise and the confined spaces, generalship was helpless. In consequence both sides found they could achieve little under these conditions and waited for the dawn.

As it began to grow light Pyrrhus was disturbed to see that the whole of the open square known as The Shield was filled with enemy troops, and then among the many votive offerings in the market-place he caught sight of the statue of a wolf and a bull carved in bronze and about to attack one another. He remembered with sudden dread an oracle which had predicted many years before that he was fated to die when he saw a wolf fighting with a bull. According to the Argives these figures were set up to commemorate a very early event in their history. When Danaus had first landed in the country near Pyramia in the district of Thyreatise and was on his way to Argos, he saw a wolf fighting with a bull. He supposed that the wolf must represent himself, since he like the wolf was a foreigner and had come like it to attack the native inhabitants. He watched the contest, and when he saw that the wolf had gained the day, he offered his prayers to Apollo Lyceius the wolf-god, attacked the city and was victorious, after Gelanor who was then the king had been driven into exile by a rival party. This, then, is the account the Argives give of how he came to dedicate the statue.

33. The sight of these animals combined with the evident failure of his plans disheartened Pyrrhus and he decided to retreat. But remembering how narrow the gates were, and fearing that he might be trapped behind them, he sent a message to his son Hellenicus, who had been left outside the city with the main body of the army: the orders were that he should break down the wall and cover the retreat of Pyrrhus and his men as they passed through the breach in case they were being hard pressed by the enemy. But in the haste and confusion the messenger failed to convey these instructions clearly, so that the young prince taking the remainder of the elephants and

the best of the troops marched through the gate into the city to rescue his father. By this time Pyrrhus was already beginning to withdraw. As long as the action remained in the main square where there was plenty of room to fight and give ground, he could retreat in good order, turning every now and then to drive off his attackers. But after he had been forced out of the market-place into the narrow street which led to the gate, he met the reinforcements who were hurrying to the rescue from the opposite direction. Some of these troops could not hear Pyrrhus when he shouted to them to retire, while those who were only too anxious to obey him were prevented from doing so by the men who kept pouring in behind them from the gate. Worse still, the largest of the elephants had fallen across the gateway, and lay there bellowing and blocking the way for those who were struggling to get out. Another elephant named Nicon, one of those which had advanced further into the city, was trying to find its rider who had been wounded and fallen off its back, and was battling against the tide of fugitives who were trying to escape. The beast crushed friend and foe together indiscriminately until, having found its master's dead body, it lifted the corpse with its trunk, laid it across its tusks, and wheeling round in a frenzy of grief, turned back, trampling and killing all who stood in its path. The crowd of soldiers was so tightly pressed and jammed side by side that nobody could help himself: the whole mass, which appeared to be bolted together into a single body, kept surging and swaying this way and that. They could scarcely move to fight those of the enemy who from time to time were caught up in their ranks or attacked them from the rear, and indeed it was themselves to whom they did most harm. Once a man had drawn his sword or aimed his spear it was impossible for him to sheathe or put it up again, but it would pierce whoever stood in its way, and so many men died from these accidental thrusts that they gave one another.

34. At length Pyrrhus, buffeted by these human waves that surged around him on every side like a stormy sea, took off the diadem which decorated his helmet, and handed it to one of his companions. Then trusting to his horse, he plunged in among the enemy who were pursuing him and was wounded by a spear which pierced his breastplate. This was not a mortal wound, nor even a serious one, and Pyrrhus at once turned to attack the man who had struck him. This

was an Argive, not a man of noble birth, but the son of a poor old woman, who like the rest was watching the battle from the roof of her house. When she saw that her son was engaged in combat with Pyrrhus, she was filled with fear and rage at the danger to him, and picking up a tile with both her hands, she hurled it at Pyrrhus. It struck him below the helmet and bruised the vertebrae at the base of his neck, so that his sight grew dim, his hands dropped the reins, and he sank down from his horse and collapsed on the ground near the tomb of Likymnius. Most of those who saw him had no idea who he was, but a man named Zopyrus who was serving with Antigonus ran up to him, recognized him, and dragged him into a doorway just as he was beginning to recover his senses. When Zopyrus drew an Illyrian short sword to cut off his head, Pyrrhus gazed at him with such a terrible look that Zopyrus lost his nerve. His hands trembled, but he forced himself to make the attempt. However, as he was half paralysed with fear and excitement, his blow was badly aimed. The first stroke fell on Pyrrhus' mouth and chin, and it was only slowly and with difficulty that he cut off the head. The news spread quickly, and presently Alcyoneus ran up and demanded to see the head so as to identify it. He took hold of it, rode off to where his father was sitting among his friends, and threw it at his feet. When he recognized it, Antigonus struck his son with his staff and drove him out of his presence, telling him that he was accursed and no better than a barbarian. He covered his face with his cloak and burst into tears as he thought of his grandfather Antigonus and his father Demetrius, who in his own family had suffered just such vicissitudes of fortune.

Then he had Pyrrhus' body prepared for burial and burned with due ceremony. Later, when Alcyoneus found Pyrrhus' son disguised in mean and threadbare clothes, he treated him kindly and brought him to Antigonus. When he saw him, Antigonus said, 'This is better my son, than what you did before, but even now you have not done well to leave him in these clothes, which are a disgrace to us now that we know ourselves the victors.' Antigonus greeted Helenus courteously, clothed him as befitted his rank, and sent him back to Epirus. He also treated Pyrrhus' friends with consideration, when the whole of his opponent's army and their camp fell into his hands.

APPENDIX

* *
*

THE events of the two decades which followed the death of Alexander in 323 are confusing to the general reader. Four of the subjects of this volume are involved in this epoch of Greek history – Phocion, Demosthenes, Demetrius and Pyrrhus – but Plutarch's account of their individual careers necessarily leaves many blank spaces in the surrounding picture. This appendix and the biographical notes which follow it attempt to fill in some of the gaps and to provide points of reference for the many unfamiliar names of which Plutarch's narrative is full at this point. After the battle of Ipsus, the end of the story of Demetrius and the career of Pyrrhus present themselves as self-contained narratives, which make few references to events in other parts of the Greek world.

Alexander had never named an heir. Moreover the Macedonian monarchy was not truly hereditary by primogeniture but elective, though in practice the same royal family always supplied the king. Normally the election may have been a formality of 'acclamation', but in 323 there was no obvious successor. The choice of one thus devolved upon the Macedonian army, and it so happened that the majority of the troops then in Asia were concentrated at Babylon when Alexander died. In the struggle for power which developed, the infantry and the cavalry, which broadly speaking represented the peasantry and the aristocracy respectively, were at first ranged on opposing sides. At the council of generals Perdiccas, the senior cavalry commander, proposed that they should await the birth of Roxane's child, which was shortly expected, and that if this was a male, he should be made king. Meleager, one of the infantry generals, argued that the king should be a Macedonian, not the son of a barbarian woman. The only candidate who satisfied these conditions was Arrhidaeus, Alexander's half-brother – the son of Philinna, a Thessalian mistress of Philip's – who was, however, mentally retarded and epileptic. A compromise was finally reached whereby Arrhidaeus was re-named Philip and proclaimed king without delay, and in August when Roxane's child proved to be a boy, a dual kingship was established, and the rulers proclaimed as Philip III and Alexander IV. Administrative power was divided between Antipater in Macedonia and Perdiccas as chief executive and commander of the forces in Asia, with Meleager as his deputy. Craterus was appointed guardian of Philip, but Perdiccas obtained the custody of his person; this arrangement left Perdiccas with the initiative, and Craterus with a mere power of veto. One of Perdiccas' first actions was to execute his rival Meleager.

The death of Alexander encouraged the Greek city states in the hope that they could throw off the Macedonian yoke. A revolt of the Greek troops whom Alexander had settled in the eastern provinces was put down, but the rising on the Greek mainland was a more serious threat. It was led by the Athenians, who quickly mobilized a strong fleet and joined forces with their allies and other mercenary troops to besiege Antipater in Lamia. But this success was short-lived. In the spring of 322 Leosthenes, the Athenian commander, was killed outside Lamia, and in the summer the Athenian fleet was defeated and lost control of the Aegean. This enabled Craterus to cross from Asia and relieve the beleaguered troops in Lamia. Thus reinforced, he and Antipater met the Greek army at Crannon, and although the battle was militarily inconclusive, its political consequence was that the rebel coalition melted away. Thereafter Antipater posted garrisons in many of the Greek cities, and curbed the Athenian democracy by reforming the constitution and limiting the franchise.

Meanwhile in Asia the struggle for power developed into a contest between Perdiccas, who aspired to hold Alexander's empire together and impose a central authority, and those generals who believed that the empire must break up and wished to establish themselves as local dynasts. One of the most active of these was Ptolemy, who had begun to carve out a kingdom for himself in Egypt and the surrounding territories. In 321 Perdiccas marched against him, leaving Eumenes to contain the invading forces of Antipater and Craterus. Eumenes carried out this task successfully, and at their first encounter near the Hellespont Craterus was killed. Meanwhile after Perdiccas had made two unsuccessful attempts to force the crossing of the Nile and suffered heavy losses, his troops mutinied and murdered him. Antipater then succeeded in rallying the Macedonian army and imposing a settlement. Antigonus was appointed senior commander in Asia Minor, and Antipater returned to Macedonia, taking the kings Philip and Alexander with him: there he died in 319 at the age of seventy-nine.

Before his death Antipater had delegated his authority as regent to one of his generals, Polyperchon, but this arrangement was promptly challenged by Antipater's son Cassander, who had expected to succeed his father. Polyperchon lacked the stature to dominate the difficult situation which he had inherited. He was unable to impose his authority over either Ptolemy or Antigonus, to whom Cassander at once appealed for help. Polyperchon reversed Antipater's treatment of the Greek city-states, removing the occupying garrisons, encouraging many of the cities to bring back their exiles, and thus strengthening the democratic factions. Cassander, on the other hand, upheld his father's repressive policy, and this was the situation in which Phocion found himself trapped. His friend Nicanor, the garrison commander of Munychia was a supporter of Cassander, but it was the democrats encouraged by Polyperchon who succeeded in seizing power, and who took their revenge by putting Phocion to death.

In the autumn of 318, however, Polyperchon's fleet was defeated off the Bosphorus, and the Athenians, recognizing that they must come to terms with whoever controlled the seas, opened negotiations with Cassander. He came to Athens, re-imposed Antipater's limitation of the franchise, and installed a benevolent autocrat, Demetrius of Phalerum, whose rule lasted for the next ten years. Cassander then proceeded to Macedonia, persuaded king Philip to appoint him regent in place of Polyperchon, and went on to consolidate his control of the Greek mainland.

Meanwhile Polyperchon had taken refuge in Epirus together with Roxane and her young son. There he sought out Olympias, Alexander the Great's mother, and persuaded her that she must join forces with him if her grandson were to have any hope of the succession. Such was the magic of Alexander's name that when she crossed the frontier the Macedonian troops at once deserted Philip and went over to her. Philip was executed and Olympias went on to order a massacre of Cassander's supporters. But here she overreached herself, and so alienated the sympathies of the Macedonians that when Cassander returned, he was able to shut her up in the city of Pella. In the spring of 316 she surrendered on an undertaking that her life would be spared, but soon afterwards Cassander, yielding to the pressure of the relatives of her victims, allowed the Macedonian army to sentence her to death. At the same time he kept Roxane and Alexander in close imprisonment, and thus, seven years after Alexander's death, his heirs had effectively ceased to exist.

It remained to be seen whether any of his military successors could take up his mantle, and the history of the next fifteen years is dominated by the struggle of the three most powerful of the Macedonian marshals, Ptolemy, Cassander and Antigonus. Of these Ptolemy was comparatively weak in man-power and Cassander in financial strength. Both men lacked the expansionist outlook which the role required, and were content to secure the possessions they already held: only Antigonus combined the resources and the ambition to reunite the empire under his rule.

While Cassander was campaigning against Polyperchon, Antigonus took the offensive against Eumenes, whom he rightly regarded as his most formidable opponent. Eumenes put up a gallant resistance, but in the following year (316), he was betrayed by his troops, captured and executed. Strengthened by this success Antigonus proceeded to assert his authority over the provincial governors of Asia Minor and their troops and annexed a large quantity of Alexander's treasure. But the result of this action was to bring about an alliance between Ptolemy, Seleucus, Cassander, and Lysimachus, the governor of Thrace. They demanded a redistribution both of territories and of the imperial treasure, and when these were refused, they declared war (315).

For this contest Antigonus by now possessed great financial resources and also the advantage of interior lines of communication. He invaded Syria, stirred up trouble for Cassander in Macedonia and for Lysimachus in Thrace and strove to win over the Greek city-states, as Polyperchon had done, by offering them self-government and freedom from Macedonian garrisons. However on each of these fronts he was able to achieve only limited success, and in 311 the five belligerents made peace: this settlement, it was generally recognized, served merely as a breathing-space to enable them to re-group and recover their strength. Cassander took advantage of this pause to end the long imprisonment of Roxane and her son Alexander by executing them.

The next four years witnessed a succession of minor campaigns and manoeuvres of political warfare. But in 307 Antigonus' son Demetrius suddenly seized the initiative: crossing from Ephesus to Athens he took Demetrius of Phalerum, Cassander's autocratic governor, completely by surprise and restored to the Athenians the outward forms at least of their democratic freedoms. Many of the institutions abolished by Demetrius of Phalerum were restored, and in their delight at their deliverance from a decade of authoritarian rule the Athenians so far forgot their egalitarian sentiments as to offer the most fulsome and obsequious compliments to their liberator.

The liberation of Athens dealt a serious blow to Cassander's prestige in mainland Greece, and accordingly Antigonus felt free to turn against Ptolemy. His first objective was the destruction of his opponent's fleet, which since Ptolemy's annexation of Phoenicia some years before had been built up to a formidable strength, and Demetrius was sent to attack its naval base on Cyprus. At the battle of Salamis, although Demetrius was outnumbered, he applied to naval warfare the tactics developed by Epaminondas and Alexander of concentrating superior strength at the point of attack and won a decisive victory. Antigonus followed up this success by conferring the title of King upon himself and Demetrius: by this action he placed his family in the direct line of succession to Alexander, thus implying his intention of establishing a dynasty which would reunite the empire.

With Ptolemy's fleet virtually annihilated, the way seemed clear for a combined invasion of Egypt by land and sea, and in the autumn of 306 Antigonus marched with an army of 88,000 men (a larger force than Alexander had ever put into the field). But this time the weather came to Ptolemy's rescue. A succession of storms made it impossible for Demetrius to land and Antigonus, unable to force the crossing of the Nile, was compelled to retire to Asia Minor. At this point and as a counter-move in the diplomatic war, Ptolemy and the other rulers of the coalition followed Antigonus' example and proclaimed themselves kings: this had the opposite effect to that of Antigonus' action, namely of denying the existence of a single imperial house and affirming the rule of a group of lesser monarchies.

In the following year (305) Demetrius was despatched to besiege

Rhodes. This operation was one of the most famous sieges of antiquity and earned Demetrius his title of Poliorcetes (Besieger of Cities). The object was to prevent Rhodes with her great ship-building capacity from helping Ptolemy to reconstruct his fleet. But Demetrius was unable to achieve quick results and the Rhodians finally obtained a negotiated peace. In 304 Antigonus resumed the strategic offensive and sent Demetrius to Greece. Here his campaign was so successful that he regained control of Attica, Central Greece and the Peloponnese and by 302 had compelled Cassander to sue for peace. Antigonus' terms, however, were so harsh that Cassander appealed to his allies for help. The coalition was once more mobilized, Lysimachus invaded Asia Minor and Antigonus in his turn was forced to recall Demetrius from Greece. The opposing forces met at full strength at Ipsus, 'the battle of the dynasts': here, thanks to Demetrius' impetuosity, the cause of Antigonus was lost and the prospect of the reunification of Alexander's empire under a single ruler was finally extinguished.

After the battle of Ipsus the map of western Asia was redrawn. Lysimachus' dominions in Thrace were enlarged so as to include western and central Asia Minor; Seleucus annexed Syria; Cassander's brother Pleistarchus was awarded the southern coast of Asia Minor from Caria to Cilicia. From this point the rest of Demetrius' career can be followed without difficulty. His reconciliation with Seleucus through a dynastic marriage (299); his return to mainland Grece and the rapid restoration of his fortunes (296–294); his reign as king of Macedon (294–288); his political irresponsibility which resulted in his deposition; his failure of strategic vision, which in his final campaign led him to throw away his command of the sea and strike recklessly inland – all these scenes in the tragedy of his career are swiftly and dramatically sketched in Plutarch's narrative.

1. MAINLAND GREECE

Chaeronea • • Orchomenus
Coronela •
• Thespiae
Leuctra • • Thebes • Rhamnus
• Plataea • Tanagra
Panactum • • Marathon
Eleusis • Phyle •
Megara • Athens
Sicyon • Piraeus •
Corinth •
Nemea • SALAMIS
Cenchreae •
AEGINA
• Argos • Calauria
Mantinea • Troezen •
Hermione •

• Epidamnus

PARAVAEA

• Aëgae
Apollonia • • Edessa • Pella
MACEDONIA
Mieza •
EPIRUS STYMPHAEA Beroea •
• Stageira

Potidaea •
MAGNESIA
Crannon • • Larisa
CORCYRA Dodona • Pharsalus •
THESSALY SCIATHOS
Cynoscephalae •
Pherae • Pagasae •

Ambracia • Aphetae •
Anactorium • Amphilochian Thermopylae • EUBOEA SCYROS
Argos
LEUCAS ACARNANIA AETOLIA LOCRIS Lamia • Cyme •
ITHACA Mt Parnassus PHOCIS
CEPHALLENIA Delphi • BOEOTIA
Oeniadae Aulis • Eretria
Rhium Naupactus • Chalcis
Patrae • Oropus ANDROS
Aegae • Corinth ATTICA
• Elis ACHAEA Lechaeum CEOS
ZACYNTHUS Olympia • ARCADIA Argos • Epidaurus
Lepreum • Tegea • AEGINA
MESSENIA LACONIA
Ithome • DELOS
Pylos • Sparta

THE PELOPONNESE
MELOS

0   50   100
miles
R. Eurotas CYTHERA

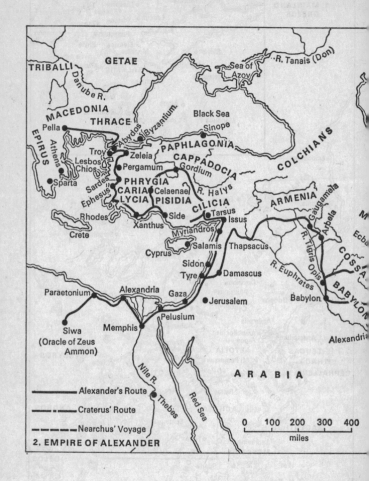

2. EMPIRE OF ALEXANDER

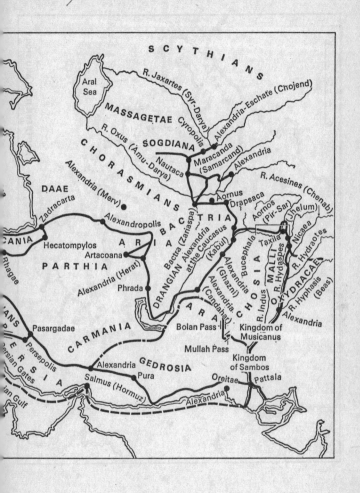

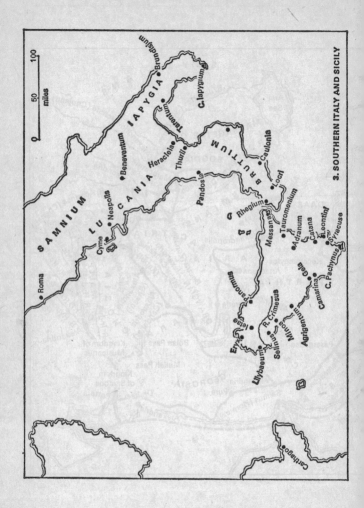

3. SOUTHERN ITALY AND SICILY

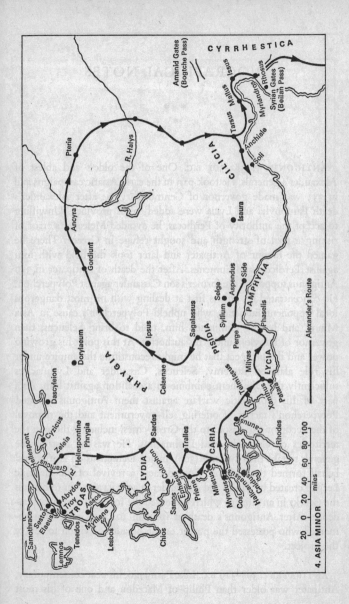

CYRRHESTICA

Amanid Gates (Bogtche Pass)
Issus
Rhosus
Myriandro
Syrian Gates (Beilan Pass)
Mallus
Tarsus
CILICIA
Anchiale
Soli
Pteria
R. Halys
Ancyra
Gordium
Dorylaeum
Ipsus
Celaenae
PHRYGIA
Sagalassus
PISIDIA
Selge
Sillium
Aspendus
Side
PAMPHYLIA
Perge
Phaselis
Milyas
Termessus
LYCIA
Telmissus
Xanthus
Patara
Dascyleion
Cyzicus
Hellespontine Phrygia
R. Granicus
Zeleia
Hellespont
Abydos
Sestos
Troy
Elaeus
TROAS
Assos
Myrtilene
Tenedos
Lesbos
Lemnos
Samothrace
Sardes
Colophon
Tralles
LYDIA
Ephesus
Samos
Priene
Miletus
Myndus
Cos
Halicarnassus
Cnidus
CARIA
Caunus
Rhodes
Chios

Isaura

Alexander's Route

0 20 40 60 80 100
miles

4. ASIA MINOR

BIOGRAPHICAL NOTES

* *
*

ANTIGONUS c. 382–301 B.C. One of the oldest and ablest of Alexander's generals. He took part in the early Asiatic campaigns and in 333 was made governor of Central Phrygia: after Alexander's death Pamphylia and Lycia were added to his province. Unwilling to accept the authority of Perdiccas, he avoided Meleager's error of risking a trial of strength and sought refuge in Greece. There he gained the favour of Antipater and later took the field with him against Perdiccas and Eumenes. After the death of Antipater in 319 Antigonus supported the former's son Cassander against Polyperchon. He concentrated his efforts first at dealing with his most dangerous local opponent Eumenes, who upheld Polyperchon's cause in Asia Minor, and having eliminated him, tried to bring Seleucus, then governor of Babylon, under his authority. At this point his growing power and the prospect that he might reconstitute the empire under his rule alarmed Ptolemy, Seleucus, Cassander and Lysimachus sufficiently to make them combine in a coalition against him. As a part of his diplomatic warfare against them Antigonus adopted Polyperchon's tactics of offering self-government and the removal of the occupying garrisons to the Greek cities, including those in the territories of Cassander and Lysimachus. He was the first of the generals to take the royal title (306). In 304 Demetrius on Antigonus' behalf formed the Hellenic Confederacy, a revival of the Hellenic League created by Philip and Alexander in 338: its aim was to harness the Greeks in an alliance which preserved the forms of their independence. After Antigonus's death at Ipsus in 301 no Greek ruler remained who possessed the power or the breadth of vision to revive the project.

ANTIPATER c. 398–319 B.C. Like Parmenio, his near contemporary, Antipater was older than Philip of Macedon and one of his most valued generals. He was sent to Athens as ambassador in 346 and negotiated peace with the Athenians after Chaeronea. When Alexander set out for Asia he left Antipater in charge of Macedonia and Greece. Here he frequently found himself opposed by Olympias, who undermined his position first with Alexander and later with Perdiccas. After Alexander's death Antipater commanded in Europe against the Greeks in the Lamian war, and for a short while after the murder of Perdiccas he restored order to the empire. His authority was accepted by the Macedonian troops in Asia, the command of whom he entrusted to Antigonus while he himself brought back the kings, Philip and Alexander, to Macedonia. His alliance with Antigonus was cemented by the marriage of his daughter Phila (the widow of Craterus) to Antigonus' son Demetrius. But by then Antipater was nearing eighty and this period of stability was cut short by his death.

CASSANDER c. 355–297 B.C. The son of Antipater, he did not accompany the Macedonian army on its invasion of Asia, but remained in Macedonia during his father's regency. He was sent to Babylon in 324 but did not find favour with Alexander. Displeased at his father's choice of Polyperchon for his successor, he set himself to oust his rival from the regency and sought help from Antigonus in Asia Minor. In 318 following the defeat of Polyperchon's fleet by that of Antigonus off the Bosphorus, Cassander returned to Macedonia, where he persuaded King Philip to depose Polyperchon. From this point his control of Macedon remained secure. In 316 he had Olympias executed and the young Alexander IV and his mother Roxane imprisoned: they were executed some years later. In the following year, alarmed by the growth of Antigonus' power, he joined the coalition of Ptolemy, Seleucus and Lysimachus against him. In mainland Greece Cassander continued the policy pursued by his father Antipater of treating the city-states as subjects rather than allies, in contrast to the policy of Antigonus and Demetrius. In Macedonia his rule was more beneficial, in that by refraining from expansionist aims he reduced the strain upon the country's man-power and financial resources. The Macedonians experienced the exact opposite of this policy during the short reign of Demetrius.

CRATERUS c. 362–321 B.C. Outstanding among the younger Macedonian generals with Alexander, he came to occupy the place which Parmenio had held in the early years. Alexander trusted him thoroughly: in 324 he was charged with the task of bringing back a large corps of veterans to Macedonia and soon afterwards was appointed to replace Antipater in Europe. Immediately after Alexander's death he was appointed guardian of Arrhidaeus. In the summer of 322 he crossed to Greece to relieve Antipater, who was then besieged in Lamia, and later engaged the Greek rebel forces at Crannon. His alliance with Antipater was confirmed by his marriage to the latter's daughter Phila. In 321 he joined Antipater in the war against Perdiccas and at a battle near the Hellespont was defeated and killed by Perdiccas' lieutenant Eumenes.

EUMENES c. 360–316 B.C. Born at Cardia in the Thracian Chersonese. Plutarch brackets Eumenes with the Roman Sertorius as soldiers endowed with genius in the handling of foreign troops: Eumenes was one of the very few Greeks born outside Macedon who commanded Macedonian armies with success. He was first employed as secretary by Philip and accompanied Alexander to Asia as chief of the royal secretariat. But Alexander seems to have recognized military talent in him too. He gave Eumenes at least one small command in India, and in 324 appointed him to one of the highest posts in the army, that of hipparch. After Alexander's death, he was made governor of Cappadocia, became the trusted lieutenant of Perdiccas and in 321 defeated an invading army from Macedonia and killed Craterus, its general. After Antipater's death Eumenes was harried by the forces of Antigonus but received support from Polyperchon. He was placed in command of the veteran corps of Macedonian infantry known as the Silver Shields and commissioned to raise forces for Polyperchon in Asia Minor. He conducted a skilful running war with Antigonus for two years, until he was finally betrayed by the Silver Shields, captured and executed.

LYSIMACHUS c. 361–281 B.C. A member of Alexander's Companion cavalry who particularly distinguished himself in India. Following Alexander's death he became governor of Thrace and the Chersonese. After Perdiccas had rejected the hand of Antipater's daughter Nicaea, Lysimachus married her. In 315 he joined the coalition of Ptolemy, Seleucus and Cassander against Antigonus. For many years he was obliged to occupy himself in pacifying his territory and consolidating his authority, but in 302 he launched a perfectly timed surprise invasion of Asia Minor, and in the following year effected a junction of his forces with Seleucus to defeat and kill Antigonus at Ipsus. Lysimachus was the principal beneficiary of the partition of Antigonus' territories which followed the battle. His newly acquired dominions stretched from north to south of Asia Minor, shut out Seleucus from the western seaboard and thus sowed the seeds of future conflict. In the last years of his reign Lysimachus' autocratic and extortionate methods of government became intensely unpopular, and when Seleucus invaded his territory in 282, he met little resistance. Lysimachus made a stand at Corupedium near Magnesia and was killed in the battle.

PERDICCAS c. 360–321 B.C. A member of a princely family of the province of Orestis in upper Macedonia. He served with distinction under Alexander, whose leading general he became after the death of Hephaestion and the return of Craterus to Europe. The dying Alexander entrusted him with the royal seal: this gave him the primacy in the Council of Generals in Babylon which disposed of the empire and the succession. In 322 he requested the hand in marriage of Antipater's daughter Nicaea, but then rejected it in favour of Alexander's sister, Cleopatra, a match offered him by Olympias. Although the marriage never took place, this action was represented by Antigonus as implying that Perdiccas aimed at usurping the crown, and caused an irreparable breach with Antipater. In 321 Antipater invaded Asia Minor, while Perdiccas had already marched south to attack Ptolemy in Egypt. He failed to force the crossing of the Nile and lost many men in the attempt, whereupon his troops mutinied and he was murdered.

POLYPERCHON c. 390/380–300? B.C. Highly born but possessing only mediocre talents, he was a divisional commander of the phalanx under Alexander, and later served with Antipater in the Lamian war. In 319 Antipater named him as regent and his own son Cassander as second in command, an arrangement which the latter deeply resented. Compelled to seek support against Cassander and Antigonus, Polyperchon reversed Antipater's repressive policy towards the Greek city-states, removing the occupying garrisons and permitting the return of many of the exiles. The effect of this action was to range himself with the democratic, and Cassander with the oligarchic factions. In 317 Cassander landed in Macedonia and Polyperchon fled to Epirus: thereafter his position deteriorated to that of a mere soldier of fortune. In 315 he accepted service under Antigonus, for whom he held the Peloponnese against Cassander's forces, and in 309 he invaded Macedonia, again at Antigonus' instigation, to support a pretender to the throne: this was one Heracles, a supposed son of Alexander and the Persian princess Barsine. Cassander bribed him to change sides, whereupon Polyperchon had the young pretender murdered. He is last heard of campaigning in the Peloponnese for Cassander in 304, shortly before the province was reconquered by Demetrius.

PTOLEMY I *c.* 360–284 B.C. Son of the Macedonian nobleman Lagus and one of the inner circle of Alexander's commanders and advisers. He fought with distinction in India and wrote a history of Alexander's campaigns which was an important source for Arrian's *Anabasis*. After Alexander's death he was appointed governor of Egypt and determined to maintain his independence of the central authority of Perdiccas. One of his first actions to this end was to divert to Egypt the cortège bearing the body of Alexander, which the army had intended to be buried in Macedonia. Ptolemy justified his acquisition of this precious relic, which was first interred with great magnificence at Memphis and subsequently at Alexandria, on the grounds that Alexander had wished to be buried at the oracle of Ammon. In 322 he allied himself with Antipater against Perdiccas and the pact was consolidated by his marriage to Antipater's daughter Eurydice. In 316 he joined forces with Cassander, Seleucus and Lysimachus to resist Antigonus' ambition to reconstitute the empire under his rule. In 306 his fleet was almost wiped out at the battle of Salamis in Cyprus, but Antigonus' and Demetrius' subsequent attempt to invade Egypt was foiled by bad weather. He took no part in the battle of Ipsus, and hence received little in the subsequent division of the spoils, but he arranged dynastic alliances by marrying his daughters, Arsinoe to Lysimachus and Lysandra to Cassander's son Alexander, and his step-daughter Antigone to Pyrrhus of Epirus. More successful as a statesman than as a soldier, he left behind him a kingdom which was to prove the most enduring of the Hellenistic monarchies. He founded the library of Alexandria and was one of the few Macedonian generals of his generation to patronize literature and the arts.

SELEUCUS *c.* 358–281 B.C. Son of Antiochus, one of Philip's generals, and a near contemporary of Alexander, he fought in the Companion cavalry and later became commander of the crack heavy infantry formation, the Hypaspistae. He took Perdiccas' side immediately after Alexander's death, but was later instrumental in his murder following the failure of the Egyptian campaign. Antipater appointed him governor of Babylon in 321. In 316 he fled to Egypt, joined Ptolemy in the war against Antigonus and commanded Egyptian squadrons in the Aegean. He returned to Babylon in 312 and steadily extended his authority over the eastern provinces. After campaigning in India he made peace with the Indian ruler Chandragupta, receiving in return a corps of elephants which played a part in his victory at Ipsus. At the partition of Antigonus' domains, Seleucus added Syria to his territories and founded his western capital at Antioch. In 285 his most threatening rival Demetrius surrendered and in 281 he turned on his former ally Lysimachus, invaded his territories in western Asia Minor and defeated and killed him at Corupedium. But when he crossed to Europe to claim Lysimachus' Thracian kingdom, he was assassinated by Ptolemy Ceraunus, the disinherited son of Ptolemy I.

MORE ABOUT PENGUINS
AND PELICANS

THE RISE AND FALL OF ATHENS

Plutarch

TRANSLATED BY IAN SCOTT-KILVERT

Writing at the turn of the first century A.D., Plutarch intentionally blended two cultures in his parallel lives of Greek and Roman heroes. The nine biographies chosen for this modern translation by Ian Scott-Kilvert illustrate the rise and fall of Athens from the legendary days of Theseus, the city's founder, to the age of Pericles and the razing of its walls by Lysander.

However unreliable in places, Plutarch's readable accounts have necessarily been a prime source of much historical knowledge.

Also Published in Penguins:
FALL OF THE ROMAN REPUBLIC
MAKERS OF ROME

PENGUIN CLASSICS

'Penguin continue to pour out the jewels of the world's classics in translation . . . There are now nearly enough to keep a man happy on a desert island until the boat comes in' – Philip Howard in *The Times*

A selection

Alexandre Dumas
THE THREE MUSKETEERS
TRANSLATED BY LORD SUDLEY

Cao Xuequin and Gao E
THE STORY OF THE STONE
Volume 4: The Debt of Tears
TRANSLATED BY JOHN MINFORD

Anton Chekhov
THE KISS AND OTHER STORIES
TRANSLATED BY RONALD WILKS

Alexander Pushkin
THE BRONZE HORSEMAN
TRANSLATED BY D. M. THOMAS

Ovid
THE EROTIC POEMS
TRANSLATED BY PETER GREENE

Madame de Sévigné
SELECTED LETTERS
TRANSLATED BY LEONARD TANCOCK